The Hide-and-Seek Children

Recollections of Jewish Survivors from Slovakia

collected and introduced by
Barbara Barnett

with Maps by
Martin Gilbert

Mansion Field

Published by
Mansion Field
an imprint of
Zeticula
57 St Vincent Crescent
Glasgow
G3 8NQ
Scotland

http://www.mansionfield.co.uk
admin@mansionfield.co.uk

ISBN 978-1-905021-10-9 Paperback

Gaspar Binet:
They wanted us to be happy

Chaja Steinmetz:
When uniformed men knocked at the Castle door the children were frightened ...
I could not play Hide-and-Seek.

Olga Grossman:
There at Clonyn Castle we learned, for the first time in our lives, to play games, Hide-and-Seek, for example. In the beginning we associated hiding with fear and running meant for us escaping. But, with the loving care of our leaders, we learned to play — and enjoy playing.

Israel Reich:
A great, huge place in beautiful grounds with a wonderful atmosphere. I remember my time there as special and our favourite game: a sort of Hide-and-Seek where the other side had to spot numbers written on cards tied round our heads, and ran off to hide in the woods.

We would like to express our gratitude to the author and the publisher for bringing our childhood stories to light. Our miraculous survival was due to Divine Providence, the resilience given to our parents and the help and assistance we received from some of our non-Jewish neighbours.

Signed: ***The Hide-and-Seek Children***

Contents

Maps   xi
Acknowledgements   xvii
Notes for the Reader   xx
Sources of Illustrations   xxi
List of Illustrations   xxiii

Part One   1
Introduction   3
    Children "At risk"   6
    "The Boys"   12
    My involvement   12
    The Schonfeld Archive   18
Chapter One   20
    Slovakia - the terrain, its history and Jewish minority   20
    Slovak Jews   22
    A massive political change   26
    From War to Peace   37
    The agony for parents - the plight of children   41
    Enter Rabbi Solomon Schonfeld   42
    A series of images of Villa Silvia and of Ohel David.   44
Chapter Two   51
    Solomon Schonfeld   51
    His father's career   52
    Solomon's youth   53
    The Rise of the Nazis and Schonfeld's response   55
    Wartime   59
    Postwar activities   61
    The schools   66
    The Legacy of Solomon Schonfeld   68
Chapter Three   70
    An Invitation   70
    Why Ireland? Irish immigration policy   77
    Reactions from Dublin's Jewish community 78
    Clonyn Castle   79
    Preparations   83
    The foundations of the Irish Venture   85
    The Administrator's initiation   94
    A journey westwards— following "The Pied Piper"   96

Chapter Four   107
   Life at the Castle   107
   Anna Katscher's Diary   110
   Housekeeping at the Castle   120
   Changes   126
   What was involved in moving on   129
   Aliyah   130
   Clonyn Castle "For sale"   131
   A tragic outcome   134
   The final months   140
   Transfer   158
   How the children remember Clonyn Castle   168
Chapter Five   174
   Reactions   185
   Some surprises   189
   Some observations   191
   Recording and Commemorating   195
   Post Script   198

Part Two   **199**
Recollections   201
Contributions from the Staff   201
   Rabbi and Mrs Israel Cohen   202
   Memories of Clonyn Castle   202
   "What Will Be With Me?" by Olga Eppel   205
   Séndi Templer   209
Recollections from the Children   217
  Hidden Children   218
    Children hidden with their mother and/or siblings   218
      Susanna and Israel Reich   219
      Oskar and Richard Reich   223
      Hedviga and Judita Friedmann   228
      Gizella, Ella and Rozsi Schwarzthal 231
      Eva Schwarz   233
      Tamáš Reif   239
      Robert Bock   243
      Erich Bock   244
      Alfred Kahan   246

Children hidden in "bunkers" without parent or sibling 252
    Emanuel Weinberger 253
    Istvan and Gyury Stahler and their sister 258
    Gyorgy Prissegi 266
    Anna Katscher 277
    Judith Mannheimer 281
    Dezider Rosenfeld 292
    Artur Weinberger 296
    Hetty Weiner-Fisch 299
Children placed in institutions 323
    Pál and Tamáš Krausz 324
    Alexander Mastbaum 328
    Judit, Olga and Alfred Ziegler 330
      Two Poems 335-6
In Auschwitz 337
    Gaspar and Robert Binet and their sister Miriam 338
    Olga and Vera Grossman 342
    Blanka Federweiss 352
    Ervin Schwarz 354
    Alfred Leicht 360
    Erika Stern 373
    Fela Cajtak Maybaum 377
Post-War Recollections 382
    Vera Wiesen 383
    Franklina Wiesen 384
    Josef Ickovitc 385
    Eva Rubinstein 386
    Ernst Rubinstein 386
    Eva Haupt 388
    Judit and Agi Wiesner 391
    Chaja Steinmetz 393
Some Other Survivors 395
    David Steiner of Bratislava 396
    Shoshana Singer Brayer of Bratislava 401
    Bertha Fischer of Rachov 403
    Edit Katz of Košice 414
    Shmuel Klein of Nitra 416
    Rachel Malmud of Bratislava 423

Appendix A
   Jona Laks and the Symposium at Kaiser Wilhelm Institutes 433
Appendix B
   The Beis Ya'acov Schools   441
Appendix C   445
   Facts and Figures: A closer look at the travel documents   445
   Observations   452
   Dispersal in April 1948   459
   Dispersal during 1949   459
   Relationships within the group   460
Appendix D   464
   The Resilience of Young Survivors   464
   A Note on Play   466
Notes   467
Bibliography   471
Glossary   477
Index   485

Maps

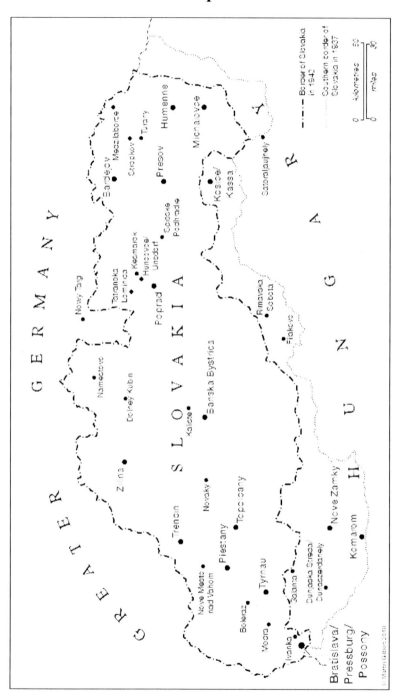

Slovakia

International borders of 1942
Greater Germany 1942

North Sea

HOLLAND

BELGIUM

FRANCE

Knokke

Aachen

Rhine

Strasbourg

Geislingen

Berne

SWITZERLAND

Montreux

ITALY

Mediterranean Sea

Lippstadt

Königshütte

GREATER GE

Bergen-Belsen

Ravensbrück

Berlin

Elbe

Oder

Les

Karlovy Vary/ Karlsbad

Cheb

Marianske Lazne/ Marianbad

Theresienstadt

Prague

Plzen/ Pilsen

Dachau

Allach

Landsberg

Munich

Adriatic Sea

CRO

Scar

Regional map to show Slovakia and neighbouring countries

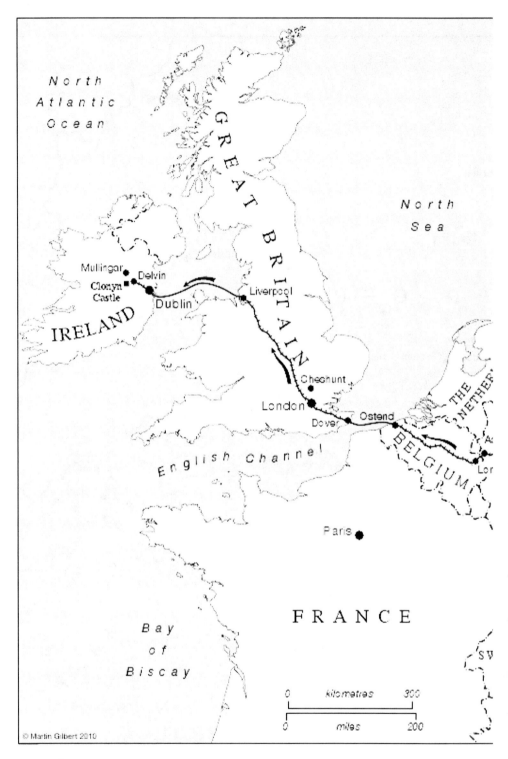

North
Atlantic
Ocean

North
Sea

GREAT BRITAIN

IRELAND

Mullingar
Clonyn
Castle
Delvin
Dublin
Liverpool

Cheshunt
London
Dover
Ostend
THE NETHER...
BELGIUM

English Channel

Paris

FRANCE

Bay
of
Biscay

SW

0   kilometres   300
0   miles   200

© Martin Gilbert 2010

The children's route across Europe to Britain – and to Ireland

These four laid the foundations for this project. Their stories are included in this book. Olga Grossman, Barbara Barnett, Bertha Fischer, Rachel Malmud in Haifa in 2000 (OG)

Acknowledgements

Many friends, old and new, colleagues and acquaintances —
as well as my children – have given me steady encouragement
throughout the many years I have worked on this project. It
developed by chance and was my first experience of producing
a book. I am not a historian, though throughout my married life
I was immersed in an academic environment seeped in history
and peopled with historians. My connection with Slovakian
survivors originated with Bertha Fischer, whom I first met in
1946. It was her sister-in-law, Rachel Malmud, who gave my
phone number to Olga Grossman and it was Olga who first told
me about the Slovakian child survivors. We have kept in close
touch ever since and she has been the inspiration for this book –
"a book that", as she said, "was born on the phone!"

Numerous people have helped me in all sorts of ways. I fear
that inevitably the list is incomplete; my memory is not as good
as it was and I apologise to everyone I have failed to mention and
any omissions are mine alone.

Jeremy Schonfeld, Rabbi Schonfeld's youngest son, has been
my mentor throughout. He has advised and encouraged me from
the start. It was his brother Jonathan who chaired the Reunion
Committee and invited me to serve on it. All three Schonfeld sons
read and approved the brief account of their father's life I wrote
for the Reunion to which I have since added a little more detail.
Jonathan has given me invaluable assistance and provided many
interesting photographs from his extensive collection.

Professor C. M. Woolgar, Archivist of the Hartley Library,
Southampton University gave me access to the Schonfeld Archive
– a crucial source of information - and provided copies of almost
all the documents in this book with permission to publish them.
This was ratified by the Schonfeld family.

It is entirely due to Irving Finkel that I found my publisher.
Irving's delightful farce, "The Last Resort Library" is all about
books that never get published. I heard about it and told him I
had one of those — and he introduced me to his publisher.

Sir Martin Gilbert, who has given wide recognition to "The
Boys", has generously provided the maps for this book despite

his many onerous responsibilities. They are designed in his own inimitable style and are crucial in providing an essential basis for the history and stories that follow. He says this is surely the first book that has maps to show every place name mentioned!

Jona Laks allowed me to publish her speech to the Max Planck Society in Berlin. Professor Shimon Shuldiner sent me comments on that event which I would otherwise not have seen. So did Juliet Dabbikeh.

Professor Martin Goodman read an early version during his holidays in 2005 and made many useful suggestions, as did Ashley Jones. Professor Vernon Trafford and his wife gave me practical ideas and were hugely encouraging. They introduced me to the memory stick! Paul Yogi Mayer added further information and useful advice. Peter Hudson saved the entire draft when Microsoft went mad and gave me lots of further help. Hugh Shaffer came to my aid whenever I was stuck with editing or computer dilemmas. It was Oron Joffe who succeeded in expelling a "gremlin" in the works when a mysterious entry appeared repeatedly. Without all these generous and able friends this book would never have appeared.

Rabbi (Emeritus) Herbert Richer, Mrs Arthur Moses and Mr N. Honig all shared with me personal memories of Rabbi Schonfeld. Enid Oppenheim Sandelson and Richard Slotover, assisted by family and friends, provided interesting information about their relative, Olga Eppel and her family. Professor Jonathan Webber, Rabbi Dr Chanan Tomlin, and Professor Derek Taylor answered queries and gave me useful guidance. Margaret Brearley invited me to talk to her women's group, as did Romee Day. Paul Griffiths, Lesley Dunn and Beth Crosland in England, and Chana Greenberg and Juliet Dabbikeh in Israel, all former colleagues of mine in the field of child welfare, have contributed to my observations and comments from their extensive professional experience.

To Frank and Sydney Baigel in England, Malcolm Gafson in Israel, The National Library of Wales, Tom French of the Irish Archives, the Irish JIG Website, Katrina Goldstone in Dublin – my thanks for their assistance and enthusiasm in matters Irish.

Bridget Astor led me to work on children's play and to George Eisen's study of this in the Concentration Camps. Chana Greenberg referred me to Judith Mishne's work. Martina

Buganova provided modern maps of Slovakia as well as translations. Shimon Levy introduced me to Henry Margulies who sent me his parents' remarkable story. Devora Speyer found for me an article about the re-establishment of Nitra Yeshiva in the USA. Emanuel Weinberger and Chanoch and Eva Kesselman told me about the achievements of Rabbi Frieder.

Rickie Burman of the Jewish Museum, Nitza Spiro of the Spiro Ark, Ita Simons of Schonfeld Square and Malcolm Gafson of the Israel Ireland Friendship League have all offered to organise Book Launches. For translations I am indebted to Alexandra Trone (German), Henia Goldberg (Hebrew), Juliet Dabbikeh (Hebrew), Julia Dehoff (German), George Dub and Martina Buganova (Slovak and Czech) and my nephew John Speyer (Yiddish) - and to Francesca Bartlett for help with editing.

My son Colin spent much time in editing the whole text at an earlier stage. He checked and corrected historical facts, added formatting and made numerous improvements throughout – and he gave me lots of encouragement.

I am deeply appreciative to my daughter Celia for her thorough work on the illustrations. To Irving Finkel and oron Oron Joffe made a final meticulous and time-consuming edit of the manuscript, correcting my many slips and oversights with the utmost patience. My son Robert offered shrewd counsel and encouragement from New York.

I am enormously indebted to Eduardo Lima Filho and his colleagues at MinaLima Design for their imaginative efforts in producing the attractive cover which adds another dimension to the contents of the book.

Above all my thanks go to the Reunion Committee for accepting me as a colleague to work with them - otherwise I would never have become involved with this project.

Finally and crucially, I would like to thank the contributors who trusted me enough to allow their personal reminiscences to be included here. I only hope I have done justice to them.

Acknowledgements for illustrations are listed separately.

Notes for the Reader

Names of contributors are those given to them on the Collective Visa of 1948. A copy of the original is included in Appendix C. This gives some protection to those who prefer not to be identified today. Many of their surnames have been Hebraised or Anglicised or have changed since marriage.

Where names appear in the text in **bold** this indicates that their story appears in Part Two.

The Glossary explains some traditions, the functions of some organisations and translations of words of foreign origin that are shown throughout the text in italics.

Maps show places mentioned in the text.

Should there be any profits from the sale of this book, they will be donated to relevant charities.

www.thehideandseekchildren.org

Sources of Illustrations

It is the illustrations that bring this book to life. I am deeply grateful to all those who contributed to this fine collection. The vast majority are documents from the Schonfeld Archive in Southampton University, thanks to Professor C.M. Woolgar and the Schonfeld family. Many come from Jonathan Schonfeld's own prodigious collection.

My sincere thanks for contributions from Rickie Burman, Louise Asher and Sarah Harel Hoshen of the Jewish Museum in London and to Dr Sharman Kadish of Jewish Heritage UK. And my thanks also to Irene Stevenson of the Irish Times, Eamon de Valera of the Irish Press Plc and Eilis Ryan of the Westmeath Examiner, all in Eire, and to the editors of Ha'aretz and Kol Ha'ir in Israel and The Jewish Tribune in London.

I deeply appreciate the generosity of contributors who provided treasured pictures to illustrate their own stories, and to Richard Slotover for pictures of Olga Eppel. My daughter Celia took several photos specially for this book and my granddaughter Hannah contributed one she took when we visited Yad Vashem together.

All uncredited documents come from the Schonfeld Archive. Initials refer to those listed below:

RC	Rachel Cooper	MN	Manfred Nussbaum
BF	Bertha Fischer	GP	Gyorgy Prissegi
OG	Olga Grossman	RR	Richard Reich
HF	Hetty Weiner-Fisch	TR	Tamas Reif
CK	Chanoch Kesselman	JS	Jonathan Schonfeld
PK	Pál Krausz	RS	Richard Slotover
TK	Tom Krausz	IS	Istvan Stahler
SK	Sonia Kummeldorfer	DS	David Steiner
AL	Alfred Leicht	EW	Emanuel Weinberger
JM	Judith Mannheimer	JW	Judit Wiesner
MM	Monica Mayer		

List of Illustrations

These four laid the foundations for this project. Their stories are
    included in this book. Olga Grossman, Barbara Barnett, Bertha
    Fischer, Rachel Malmud in Haifa in 2000 (OG)   *xvi*

Part One
Introduction

The sign of the original Jews' Temporary Shelter in the East End of
    London with Yiddish transliteration ©The Jewish Museum   3
The bronze memorial to the Kindertransport by Frank Meisler and
    Arie Ovadia erected in 2006 at Liverpool Street Station, London.
    (CB)   7
Commemorative plaques in Hope Square at Liverpool Street Station.
    (CB)   8
Three hundred young people gathered in Old Town Square,
    Prague. The first group of child survivors known later as
    "The Boys", about to make the journey to London in 1945.
    © The Jewish Museum   10-11
The Primrose Club, a social and residential Youth Club for "The
    Boys", was established in these two properties at 26-27 Belsize
    Park in North London in 1947. (CB)   14
Paul Yogi Mayer MBE. (MM)   16

Chapter 1

Bratislava Castle c.1930, since restored.   20
In the High Tatra Mountains. (TK)   21
Bratislava Orthodox Synagogue, Heydukova Street, built 1923-26.
    The only synagogue still in use. (Michal Kelovy/Wikipedia). 23
Gustav Steiner, uncle of David Steiner, served in the Austro-
    Hungarian army among numerous fellow Jews. (DS)   24
50 koruna coin issued by the Fascist regime showing Tiso.
    (Sebastian Wallroth/Wikipedia).   27
Dr. Fisch, father of Hetty Weiner-Fisch, an oculist in a protected
    occupation. Note "zid" (Jew). A prescription he gave for
    spectacles and below another for medication, 1944. (HF)   30
Košice Synagogue built in 1926. (Marion Gladis/Wikipedia)   32
Gisi Fleischman, close friend of Hetty Fisch's mother, wearing a
    hat, beside Hetty Fisch's aunt Beate Weiner on the left. (HF) 35

At Villa Silvia. Judith Mannheimer helping out with the small
    children. Marianna Stahler beside her wearing a bow. (JM)   44
Friday evening at Villa Silvia. Sabbath loaves - but no candles!
    Taken for American benefactors in 1946.   45
Headed notepaper for Detsky Domov (Children's Home) - Ohel
    David (David's Tent) established by Rabbi Frieder.   45
Recuperating at Villa Silvia in the High Tatra Mountains, 1946.
    (CK, TK, IS)   46
Mr Vogel and Mrs Vogel. (JM)   48
Children from Villa Silvia after moving to Rabbi Frieder's
    facilities at Ohel David, including his nephew, Amiel; the
    three Schwarzthal girls are on the left. In charge were Mr Vogel
    (wearing a hat) and Mrs Vogel. (CK, TK, IS)   49
Israeli dancing at Ohel David (TK)   50
Shooting practice said to be in preparation for life in Israel! (TK)   50

Chapter 2

An unusual example of CRREC notepaper with an impressive
    tally of their achievements   51
The office of the Chief Rabbi's Religious Emergency Council at 86
    Amhurst Park, North London. (JS)   58
Mrs Schonfeld's house at 35 Lordship Park, North London, which
    her son often crammed with newly-arrived children. (CB)   60
Mobile Synagogue Ambulance sent by Rabbi Schonfeld for the
    use of Jewish servicemen. (JS)   62
Rabbi Dr Solomon Schonfeld in the uniform he designed for his
    journeys in post-war Europe. (JS)   65
Rabbi Dr Solomon Schonfeld at his desk. © Douglas Glass   67

Chapter 3

Main Railway Station, Prague where the children met for their
    journey to London. (Lucy Abel Smith/John Murray)   70
11th April 1948 American "Joint" confirming Rabbi Schonfeld's
    credentials to the Czech officials.   72
American "Joint's" letter of support for Rabbi Schonfeld's
    application and confirmation of the details – probably a copy. 73
A typical form used to register applicants to Rabbi Schonfeld's
    transport, this one for Eva Schwarz.   76
Official letter dated 16th August 1947 from the Irish Government
    listing the conditions for the admission of Rabbi Schonfeld's
    Slovakian group.   80

A detail from Sonja Kummeldorfer's Irish passport with an
    unexpected comment. (SK)   81
Clonyn Castle in 2007. (RR)   84
The entrance hall of Clonyn Castle taken on our visit in 1998. Very
    little had changed. (JS)   86
The imposing main staircase that confronts the visitor. (JS)   87
The marble stairs leading to the broad first floor gallery. (JS)   88
Henry Pels, Executive Secretary to the Chief Rabbi's Religious
    Emergency Council. (Rachel Cooper)   90
Olga Eppel with her great niece Peggy Slotover and Peggy's daughter
    Jill 1956-7. (RS)   92
Olga Eppel with great-great nephews, Robert (left) and Richard
    Slotover in 1958. (RS)   93
Arriving in Britain.   100-101
Preparing to disembark (Key on next page)   102-103
Greenville Hall Synagogue, Dublin. © Nigel Corrie, courtesy
    of Jewish Heritage UK.   106

Chapter 4

Headed notepaper showing the later move from the Castle to Dun
    Laoghaire, 1949.   107
Group of boys and girls on the Castle steps in 1948. (JS)
    © Irish Press PLC.   112-113
Benjamin Pels alludes to difficulties in a letter to Rabbi Schonfeld. 118-9
Anna Katscher, Blanka Federweiss, Lily Lowinger and Ella or
    Rozsi Schwartzthal read letters (JS) ©Irish Press PLC   121
More letters arrive. (JS) ©Irish Press PLC   122
Clonyn Castle Football Team and Supporters (JS) ©Irish Press PLC 124-125
January 8th 1949. *The Times Pictorial* reports on the first group
    leaving for Israel © The Irish Times.   132
February 24th approval requested for another group of children
    to go to Israel. See the Rabbi's handwritten comment: parents'
    agreement also required.   133
February 11th Mrs Eppel reports on rumours of a CBF take-over
    and her negotiations for a smaller property.   135-136
February 16th, Mr Pels' reply to damaging rumours circulating in
    Dublin.   137-138
February 21st - Rabbi Schonfeld's reassurance.   139
Clonyn Castle still for sale in 1969 © The Irish Times   141
"Clonyn House", 9 Vesey Place, Dun Laoghaire where the
    remaining remaining children moved when Clonyn Castle
    was vacated. (JS)   142
Clonyn House, Rules and Regulations.   143

Mention in the Minutes of the purchase of Clonyn House
    (wrongly dated). Note "Clonyn free" written across the page
    by the Rabbi.   144
March 29th. Note that the impression is given that debts were to
    be settled before leaving the Castle. Later information
    questions this.   145
Page from Mrs Eppel's accounts. A summary of essential
    purchases. Note coal usage.   146
 P.S. A welcome compliment from the children's new headmaster. 147
April 6th. About a gift of *kosher* food supplies for Passover and an
    audit of her accounts.   148
June 10th. A suggestion for settling the rest of the debts.   150-151
The list of outstanding debts that so shocked Mr Pels.   152-153
June 21st. Here is Mr Pels' reaction.   154
Undated but soon after the move to Vesey Place. A glimpse at the
    complexity faced in arranging every child's future.   155
June 15th. Future of the last group of children.   156
June 23rd. Mrs Eppel's exasperation at further delays and
    concern for the frustrated girls.   157
Five of the older girls express their concern.   159
Telegram typical of several from an exasperated Mrs Eppel.   160
August 25th. Notice the Rabbi's comment.   160
July 27th. A holiday?   162
"… and when the last child leaves shall the house be sold?"   164
The Chief Rabbi, Dr Israel Brodie, approves the CBF take-over.   165
August 3rd. Concern over children's travel arrangements.   166-167
A treasured memento of Clonyn Castle from 1948.   169
Sonja and Ervin Kummeldorfer aged 8 and 10 at the Castle in
    1948. (SK)   171
Gyorgy Prissegi with Lily Lowinger and another girl (GP)   172

Chapter 5

Headed notepaper of the Jubilee Reunion Committee.   174
At the grave of Rabbi Schonfeld. Behind, Gertuda Muller with
    Eva Schwarz. (TR)   175
Rabbi Israel Cohen and Barbara Barnett at the Reunion. (JS)   177
Invitation to the Reunion Dinner, April 26th 1998. (TR)   177
From the *Bulletin of the Association of Jewish Refugees*, March 1998. 179
The Consecration of a new Sepher Torah during Schonfeld
Children's Reunion (from *The Jewish Tribune*, April 30th 1988).   180-181
April 28th. Istvan Stahler arrives at Dublin Airport. (JS)   182
Anna Katscher's husband Manfred Nussbaum points the way. (JS) 183
Friends reunited on the steps.   184

Dining Room used as the synagogue. (JS)   186
Agi Weisner, with her husband, pointing to the mark left by a
     mezuzah. (JS)   186
Doorpost on the top landing where the boys slept, showing where
     there had been another mezuzah. (JS)   187
 Another clue to the past: Bell Board in the servants' basement. (JS) 187
Jonathan Schonfeld shows the present owner the architect's
     plans of the building. Chaja Steinmetz's husband looks on. (JS) 188
The Two Alfreds; a lifelong friendship. May 6th 2000
     © The Irish Times   190
Memorial at Yad Vashem to all who rebelled, fought and died
     in the Holocaust. (HB)   196

Part Two

Séndi Templer's Application Form.   211
Séndi's wedding to Benjamin, son of Henry Pels, London, 1949. (JM)
                                                                        214-215
Rabbi Schonfeld with the youngest wedding guests. (JM, MN)   216
Yad Vashem Award of "Righteous among the Nations". (RR)   225
Oskar and Richard Reich at the Castle. (RR)   227
A page from Eva Schwarz's Application Form with her story in
     German.   235
Eva Schwarz's Application Form in Czech.   236
An unusual definition used by Rabbi Schonfeld.   252
Emanuel Weinberger's British Certificate of Identity. (EW)   257
At Villa Silvia: Amiel Lucknar leading Gyury Stahler, second from
      front, his brother Istvan fourth, Tamáš Krausz at the back. (IS) 261
Cover of Istvan Stahler's Certificate of Identity for the newly
     established Republic of Ireland. (IS)   263
The details inside the Certificate, stamped on his departure   264-265
Gyorgy with the Prissegi family in 1946. (GP)   268
Gyorgy on a rocking horse. (GP)   269
The postcard from Gyorgy's mother in Birkenau Concentration
     Camp, May 15th, 1943. (Gp)   270
Gyorgy with Mrs. Prissegi wearing the sailor suit sent by his
     mother. (GP)   272
Soon after the war ended the Prissegi and Engel families together
     again relaxing in their garden with Gyorgy. (GP)   273
Gyorgy at Clonyn Castle. (GP)   274
Gyorgy with "big sister" Lily Lowinger and two other girls at
     Clonyn Castle. (GP)   275
Gyorgy and Rita had a joyful reunion with foster sister
     Magda Pichler, *née* Prissegen in Bratislava in 2009. (GP)   276

Anna Katscher with her cousin Judith Mannheimer on the left. (JM) 280
"My mother with her six children. I am the youngest." (JM).   283
Bella, Moshe (Morris), Asher (Arthur), Rena (Renka), Robi (Robert)
    and Judith the youngest. (JM)   283
The four who survived – Bella, Morris, Arthur and Judith. (JM)   285
Judith at the Hasmonean School. (JM)   288
Judith with her foster sister Helen Warhaftig in London. (JM)   289
Judith on holiday with Eva Steiner also from the Bratislava group,
    who was placed with a family in Cardiff. (JM)   290
Judith with Moses Schonfeld in the USA. He was an international
    journalist at the UN and a brother of Rabbi Schonfeld. (JM) 291
"Condolence letter from Gisi Fleischman to my father after my
    mother died in 1932." (HF)   301-3
"On one side she writes that she is sorry and that she is sending
    him a copy of what she intends to say at my mother's grave." {HF)
                                                                 302
"My parents Dr Geza and Jeanette Fisch (Hartvig) in the late 1920s."
    (HF)   305
"With my grandparents Jakob and Thekla Hartvig in Berlin 1933." (HF)
                                                                 306
"Daddy and I in 1933." (HF)   307
"A visit to my cousins Egon and Ursel Hartvig in Berlin, 1934" (HF) 308
Dr and Mrs Majercik, newly-weds. (HF)   311
The Majercik family during May 1945. (HF)   314
"This picture taken two or three days after my liberation." (HF) 315
The exhibit at Yad Vashem honouring Dr and Mrs Majercik. (HF)   320
"Four of my children and nine grandchildren". (HF)   321
The Krausz brothers with Sister Zofia, who protected them in her
    convent. (TK)   325
Tamáš Krausz returns to the High Tatras in 2008. (TK)   327
The Two Alfreds visit the Castle again. They were interviewed by
    the Westmeath Examiner. © John Mulvihill.   370
Erika in 2007 beside an antique Czech cupboard in a Jerusalem
    café. (BB)   376
Fela Maybaum's obituary in Ha'aretz, 2005.   381
Judit Wiesner with sixteen grandchildren in 1996. (JW)   392
The Steiner Family Bookshop and Lending Library, founded in
    1847 moved here to 22 Venturgasse, Bratislava in 1880. (DS) 397
David Steiner. (DS)   399
Rachov in the Carpathian Mountains, now in the Ukraine, where
    Bertha's father was head of the Jewish Community. (BF)   404
The Fischer family home beside the river in Rachov next to Bertha's
    father's wholesale dry goods store. (BF)   404

Bertha's paternal grandmother, Henja Geitel Fischer, on the left with
    her cousin. (BF)   405
These are the pupils of the "Jewish School at Rachov, June 25th, 1940". (BF)
    408

Appendix A

Jona Laks, representative for the surviving Mengele Twins.
    "Human beings and not metaphors made Auschwitz. Dr
    Mengele was a human being born from human beings and
    not a symbol. I cannot forgive." © Naor Rahav.   440

Appendix C

Collective Visas

The Collective and Transit Visas from Prague to London.   446
14th April 1948. Czech Ministry of the Interior approved 148
    persons of uncertain citizenship to travel abroad between
    20th and 29th April. Countersigned in Germany.   449
1st January 1948. Letter permitting transit via the UK for 100
    children travelling from Czechoslovakia to Eire.   450
14th April 1948. British Embassy approval for 50 children, orphans
    under 16, to be admitted to the UK   451
Names covered by the Collective Visas - Pages 1 to 6   453-458

Dispersal in 1949

Early summer 1949. Plans for the remaining children show
    those who went to Israel in January and suggested
    destinations for the rest   (Pages 1 to 3)   461-463

Part One

Introduction

The sign of the original Jews' Temporary Shelter in the East End of London with Yiddish transliteration ©The Jewish Museum

There has been a flurry of writings from survivors of the Nazi Holocaust during the past ten years or so but this collection differs from the rest in a number of ways. The contributors to this book are survivors of anti-Semitic atrocities inflicted by the Slovak fascists from 1939 until 1944 and then from the invading Nazis who took over that role till the Allies finally overcame them. Slovakia is a country we hear little about, one of the least industrialised and the most impoverished in Eastern Europe. In 1948, just as a Communist regime was about to take over their country and present a new and imminent danger to the Jewish community, the contributors of these memoirs were brought to London by an English Rabbi, Dr Solomon Schonfeld.

Dr. Schonfeld's mission was to protect and sustain surviving Jewish children; he offered a year of recuperation and traditional Jewish education in England or the Republic of Ireland for 150 Jewish child survivors. His message drew children and teenagers in towns and villages from across Slovakia to apply for places. 148 were accepted and they all met up with him at Prague railway station to commence a new chapter in their lives. Here follow details of that venture, not previously published, with an account of its ups and downs and of the impact it had on them.

Part One of this book provides an introduction to the personal reminiscences that follow. A glimpse at the geography of Slovakia and a brief resume of some relevant Slovak and Jewish Slovak history provides a setting necessary for appreciating the stories. Events there during World War Two are not widely known. The heroic Jewish leaders made immense efforts that halted deportations to the death camps for two years – unlike anywhere else in Europe. They exploited the vulnerability of the Nazi chief based in Bratislava and they made deals with the Fascists to alleviate some of the intense stress on their community; but only a remnant of the pre-war Jewish community survived these ordeals.

Before the war and during it, Rabbi Schonfeld had worked tirelessly to save Jewish lives and help retain their religious heritage. Derek Taylor has published a full study of his life and achievements.[1] In Chapter Two I have provided a brief account of his life.

He had an extraordinary reputation, a charismatic figure deeply revered by the numerous people whose lives he saved, respected for the schools he established, but seen as something of a maverick by others.

Copious correspondence and documents in the Schonfeld Archives provide vivid details about the Children's Home the Rabbi established at Clonyn Castle in Eire, where one hundred of them stayed for up to a year. From the same source we learn about the complicated arrangements made for every one of these young people to join surviving relatives or make their own way ahead.

In 1998 a Reunion was organised by some of the group settled in London to celebrate fifty years since their arrival and to pay homage to the Rabbi who had brought them there. That is described in Chapter Five. By chance I became involved with this occasion and it was from stories I collected then, from those present and others sent later from far and wide, that this collection emerged. More suggestions are offered for further reading.

The memoirs appear in Part Two. They are introduced by senior staff at Clonyn Castle. Séndi Pels and her husband have survived to see this account of their endeavours published and appreciated but sadly Mrs Eppel and Rabbi and Mrs Cohen have all passed on. We are fortunate to have original contributions from the Principal and the Administrator. The children's contributions follow. They represent, albeit by chance, a cross-section of the Slovak Jewish population, a mix of town and country origin and of social levels, a minority settled there for centuries past. Most of the teenagers were among the few who survived the death camps, abused as slave labourers and held in appalling conditions. The younger ones were "Hidden Children" – a group among survivors that has seldom been heard about, with the notable exception of Anne Frank.

Only in 1991 was there a first gathering of "Hidden Children", by then mature adults. It emerged that most of them had never before shared their wartime experiences, maintaining those strict restraints that had safeguarded them in their hiding places. On this notable occasion that silence was at last broken – a most extraordinary happening. The Conference was initiated and organised by Nicole David, herself a Hidden Child from Belgium, and the proceedings published.[2] This drew much interest. "The war has been over for fifty years and yet we are still in hiding – but now we can face the dawn of a new day."

The stories that follow bring to light further examples. These children emerged from hiding places found by frantic parents where they were protected by non-Jews – families of partisans, anti-Fascists, monks and nuns. They lived under false identities, with or without forged papers, in unfamiliar surroundings at constant risk of detection. Any divergence from this pretence could bring certain death not just for them but also for their courageous protectors. We shall never know how many shared that fate for no records were kept of those who were caught and killed without trial.

None of the Hide-and-Seek Children went back to Slovakia where the new Communist government had forbidden all religious practice, as Rabbi Schonfeld had predicted. After some months recuperation they scattered to settle in the newly created State of Israel, in North America or in England. We discover how their lives developed. We learn of their achievements in gaining financial independence, managing impressive careers and creating new families – while adhering, as the Rabbi had hoped, to Jewish religious practice. It is an inspiring record.

Further material I collected in the course of research for this book is added at the end. Appendix A records the history of the Beis Ya'acov Schools. This education system had a strong impact on so many of the girls both in Slovakia and in London where it was introduced by Dr Judith Grunfeld. Appendix B contains a response to apologies from the Max Planck Institute for the activities of the diabolical Dr Josef Mengele. It was powerfully presented by Jona Laks, another Slovak survivor also brought to London by Rabbi Schonfeld. Appendix C contains some facts and figures from a range of sources relating to the Slovak children in the 1948 transport. Appendix D draws attention to studies of resilience among young survivors and to the importance of play for children.

Children "At risk"

Rabbi Schonfeld was not alone in voicing concern for the welfare of children in wartime. There were three notable measures authorised by the British Government: the *Kindertransport* just before the war, the evacuation of British school children at the start of the war, and the acceptance of Concentration Camp survivors after the war ended.

Anti-Semitic activity grew rapidly in Germany from 1933 but it was not easy for Jews to emigrate. Some fifty thousand German Refugees were were admitted to Britain by 1939, all of them fortunate enough to acquire guarantees from British subjects. They were restricted to taking only unskilled work.[3] Most countries, including the United States, were unwilling to grant entry permits. When conditions worsened after *Kristallnacht* in 1938 the British Government became more concerned. As an exceptional case, they agreed to a project under which 10,000 unaccompanied Jewish refugee children between the ages of 3 and 17 would be admitted. It became known as the *Kindertransport*.[4] Few of these children ever saw their parents again.

Frank Meisler, today well known as a sculptor, arrived in London aged 9, on one of those transports. His statue marks the arrival point of the young people.

The British required some provisos. Financial responsibility and a bond of £50 had to be guaranteed for each child. They were to be assisted to emigrate elsewhere at a later date, should the Government require it – though that was never enforced. As conditions worsened in Europe, more and more children arrived so schemes were hurriedly set up to accept them. This put huge

The bronze memorial to the Kindertransport by Frank Meisler and Arie Ovadia erected in 2006 at Liverpool Street Station, London. They made a companion statue at Friedrichstrasse Station in Berlin, where the children bravely look forward, with their backs to another group that are left behind. (CB)

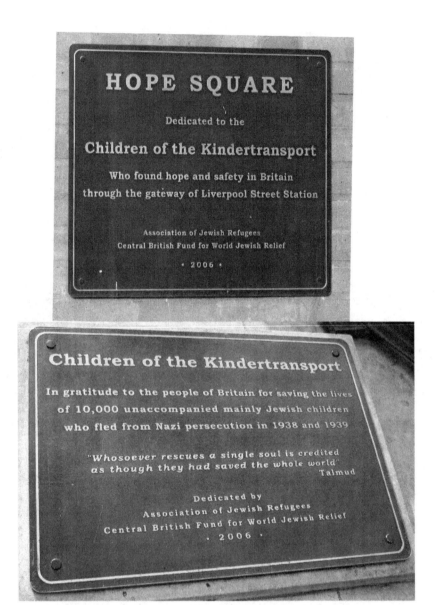

Commemorative plaques in Hope Square at Liverpool Street Station. (CB)

pressures, financial and practical, on the Central British Fund for German Jewry (CBF) and other organisations, both Jewish and non-Jewish. Not all of their efforts have been publicly recognised.[5]

Among them was that of Rabbi Schonfeld who later brought the group to England which is the subject of this book. He conveyed about 1500 refugees to Britain before the declaration of war in 1939 cut off communications.[6] He was particularly concerned that children from observant Jewish families should be found equally observant placements. Where these were insufficient his response was to set up hostels but the urgency of the situation caused some children to be placed with non-Jewish families. Most, if not all, fared well. The Rabbi's protests in this dilemma were deemed unreasonable.

Ironically it now was the turn of children in Allied territory to face displacement and separation, although their experiences were incomparably gentler. The British Government anticipated the German bombing campaign of cities and organised a massive evacuation programme to remove urban schoolchildren with their teachers to the safety of the countryside. See further comment in Appendix D.

Several diplomats were prominent among those who took huge personal risks to rescue as many Jews as possible. Among them were the activities of two British officials: Nicholas Winton in Prague[7] for which he was nominated in 2008 for the Nobel Peace Prize - and Frank Foley[8] in Berlin. It is shocking that it has taken so many years for knowledge of these outstanding individuals to come to light. In Budapest the Swiss representative gave protection to numerous Jewish families. Raoul Wallenberg, a Swedish diplomat, saved thousands and then disappeared in Russian hands.[9] All of these, and others less well known, saved countless Jewish lives in defiance of their official duties, often providing papers of doubtful validity while putting their own lives at risk.

Extraordinary and heroic stories continue to emerge. In 1999, research by some Kansas schoolgirls discovered that a Polish Catholic social worker, Irena Sendler, with the assistance of a dedicated team of helpers, had organised the placement of about 2,500 children from the Warsaw Ghetto into the care of gentile families. She carefully recorded their true names in a safe place in the hope that after the war, they could be reunited with their families. By then most of the parents had been murdered.[10]

Three hundred young people gathered in Old Town Square, Prague. The first group of child survivors known later as "The Boys", about to make the journey to London in 1945.
© *The Jewish Museum*

"The Boys"

After the war was over the British authorities offered visas to 1,000 homeless young Jewish survivors rescued from Concentration Camps; 732 took up this invitation. They had to be orphans aged under 16, and they needed British guarantors to ensure they would not become dependents of the state. The Committee for the Care of Children from the Concentration Camps (CCCCC) was set up by the CBF to receive them.[11]

The initial group was housed for the first few months at a hostel at Windermere in the Lake District in North East England. There began the long process of recuperation from years of malnutrition and unimaginable trauma. They were fitted with new clothes, nourished with regular meals, and given single rooms with real bedding – conditions that seemed like paradise - while they began to recover their health and to learn English and English ways. During their stay strong relationships grew between them. They shared a horrendous history. They gained new strength and hope for the future from supporting each other in a strange environment.

The first group of 80 boys and girls moved on to the next stage: the Temporary Shelter for Jewish Immigrants in the East End of London. Future plans were discussed individually; they could chose to seek work or to study or to take a vocational training course. The CBF then found them room and board with a Jewish family or a place in a hostel, and provided a minimal living allowance until they earned enough to be independent.

My involvement

In 1946 I was a social work student at London School of Economics, specialising in child welfare. One day I was approached after a synagogue service by a stranger. She asked me if I would volunteer to socialise with children rescued from the Concentration Camps. I said that, much as I would like to help, I was only a student and did not know anything about helping Holocaust survivors. She answered: "Well – nor does anyone else!" I never met her again but I went to the Jewish Temporary Shelter to meet the group – "The Boys" –

as they dubbed themselves later (although there were some girls, too!) – and immortalised by Sir Martin Gilbert's volume of that name.[12]

My background was very different from theirs. My roots were long-established in Britain: fifth generation on my Sephardi father's side and fourth on my Ashkenazi mother's side. We were brought up to be proud of being British and of belonging to the oldest British Jewish community.

After "The Boys" left the Shelter and in recognition of the strong bonds that had developed between these young people, the CBF and the CCCCC opened a Youth Club in 1947 where they could continue to meet. It became known as The Primrose Club and was based in Belsize Park in North West London.

It was led by the gifted and experienced youth worker, Dr Paul Yogi Mayer, a refugee from pre-war Germany. He had been a community worker in Germany and he was a keen athlete. He had been a volunteer in the British Army then served in the renowned Special Operations Executive. He became a personal mentor to "The Boys". They have deeply appreciated his sensitive understanding and involvement ever since.

I became regularly involved at The Primrose Club along with Richard Barnett. Richard found that the club members responded with enthusiasm to classical music so he organised weekly concerts on gramophone records. This had a lasting impact, as many recall today. I introduced a drama group and produced a play. Richard and I were married in 1948.

It was through Richard that I came to know some of the Schonfeld family. One of his oldest school friends was Leon Hertz, a son of the Chief Rabbi. Leon's sister Judith became Rabbi Solomon Schonfeld's wife. Leon's wife, Irene introduced me to her and her sons; but, to my regret, I never met her husband. Jeremy, the youngest son, has been in touch with me and my family ever since and encouraged me to produce this book.

As "The Boys" grew into adulthood they formed their own mutual support group, the '45 Aid Society. "The Boys" – and the girls, too – have become like a family, sharing each other's celebrations and sorrows. They turned to helping others, giving generously to a range of charities. Their chairman became Treasurer of the CBF - the organisation that had brought them to England and supported them in the early years. A number are among my oldest friends. **Bertha Fischer** is one of them. We

*The Primrose Club, a social and residential Youth Club for "The Boys",
was established in these two properties at 26-27 Belsize Park in North
London in 1947. (CB)*

met when she joined my husband's music group. It was through Bertha and her sister-in-law, **Rachel Malmud**, whose stories appear later, that **Olga Grossman** got in touch with me.

This happened in 1996 during the six months that I was working in Jerusalem annually as a social work consultant. Olga was the first to tell me about the Slovakian group and the Reunion they were planning. **Anna Katscher,** whose idea it was, also suggested people write about their experiences for this occasion. Olga was finding that quite difficult. So I offered to assist her. We became close friends and have stayed in touch ever since.

On my return to London I offered my services to the Reunion Committee. This was chaired by Jonathan Schonfeld, middle son of the Rabbi, and made up of several of the original group. My personal and professional experience differed widely from theirs and they all belong to ultra-orthodox communities; nevertheless they welcomed me and invited me to work with them.

The hardest task was to trace the present whereabouts of the original group. Extensive correspondence was involved. I collected material for two booklets. One was to mark the occasion about the group as a whole, the other containing a dozen personal stories, three transcribed from interviews. Some people avoided talking about their history altogether because of a belief that it is unpropitious to name the dead. Several had encountered exploitative journalists "Tell me your story and we'll share the profits". I heard of similar stories in which lengthy interviews were given but the reporter was never heard of again. I had to answer some very direct questions and faced some suspicion. "Are you a survivor? A Slovak?" I am neither. "So what are you going to get out of this? Why are you so interested?" My integrity was seriously tested. I saw my role as an enabler, to provide an opportunity for people to share their previously untold experiences during the war and how successfully they had rebuilt their lives since. At the Reunion someone asked if I was going to publish their stories. "Do you want me to?" I replied. And that is how this project began.

Two years after the Reunion I had traced two-thirds of those named on the Group Visa (See Appendix C) that had allowed them to leave Czechoslovakia and written to them all. Eventually I collected a further 26 contributions to add to the original dozen. Many of these experiences were shared by siblings so statistically

Paul Yogi Mayer, MBE, 1912-2011, a pre-war German refugee. He served as a volunteer in the SOE, was the eminent manager of The Primrose and The Brady Clubs, and life-long mentor to "The Boys". (MM)

these accounts represent about a third of the original group. Another third chose not to take part, personal decisions that I treated with respect. The last third remain untraced.

Some had, until then, avoided all comment on the war years. For the majority the recollection process was an ordeal. What they have offered here is as much as they feel able to share. Owing to the sensitivity of the experience I refrained from using a tape recorder and I chose not to question or discuss what I was told. Some contributors gave me written accounts, others accepted my offer to write on their behalf. I made notes from conversations, many of them on coach journeys during that momentous weekend of the Reunion. Others resulted from meetings in Israel and in London, in their home or mine, during the following year or two.

Inevitably mistakes and inaccuracies arose during the process of transcription. I tried to correct them by contacting the contributors. Here is a typical letter I wrote on 9th August 1998:

"I so much enjoyed meeting you at the Reunion in April. Here is a copy of the notes I made when you told me some stories about your life. That was when we sat together on the coach to London. When you see this, I expect you will find mistakes I have made; and I am sure you will remember more about your experiences and your feelings that you could add. Perhaps one of your family or a friend would make some more notes and any alterations. Then you will have a full account to pass on to your grandchildren. I will gladly add anything you send – or alter anything – and send it back to you. I am collecting as many stories as I can about the 'Schonfeld Children'. Maybe they could be put in a book – if you and others agree – as a memorial to Rabbi Schonfeld. At present I am just encouraging people to write their stories for their own family records.
Best wishes to you and your family. Keep well!"

Very few replies ever reached me. I slowly realized that I had to accept that the subject was perhaps too painful to look at again. That is why few of the stories that follow have been checked by their contributor. They are published here are as they were presented, whether spoken or in writing, most for the first time. I made no attempt to query any details; and any errors are mine and mine alone.

Very few survivors chose to tell others about their past before reaching retirement. Jona Laks was an exception. Even in 1946 the Rabbi found her willing to talk about her almost unspeakable experiences. She has yet to publish her memoirs. (See Appendix A.) We hear, too, of those who firmly avoided any mention of their wartime ordeals to their children or even to their spouses in a determined effort to shelter them from the anguish that these had provoked.

Frequently today the subject arises when grandchildren ask questions for a school project on their family history. This has become wide spread practice for Jewish children approaching *Barmitzvah*. For Jews this is reminiscent of the duty of parents when celebrating the Passover to tell their children how their ancestors were freed from slavery in ancient Egypt. Survivors are told these days that they have a duty to describe what happened to them.

Steven Spielberg's Shoah Foundation, Yad Vashem and others have recorded interviews with witnesses of the Holocaust. The redesigned museum at Yad Vashem makes spectacular use of tapes like these. Former slave labourers, camp inmates and Hidden Children have become committed to passing on their stories as a legacy to the Second Generation.

The Schonfeld Archive

Rabbi Schonfeld's personal papers are housed in the Anglo-Jewish Archives at Southampton University. They have painstakingly been catalogued and made available by Professor C. M. Woolgar and his helpful staff. I spent a couple of days reading through all the material covering 1948 and 1949. There is a mound of miscellaneous documents about the administration and financing of the Slovakian venture but only a few thumb-nail reports about individual children.

A large part comprises an almost daily correspondence between the administrators: Henry Pels, the Rabbi's Executive Secretary in London and Olga Eppel, his Administrator in Dublin – two determined and indefatigable individuals. They were often at loggerheads over money matters but shared a determination to see the project through whatever the difficulties.

Another source is the volume the Rabbi published himself[13] in which he gives some idea of his many activities and accomplishments. Much more derives from those who had personal contact with him: his family and his colleagues, his congregants and employees and the refugees themselves.

It is appropriate to gain some impression of the Slovak environment, the Jewish community and their situation prior to and during the Second World War as a background to the stories that follow.

Chapter One

Slovakia - the terrain, its history and Jewish minority

Bratislava Castle c.1930, since restored.

Slovakia is not to be found on an atlas until after the First World War. It was then that the Austro-Hungarian Empire was split up and its Slovak minority, present in Hungary for near one thousand years, was granted the eastern half of the newly-created Republic of Czechoslovakia. In 1938 a Fascist party took over the Slovak area till they were ousted by the Russians in 1945. Only in 1993 did Slovakia become an independent state.

The map shows its position, land-locked in Eastern Europe with Bratislava, formerly known as Pressburg, as its major city. Bratislava stands on the flood plains of the Danube River between two other capital cities. To the west is Vienna only 55 km (34 miles) away. The Hungarian capital, Budapest, is 163 km (101 miles) to the east.

The central area of the country contains the gently rounded and densely forested limestone range of the Carpathian Mountains divided by two deep river valleys; and above them tower the majestic granite peaks of the High Tatras.

In peace time this region is popular for health spas and winter sports. But it had more sombre uses during the Second World War when it was unfriendly territory, forbidding for strangers. It was from here that the Slovak Partisans organised guerrilla warfare against the Fascists. And here, too, numerous Jewish fugitives found hiding places in primitive conditions.

In the High Tatra Mountains. (TK)

Eastern Slovakia is covered with conifer and beech woods and is noted for its minority groups – Romanies (Gypsies), Hungarians, Rusyns and - until World War Two - for its Jews. Its principal towns are Košice and Prešov.

In the western half of Czechoslovakia the largely Protestant Czechs built up a stronger and more industrial economy with a more liberal outlook and closer links with Western Europe than the predominantly Slovak and Catholic east. This eastern terrain was, and still is, far less developed. In rural areas electricity did not arrive until after the Second World War, roads were unpaved and health services primitive and sparse. Yet from 1918 Tomas Masaryk, followed later by Edvard Benes, skillfully led a democratic and liberal regime that gave Jews and other minorities equal rights.

Slovak Jews

Slovakia has had a Jewish presence for at least ten centuries. Records refer to Jews living in the area in 1251 and of a synagogue in Pressburg (later Bratislava) in 1399. In the sixteenth century the Jews of Pressburg were given refuge in Podhradie – literally "under the castle" just outside the city walls. There is evidence that attitudes towards Jews fluctuated over the years between acceptance and expulsion. Nevertheless communities steadily developed across the country. In 1806 a *yeshiva* opened in Pressburg. It drew students from far afield. It was a stronghold of Hungarian Jewish orthodoxy led by a succession of distinguished Rabbis. Riots broke out in 1848 when the city council granted Jews equal rights, and again in 1851 when some Jews opened businesses within the city. Yet Slovak Jews remained.

In 1872 a Neolog congregation made some reforms to synagogue services, introduced a Jewish education that included secular subjects, and expressed sympathy with Zionism. Orthodox Rabbis were naturally conservative; most of them opposed Zionism as a secularist misinterpretation. A third community stood between the two known as the Status Quo. Similar divisions were also developing in Vienna and Budapest but the majority adhered to Orthodox practice. Jews saw themselves as loyal to the state. Some 320,000 Jewish men served in the Austro-Hungarian forces during the First World War and 40,000 died in that conflict.

Anti-Semitism came to the surface several times during the economic crisis of the 1930s. Poor economic and social conditions readily exacerbated racial prejudice. Zionism offered fresh hope for more assimilated Jews and those in Reform communities. Yet in contrast to what was to follow, conditions seemed fairly good for Slovakian Jews during the years between the two World Wars.

Bratislava Orthodox Synagogue, Heydukova Street, built 1923-26. The only synagogue still in use. (Michal Kelovy/Wikipedia).

Seine Majestät
Der Kaiser von Oesterreich
König von Böhmen u.s.w.
und Apostolische König von Ungarn

haben mit Allerhöchster Entschließung

vom 27.Mai 1918

dem san.Leutnant i.d.R.

G U S T A V   S T E I N E R

des IR.72,beim perm.Krankenzug 54,

in Anerkennung vorzüglicher und aufopferungsvoller Dienstleistung im Kriege,

das Goldene Verdienstkreuz mit der Krone
am Bande der Tapferkeitsmedaille

Allergnädigst zu verleihen geruht.

Was hiermit beurkundet wird.

Wien, am 4.Juni 1918.

Von Seiner k. u. k. Apostolischen Majestät

Obersthofmeisteramt:

Gustav Steiner, uncle of David Steiner, served in the Austro-Hungarian army among numerous fellow Jews. He received the Golden Cross for Bravery. From 1919 he worked as a General Practitioner in Bratislava. He died in Dachau in 1944. (DS)

Daily life was punctuated by orthodox teachings and routines. Children attended *cheder* in places too small to provide a Jewish school. The Sabbath and the dietary laws were widely observed. Where many shops were shut on a Saturday there was clear evidence of an established Jewish community. The wider population, largely Roman Catholic, relied on their Jewish neighbours for numerous goods and services and broadly accepted them. They rarely mixed socially because the rules of *kashrut* precluded Jews from eating outside their community. Some children met unpleasantness particularly in village schools where Catholic priests spread old prejudices and teachings; but on the whole, following Tomáš Masaryk's upholding of equal rights, Jewish communities were free to follow their own life style and religious practices.

I was born in Bratislava at a time when we Jews were proud to live in Czechoslovakia among enterprising and tolerant people with a rich culture. We were free to follow our own practices and Jews prospered. That was why my parents named me Tamáš, in honour of President Masaryk.

Tamáš Reif

He describes Jewish life in Bratislava during the late 1930s:

Our community was well organised, with both Orthodox and Reform congregations settled in a centuries-old area of the city built in Hapsburg times. It was near the bridge across the Danube by the great Cathedral and the fish market. When the war came and throughout the ghetto years the community centre remained active; the soup kitchen was open every day, *shabat* meals pre-paid. There was true charity above all else.

The census of 1938 counted about 95,000 Jews in Slovakia in numerous long-established Jewish communities scattered in towns and villages across the country. They served in a wide range of occupations and professions. There were a few who owned large properties:

Our grandfather was a timber merchant with large concerns in the forest.

Hedviga Friedmann

Our father and his three brothers were builders and he owned a lot of property, farms and forests.

Olga Grossman

Our father was very rich before the war. He owned a five-storey house with 28 rooms and was in the clothing business.

Gaspar Binet

I have a vague picture of my father. He provided wholesale supplies for the bakery trade.

Tamáš Reif

I was born in a small place in the Tokai district noted for its vineyards. My father was in the wine business and had a grocery shop. We were kings of the place, one of about 35 Jewish families living there.

Ervin Schwarz

The great majority were modest artisans and shopkeepers providing crucial services; but there was widespread poverty. In larger towns there were Jewish schools and *yeshivot* and numerous communal organisations. Those better off helped the needy where they could. For most Jewish families, particularly those in remote villages and hamlets, life was a struggle. Living conditions were harsh, toilets were outside, bathrooms unknown, medical services primitive. **Tamáš Reif** mentions that even in 1945 his mother was treated with leeches at the Jewish Hospital in Bratislava. Yet there was a rich Jewish life that is remembered in retrospect as steady and serene.

A massive political change

In the background, however, a sinister movement was quietly coming to life. In 1918 Andreas Hlinka, a Roman Catholic priest, had inaugurated a small Fascist party that was wildly anti-Semitic. This group slowly but steadily gathered strength until 1938 when they abruptly threw out the liberal government of Benes and took control of the country. This occurred just when the Allies had forsaken Czechoslovakia and the Germans had occupied Sudetenland. Benes fled to Britain. So did Masaryk's son. Hlinka died in 1938, Josef Tiso, another anti-Semitic priest, took his place and on March 14[th,] 1939 Hitler "persuaded"[1] Tiso's

50 koruna coin issued by the Fascist regime showing Tiso. (Sebastian Wallroth/Wikipedia).

Nationalists to break away. Thus an independent Slovakia was born under German "protection" and declared itself an ally of Nazi Germany. Czechoslovakia was completely dismembered. Moravia and Bohemia were renamed as a Protectorate on a pretext by Hitler that this was necessary to deal with local instability. The next day Hungary annexed a wide strip of southern and eastern Slovakia, including Košice. This ancient city, the next in importance and size to Bratislava, had been part of the Austro-Hungarian Empire before 1920.

These abrupt changes had a devastating impact on the Jewish population. At first there was Slovak resistance to Tiso's rule but any opposition was harshly subdued. Vojtech Tuka was appointed Prime Minister, another pro-Nazi. Political propaganda rapidly appeared depicting Jews as commercial thieves, accused of expropriating Slovakian property and promoting Hungarian influence and language. All holders of Hungarian nationality, some 40,000, most of them Jews, were summarily expelled along with their families.

In 1941, a system of anti-Semitic regulations was instituted. It was modeled on the Nuremberg Laws and enforced by the Hlinka Guards, the Slovak equivalent of the Gestapo. Jews were required to wear yellow armbands, banned from using public transport, expelled from schools, from the army and the civil service, and their legal rights abolished. For a while some occupations were "reserved" if their expertise was in short supply, doctors and engineers among them.

All debts due to Jews were cancelled. Jewish property, commercial and private, was confiscated. Initially high officials took possession of it; then Hlinka Guards helped themselves and finally the local population was free to loot and sabotage what was left. By 1941 ten thousand Jewish enterprises had been expropriated or destroyed. A further 2,223 businesses were taken over by appointees known as *arisators*. Most of these floundered through the lack of experience of their new managers.

Several thousands emigrated; but to move abroad involved lengthy procedures and heavy expense, out of the question for most people. Before the war began my parents had a visa for us to go to the States but my father was the eldest son and would not leave his elderly parents.

Eva Schwarz

An aunt in America sent us an affidavit but unfortunately we were unable to validate it because of formalities. Another option was to make *aliyah*; but that was fraught with hazards. We were like fish in an aquarium. For an individual, flight might still be possible; but for a close little group like ours, this was no longer credible.

In a letter from **Ivan Stahler**'s uncle

Too many waited too long – in the hope that the situation was transient. But that was not to be. Increasing pressures demanded immediate means of escape. It was more reasonable to seek ways to cross the southern border in to Hungary where conditions were less alarming. Many children, like the **Reichs** and the **Malmud** sisters, were escorted by local peasants paid to lead them across remote border crossings to the care of relatives. It was a risky venture. Yet at Kežmarok some 2,200 refugees were led into Hungary by plucky loyalists. However once there refugees without identity documents or ration books were at risk from the Hungarian authorities as were their hosts.

A secret network of Partisans, Jewish and gentile, developed to provide guides, safe houses and forged identity documents to assist those trying to escape. In Bratislava a hiding place was devised under the main synagogue.[2] Košice synagogue had similar facilities.

Nitra yeshiva became a safe house nicknamed "The Vatican". Students dug hideouts below their study rooms where fugitives could rest while lectures continued overhead. They were advised always to carry a knife hidden in their shoe. By such means their eminent teacher, Rabbi Weissmandl managed to escape later from a cattle truck en route to Auschwitz. **Alfred Kahan** describes his family home, the "Goldring House", as a safe haven:

The goal was to get people, especially the Zionist youth, to Romania and thence to Palestine. The route was through the Goldring House … I recall people arriving one night, and disappearing during the next …

Many of the **Kahan** family were involved in organising escape networks.

… but two of my uncles were caught and, with their wives and children, died in Auschwitz. Another one boarded a boat bound for Palestine with

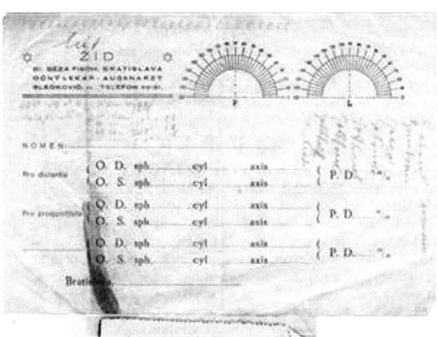

Dr. Fisch, father of Hetty Weiner-Fisch, an oculist in a protected occupation. Note "zid" (Jew). A prescription he gave for spectacles and below another for medication, 1944. (HF)

his family, but a German torpedo sunk the ship and they all perished. Somehow five of the eight Goldring families did survive - and without entering Auschwitz.

Many of the fugitives fled deep into the mountain region among the Partisans. Shmuel Klein's friend, Romi Cohn left Nitra yeshiva to live in continual danger in Bratislava. He vividly describes his experiences there and how he went on to join the Partisans and fought with them.[3] He met up with a tough band of older men, struggling to survive in conditions that were hazardous at the best of times, and bitterly cold, exceptionally so during the winter of 1944. They were resolute in their determination to cause disarray among the Fascists. He tells how Jewish fugitives and Partisans alike were dependent for essential supplies from villagers willing to risk their lives. Those caught were shot without trial.

In the towns small underground industries developed to forge documents and distribute them, making it possible for their holders to live and work as Christians. They did so in an atmosphere where they could never relax, always at risk of discovery. In Hungary as conditions worsened there were similar activities.

In the autumn of 1941 Tiso and Tuka met Hitler to plan the elimination of all remaining Slovak Jews. Those with German, Sudeten or Hungarian papers were expelled. Measures were taken to exploit the working capacity of those who were able-bodied. First youths, and then girls, aged 16-35, were rounded up and deported for "war work" within German territory.

David Steiner showed me at Yad Vashem German documents recording the deportations of 58,000 Slovakian Jews between March and October 1942. **Rachel Malmud** gives a vivid account of how she and her sister narrowly escaped being among them. They did not know their destination.

By 1941 ten thousand Jews from Bratislava had been forcibly deported, ostensibly to make available housing for non-Jews. Thousands, deprived of any income, had registered for aid from Jewish community funds. By May numbers nearly doubled those recorded seven months earlier.

Men were deported to build Transit Camps at Sered, Vyhne and Nováky. The Vatican criticised this break-up of families

Košice Synagogue built in 1926. (Marion Gladis/Wikipedia)

so wives and children were sent after them, the **Schwarzthal** family and **Erich Bock** among them. Jewish community leaders organised industrial workshops in the Transit Camps. These made a substantial contribution to the war effort and stemmed the flow of deportees into German occupied territory. The Fascists had prepared Jews for deportation by fooling them into believing there would be better conditions at their destination. Those remaining in the Transit Camps faced a severe shortage of food and water and overcrowded and insanitary conditions that killed many and weakened the rest.

In January 1942 at the Wannsee Conference "The Final Solution of the Jewish Problem" was mapped out. Eichmann boasted that in Slovakia "... the matter (of preparing the ground for the 'Final Solution') is no longer so difficult." The Slovak government had entered into a monstrous agreement to pay the Nazis 500 Reichmarks for every Jew "relocated" to Nazi territory, ostensibly to cover their food, clothing and housing. In return the Slovaks received a guarantee that the deportees would not return or make any future claims on their confiscated property.[4] In Eichmann's confession at his trial he said "Slovakian officials offered their Jews to us like someone throwing away sour beer ".

Then came a dramatic change. From October 1942 until September 1944 there were no deportations from Slovakia. Nothing like this occurred anywhere else in Europe. Various explanations have been offered. Livia Rothkirchen, the eminent Slovak historian, suggests three contributory factors.[5] The first was public opinion. Large numbers in the wider population had made material gains from "aryanisation" of Jewish property; but the witnessing of mass deportations and the cruelty inflicted by the Hlinka Guard began to alter initial indifference. In addition news was emerging from escaped prisoners and soldiers returning from the battle fronts of appalling conditions, torture and systematic mass murder by the Germans.

Secondly, correspondence found after the war between the Papal Nuncio in Bratislava and the Vatican expressed some concern about the verdict of history in a post-war world. Tiso was warned that the treatment of the Jews (particularly of those who had converted to Catholicism) could be judged as contrary to Roman Catholic teachings. There were long delays before these letters were answered when the German ambassador accused the Vatican of meddling in Slovak Jewish policy.

The dominant reason for the halt in deportations was due to the strategies of the representatives of the Slovak Jewish community. They had to work with a certain Dieter Wisliceny, the German Nazi sent to Bratislava to oversee deportations. A full account of their remarkable tactics has been published by Abraham Fuchs.[6] The Committee of Six, as they named themselves was led by two outstanding individuals: Rabbi Chaim Michael Dov Weissmandl, teacher and friend of Rabbi Schonfeld, and Mrs Gisi Fleischman, an able leader in the Zionist movement.

They worked intensively to ameliorate conditions at Transit Camps. They urged that these be sited within Slovakia. And they devised the Europa Plan.

The Europa Plan was an ambitious scheme to save European Jewry. They secretly sent couriers to Jewish communities in the free world - including Rabbi Schonfeld - with reports about what was really happening to the thousands deported, urging them to convince the Allies to destroy railroad access. Their concern was for all the besieged Jewish communities of Eastern Europe. Their plea was for substantial sums of money to bribe the Nazi warlords. Tragically, the response was too slow and inadequate. Some thought the reports to be wildly exaggerated and the sums demanded extortionate. The reaction of a Swiss representative demonstrates this: he offered payment but insisted it would be handed over only after the war.

In Bratislava the Committee of Six lured Dieter Wisliceny with promises of large cash payments if he halted the trains to Auschwitz. They kept rapacious officials on a string for as long as they could. Gisi Fleischman succeeded in bribing a top official's wife until this was discovered. They had uncovered Wisliceny's weaknesses: his delusions of grandeur, his ambition to enrich himself and his belief in hugely wealthy Jews. They invented a fantasy figure in Switzerland and forged letters purporting to come from him, offering massive payments. It was a very risky strategy. and succeeded in playing for time.

Abraham Fuchs quotes the concluding words of Rabbi Weissmandl's own report on these negotiations: "From the day after *Yom Kippur* 5703 (1942) until the day after *Yom Kippur* 5705 (1944) and the war of the Partisans there was respite from the expulsions in Slovakia." Livia Rothkirchen has uncovered more details of this intense situation and there continues to be

Gisi Fleischman, close friend of Hetty Fisch's mother, wearing a hat, beside Hetty Fisch's aunt Beate Weiner on the left. (HF)

controversy among historians about other factors current at the time.[7]

Another member of the Committee of Six was Rabbi Armin Frieder. He had developed at Nové Mesto a community centre known as "Ohel David" – in Hebrew meaning "David's Tent". There was an Old Age Home and a Soup Kitchen as well as cultural and educational facilities. The Fascist authorities recognised Rabbi Frieder as manager of the complex . Somehow the Rabbi built up so trusting a relationship with the Minister of Education that he was able to negotiate with him. He even had access to government files on the Jewish community. During the lull in deportations he succeeded in transferring many elderly from Transit Camps to Ohel David, then still a place of safety. He saved many lives. Twice he was arrested and twice he escaped.

In April 1942 Rudolf Vrba and Alfred Wetzler were among 2000 Slovak Jewish men deported to Auschwitz. They set themselves to make a thorough study of the death camp, its activities and organisation. Two years later by dint of masterly tactics they managed to escape and amazingly avoided recapture. They reached Zilina in April 1944 where they immediately dictated "The Auschwitz Protocols" from the mass of information they had memorised. This unique report eventually reached leaders among the Allies but tragically failed to have any impact on their tactics. Their ardent hope was to forewarn the Jews of Hungary of their impending deportation. Tragically, too, this did not happen. Explanations continue to be debated, most recently by Martin Gilbert.[8] After the war Vrba published his story.[9]

There is no doubt that all these activities played some part in holding back the deportations. That increasingly uneasy balance was abruptly destroyed in 1944 by the Slovak National Uprising - a heroic but futile attempt to oust the Fascists. On August 29th 1944 the free radio from Banská Bystrica announced The Uprising. The response was widespread and enthusiastic but it was a military disaster. Some Palestinian Jews were dropped by parachute to assist. Havivah Reik was one of them. She was caught and executed.[10] A Jewish resistance movement inside Nováky Camp overpowered the prison guards and the entire camp was liberated. Escapees joined the fugitives in the forests. The Germans reacted rapidly to subdue the insurgents and to track down all remaining Jews. The invading army quelled the riots and occupied the rest of the country. Thousands of resistance fighters were killed.

Large-scale deportations of Jews began again. They were imprisoned in Transit Camps; mostly in Theresienstadt where the Germans for one brief period dressed up a bit of it to fool Red Cross officials into believing it was a "model" camp. By the time the war ended in March 1945 no more than four or five thousand Jews remained in Slovakia, all living in hiding.[11]

From War to Peace

It was early December. Ours was the last transport to leave Sered. We spent seven days on that awful train scheduled to take us to Auschwitz. My mother tells me it was a horrendous experience. The Russians were advancing so the train turned back to Theresienstadt.

Israel Reich

By 1945 the Allies were gaining the upper hand and steadily ousting the Axis powers across Europe. They were confronted with the full horror of the Concentration Camps. Gordon Langner, a young cousin of mine, died from a disease he caught in this horrendous exercise. The most vivid and stark record, perhaps, is to be found in the books of Primo Levi[12] where he recounts his experiences within Auschwitz and during the chaotic conditions that followed liberation.

The Russians finally drove out the Germans from Prague on May 9th 1945. The people of Czechoslovakia flocked to welcome them as liberators, unaware of the true nature of a Communist regime. A second Republic of Czechoslovakia was declared without Carpathian Ruthenia which was ceded to the Ukraine.

Against all odds some Jews had managed to remain free and were emerging from hiding places.

In April 1945 we were liberated from a bunker where we were hidden. There was chaos across the continent. Basic services had collapsed. Journeys took circuitous routes to avoid wrecked bridges and bombed intersections.

Erich Bock

> We (Camp survivors) could travel for free but trains were so packed:
> we lay in peril on the roof; some were killed by overhead wires.

Ervin Schwarz

Essential supplies were severely restricted. Soldiers and civilians, refugees and released prisoners were all struggling to reach their homes desperate to discover whether any of their family was still alive. A grapevine rapidly developed to distribute any news. Lists of survivors were displayed wherever a temporary shelter was established but the lists of those who known to have perished were far longer. 95,000 Jews had been resident in Slovakia in 1938. When the war ended only 25,000 remained. 13,000 had been starved or murdered in the Death camps and many others succumbed to the wretched conditions in their hiding places.

Hetty Weiner-Fisch describes finding her aunt again:

> She weighed no more than 27 kilos. She smelt of vomit and sweat. She
> was in shock but so HAPPY. I froze before going near her.

Relief for survivors was rapidly organised by local, national and international charities. Disturbing information has come to light about the International Committee of the Red Cross's attitude to Nazi activities. In 1997 John Simpson, the BBC's World Affairs Editor explored their wartime record.[13] Their Chairman, Cecil Burkhardt, had visited Camps and met Hitler in the 1930s. He ended a letter to Hitler:

> ".... What especially and permanently impressed itself upon me was the spirit of co-operation which informed everything. Your deeply devoted, etc..."

In 1942 the ICRC was informed about the Extermination Camps. Most members were shocked. Cecil Burkhardt insisted that their role was to stay impartial and that their duty was only to combatants. An appeal to one side would negate this and anger Germany, endanger Switzerland and risk invasion. The result was that no action was taken. In 1997 Simpson interviewed a retired senior officer. "I didn't want to get the ICRC into trouble," he said. "Can you be proud of what you did?" asked Simpson.

"I'm not ashamed. These people were proud of their work. They were convinced they were purifying Europe."

Displaced Person Camps were set up. Food, clothing, and pocket money were distributed. Free travel was granted to survivors of the death camps. The Allies' armies of occupation gave every possible assistance. Complexes previously assigned for military use were rapidly adapted to house and care for struggling survivors. Medical facilities were rapidly packed with the very sick from the Camps. For some the armistice came too late. They were too damaged to recover. Others needed long-term medical care before they could lead independent lives again.

Numerous accounts tell of survivors' arduous journeys to their former homes only to discover not one of their family had returned, of finding hostile neighbours in possession who greeted them with anger, disdain and hatred. At Kielce in Poland they were confronted by a shocking *pogrom.*

Alfred Leicht tells what it felt like and **Ervin Schwarz** records how he was treated on return to his home town. A mere ten per cent survived in Topoľčany, north of Nitra. It is a town of 15,000 today. Some 3,000 Jews lived there when the war began including the **Schwarzthal** family. But when they returned in the autumn of 1945 they were attacked by their former neighbours and many were severely injured. "The Jerusalem Report", on November 28th 2005 reported that present leaders expressed their "deep regret at the tragic event … which has no equivalent in our modern history in terms of its evil and inhuman character."

But there were some loyal gentile friends, too:

Our former landlady returned to us all the furniture and other items we had asked her to hold for us.

Erich Bock

And another pleasant surprise:

One of my father's patients, the flower man, presented me with a bag of ducats he had saved till my return.

Hetty Weiner-Fisch

Such incidents were rare. Most survivors found it was safer to stay together in larger towns like Bratislava and Košice. They were destitute, physically and emotionally drained. Fellow citizens, formerly affable clients, customers and neighbours, were no longer so and with few exceptions could not be trusted. The outlook was bleak. The threat of a Communist take-over introduced yet another danger for Jews. It became a reality when the USSR took over all of Czechoslovakia from April 1948. They gave Jews two options: to completely assimilate or leave for Palestine. So there was intense interest in emigration, particularly to Israel.

We knew the Russians were coming and we would be hemmed in.
Blanka Federweiss

There was also the problem of Communism. We heard about horrors in Russia, from prisoners returning from there, and from Jewish Red Army officers who awaited the first opportunity to escape to the west.
Alfred Kahan

Everyone was very much alarmed by the Communist take-over and knew what it meant for the Jewish people.
Ervin Kummeldorfer

The Communist take-over was horrifying. Enough that the war had ravaged the Jewish community. Now we were jumping from the frying pan into the fire.
Tamáš Reif

We had returned to a Czechoslovakia we didn't recognise. The Communists were controlling more every day. Life for Jews was difficult.
Vera Wiesen

Communist control was to continue until the "Velvet Revolution" in 1989 which was, as John Simpson revealed only in 2009, allowed to happen by the Secret Police. It took till 1993 before the independent Slovak Republic was established under the liberal leader, Vaclav Havel and by then few Jews remained. Avi Becker wrote in the Israeli daily paper, "Ha'aretz" on 11th January 2006:
"After 50 years of war and life under a totalitarian Communist regime in Slovakia, most Jews have totally assimilated. Jewish

education was banned by a dictatorial government that cast terror on its citizens and provoked anti-Semitic violence. Today young people are coming forward eager to re-establish Jewish traditional life, something they have never experienced."

"The Jerusalem Report" on 23rd January, 2006 wrote that in 2002 the government of Slovakia had set up a fund of $26.5 million to pay reparations to individuals and the Jewish community. The nation's Memory Institute was establishing lists of Slovak Jews imprisoned, deported or murdered during the Holocaust and a list of Jewish-owned companies shut down by the Nazi puppet government of 1939-45.[14]

Today the country has only some 2,000 Jews.

Of the old Jewish Quarter of Bratislava nothing remains but a plaque. Jan Morris, the renowned travel writer, comments nostalgically about the huge loss across Europe of previously flourishing and industrious cultured Jewish communities. She reminds us how for centuries past Jews had influenced and enriched the countries where they had settled in so many ways.

The agony for parents - the plight of children

That any children survived the war is astonishing. Urban hideouts in cellars and outhouses had been hurriedly improvised, but no baby or toddler could be kept silent in such places. At least one crying infant was suffocated to save the rest. **Shoshana Brayer** mentions this. So does **Judit Ziegler** in her poem:

> "But my baby sister, have you heard of her?
> They wanted to kill her because she cried."

In a desperate situation parents had made rapid and difficult decisions. An unknown number of children were placed in convents and monasteries or in foster homes with former neighbours or employees. Others lived with families loyal to the Partisans. Martin Gilbert records that by 2008 Yad Vashem had honoured 22,211 Christians as "Righteous Gentiles" for saving Jewish lives - among them are 478 Slovak families.[15] In all these placements children had to play a role. Even their names were changed. They are spoken of today as "Hidden Children".

Without warning or preparation they were required to merge into an unfamiliar environment where they and their protectors lived in constant danger at every hour of the day and night. Nowhere was fully safe and new Fascist regulations continually added fresh constraints throughout the war. Wherever the Hlinka discovered a Hidden Child the whole household would be shot without trial and nothing recorded.

After the armistice was declared in May 1945 any surviving children were faced with another grim and bewildering situation. Many never found their parents again Adult survivors were all in poor shape and children saw them struggling to cope. At the same time possibilities for emigrating were being explored, complex processes that took time, perseverance and patience. Meanwhile there were fresh dangers to face every day in a hostile environment.

Schools and youth groups and residential Children's Homes were established. **Edit Katz** told of her embarrassment in finding herself in an orphanage where her mother had been a benefactor. Many child survivors were housed in hostels organised by *World Agudath Israel*, *World Jewish Congress* and *Beis Ya'acov* schools, and training centres were set up to prepare young people for *aliyah.*

Some very sick and frail children were sent to convalescent homes, previously spas and resorts in the Tatras Mountains. One of these, at Villa Silvia, later moved into Rabbi Frieder's centre[16] in Nové Mesto, some miles north of Bratislava where he had hidden Jewish fugitives and protected many of the elderly during the worst times. Several children from Nové Mesto were among those brought to London by Rabbi Schonfeld in 1948.

Enter Rabbi Solomon Schonfeld.

Soon after peace was proclaimed on May 8th 1945, Rabbi Solomon Schonfeld came from London and toured the Continent. He saw what a vast task lay ahead for Jewish survivors and in particular for those with children. Parents needed time to recover their own health and strength before they could explore possibilities for rebuilding their family lives. Immediate conditions denied them the wherewithal to offer a traditional

Jewish setting for their families. Rabbi Schonfeld maintained there was an urgent need to provide this, a right they had been denied too long, in addition to immediate and good physical care. So he presented for children or young people a programme of recuperation in an Orthodox Jewish milieu, a fully traditional life and education long denied them.

His invitation extended their care until such time as relatives informed him they were ready for the children to join them again. If no family had survived he promised to assist lone children to settle where they chose – a promise he kept and took very seriously in his role *in loco parentis* to the end of his days. Since the armistice Rabbi Schonfeld had brought several groups of young people from Europe to recuperate in Britain. The last group was that from Slovakia and is the subject of this book.

Who was this man?

A series of images of Villa Silvia and of Ohel David.

At Villa Silvia. Judith Mannheimer helping out with the small children. Marianna Stahler is beside her wearing a bow. (JM)

Friday evening at Villa Silvia. Sabbath loaves - but no candles! Taken for American benefactors in 1946.
Note school folders on the shelf and portraits on the wall:
i. Tomáš Masaryk
ii. Edvard Beneš, both benevolent presidents
iii. Josef Stalin - The Russians as liberators from the Nazis were seen as heroes at this time. (TK)

DETSKÝ DOMOV

OHEL DÁVID
NOVÉ MESTO NAD VÁHOM
Kláštorská 60   Telefon 162

Č. j. ....

Predmet: ....
....

Nové Mesto n.Váh., 6/IV.1948.   194...

Dôstojný pán

Dr.N. Schönfeld,

P r a h a.
Hotel Paríž

Headed Notepaper for Detsky Domov (Children's Home) - Ohel David (David's Tent) established by Rabbi Frieder.

Recuperating at Villa Silvia in the High Tatra Mountains, 1946 (CK, TK, SL)

46

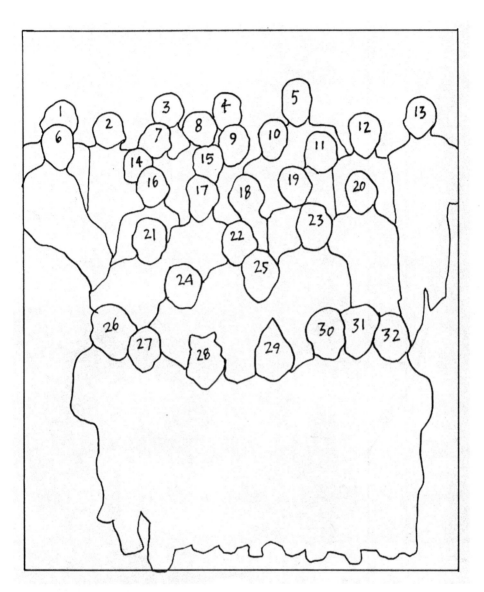

6. *Pál Krausz, now in London; 13. Tamáš, his brother, now in Bournemouth; 15. Istvan Stahler, now in London; 17. Gyurgy Stahler, his brother, deceased; 18. Eva Steiner, now in London; 19 Gizella Schwarzthal, now in Israel with sisters 20. Ella? Schwarzthal; 23. Rozsi? Schwarzthal (twin of 20); 25. Amiel Luknar (Schwartz), nephew of Rabbi Armin Frieder; 26. Oscar; 27. Duro Alexander, son of Iby Alexander, now cellist in Slovak Philharmonic Orchestra; 28. Marianna Stahler (sister of 15 and 17 above) now in London; 29. Pálo Weil; 30. Ivan Fried; 31. Sarolta Weinberger (the Stahlers' late grandmother).*

Mr Vogel and Mrs Vogel (JM)

Children from Villa Silvia after moving to Rabbi Frieder's facilities at Ohel David, including his nephew, Amiel; the three Schwarzthal girls are on the left. In charge were Mr Vogel (wearing a hat) and Mrs Vogel. (CK, TK, SL)

Israeli dancing at Ohel David (TK)

Shooting practice said to be in preparation for life in Israel! (TK)

Chapter Two

Solomon Schonfeld

An unusual example of CRREC notepaper with an impressive tally of their achievements.

This brief summary of Solomon Schonfeld's life is expanded from the one I prepared for the Reunion in 1998. It is based on an interview with his youngest son, Jeremy, further developed by his older brothers, Victor and Jonathan. Since I wrote this Professor Derek Taylor has published a full and fascinating biography. He tells some of the same legendary stories but his is a far more extensive study of the man and his many activities.

Solomon Schonfeld was born on February 21st, 1912 in Stoke Newington, North London and died in Highgate on February 6th, 1984. His father, Rabbi Dr Avigdor (Victor) Schonfeld, was born in 1880 at Sutto on the River Danube, a town between Bratislava (then Pressburg) and Budapest. His was a poor but learned family; he had one brother and six sisters. He won scholarships that financed his secondary education at a gymnasium in Pressburg where he also attended the *yeshiva*.

He moved on to the Universities of Vienna and of Giessen. His Ph.D thesis was about the similarities between some Rabbinical thinking and the philosophy of the eighteenth century British deist, Anthony Ashley Cooper, the Third Earl of Shaftesbury.

His father's career

Victor Schonfeld's first appointment as Rabbi was to Vienna at the age of 24. In 1909 he was called to the modest North London Beth Hamidrash, a congregation he transformed into a community. It became known as Adath Yisroel and was inspired by the teaching of Rabbi Samson Raphael Hirsch. He taught that the *Torah* and everyday life were inseparable. Victor Schonfeld had frequent disagreements with the Chief Rabbi of the United Synagogue. He generally took a stricter or more orthodox view. His son later described their stance: "We are on the right wing of Orthodoxy – Orthodox meaning correct".

Victor Schonfeld married Rachel Leah Sternberg who also came from a learned family, descendants of Rabbi Akiva Eger. They were antique dealers, well-to-do and very religious. It was a good match. The Rebbitzen had a strong personality and was a notable figure in her own right. She proved to be a capable organiser with a sense of humour. Solomon was their second son and one of seven children. All of them were strong-minded and forthright, and successful in their professions.

There were no Orthodox Jewish schools in Britain at that time, so Solomon was sent to the local Primary School and then to Highbury County School. August Gomez de Mesquita, who was a fellow pupil, told me he recalls him leading Jewish prayers there. In 1919 the whole Schonfeld family moved to Jerusalem following Rabbi Kook who had been appointed the first Ashkenazi Chief Rabbi of Palestine. He set up an education system and appointed Rabbi Victor Schonfeld as the Director. The Schonfeld family lived first at the famous Petra Hotel in the Old City and then in the Bukharan Quarter. But after only three years Rabbi Schonfeld resigned, disenchanted by the endless conflicts between secular and religious groups and continual squabbles about funding. So the family went back to England.

Rabbi Schonfeld chose to return to Adath Yisroel where he remained till his death although he had been offered several alternative and attractive appointments. One was in New York, another in Frankfurt am Main and a third that of Chief Rabbi of Salonika. In 1926 he inaugurated The Union of Orthodox Congregations and he threw his energies into developing the first Orthodox Jewish Day School in London. This school, later known as the Avigdor High School, was established in 1929. It became the kernel of the Jewish Secondary School Movement.

Solomon's Youth

In many ways Solomon's development emulated his father's. In 1927, aged just 15, he was sent to study at the *yeshiva* at Tyrnau in Slovakia, led by Rabbi Solomon David Ungar whose philosophy and enthusiasm made a profound impact on him. So did his renowned assistant, Michael Ber Weissmandl. In 1929 Victor became seriously ill and in a matter of days had died. The congregation voted that Solomon, young as he was, should take his father's place. He had by then signed up for courses in law at the London School of Economics and was articled to Lord Nathan in preparation for entering the legal profession. So, in 1930, these plans were abandoned. Rabbi Eli Munk was put in charge of Adath Yisroel while Solomon returned to Slovakia to finish his rabbinical studies.

There followed some controversy within the community over its future leadership. I am indebted to Rabbi Chanan Tomlin for clarifying this situation. He explains that there was some uncertainty about the terms of Rabbi Munk's appointment. One faction wanted it to be permanent. Mrs Schonfeld, a figure of consequence in the community, arranged an informal meeting to avert growing disunity. It was confirmed that Rabbi Munk had been appointed only until Solomon Schonfeld was fully qualified.

Solomon returned to Rabbi Ungar's *yeshiva* which had by then moved from Tyrnau to Nitra. There his study partner was Michael Weissmandl, mentioned earlier. He was a war hero who survived to re-establish the Nitra Yeshiva at Mount Kisco, New York State.[3] The two were life-long friends. Solomon moved on to study at the famous *yeshiva* at Slobodka in Lithuania. Like his father, he also took up secular subjects. At the University of Koenisberg he studied English literature, oriental languages and pedagogy and obtained a Ph.D with a thesis on Milton's use of Rashi. In 1933 Solomon Schonfeld, now Doctor, came back to London with his rabbinical diploma to follow in his father's footsteps. The new Rabbi comfortably straddled both worlds, the religious and the secular, and quickly adjusted to taking up his new responsibilities.

Rabbi Emeritus Herbert Richer (of the Liberal Jewish Movement) was brought up at the Adath Yisroel Synagogue in Green Lanes where his father was the *shammas*. He told me that many of the local shopkeepers belonged there and it was a community of cultured people. He recalls Rabbi Schonfeld as a typical English gentlemen, very handsome and clean-shaven and that he maintained a modest life-style - but he habitually wrote in green ink! "I remember him in 1936 at my *Barmitzvah* wearing a top hat and frock coat. He was only 24 years old at that time but he was so charismatic that everyone stood up when he entered. A few years later, when he brought refugees from the Continent we dubbed him "The Scarlet Pimpernel."[4]

At the same time the young Rabbi Schonfeld became Principal of the Avigdor High School his father had founded. During the next decade five more schools were opened, both primary and secondary. Their curriculum was based on a deliberate idea: to combine religious and secular education for Jewish children and remove the need for Hebrew Classes outside school hours (known as *cheder*). He wanted children to grow up with Judaism as an essential part of their lives and be confident and comfortable with their inheritance. To be a good Jew also meant being a good citizen.

From his father he inherited and continued to have clashes of opinion with the Dr J. H. Hertz, the Chief Rabbi of the United Synagogues of Great Britain, the central core of Ashkenazi communities. But if there was any animosity, that was soon to change. In 1939 Rabbi Schonfeld became engaged to be married. At that stressful time few were aware of this remarkable match. A letter from Dr Hertz tells his sister how he learned about it.

"....My daughter Judith told me a day after Yom Kippur: 'Father, I have promised to marry Dr Schonfeld.'

My reply was: 'If you have promised, then you must keep your promise.' And she did!"

He conducted the marriage ceremony on January 16th 1940 at his home in St John's Wood, in London. Most of their married life was spent at 73 Shepherd's Hill in Highgate, an attractive family house bought with a part of Judith's dowry. The Chief Rabbi described his new son-in-law in another letter to his sister:

"Of all the clergy he possesses most personality, common sense and fearlessness towards the assimilated aristocrats. His help proved invaluable. I could never have ventured to rescue 250 German Rabbis and their families without him as my *shammas*, representative and "Cossack". Add to this he is an exceptionally handsome man, six-foot high, blue-eyed and a renowned *shnorrer*, persuasive and affable. It is understandable that he could have won Judith. They are very happy."

Judith chose not to take any role in her husband's professional life and spent a lot of the war years at their cottage in Essex. Victor was born in 1940 followed by Jonathan in 1944, and Jeremy in 1951. In later years the country cottage became the boys' holiday haunt and their father's retreat. Judith preferred to stay in London; she had had enough of country life in wartime. So the boys would go there with their father. Rabbi Schonfeld delighted in relaxing with them, cycling, exploring the countryside, playing cricket and returning to cook a meal for them, all tired, muddy and happy. They recall him, too, spending a lot of time sitting on a deckchair in the garden having loud and heated discussions on the telephone. But he always tried to find time to read them a bedtime story. No wonder he was much-loved by his own children, too.

The rise of the Nazis and Schonfeld's response

News from Hitler's Germany of the rapid growth of Nazi power and anti-Semitism was reaching Jewish leaders in Britain and demanded their close attention. As conditions worsened

Anglo-Jewish communities organised relief efforts. The Jewish Refugee Committee (JRC) was established in March 1933 by Otto Schiff and was followed by the Central British Fund (CBF) which raised funds and channeled them to other relevant charities. The Zionist organisations focused on drawing refugees to Palestine.

Rabbi Schonfeld was determined to act before it was too late. During his travels on the Continent he had personally experienced an assault and witnessed attacks. He was deluged with requests for help. He realised how acute the situation was and how rapidly it was deteriorating. He doubted whether others fully recognised the urgency. There was no time to sit and plan but he speedily devised creative ways of operating. He personally improvised grounds for more than 1000 Jewish families to acquire British Visas in order to escape the Nazis. These were designed for rabbis, *shochetim*, teachers and *yeshiva* students ostensibly coming to train for work abroad which would involve a temporary stay. He successfully arranged Transit Visas for them and their families and chartered boats under the benign eye of tolerant officials. He used whatever means he could to achieve his aim of saving Jewish lives and finding suitable places of refuge before it was too late. On this he worked closely with Chief Rabbi Hertz. This was a liaison they both appreciated. In 1938 they set up the Chief Rabbi's Religious Emergency Council (CRREC). It was registered as a War Charity with Rabbi Schonfeld as its Executive Director. He worked from his London office at 86 Amhurst Park in Stamford Hill with a tiny staff.

In 1938 Rabbi Schonfeld brought to Britain twelve unaccompanied children, most from the main Orthodox Synagogue in Vienna.[5] He continued bringing increasing numbers till September 1939 when parents desperate to save them from worsening persecution could no longer do so. He assured their families he would look after them in a strictly religious milieu and give them a sound Jewish education. A mother later recalled how, in the anguish of letting her child go, the tall and imposing figure of the Rabbi was pointed out to her. "If that's the man who offers to look after you, I entrust you to him". In London the Rabbi frequently went the rounds of his congregation, standing at their doors, a clipboard in hand, waiting to know how many each would cram into their home. He refused to take no for an answer, saying "and do you expect me to leave them in the street?" He would reach London with coach-loads of children. He personally brought 250 children from Vienna. He converted the Avigdor High School into a temporary hostel filling it with camp beds and accommodated others in his mother's home. He gave up his own room to sleep in the attic or even, it is said, in his car. Thea Ginsberg describes how she helped turn the elegant parlour into a dormitory with a row of beds on one side, and cots on the other.[6] Mr Honig, the Stamford Hill bookseller, told me he recalls finding the Rabbi feeding a number of newly-arrived babies and changing their nappies while waiting for others to take over their care.

British Visas for adults or children were issued only if every one was personally sponsored. This demanded strenuous activity by the Rabbi and his hard-working team. Who could refuse a direct appeal from the Rabbi? With war becoming imminent and inevitable, escape routes were being blocked. It was an increasingly worsening situation.

The Refugee Children's Movement (RCM) campaigned for and organised the *Kindertransport*. It was an association of Christian and secular charities as well as Jewish ones that collaborated to share the effort, the CRREC among them. The motivation of most was humanitarian rather than religious. They were faced with an overwhelming flood of unaccompanied children and were hard pressed to locate enough Jewish foster homes. The urgency of the situation demanded immediate action and so some Jewish children were placed in non-Orthodox settings or where Jewish practice had lapsed. This did not sit happily with Rabbi Schonfeld and he made his views widely known. He felt that preference was being given to non-Jewish hosts "as ambassadors offering good possibilities for Jewish children." Many in the Jewish community felt that such criticism was inappropriate at a time of urgency and crisis. Dr Hertz's response was that *kosher* food and Orthodox practice be made available at least for those refugees who came from Orthodox families. Rabbi Schonfeld took this matter much further. Here are some extracts from a leaflet (published by the Union of Orthodox Hebrew Congregations, 26 Green Lanes, London N16) that he issued in January 1944, written in his rather strident style:

"The Child-Estranging Movement: an expose of the alienation of Jewish refugee children in Great Britain

The office of the Chief Rabbi's Religious Emergency Council at 86
Amhurst Park, North London. (JS)

from Judaism. Defend the rights of Jewish orphans! Legal guardians are about to be appointed by the Home Office. There is a veiled tendency to move them away from Orthodoxy. Funding is from Anglo-Jewry and non-state sources and run by self-appointed people disinterested in the religious question...."

The CBF on behalf of the RCM had to face Rabbi Schonfeld's concerns over their policies.[7] In response the CBF questionnaire of refugee parents asked them about their religious affiliation - in effect how orthodox they were. But Rabbi Schonfeld was still not satisfied. He felt that many refrained from stipulating Orthodox practice in case this might reduce their children's chance of rescue. However, practical considerations took priority.

Perhaps it was as a result of these differences of opinion that Rabbi Schonfeld preferred to work alone. He had no use for committees. He was very effective as a man of action but he also gained a reputation as a maverick. The CBF was often drawn in to sort out bureaucratic tangles with the Immigration Authority that resulted from the Rabbi's unconventional methods. Otto Schiff was its indefatigable Director, ably assisted by Joan Steibel. She recalls how Mr Schiff described Rabbi Schonfeld, with some truth, as a frustrated lawyer - a controversial figure but widely admired. He once told him "you do marvelous work but go about it in the wrong way". For Rabbi Schonfeld the goals were very clear and any obstacles had to be surmounted whatever the costs.

Wartime

On the outbreak of war it became almost impossible to bring out any more children or adults though there were some notable exceptions using remote and dangerous means. 550 boys and girls from the Avigdor High Schools were evacuated, a third of them recently arrived refugees and he kept in close touch with them. This was another demanding exercise described in Appendix B.

The war years brought other problems. He visited and supported servicemen and others as an unofficial chaplain. He tended to the religious needs of service personnel from all

Mrs Schonfeld's house at 35 Lordship Park, North London, which her son often crammed with newly-arrived children. (CB)

over the globe posted to Britain and of those interned as enemy aliens. He vouched for the credentials of any internee for whom he could secure a release. During the blitz, Rabbi Schonfeld often took advantage of air raids to reach those he wanted to see and any who needed assistance. He argued it was far quicker to move around when everyone else was tucked away in shelters. He seems to have been oblivious to danger and even saw some beauty amidst the awful destruction when explosions lit up the City of London. Somehow Rabbi Schonfeld also retained contact with some of his fellow students in Europe, even during the war.

He designed and equipped Mobile Synagogue Ambulances. These were converted army trucks adapted for multiple usage as a synagogue, ambulance or canteen and were provided to assist the work of Jewish chaplains on active service. They were stocked with *kosher* foods and medical supplies, prayer books and the religious requisites. Each had an Ark with a Scroll of the Law; and behind a partition, a kitchen and storage space. They were inscribed with a banner "Your Messenger-on-Wheels to bring Hope, Relief and Rehabilitation to our Brethren in Europe". The first ambulance was consecrated in November 1944 by the Chief Rabbi. His text was Genesis 45, v.27:

"And when he (Jacob) saw the wagons that Joseph had sent to carry him, the spirit of Jacob their father revived."

Postwar activities

In the chaotic conditions following the armistice and the liberation of the Concentration Camps in Europe, welfare organisations established Displaced Person Camps and hospital services, some specially for children. At the same time a huge exercise was taking place to put survivors, in poor health and destitute, in touch with any surviving relatives and assist them to find their way back into an unknown and frightening world.

Rabbi Schonfeld was among the first to take action when the horrendous sights and appalling truths about the Concentration Camps became known. He then turned his attention to the survivors.

Mobile Synagogue Ambulance sent by Rabbi Schonfeld for the use of Jewish servicemen. (JS)

"In order for me to bring from Poland my fourth transport of up to 100 Jewish orphans I require one thousand persons, each of them to promise to pay £1 per month for a period. This time the children are to be accommodated in Clonyn Castle near Dublin, a large mansion that has been put at our disposal and specially adapted for the purpose. The Irish authorities have extended every facility and we hope that under the favourable conditions existing in Ireland the children will grow up healthy in mind and body and eventually emigrate to Palestine and overseas countries.

Many of the children in our previous groups have relatives who can and are looking after them. These kiddies have no one except you if you will agree to be one of their guardians. I do not stress the worthiness of this cause; unless it speaks for itself, words will be useless."

This appeal raised £50,000. Despite mention of Clonyn Castle, in fact negotiations with the Irish government broke down after this letter was written. The Polish group was accommodated in England instead and it was the Slovakian transport that in the following year occupied Clonyn Castle.

The Rabbi searched far and wide for any Hidden Children. Their names had usually been changed and their identity altered. Some had settled well and become closely attached to their substitute family but he ignored this in his determination to return Jewish children to a Jewish setting. By his striking presence and strong and attractive personality, he nevertheless succeeded in collecting hundreds of children on every expedition. He chartered ships to cross the Channel, sometimes paying with gold sovereigns; often he was the sole adult in charge of a boatload of youngsters. A young Polish survivor wrote a vivid description of his experience on one of these journeys. See AJR Journal: December 2007.

On visits abroad he was advised to wear a uniform for his own safety. He saw that this would be an advantage. So he devised his own uniform and designed a badge for the cap. He looked very impressive in it and, with his neatly trimmed beard some people mistook him for King George V!

On one occasion the Rabbi heard rumours of a plan to assassinate him. He survived by changing his itinerary at the last moment. But some of the occupants of the car he was to have used were killed and he reached his destination to hear his own death announced amongst them on the radio.

When bringing refugees from Europe, both before and after the war, he had to adhere to the rigid exit requirements as well as strict entry conditions imposed by the British authorities. In a letter to "The Times" in December 1946 he wrote about his fourth visit to the Continent in twelve months and how the Foreign Office had often eased the path for refugees to enter Britain. This island, he wrote, offers people in a desperate state the chance to recuperate and helps them to look for any surviving relatives.

He wrote on one occasion:

"It is a most encouraging sign of the times that while Britain's very existence was threatened the authorities did not fail to give attention to Jewish questions that arose during and after the emergency."

Rabbi Schonfeld even bought with charitable funds a small uninhabited island in the Bahamas called Strangers Cay. He planned to use it as a place of convalescence and rehabilitation for Holocaust survivors. His thinking was that, once there, safely within the British Empire, residents could claim British citizenship and the right to settle in Britain. The plan failed through lack of support and he sold it years later; the proceeds went to Jewish Secondary School funds. At that time stringent controls on immigration to Palestine impeded efforts by the Zionists to attract survivors there.

His son Jonathan told me that his father kept a range of notepaper headed for his various activities. When asked to provide a letter he would sign the appropriate sheet (always in green ink) and suggest that the petitioner fill in the rest "... as he knows best what he wants me to say!"

He worked round the clock with the minimum of sleep and seems to have considered that this was nothing unusual and rather unreasonably expected others to do the same. His staff would often receive phone calls at unsocial hours requiring them to meet him or undertake some task at once, regardless of their private lives. The Rabbi was an extremely demanding manager but he inspired allegiance and generally obtained it.

Altogether some 800 war-damaged children were brought to Britain by his endeavours. Most were from Poland but the last group, the subject of this book, were from Czechoslovakia.

14/12/46

Rabbi Dr Solomon Schonfeld in the uniform he designed for his journeys in post-war Europe. (JS)

Somehow he maintained throughout his life the inner resources to bestow continuing concern and affection on these lone children that he had sheltered in Britain. He was for ever after, aware of his responsibility for them *in loco parentis*, a duty he maintained very seriously indeed. His chosen reward was to witness his charges' successes and, ultimately, their marriages. He kept a small black notebook in which to jot down names and birth dates. From these he would calculate a numerical value and translate that into a blessing on their compatibility in the ancient practice of *Gematria*.[8]

He used the same little book, his son Jeremy told me, to make a note of phone numbers, inventing acronyms based on biblical quotations, some slyly satirical, to assist his memory. Many still lovingly recall when he would remember every one of their names and history even at chance meetings, many years later. Boys and girls alike felt an intimate and personal bond with him. He became a role model that restored their faith in humanity after years of deprivation.

The schools

After the war Rabbi Schonfeld focused his attention on further developing the Jewish Secondary Schools Movement. In 1930, when his father inaugurated the first Jewish Secondary School, Anglo-Jewry had been unenthusiastic. Most British Jews considered their children needed to grow up in the culture and ambience of their neighbours and attend secular schools. Their Jewish education was provided at *cheder* or through the synagogues. There was resentment against the Movement for a long time. Yet Rabbi Schonfeld, as was his way, worked steadily on. His schools provided a curriculum that balanced a secular education of high standard alongside an equally sound religious one. Some of his views were seen as unduly tolerant by his Orthodox colleagues. For example, he considered that *yeshiva* boys should be prepared to earn their living alongside their studies. And he told Paul Yogi Mayer, then a sports master at the Hasmonean School, that he considered physical education and exercise essential for the good health of young people.

By 1939 there were three separate schools; one for Boys, one

RABBI DR SOLOMON SCHONFELD זצ"ל
4th Adar 5672 - 4th Adar 5744
21st February 1912 - 2nd June 1984

Rabbi Dr Solomon Schonfeld at his desk. © *Douglas Glass*

for Girls and the Preparatory section which was co-educational. As part of the Government Evacuation Scheme the three schools merged. 550 children, one third of them recently arrived from Nazi Europe, were evacuated to villages in Bedfordshire, 40 miles from the metropolis.[9] When peace came the schools returned to London and rapidly developed. By 1956 there were two Grammar Schools with optional boarding facilities, the Avigdor in Stamford Hill and the Hasmonean in Hendon as well as three primary schools together providing nearly 2000 places. There were many difficulties, legal and administrative, but particularly financial ones. Yet the Movement grew and became the system that continues to be widely respected today.

Some time after 1959 Rabbi Schonfeld initiated a project in Israel. He established a Community Centre in Ashdod. He was not a Zionist himself and he never felt completely comfortable in Israel, preferring the culture and ethos that prevailed in Britain.

In his later years Solomon Schonfeld became isolated from the Adath Yisroel Community. It lost that flavour of British life style and Western culture that marked the earlier years under father and son. It is still active but with a different membership and a different emphasis that follows a strongly Eastern European tradition.

In 1965 Rabbi Schonfeld had a benign tumour removed from his middle ear. Although he carried on to a remarkable extent, his activities were curtailed and his energies diminished. Serious difficulties and disagreements developed within the community and in the administration of the schools. He was no longer allowed to drive. Then came a stroke. His wife was determined to nurse him at home for as long as possible. She coped alone until Dr Judith Grunfeld realised the strain had become too heavy. She consulted his cousin, Sir Sigmund Sternberg, who made funds available for his care throughout his final illness. He died in February 1984, aged 72 on his Hebrew birthday - 4th Adar 5744 in the Jewish calendar. His date of birth was 4th Adar 5672.

The Legacy of Solomon Schonfeld

His Schools continue to develop and are a source of pride to the community today. His name lives on in Schonfeld Square in Stamford Hill where a range of establishments have been founded in his memory. These offer loving care in comfortable surroundings for the aged, the disabled and the sick. Above all he is revered by those he brought to a safe haven, their children, grandchildren and great-grandchildren who continue to pay their respects to the memory of this outstanding and extraordinary personality.

Rabbi Solomon Schonfeld held a rather unusual view of himself and his mission. He saw himself as a brinksman who put his trust in the Almighty and had a direct line to his Creator. Some suggested he should write his memoirs but he answered with gentle irony "Certainly not! If I blow my own trumpet, do you think the Almighty will still do what I want?" But, humour aside, he seems to have genuinely seen himself as God's messenger and to have feared the loss of that special role. When asked how many lives he had saved he replied "But do you know how many I didn't save?" He preferred to distance himself from thanks or acknowledgement of any kind.

Rabbi Schonfeld was a man of many parts. His activities were informed by deep religious conviction and a wish to draw others in the same direction. He avoided, though, any criticism of other people's personal beliefs or practice and always respected those of his young charges. Posterity will recognise debatable aspects of his activities alongside remarkable achievements. One of these is recorded here and brought up-to-date by those involved in the story of "The Hide-and-Seek Children".

Chapter Three

An Invitation

Main Railway Station, Prague where the children met for their journey to London. (Lucy Abel Smith/John Murray)

Rabbi Schonfeld had obtained permission from the Allied Forces to visit the Continent soon after fighting ended. He found exhausted survivors struggling to cope but determined in their efforts to re-establish Jewish communities; a serious pogrom in Kielce alerted him to continuing overt anti-Semitism. At the same time a new danger was threatening Czechoslovakia: the Communists were taking over in Prague, with Soviet backing. They would permit no religious practice. The Iron Curtain was about to descend.

Rabbi Schonfeld applied his energies and resourcefulness to draw to safety as many children as he could. He offered an invitation to war-damaged children to spend a year or so in Britain until such time as any surviving family had re-established themselves. His offer provided that until then he would be responsible for their care and that would be in a traditional Jewish setting. As for orphaned children, he would assist them in planning their future.

It is not entirely clear how Rabbi Schonfeld operated in Europe or how he selected the Slovakian group. He had made a whistle stop visit to Poland in March 1946, giving whatever advice and assistance he could. Some idea of how he worked can be gleaned from his book "Message to Jewry".where he quotes a few pages from his diary. He delivered food to struggling survivors across Poland. He found them in a pitiful condition and facing huge difficulties. He made four similar visits. On two occasions he returned with 100 orphan children single-handed He eventually brought back 500 orphan children from Poland and 300 from Hungary and Romania and finally, this group of 148, from Czechoslovakia.

In 1945 he had set up an office of the Religious Emergency Council in Prague under the guidance of Rabbi H. Vorhand, the post-war Chief Rabbi of Prague. Arthur Moses was sent there as his representative on a number of occasions. His widow spoke to me about him.[2]

Arthur Moses endeavoured all his life to repay kindnesses he had received by helping others. In 1945 he was among the first who visited survivors in the Camps and took letters for their relatives. Very early one morning during 1948 he received a phone call from Rabbi Schonfeld. On this occasion he instructed Arthur to go to Prague forthwith. He demurred because his young wife was heavily pregnant. Rabbi Schonfeld replied that she had parents to support her while those in Prague were destitute and in dire trouble.

The Rabbi's invitation was sent across Slovakia wherever Jewish communities were attempting to re-establish themselves. Several were led by his former teachers or classmates. The Schonfeld Archives show that some of the boys were collected from Bratislava and Karlsbad (Karlovy Vary) *yeshivot* and several girls from Beis Ya'acov Schools in Bratislava and Košice, the largest post-war communities. Other children came from the Children's Home at Ohel David.

He also searched monasteries for any Jewish children. He is said to have visited a convent where the Mother Superior told him she had no Jewish children. He asked to accompany her on her 'good night' tour of the dormitories. At each doorway he quietly pronounced the opening words of the *Shema*. Several times little voices joined in. He left with a contingent in tow.

News of his invitation passed quickly by word of mouth. There was intense pressure on families to make a quick and agonising decision, often overnight, whether to separate from their child yet again. It meant sending them to an unknown destination in a foreign land with no idea when they would next see them. Yet all places were quickly filled.

Alongside these activities the Rabbi had to initiate a series of complex bureaucratic operations. Exit visas for the children had to be negotiated. Initial applications were made late in 1947 but by the time they were needed the Communists were about to take control. The authorities began to introduce new measures, refusing to allow any nationals to leave. The essential documents were valid for just a few days and were only approved at the very last moment. This was assisted by a letter from the American Joint Distribution Committee (known as "The Joint"). See Appendix C.

MS 193 / 1002 / 3

CABLES: JOINTFUND PRAGUE

Tel. 206-90
397-03

AMERICAN JOINT DISTRIBUTION COMMITTEE

ADMINISTRATIVE OFFICE
Praha I., Příkopy 27.
CZECHOSLOVAKIA

REGIONAL OFFICES
PRAHA V. Josefovská 7
Tel. 619-94, 614-13
BRATISLAVA, Molotovova 7.
Tel 7214

April 11th, 1948.

Dr. K. Slapak,
Ministry for Social Welfare,
PRAHA.

Dear Dr. Slapak,

The American Joint Distribution Committee is interested, as you know, in helping orphan children to resettle. We would, therefore, appreciate any assistance you may be able to give to the project of the Chief Rabbis Council, involving the care of a group of Jewish children.

With best thanks and kind regards,

Yours sincerely,

Miss Helen Kohn.
Director of Emigration.

11th April 1948 American "Joint" confirming Rabbi Schonfeld's credentials to the Czech officials.

13.dubna 1948.

Dr Bs/Li.

Titl.
Ministerstvo sociální péče,
k rukám pana ministerského rady dra Šlapáka,
P r a h a II.

Chief Rabbis Emergency Council má zájem umístit v Iraku
a v Anglii židovské sirotky ve věku do 16 let,jejichž seznam
je připojen.Visa pro tyto sirotky byla přislíbena ihned jak-
mile bude předložen hromadný cestovní průkaz.

Chief Rabbis Emergency Council je zodpovědná instituce dobře
známá American Joint Distribution Committee a zavázala se
starat o děti v Iraku.O děti,které mají jeti do Anglie bude
se starat naše spolupracující organisace,která je obeznámena s
celou záležitostí a schválila ji.

Pobyt a úhrada je dostatečně zajištěna,takže děti nepřipadnou
nikomu na obtíž.

Byli bychom Vám povděčni,kdybyste byli nápomocni při uskuteč-
nění vystěhování těchto sirotků.

Děkujíce Vám předem za Vaši ochotu,jsme

                                    v dokonalé úctě:

                                    American Joint.
                                    Praha.

American "Joint's" letter of support for Rabbi Schonfeld's application
and confirmation of the details – probably a copy.

Translation of the letter from "The Joint":

13th April 1948
The Ministry of Social Care
For attention of: Minister Dr Slopak
Prague

The Chief Rabbi's Emergency Council is interested
in placing Jewish orphans up to the age of 16 in
England and Ireland. We enclose the list of names.
The visas for these orphans have been promised as
soon as a multiple travel document is presented.

The Chief Rabbi's Emergency Council is a responsible
institution well known to the American Joint
Distribution Committee and has pledged to take care
of these children in Ireland. Children travelling to
England will be looked after by our co-organisation
which is familiar with the whole project and in
agreement with it.

Accommodation and expenses are taken care of and
the children will not be a hindrance to anyone. We
would be grateful to you for your help in realizing
the emigration of these orphans.

Thanking you in advance for your willingness, we
remain, yours
American Joint, Prague.

Details of the Collective Visas required numerous changes to satisfy the authorities. Names and birth places were altered to show that none of the children was Czech. Many dates of birth were altered to say all were under 16 and when some children were withdrawn by worried parents late in the day others took not just their places but their names, too.

A perusal of the Schonfeld Archive for the years 1948 and 1949 produced a mass of miscellaneous correspondence with numerous lists and forms frequently lacking headings but their purpose can often be surmised. Many are marked and annotated in Rabbi Schonfeld's familiar hand. For example his method of indicating family status:

F = father survived, M = mother survived, O = orphan and Y = youth over 16 years old. Occasionally some personal details like "looks younger". "Auschwitz", or another place name.

I found about seventy application forms relating to the Slovak group. The forms were surely used as a basis for selection and to provide essential information for identity documents. These were needed in lieu of a passport and in the absence of any birth certificates. I made copies for the original applicants.

There were other bureaucratic hurdles to confront. Permission had to be given by the Allied Forces in Germany and Belgium to cross Occupied Europe and visas obtained for admission to Britain. See Appendix C. Rabbi Schonfeld adhered more or less to these rules and found officials supportive. He expressed his appreciation to the Home Office.

From Dr Solomon Schonfeld to Miss M. Wellstead, Home Office,
8th May,1948

We, (137 and me) arrived from Prague on April 22. Without your help and co-operation this "operation" could not have been carried out. One hundred children are now in transit to Eire – 84 in Clonyn Castle and 16 older ones in Dublin. I am deeply indebted to you for enabling me to accomplish this difficult piece of work. These youngsters deprived of a normal home life by the war will receive an education and training conducive to their complete rehabilitation.
May God bless you.

Information is sparse on the forty-eight young people allowed to remain in England. The given age of half this group was around 16 and I believe all of them were orphans. Records show that four were born during the war; one boy was *quasi*-adopted and it is very possible the other three very young ones were, too. At least six joined relatives already in Britain.

The other one hundred were *en route* for Ireland. Correspondence shows that the Rabbi had been negotiating to bring children there as early as 1946. But what led the Rabbi to take them to The Irish Republic?[3]

CHILD QUESTIONNAIRE

No.

1. Family name: Schwartz   2. First name: Eva Viera

3. Sex: girl   4. Citizenship: ČSR

5. Birthplace: Bratislava   6. Year, month, date of birth: 6.V.1934

7. Present residence: Bratislava Uzka ul.1

8. School attended: gymnazium   9. Which Grade: III.class

10. Father's name: Dr Julius Schwarz   advokat

11. His present residence:

12. His age: 56   13. His occupation: advokat

14. If not alive, when did he die: 1942 Poland   15. Under which circumstances: dep.Poland

16. Mother's name: Marta Schwarz geb.Majer

17. Her present residence: Bratislava, Uzka ul.1

18. Her age: 41 year   19. Her occupation: houswife

20. If not alive, when did she die: 21. Under which circumstances:

22. Data of brothers and sisters:

Name	Age	Present residence	Occupation

23. If both parents defunct give trustee's name and address:

24. With whom is the child living presently? with mother

with parents, - brothers, sisters, - relatives - friends, -

in a Home - or:

25. Occupation of householder:

26. If half - orphan, reason why transfer to home desirable

A typical form used to register applicants to Rabbi Schonfeld's transport, this one for Eva Schwarz.

Why Ireland? Irish immigration policy

A tiny Jewish presence, mostly in Dublin, had existed in Ireland since the seventeenth century when Oliver Cromwell gave tacit approval for their return to England. The earliest to arrive formed a Sephardi community. Others followed both from Western and Eastern Europe but not in large numbers.[4]

Some affinity grew between Catholics and Jews in the struggle both faced for political emancipation. But in the 1880s pogroms in Russia brought a new wave of poverty-stricken Jewish immigrants. Many lived as peddlers, travelling with their wares by the week, and returning to their families in the towns for the Sabbath. They were often the victims of prejudice and of civil disturbances in Dublin, Limerick and Cork. So strong were the complaints against the Jewish immigrants that a government inquiry was set up. The police reported that they had met no problems with the newcomers, who were, on the contrary, law-abiding citizens. But anti-Semitic propaganda continued, often fuelled by Catholic preachers.

By 1891 the British Administration estimated from census reports there were some 1,779 Jews, rising to nearly four thousand in 1901, around 80 per cent resident in Dublin. By 1946 there was no increase. In 1991 that number had dwindled to 1,581.

Ireland had until recently a strict policy on immigration.[5] Neither refugees or asylum seekers were welcome. Ireland was officially neutral during the War but there were Nazi sympathisers who overtly backed the Germans, believing they would win the war. The Chief Rabbi of Palestine, Rabbi Isaac Herzog, was a previous Chief Rabbi of Ireland and a friend of Eamon de Valera. He had pressed for the admission of those under threat of annihilation – but without success. He was accused of interfering in government policy. After the war, de Valera agreed to allow entry for one thousand war orphans. A venture called Operation Shamrock was initiated by Dr Kathleen Murphy, a pediatrician, in collaboration with the Irish Red Cross and permission was granted to bring in 462 German gentile children for convalescence.[5] But when the Concentration Camps were opened up Ireland was reluctant to admit any survivors. [6]

In 1946 Rabbi Schonfeld, on a earlier project, had sought permission to bring one hundred Jewish orphans from Austria, survivors of Bergen-Belsen. The Justice Minister made it known that he feared that "any substantial increase in our Jewish population might give rise to an anti-Semitic problem." So he was turned down. The Rabbi found alternative placements for the Austrian children.

No record has been found to explain why Rabbi Schonfeld chose Ireland as a destination. It seems a curious choice for, like Slovakia, it is predominantly Roman Catholic, dominated by more prosperous neighbours, and with a history of anti-Semitism. Perhaps it was because Irish neutrality meant that provisions were more readily available there, while Britain continued to suffer shortages and food rationing until 1956.

But he was not easily deterred and continued negotiations to bring another group to Ireland. Robert Briscoe took up his cause. He was the first Jew to win a seat in the Irish Parliament and was later to become the first Jewish Lord Mayor of Dublin. He had met Jabotinsky during a visit to Dublin in 1938 and tried to arrange a refuge for Polish Jews without success. But not until 1947 was Briscoe able to exercise a decisive influence and persevere till a permit was issued in August that allowed Schonfeld to go ahead.[7] This granted permission for one hundred war orphans to enter Ireland. Their stay was strictly limited to twelve months.

Only in January 1948 was there official recognition of this decision by the British Home Office. It was ratified by the Embassy in Prague just before the group's departure.

Reactions from Dublin's Jewish community

There were mixed feelings within Dublin's Jewish community when Rabbi Schonfeld's plans became known. He selected Mrs Olga Eppel to be Administrator of the scheme. She was chair of the Dublin Jewish Ladies' Society (DJLS). The majority welcomed an opportunity to play a part in the recuperation of the Holocaust survivors. He asked for their support and they responded. They were encouraged by his oratory and impressive appearance. Contributions in cash and in kind rolled in. Mrs Erwin Goldwater formed and chaired the Dublin Jewish Ladies Voluntary Aid

Committee as a branch of the DJLS specifically to provide any backing needed for the newcomers. The Dublin Congregation and their Ladies Committee, as it came to be called, raised a substantial percentage of the cost of the children's maintenance and of their later dispersal. Many Dublin families extended warm hospitality and continued support throughout their stay.

Some of the Dublin Jewish community were less enthusiastic. They had learned over the years to maintain a low profile in an environment where anti-Semitism was latent and easily provoked. There were few ultra-Orthodox Jews in Ireland. The majority adhered to the practice followed by the United Synagogue in London. These children would be following orthodoxy as practised by Rabbi Schonfeld. Harry Goodman arrived from London to explain the project. He was Secretary of World Agudath Israel, a non-Zionist political and welfare organisation supported by Orthodox Jews. The Dublin community, however, was strongly Zionist and Harry Goodman irritated them both by his attitude and his manner. Over the years their Immigration Committee had collected £6,000 for Youth Aliyah, the organisation that assisted young people to settle in Israel. The Chairman was Professor Leonard Abrahamson. He held strong views. During the First World War his family had been subjected to heavy anti-Semitism when a widely held belief among the Irish was that all Jews were German and so were suspect. He opposed Rabbi Schonfeld's scheme and insisted that his Committee's funds were neither for refugees nor for the Orthodox although contributions had been sent to Millisle Farm Children's Home in Protestant Northern Ireland.[8] It was designated as preparation for children on the *Kindertransport* for life in Israel. Mrs Eppel was seriously impeded by Abrahamson's dislike of the plan. He was angry, too, that his advice had not been sought. The situation was further complicated as his daughter was married to Mrs Eppel's nephew. He remained critical throughout the entire project.

Clonyn Castle

Some months earlier Rabbi Schonfeld had discussed a plan to bring child survivors to Ireland with Jacob (Yankel) Levy. He was a qualified pharmacist and optician who had inherited

éıяe

TO WHOM IT MAY CONCERN

    This is to confirm that the Government of Ireland has decided to admit to Ireland up to one hundred Jewish war orphans from Central and Eastern Europe, selected by Rabbi Dr. Solomon Schonfeld, Executive Director of the Chief Rabbi's Religious Emergency Council.   The orphans are aged between 7 and 16 years.

    It has been agreed that all costs of this scheme will be borne by the above mentioned Chief Rabbi's Council.

High Commissioner

16th August, 1947.

Official letter dated 16th August 1947 from the Irish Government listing the conditions for the admission of Rabbi Schonfeld's Slovakian group.

Surname and forenames of mother / Nom de famille et prénoms de la mère } *Waner, Margita*

Ainm a mhná (fir) chéile / Name of wife (husband) / Nom de la femme (mari) }

Ainmneacha clainne / Names of children / Noms des enfants }

Comhnaí i gcoigrích roimhe seo / Former residence abroad / Ancien domicile à l'étranger } *Czechoslovakia*

Comhnaí fó láthair in Éirinn / Present residence in Ireland / Résidence actuelle dans l'Irlande } *Clonyn Castle, Delvin, Co. Westmeath.*

Deimhniú clárathachta / Police Registration Certificate / Certificat d'enregistrement délivré par la Police } *Nil*

COMHARTHAI.
DESCRIPTION.
SIGNALEMENT.

Airde / Height / Taille } *4 ft. 1 in.*   Aghaidh / Face / Visage } *Oval*

Remarks / Observations } *The holder of this certificate, being under the age of 16 years, does not require a visa to return to Ireland.*

Síghniú an tSealbhóra. / Signature of holder. / Signature du titulaire.

Sonja Kümmeldorfer

A detail from Sonja Kummeldorfer's Irish passport with an unexpected comment. (SK) a prosperous wine business in Manchester. He and his wife, Malkeh, gave generous hospitality in their strictly observant home and readily assisted any needy individual or worthy Jewish cause. He supported *yeshivot* in Britain and in Israel, in Shanghai and in Rome. He established the first Jewish Primary School in Manchester, the "Broughton Jewish Prep". He was very fond of children and had seven of his own. When the Concentration Camps were liberated he was among the first to visit survivors and spent six weeks distributing medication there. He gave guarantees to a number of Jews so they could settle in Britain.

Rabbi Schonfeld persuaded Yankel Levy to provide premises for a temporary Children's Home. Shula, one of Yankel Levy's daughters, told me that when she was a young child, she flew to Ireland with her parents in a light aircraft to view Clonyn Castle. It was a tiny plane and the pilot told her to sit near the middle to avoid it tipping! She remembers the beautiful countryside and that the owner at that time was an elderly widow who had re-married her young chauffeur. So Clonyn Castle was purchased as a home for refugee children through the Levy family's "generosity". The Daily Telegraph reported that it cost him £30,000.

The present Castle is an imposing and austere castellated structure with towers at each corner. It was built in 1870 in neo-Gothic style by Lord Fulke Southwell Greville, later Lord Lieutenant of Westmeath, and his wife Lady Rosa Nugent, who inherited the place.[9] The ruins of an earlier Castle built in 1639 by her ancestors and burned down in 1923, are still visible in the grounds. In 1928 the Castle, with 1600 acres, was sold by their descendants to an Order of Australian nuns who never used it. It lies half-a-mile from the village of Delvin, in County Westmeath and is surrounded by one hundred acres of gardens, fields and woods.

The great front door opens on to a large hall with a huge fireplace. Ahead is an imposing staircase that divides at mezzanine level to left and to right. These flights lead up to a circular balcony, the inner side overlooking the hall, the outer side lined with doors to a dozen rooms. This was where the girls and small children slept. Two modest sets of stairs, intended for servants' use, lead to the upper floor where the boys and some of the staff slept. The ground floor contains spacious rooms with big windows giving splendid views of the grounds and the countryside beyond. One was used as a synagogue, others as classrooms. The dining room still has a butler's lift, "the dumb waiter", to bring up food from the kitchens on the floor below, which became a source of much amusement to the children.

Preparations

A crucial part of the Irish government's granting of these temporary visas was that the CRREC be held entirely responsible for all the expenses of the venture. A similar undertaking was made by the CBF with the British government when children were admitted to Britain both before and after the war. There was a major difference between the two undertakings. Whereas the CBF had widespread backing from the Jewish public, the CRREC was a tiny organisation, Rabbi Schonfeld's personal brainchild. True, he had the blessing of the Chief Rabbi of the United Synagogue, but in reality his followers were small in number and few were affluent.

In Britain, and later in Dublin, Rabbi Schonfeld urged his congregants, acquaintances and friends to assist in any and every way. He asked for, and received, donations of furniture and furnishings and clothing. But above all a regular commitment was required to make a payment, however small, towards the upkeep of every child. Jeremy Schonfeld told me that hosts of big functions, weddings, *barmitzvahs* and the like, would be asked to allow collectors to approach their guests, presumed to be in a generous mood, to sign up as guarantors. Lists show benefactors from far and wide, some contributing as little as one shilling a week. Against their names is shown that of the child they wholly or partly guaranteed. Collectors called weekly for payments both in Britain and in Ireland but the revenue raised was always irregular and frequently inadequate. The records show that there was a continual struggle to finance the enterprise but for Rabbi Schonfeld and his loyal staff there was only one goal: to see the scheme through to the end with every child and young person settled wherever they wanted to be.

Clonyn Castle in 2007 (RR)

The foundations of the Irish Venture

The Irish venture depended largely on its four key staff members:

Henry Pels was the Executive Secretary of the CRREC. He worked intensively in managing Rabbi Schonfeld's ambitious projects assisted by only a tiny staff. He was dedicated to the task. It lay upon him heavy and many-sided responsibilities which he handled with impressive capability and confidence.

I have learned little about his history. His son, Rabbi Benjamin Pels, who married **Séndi Templer,** told me he did not talk about his earlier life. Amongst his many responsibilities lay the daunting task of dealing with the needs of the young people from Slovakia. This involved close collaboration with Mrs Olga Eppel.

Olga Eppel (1898-1959) had been interviewed by Rabbi Schonfeld, Robert Briscoe and Henry Pels on February 23rd, 1948 and selected to represent the CRREC in Eire. She was made responsible for the administration and welfare of Clonyn Castle staff and residents. She was described as powerfully-built, grey-haired and rather "Sergeant-Major-ish" but her formidable manner brought remarkable achievements. Her almost daily correspondence with Mr Pels in London survives in the Schonfeld Archive held at Southampton University. This reveals the numerous problems they confronted and how they coped with them. Yet this was only a temporary enterprise. At the same time plans had to be made for every child to move on within the year. This clearly involved an extensive exchange of letters with any surviving family and with officials in several different languages. (Surprisingly I have come across none of this correspondence.) There is a likelihood that Mrs Eppel understood Yiddish and may have spoken it, too, for Rachel, her eldest sister, is known to have been a Yiddish speaker.

What is apparent is Mrs Eppel's expertise in managing an extraordinarily wide range of activities whilst under considerable pressure. I tried to find out more about this remarkable woman. Enid Oppenheim Sandelson, a great-niece, showed me a history of the family.[10] Olga's father, Avrom Behr Eppel, was born in Vexnia, Lithuania in 1845. After his parents died in a cholera epidemic he was brought up by his grandfather, Reb Baruch Eppel, who sent him to study at the famous Slobodka Yeshiva.

*The entrance hall of Clonyn Castle taken on our visit in 1998. Very
little had changed. (JS)*

The imposing main staircase that confronts the visitor. (JS)

The marble stairs leading to the broad first floor gallery. (JS)

There the students were required to study the *Torah*, adhere to high ethical standards of behaviour and dress fashionably. That is where much later Rabbi Schonfeld also studied and qualified as a Rabbi. Avrom Eppel married Malka Shishi and became the State Rabbi of Vexnia. After relatives of his wife emigrated to Ireland he followed them there in 1870, and with his wife and five children settled in Dublin. He died in Dublin in 1939.

Dublin is where Olga was born, the tenth in a family of eleven children. They grew up in a strictly Orthodox milieu. Her father spent his time studying. There was always a shortage of money in that large family and Olga continued to be hard up during her later life. Despite that, the following generation prospered. Her four brothers became successful doctors and so did several of the next generation. Olga was once married but soon divorced and had no children of her own. After that she was always known as "Mrs" Eppel but this was an honorary title as a divorcée. Eppel was her maiden name.

Relatives recall her strong personality and devotion to her family, especially to the children. Richard Slotover, a great-great-nephew, told me she was much loved by her numerous nieces and nephews. He showed me affectionate letters she sent to him during his schooldays that tell how much she enjoyed that role. He recalled happy times when his parents were away and "Auntie Olga" took charge.

I had hoped to discover how Mrs Eppel had acquired the knowledge and expertise that enabled her to cope so successfully with the complex task that Rabbi Schonfeld assigned to her. But no one today knows anything about her activities prior to 1939. Dr.Lionel Koplewitz, a family friend and at times her doctor, recalls that during the Second World War she worked for the (perhaps American) Red Cross at Tidworth near Andover, Hampshire and at another time in Tewkesbury. In a letter to Benjamin Pels in July 1949 she mentioned working in England throughout the war then retiring to Dublin. So much had she enjoyed working for Rabbi Schonfeld that she asks him to find her more work of a similar sort. Did he do so? We are left guessing.

Enid Oppenheim Sandelson says that later Olga was an Administrator for the British Friends of Magen David Adom, the Israeli equivalent of the Red Cross and Dr Koplewitz remembers

Henry Pels, Executive Secretary to the Chief Rabbi's Religious Emergency Council. With thanks to his daughter, Rachel Cooper.

that she worked for the British Branch of the Anti-Tuberculosis League of Israel which was established in Israel in 1953. Richard Slotover told me that she spent her later years in London not far from his family home. He kept closely in touch with her till the end of her life. She spent her last years in Newcastle to be near Leah, her much loved younger sister and died there in 1959.

Mrs Eppel was outstandingly capable. I learned that she was always convincing in her arguments and determined to get what she wanted – and she usually did! She was incredibly well suited to work with Rabbi Schonfeld who was another strong figure. What is evident is that she excelled, too, in the role of "favourite auntie" not only within her family but also to the Hide-and-Seek Children in her selfless care and concern for them.

A year after the children first arrived Olga Eppel wrote a lively account of her experiences with them. It appears in Part Two.

Rabbi Israel Cohen (1922–2006) with his wife **Trudi** (1922-2006) had been torn away from teaching in London by Rabbi Schonfeld to take charge of Clonyn Castle. They had a toddler and a second baby was on the way. Rabbi Cohen was born in Manchester to parents who had settled there from Lodizhin in Russia at the turn of the century. His father, a devout Rabbi, sent him at the age of six to an Orthodox school in Antwerp, Belgium. Such early separation from his family may have helped him to identify with his young charges who had experienced far greater deprivation. From this foundation Rabbi Cohen travelled around England serving small congregations as a visiting minister and became known for his oratory and devout Orthodox practice - proffered with a warm smile and a glow of affection. It was at the establishment set up by the CBF for young Holocaust survivors at Windermere that he met his future wife.[11]

Trudi Cohen was born in Frankfurt am Main. In 1939 when she was 17, her parents sent her to safety in Britain. Her sister followed on one of Rabbi Schonfeld's transports. Their parents, grandmother and younger brother were deported and never heard of again. Trudi was fortunate to find domestic employment (the only work permitted her as a refugee) near friends. Following the outbreak of war, she was evacuated with the Jewish Secondary Schools and became a valued staff member. A year or so later she trained as a psychiatric nurse at Oxford's famous Radcliffe Infirmary – an unusual career for an Orthodox girl.

Olga Eppel with her great niece Peggy Slotover and Peggy's daughter Jill 1956-7. (RS)

Olga Eppel with great-great nephews, Robert (left) and Richard Slotover in 1958. (RS)

They both worked at Windermere with the group of adolescent survivors known as "The Boys". Oscar Friedmann was in charge. As a young child he had suffered harsh treatment in a hostile German institution. He trained as a social worker and teacher and then managed an establishment for young delinquents. In 1933 the Nazis imprisoned him and his charges in Sachsenhausen Concentration Camp for some months. He was left with permanent physical damage but continued to work. Later he escorted a large number of German Jewish boys to Britain. The CBF persuaded him to stay. He turned his attention to the welfare of refugees and in 1945 to young survivors of the Camps. At Windermere he devised a regime for their rehabilitation that was unique and proved highly successful. The Cohens' experience there no doubt served as a valuable model when they came to Clonyn Castle. He as Principal held overall responsibility, particularly for education, while Trudi oversaw all health, welfare and domestic matters. The young Rabbi and his wife were faced with creating, from scratch and without preparation, a successful Children's Home. The managing of any residential establishment is complex and demanding at the best of times and these were exceptional circumstances.

The Administrator's initiation

Olga Eppel's role began abruptly. One hundred children and young people were due to arrive in a few weeks' time with staff and volunteers. So her first act was to view Clonyn Castle. She drove her ancient vehicle the sixty miles from her Dublin home through heavy snow, a journey she was to take several times a week in the months to follow. She found a splendid mansion but entirely bare. The top floor was "terribly wet". There was no electricity, the existing generator was not working and oil supplies were inadequate. Meanwhile a log fire was kept burning in the huge fireplace in the main hall. The place was thick with dust. Upper rooms were being repaired by Yankel Levy's workmen but lots more had to be done before the place was habitable. A " beautiful but useless " fire escape had, unfortunately, been built, too narrow and of wood (because Mr Levy found metal ugly!). This had to be removed.

Mrs Eppel had introduced herself and the project to local tradesmen in Delvin, the closest village, half-a-mile away. She found them friendly and keen to co-operate with the Castle's new occupants. Throughout the period she found local farmers to provide fresh dairy products to meet *kosher* requirements. Only one incident spoilt that impression. Shortly before the children arrived, someone attempted to start a fire in the Castle. Little damage was done and the culprit was never identified. Mrs Eppel tried to avoid publicity but it had to be reported. The police called it a "mad effort" but from then on were vigilant in keeping an eye on the place.

So, the children were now due and their needs had to be met: food and clothing, health and educational facilities, skilled staff and domestics for work inside and out. A new generator was installed. When it worked the lights could be seen at night among the trees, a wondrous sight for local people who had no electricity.

The Castle had no furnishings whatsoever. Rabbi Schonfeld addressed a meeting of the Dublin Jewish community. "We turn to generous-hearted friends for their ready and liberal assistance. These children deserve our care to make up for the homes they have lost." The cry was "Comforts for the Castle!" There was an enthusiastic response. Large consignments of furniture, bedding and kitchen equipment were also sent from London. These required Export Licenses and permits for Utility articles, controls continuing from wartime, then transport by ferry to Dublin and on to the Castle. Every donation had to be acknowledged, another task thrust on the Rabbi's overworked staff.

At the last moment Mrs Eppel had to borrow iron bedsteads from Irish Army stores. When the Castle closed down these were sold and the Army reimbursed. A list shows how rooms were allocated, and what furniture was still needed. There were 87 beds: 52 for girls and staff in ten rooms on the first floor and 33 for boys in seven rooms on the floor above. There was a recreation room, dining room and serving room, the synagogue and the library. Two rooms were set aside as sick bays. Rabbi and Mrs Cohen had two rooms and an office, and another was for the Bleier family. One was marked for the cook and one was for "2 sleeping-in staff"; four rooms were to be used as classrooms. There was a dire shortage of chairs, but later Rabbi Cohen had the bright idea of having benches made by a local carpenter from timber that was freely available. Only thirty days after starting work Mrs Eppel reported the place as clean and dry and on March 30 she wrote to Rabbi Schonfeld in Prague: "Please bring the children".

Rabbi and Mrs Cohen and their child arrived shortly before the Slovakian children. They formed a sound partnership with Mrs Eppel.

Rabbi Schonfeld stipulated that strict *kashrut* must be maintained. The older girls and boys were separated and daily life followed Orthodox practice with services and prayers defining the day and all Fasts and Festivals faithfully observed.

A journey westwards — following "The Pied Piper"

With preparations at last in hand, Rabbi Schonfeld was in Prague collecting the essential documentation and meeting his young charges. Many came via Bratislava on the night train to Prague, some with siblings, a few with cousins but most had never met before. Their departure on April 20th was fraught with anxiety as parents and children faced yet another separation, albeit this time voluntarily. For the younger children it was something of an adventure but the older ones were anxious about travelling once again into the unknown. There was also a degree of disarray. Numbers fluctuated until the last moment.

At the last moment a family of three had failed to turn up and we were accepted instead. That was how Rabbi Schonfeld came to alter our names to those of the missing family shown on the visa.

Istvan Stahler

The situation was tense while the Czech authorities examined their credentials. No Czech nationals were permitted to leave so the children were warned not to speak Czech, and the older ones were made responsible. The Collective Visa shows fifty-one young people as born in 1932. Later information reveals that many were in fact older although no one over 16 was supposed to leave. So on the journey taller lads were told to crouch down to appear younger. There was immense relief for the whole party once they crossed the Czech border.

> The departure from Prague was very scary. I still remember how I felt at the time. I was eight-and-a-half years old.
>
> **Judit Ziegler**

Every child carried a small bag with clothes and other items hastily assembled by family or friends.

> All our cherished possessions, including my stamp collection, disappeared on the journey.
>
> **Istvan Stahler**

This was a tragedy for Istvan and his sister because their clothing had been collected with great difficulty by their devoted father.

Later the sight of the sea brought great excitement, as they all came from land-locked countries. Red Cross Volunteers met their train in Belgium and offered them another new experience: bananas. The Orthodox wanted to know what blessing to say and many ate them skin and all! But there were still anxieties. Numbers on the Visas did not quite tally. So, as they walked towards the ferry at Ostende, Rabbi Schonfeld told the boys to run around to confuse the officials who were trying to count them. On the boat they relaxed and he taught them some English poems and popular songs including "Daisy, Daisy".

Their arrival coincided with the week of the Passover Festival and they were hurriedly distributed among families, in hostels and schools in London and further afield. Some spent the week in Brighton; another group stayed at the Primrose Club established for an earlier group of young Holocaust survivors.[12]

> I remember *Seder* at the hostel for young Polish refugees at 32 Woodberry Down, led by one of Rabbi Schonfeld's uncles.
>
> **Pál Krausz**

The Passover Festival was over and there were 148 children to settle. Forty-eight remained in Britain. The rest were brought together again for medical examinations prior to travelling on to Ireland.

Bertha Myer[13] was aged 19, and a kindergarten teacher in Stamford Hill when she was called upon by Rabbi Schonfeld to assist him. She recalls the whole group being examined by Dr Sherwood, a General Practitioner in North London. He knew Yiddish, unlike most of the helpers, so could communicate with some of the children. Bertha recalls how nervous they were and petrified of the doctor. He found the four youngest had impetigo. Every one was undernourished and several had rickets.

They travelled by coach to Liverpool and took the night ferry across the Irish Sea. Bertha went with them. Rabbi Schonfeld insisted that boys and girls were separated on the ship to reassure any that were very observant.

A telegram informed Mrs Eppel: "Transport left. Stop. Arrival Dublin Thursday 7.30 a.m. Stop. You need 3 coaches with 104 seats…"

The travellers woke on May 5th to be met at the Irish docks by Rabbi and Mrs Cohen with Mrs Eppel. They found their charges in shock and confusion, speaking several languages but no English. All were conveyed to the Greenville Hall Synagogue in Dublin.

There Rabbi Alony and Rabbi Lewis, with the members of the Ladies' Committee, welcomed them on behalf of the local community with a plentiful and hot breakfast. Many of the children recall to this day how they were offered tea with milk, unheard of on the Continent, and were afraid they were being poisoned! Every one was given sixpence pocket money and a packet of sweets, but several were too anxious even to accept these treats.

Sixteen of the older boys were whisked away in smart private cars, much to their delight. Local families were offering them hospitality till a hostel was ready. By May a Dublin property had been found. This was at 143 Kimmage Road. It was rented from a member of the Jewish community. Rabbi Artur Pollak and Mrs Olga Pollak, who were Hungarian refugees, moved in to take charge. **Chaja Steinmetz**, one of the older girls, came daily to cook for them. She was lodged with the Wolfson family and married from their home in December 1949.

Buses arrived to take the rest of the party to Clonyn Castle.

Key to following photograph

Those identified: 1. Rachel Grunfeld; 2. Pál Krausz; 3.Tamáš Krausz; 6. Istvan Stahler; 11.Tamáš Steiner; 12. Séndi Templer; 16. Blanka Federweiss; 21. Roszi or Ella Schwarzthal twin; 22. Marianna Stahler; 24. Emanuel Weinberger; 25. Gyorgy Prissegi; 26. Richard Fischer; 27. Helena Sichermann; 28. Max Klein; 31. Vera Fischer; 33. Artur Weinberger; 34. Alfred Herz.

Arriving in Britain. (Key on previous page)

Preparing to disembark (Key on next page)

Key to previous photograph

Those recognised: 1. Pál Krausz; 10. Maximilian Rubin; 13. Lenke Rubin; 17. Richard Fischer; 18. Rachel Grunfeld; 20. Istvan Stahler; 25. Eva Rubinstein; 26. Judith Mannheimer; 29. Marianna Stahler; 32. Artur Weinberger

Some of the weary and confused children were reluctant to get into them. After an hour's drive through unfamiliar countryside they caught their first sight of the imposing Castle and that aroused further misgivings. What sort of institution was this? And doubts intensified later at the sight of iron-framed bunk beds. It was difficult enough to try to explain or reassure them without the additional handicap of the language barrier. Yet Mrs Eppel wrote to Rabbi Schonfeld that within an hour or so of their arrival she was watching them play football on the grass as if they had been there for ages.

Rabbi and Mrs Cohen and their helpers, some from London, some from Dublin, some paid, some volunteers, were confronted with a host of uncertainties. There was even confusion over personal names. Several children would come running whatever name was called! There was a range of explanations. Hidden Children had been assigned non-Jewish names by foster parents. Others had been re-named to match those on forged identity papers. On the journey to Britain any Czech names had to be changed and a few were given the name of those who had dropped out at the last moment. Several examples of these confusing situations were only finally sorted out at the Jubilee Reunion fifty years later!

So began a new experience for these young survivors, one that they were to recall later as a period of unparalleled calm in their tumultuous lives.

Greenville Hall Synagogue, Dublin. © Nigel Corrie, courtesy of Jewish Heritage UK.

Chapter Four

Life at the Castle

Headed Notepaper showing the later move from the Castle to Dun Laoghaire, 1949.

This is how **Alfred Leicht**, probably at 18 the oldest of the Dublin boys, described life at the Castle:

It was a remarkable experience to live alongside one hundred children ranging in age from six to seventeen, from different countries, with varying degrees of religious commitment, differing customs and endless stories of trials and tribulations. You could say we were an abstract tapestry, woven together yet unique in colour and contrast, symmetry and contradiction, too varied to fully comprehend. Our personalities and demeanour reflected the vagaries of an utterly confused past and a lost childhood. We wore our misery on our faces.

Rabbi Cohen and his wife, Trudi, created a relaxed and gentle routine to allow the children to recover their physical and mental strength and enjoy a tranquil life style they had lacked for years or never experienced. There were few demands and the minimum of restrictions. Rabbi Cohen led services, both morning and evening and the Sabbath, Fasts and Festivals were observed with much fervour. The children responded warmly under his guidance and enjoyed his informal sermons.

Classes organised by Rabbi Cohen concentrated on teaching English, Jewish history and religion but his timetable allowed plenty of opportunities for relaxation and leisure pursuits. Teachers, however, were hard to find. Volunteers came and went from Britain, among them Bertha Goodman, daughter of Harry Goodman, E. Shakovitsky and Judith Sternbuch. Judy was popular and warmly remembered.

I came fresh from seminary, aged 18, full of life and idealism to be a helper at Clonyn Castle. I taught English there. It was a shock to meet these children. They were suspicious of everyone! They were fearful in case the next meal failed to appear and some hid away bread. A 12 year old girl had been hidden in a convent and used to cross herself frequently, mystifying the others. But how Séndi spoilt them! She was a strong and powerful person. Benjamin fell in love with her. I remember that a local boy came to stoke the boiler to warm the water for our baths. He was a firm Catholic and he disliked Jews.

Judith Sternbuch

We were taught to take religion very seriously. But Judy's *shiurim* included a lot of humour and laughter. **Blanche Federweiss** prayed with us and told us we must not talk after that. But it was difficult to resist talking so we invented a secret sign language.

Judit Ziegler

Judith's friend, Bertha Goodman, another volunteer, showed me snaps of them both with lively groups of children exploring Delvin, the local village, and of Judy leaving to return to England. There she taught at the Hasmonean School where several of the group met her again later. Today Judit is a grandmother and a Rebbitzen settled in Jerusalem.

Benjamin Pels, son of Henry Pels, came too, fell in love with and later married **Séndi Templer,** the *metepelet* from Beis Ya'acov who had escorted them from Prague. She alone among the staff spoke the mother tongues of the children, and had suffered intensely herself during the war. The volunteers, in contrast, were young students with little or no experience to offer. Rabbi and Mrs Bleier, refugees from Europe, came with their child. They knew little English and discipline was a problem. He had difficulties teaching the older boys who became increasingly restless. Irish law forbade corporal punishment without agreement from Head Teacher and parents; but on the Continent it was usual. This raised issues.

A few local people provided English classes and made important contributions. Mr Mundheim from Dublin, an elderly refugee, was particularly popular and successful. Others came and went. There were language barriers, cultural differences and difficulties over discipline. Yet Mrs Eppel wrote five weeks after they arrived: "The children have made remarkable progress with their English".

All of them suffered from malnutrition but there is suprisingly little written in the Archives of any illness, health or psychological problems. Many, of course, had colds and, as was recommended at that time, one after another had their tonsils and adenoids removed. Several remember waking from the anaesthetic to find Mrs Eppel offering ice cream to soothe their burning throats. Visits to the dentist provoked much anxiety and were exacerbated by the language barrier.

Mrs Bleier took charge of the kitchen. Chaja Kurtz and Klara Kalman, two of the older girls, assisted her. In later months they took over a lot of that responsibility. Mrs Cohen commented that Mrs Bleier worked from morning till night to produce marvellous meals. After she left Mr and Mrs Margulies took over. They were recent arrivals from Poland. Incredibly they had survived by hiding in the sewers under the Lvov Ghetto in horrendous conditions and in perpetual danger.[1] Yet they put the past behind them and dedicated themselves to provide the best possible meals for the children and did so until the last had left. Then they settled in London where they ran a very successful catering business.

Milk was collected from a farm every morning fresh from the cows to ensure that it was *kosher*. Children took turns to ride on the pony cart to fetch it; that was a great treat. Meals were served in two sittings. It was hard to put limits on how much they could eat but Mrs Eppel became concerned by increasingly heavy bills. She comments that the younger children at the first sitting were leaving no fruit for the older ones who would then raid the stores.

Impecunious parents had provided clothing but this was soon outgrown. Lots of garments were collected by the Dublin community and the Irish Red Cross and even sent from London where it was still severely rationed. Mrs Eppel's brother-in law, Mr Green, generously provided £5 a week to be spent on outfitting one or two children at a time. The Dublin Ladies dealt with many other requirements. More blankets had to be found and were. There was a request for bicycles, too, but no record of the response.

Anna Katscher kept a diary, remarkable in many ways, particularly for her extensive knowledge of English. She contributed the following extracts. They give a detailed glimpse from a child's perspective of daily life at the Castle and how her personal attitude to being there changed as time went on.

Anna Katscher's Diary

These extracts were written when she was 12 years old. (Translations of Hebrew and Yiddish terms and explanations of customs and religious practices are given in the Glossary.)

Sunday 3rd October 1948: *Rosh Hashanah* today. I decided that I shall write a diary from the beginning of year 5709. That is my autobiography of what happened in Ireland in Clonyn Castle near Dublin. I am 12 years old. We got to Delvin on the 6th May 1948 and it is *Rosh Hashanah* G-ds will I have to spend here our big *Yom Tov*. It is the first evening of *Rosh Hashana* and at 6 pm we had to be ready to go downstairs to the dining room. There Agi started to talk about the *Yom Tov*. Later they distributed prayer books and showed us in which order to pray and then we went to the synagogue. We finished praying in the synagogue at 10.15 pm. Then we had supper till 11 pm. After supper we went to sleep.

Monday 4th October: I woke up at 8.30 am and then started to dress. When I was ready I went to the synagogue. I came a bit late but I soon caught up. We prayed till 11.30 am then we all got a cup of milk and a piece of cake. After a 10 minute break we had to go back to *shul*. At 4

Key to following photograph

Those identified:
1. Gyury Stahler: 2. Peter Steiner; 10. Alfred Herz; 12. Istvan Stahler; 13. Anna Katscher; 14. Franklina Wiesen; 15. Ella Schwarzthal; 16. or Rozie Schwarthal (twins); 18. Richard Fischer; 19. Erich Bock; 20. Richard Reich; 21. Vera Wiesen; 22. Gyorgy Prissegi; 23. Dezider Rosenfeld; 24. Emanuel Weinberger

Group of boys and girls on the Castle steps in 1948 (JS) © Irish Press PLC.

pm we had dinner. After one hour we went to *tashlich* to give our sins to the fish. The journey there took 1 hour. When we came back we had to go again to pray. We prayed till supper time. Supper was a meat meal. It ended at 10.30 pm. This was the first day of *Rosh Hashanah*.

Tuesday 5th October: Today we had to get up earlier than yesterday, but I got up at the same time at 8.30. To the service. I did not miss too much. At 11.30 we again had a 10 minute break. Today lunch was much earlier than yesterday. At 3.30 already it was finished. Straight after lunch I went for a walk with Eva Schwarz and Gita Strauss from which we returned quickly. During that time something happened. Miss Agi sat outside and was looking at the boys (mainly at Robi Muller and Rubin Max). Suddenly Robi started a nosebleed. He laid down on the floor and when it stopped bleeding, he stood up and went to change his outfit.

When he left then Agi also stood up and also left. After this we also went upstairs. Later we went to help in the office to make tea. We cleaned grapes - pears - bananas. After we handed them out at the tables we had some pears left over. Eva took 3 to our room and the rest we gave to the boys. At that time we had no *madrichot*. Mrs Cohen asked me to bring the leftovers. When I told her there were none she asked me what happened to the rest on the tray? To this we answered the boys took them. She told us to watch the table next time so that the boys should not steal them. Thus the time passed at teatime which was at 6.30 boys went to pray and we danced outside during this time, the *hora*. When the boys came they did not leave us alone, but we did not stop dancing. Agi just watched us but did not say a word. Then they got us very mad so we went elsewhere to dance the *hora*. After the dancing we started playing "Tretieho" when two boys joined us, Peter Steiner and Ernest Rubinstein. We were just playing then Peter and I went running together. At this they started teasing us and the girls sang about us. Rubin came and called the boys to prayers, this they finished at 9 pm. At about 10 pm we had supper because till then we were not *milchig*. Thus passed the second day of *Rosh Hashana*.

Wednesday 6th October: It is Wednesday a working day. Today (our room and also a few girls) we are getting ready for washing and having a bath, because we can only do that once a week. I could not have a bath because there was no water, but I washed between lunch and teatime.

After that I wrote four letters till dinner, after dinner I went to play ping-pong.

<u>Wednesday 13th October</u>: Today is *Yom Kippur* a fast day. All day we were in synagogue, except when we had a break for *Mazkir* (me too). In the evening I was very happy, because I received a parcel - it took 1 month and 10 days to arrive. At 7.30 pm we could eat and afterwards I went to play.

Friday 15th October: This day was really great, because I wanted to go to the village. Not planned. I went to the office for mail. When I was going away Mrs Eppel called me and asked me about blouses which I received in the parcel. Then I sold her 2 for a lot of money. I got 6 pounds for the two. Today Sabbath started at 6.45 pm so we had to return quickly. After supper I went with Eva for a little walk.

<u>Saturday 16th October</u>: Today I did not go to pray, because I woke up too late. When I prayed a bit they called me for *Kiddush*. Just after *Kiddush* is lunch and it finished a 2.30 pm. After lunch we went to dance the *hora*. Later we went for a walk, when we came back it started to rain.

We did not want to get wet so we went to buy ice cream to Norin where we ate it. I bought a bottle of lemonade. We carried on to different shops, just to look around and ask for things as we had no intention of buying.

We returned about teatime, it was later than usual; I read "Madame Curie", a book I borrowed from Hedy Friedmann. Sabbath was finished early so we went to play ping-pong. Today we played doubles – mixed.

We went to sleep at 11.30 pm.

Sunday 17th October: Today early in the morning I went to the office to borrow keys to the sewing room. I washed my clothes till 12.30 pm then I played ping-pong. I played with Trudi Mangel and I lost 21-7 and the second game 21-4. After lunch I washed again and finished around 3 pm. At 3 I started getting ready for *Yom Tov*. I was ready at 6 pm, so I went to iron my brother's things. When I finished I still had time to iron my apron. *Sukkes* started at 6.30 pm. We prayed very quickly and today only us girls ate in the dining-room, boys ate in the *Succah*. After dinner we danced the *hora* and other dances. One girl Saba Kumelmann taught me how to dance *Jadin gadin gadol*.

Monday 18th October: Today I woke up late so I did not go to synagogue. I prayed but not everything. Later I went to *Kiddush* which was together with lunch. During lunch we sang and after we danced for half an hour.

At 3 pm I went for a walk by myself. When I left I met Jutka with Lili by the gate. Jutka is false to me and accused me of spying on her. I made nothing out of it but deep down I ask myself why she thinks so badly of me. I went round the Castle. Eva was in the library when I went to look for her. It was very warm in there so I went for my book and read by the fireplace. Then my brother came and told me we got stamps. I was very pleased and ran upstairs to look at them. When I got there some of them were already sorted. Two series I put in the album and another I left out. I worried I would be late for a *Siur* given by Séndi because I like to hear her. She talked about the festival and about *esrog*, praying - why we do it - and the meaning of *esrog*, *lulev* and another two things (*arba minim*). But this *Siur* was after dinner. At 11 pm the lights went off so we had to go early to sleep.

Tuesday 19th October: This morning again I did not go to synagogue because I went to get the milk. Today was the same as yesterday. After lunch I sat by the fireplace next to the library. Later I spent time with Agi and Esti because they came to sit next to the fireplace. But I continued to read. When it became dark and I could not see to read I went to watch the boys playing. I stayed there till we had to go to pray. After that was dinner. After dinner and *Havdole* I went to play ping-pong as usual. I could not stay because Rabbi Cohen sent me to sleep, when I went up I still read.

Thursday 20th October: Today is already six months since we left Prague. Six months ago I still saw my dearest parents and at that time I decided to go into the world to try my luck. Just one word and I would not have to be here today. I could be going to school and have stayed next to my parents. I will never forget how it was with my father in the train and when we said goodbye. My father was crying and I also felt like it but I held back the tears. His last words were - be a good girl - do not forget your parents. Even if these were not the exact words, this is what he meant.

Now instead of that, at home where I could have gone to school and learn. I am lying down because I have a cold. Today I am lying down and did nothing useful. After lunch I played a bit dominoes by myself and then I was talking to Heda about our home comparing to our life now.

Throughout the year Rabbi Alony and Rabbi Lewis in Dublin encouraged and assisted Rabbi Cohen and Mrs Eppel. Rabbi Schonfeld let them know that the overall responsibility was his, as he was the children's official guardian. There were some problems between volunteers. There was a conflict when children were urged by Irish helpers to join their youth groups, the Zionist B'nei Akiva or Mizrachi, (akin to the Scout and Guide movements) rather than Agudath Israel that was not Zionist, and favoured by those from Britain. Then, at the close of a function at the Castle, when Dublin visitors began to sing the Israeli National Anthem, as was their custom, they were halted by a London volunteer. Rabbi Cohen was concerned to prevent any political pressure on the children; and so it was agreed that politics should be avoided in future.

Séndi Templer and **Blanka Federweiss** had a major impact on all the children. Blanka was born in 1927 (and not 1932 as stated on the Visa). These two became mother-substitutes to the youngest children, and role-models to the older girls. They instilled a love and respect for Jewish practice and history that has remained with them all. They soothed the troubled and comforted the homesick, singing songs, telling bedtime stories and leading night time prayers. They had far closer ties than was possible for the rest of the staff as they spoke the children's mother tongues, came from the same backgrounds and had suffered like them. They helped those who had families to write weekly letters. Rabbi Schonfeld insisted on this and two stamps a week were provided for every child. The village post office was delighted with the influx of answers these brought from abroad and the letters gave great joy to those who had family surviving.

The children enjoyed the half-hour walk to the village and they became popular with the local people. They collected the mail and spent their pocket money, an innovation in itself, in the village shops. Chocolate was a luxury they had not met before. **Eva Schwarz** told me how friendly the villagers were, how she would point to something and they would teach her the English word. An older boy was given English lessons by the police chief's wife at the Police Station. And **Rabbi Cohen** told me he occasionally found time to play chess with Mr Fitzsimmons, the local publican. There were escapades, too; **Josef Ickovitc** is recalled falling off a roof! The boys established their own football team and played the village school. The goal-keeper was their hero.

עב

Clonyn Castle
Delvin
West Meath
EIRE

Dear Dr. Shonfeld וכו׳ לה

The Madrichans are putting up a terrific fight for their young "wards". You would be really pleased to see how Miss Sh. Temple and others, often near to tears, fight to keep real "heimishe" 100% orthodoxy for 'our' children. They work extremely hard: education general welfare, service at meal-times and, I think, a bit in the kitchen.

Some of the bigger girls are really undermining the Madrichans' efforts: a little girl, for example, was told to comb her hair on שבת "and don't let the Madrichah see you"; the boys are ashamed to learn בהמ״ז at meal-times "because the big girls laugh"! I have not yet met a single person here who thinks is not convince that this split must be healed and the big girls leave as soon as the necessary permits are obtained.

Rabbi Kohn I admire and like; he seems to me deeply religious, quiet and efficient, and pretty conciliatory. But we all (incl. Mrs Kohn) feel that politics must be kept away from Castle;

Benjamin Pels in a letter to Rabbi Schonfeld.
Page 2 is opposite.

118

Last night we informed Rabbi Kohn of our attitude and intention of writing to you; only after the letter was sent off did he change his mind and announce semi-publicly that he was "against politics and the formation of a Bne Akiva group".

I think that all points of our joint letter should be cleared up at your very earliest, in the 'peace-spirit' which reigns at present. [There was and אי"ה never will be any personal מחלוקת]

Otherwise it is wonderful out here, I really admire your efficiency.

Yours Truly

בנימין פעלס

P.S. Brisko was here last night; sends regards to father will write to you.

Page 2 of Benjamin Pels' letter to Rabbi Schonfeld.

Housekeeping at the Castle

No estimates have surfaced to show what costs were envisaged for the Irish venture. Almost from the very beginning the entire scheme tottered from crisis to crisis because of inadequate and unreliable funding. Mrs Eppel certainly demonstrated an impressive ability and had strategies to deal with every exigency. Bills came tumbling in. Mention had been made in April 1948 of allowing £100 per week for food but it soon became evident this was not enough. One note records: "Cost of maintenance at the Castle amounts to £3-6-0d per head." Another states that weekly expenditure at the Dublin Hostel "is about £150 a week". Prices in Ireland were heavier than in Britain where substantial wartime subsidies remained in place. And even in Ireland, Mrs Eppel informs Mr Pels, there was some rationing: four ounces of butter and three-quarters of a pound of sugar per person per week. She mentions that she had to obtain some sugar on the black market. *Kosher* margarine had to be sent from England.

Lighting and heating required continuous supplies of fuel and onerous duties. The new generator caused endless problems. Rooms were heated by open fires that ate up logs. The girls naturally enjoyed sitting by the fire in their bedrooms to read and chat and seem to have been unaware that this was a luxury. Letters and telegrams show that the weekly cheque due from London was frequently delayed. An exasperated Mrs Eppel would complain to Mr Pels. He in turn often queried her expenditure. Yet somehow she succeeded in maintaining essential supplies despite steadily mounting debts.

At first eight local girls were employed, four living in and four coming daily to deal with laundry, cleaning and kitchen duties at 10/- each a week. For the month of June 1948, Mrs Eppel paid them £65 in wages. From August only one was retained and several of the older Slovak girls replaced the others. Two gardeners kept some order in the grounds, planted summer vegetables and two acres of potatoes, but not enough, they advised, to feed a hundred for a year. Rabbi Cohen was quick to adapt and to improvise. His most valued assistant was Oliver, the handyman, who took on numerous tasks and solved all manner of problems.

Reading letters
Anna Katscher, Blanka Federweiss, Lily Lowinger and Ella or Rozsi
Schwartzthal. (JS) ©Irish Press PLC

More letters arrive. Second from left, Lily Lowinger, Anna Katscher, Max Rubin, Ervin Schwarz, and Victor Mangel (JS)
©*Irish Press PLC*

Key to following photograph

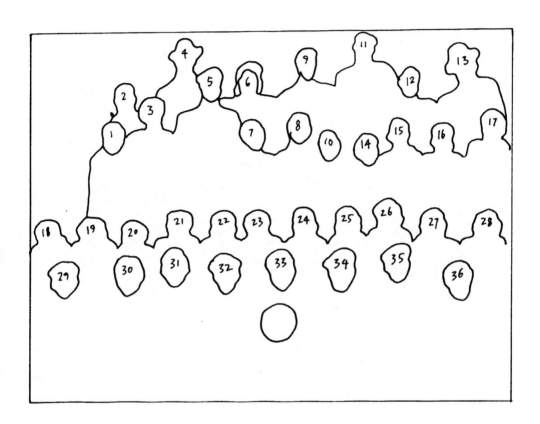

Those identified:
1. Visitor; 2. Visitor; 3. Erich Bock; 4. Maximilian (Max) Rubin; 5.
Ivan Katscher; 6. Lady Visitor; 7. Ervin Kummeldorfer; 8. Dezider
Rosenfeld; 9. Rabbi Israel Cohen; 10. Visitor; 11. Robert Muller; 12.
Ernst Rubinstein; 13. Ervin Schwarz; 14. Emanuel Weinberger; 15.
Gyury Stahler; 16. Alexander Lowy; 17. Richard Reich; 18. Tamáš
Gottlieb; 19. Manfred Hochhauser; 20. Israel Reich; 21. Robert Bock;
22. Alexander Mastbaum; 23. Robert Binet; 24. Gaspar Binet; 25.
Istvan Stahler; 26. Alexander Strausz; 27. Tibor Danzig; 28. Mihaly
Steiner; 29. Richard Fischer; 30. Alfred Herz; 31. Tamáš Steiner;
32. blank; 33. Emerich Grossmann; 34. Artur Weinberger; 35. Oskar
Reich; 36. Alfred Ziegler.

Clonyn Castle Football Team and Supporters (JS) ©Irish Press PLC

Resident staff wanted to spend their days off in Dublin; but fares cost 10/6d and meals were expensive. So Mrs Eppel allowed them £2 a month extra "though we can hardly afford an additional burden". Miss Isaacson, and in her absence Miss Smith, both members of the Dublin community, were employed to keep the monthly accounts for Mrs Eppel and the London office. Mrs Eppel's Dublin landlady raised her rent by two pounds a week on the grounds that so many people were coming in and out of her home. The Ladies Committee continued to raise funds and give practical help that was crucial throughout the whole scheme. They stood firmly behind Mrs Eppel every step of the way.

Changes

In August 1948, Rabbi Cohen resigned and in September he and his family left Ireland. He wrote to Rabbi Schonfeld "...that expenses were inevitably exorbitant for running a residential home in such an exotic setting" and that many of the volunteers and staff had left or were about do so. He felt he lacked any authority over the staff on religious questions, that he was concerned about the future and could not continue. His wife was expecting another child in December and he had been offered back his job in London. So ended the first phase of the Irish venture.

The departure of the Cohen family was devastating for the young people. They expressed this in the words of a song I came across, tucked into a photo album lent to me by Bertha Goodman.

Farewell
An anonymous song dedicated to Rabbi and Mrs Israel Cohen, September 1948, translated from the German.

We sing this song so often, this sad, repeated farewell
Now it's more difficult than ever, as more and more depart.
So many go away now. We hope this is all to the good.
It must be, because our leader is accompanying his students.
We begin with the chief who everyone respects.

We want to remind you of all the good advice he's given us.
We have many worries from early morning every day - big and little.

How will we manage when you are no longer here?
We shall miss your singing of prayers and psalms and weekly sermons.
Oh! Something has just occurred to us - maybe a good idea:
We would like you to send us a weekly Sabbath address.

He is a man of many talents, from ping-pong to business.
Nothing is too difficult for him -though 'tis true that the ball
Often falls off the table. Never mind, as long as he plays the game.
Rabbi Cohen has been here only six months but he has learned
All our languages. But there is one thing we must emphasize:
Make sure that his appetite does not leave him. That's important.
Suke goes with him everywhere. Don't let our worries get us down,
Don't be afraid. Rabbi Cohen will come back soon.
So be happy, don't make trouble.

Now it's our caring Mrs Cohen's turn for our appreciation.
What she does and who she is we cannot find words to describe.
There are few people to equal her. She is always content with everything.
Whoever comes to her with their troubles or guilt she always has a remedy
And the patience of Hillel. Whether in sorrow or in joy
She always finds comforting words. In one word - she's irreplaceable
And for us unforgettable. She has a daughter, "Suksuk" is her name.
We will miss her a lot. Without her the house will seem empty.
We thank you both for everything. The Lord grant you much happiness,
A reward for your goodness - all your trouble looking after us.

We will have to go on singing a long time to express our gratitude.
The words are not the main thing but what every one thinks and believes.
Take these few words from the bottom of our hearts.
May the Lord bless you with all things good. May we meet again soon.

The departure of the Cohen family marked the end of a
tranquil period. It revived in the children their latent insecurity.
The joys of the Irish countryside had boosted their spirits initially
but the charm faded as concern grew about what the future
held for them. There was intense longing to be reunited with
surviving family members and, especially among the older ones,
an impatience to move into a more stimulating environment.
They longed to make up for lost years of schooling, and had an
ardent desire to work and achieve independence. They all knew
that Mr Pels was corresponding with parents about plans to join
them and making arrangements for orphaned children. And, one
by one, children were leaving for Britain, for the USA or Canada,
or for Palestine via France - to the increasing frustration of those
left behind.

This was the scenario faced by Moishe Lozor Zahn who was sent to replace Rabbi Cohen. He was a son of the Rabbi of the Sunderland Yeshiva. It was quickly evident that he lacked the experience and maturity needed to handle an increasingly difficult situation. Mrs Eppel was dismayed by a lack of discipline. Meals were served late and the cleaners' work impeded because children were staying in bed. She complained that Mr Zahn's inexperience and the lax routine were a direct cause of the disorderly behaviour of the youngsters.

In her almost daily letters to Mr Pels, Mrs Eppel also complained about unnecessary extravagances and "massive waste". She asked Rabbi Schonfeld to intervene and urged him to send a matron to take charge of the household. Rabbi Schonfeld responded with a serious letter to Mr Zahn for his "immediate attention", written by hand and in German. There is the first mention of vacating the Castle. Above all Rabbi Schonfeld required the young man to:

"Think very carefully before spending any money at all, and delegate responsibility. You must work together, maintain order and keep to regular meal times. Rooms should be comfortably warm but not overheated; it is cold in the Castle but heat costs a fortune and must be reduced. Travel into Dublin only if really necessary. Restrict purchases from the Delvin chemist to children spending pocket money. Phone only when important, avoid long telegrams to Dublin. A smaller house is being sought in Dublin now there are fewer children. Seems to me these problems must be overcome. You must all work with Mrs Eppel. When she sees you are pulling together, she will be better pleased. Consider the expenses for January amounted to £1,291. The young people must be drawn into our confidence. If they can earn something to support themselves they should do so and take any jobs they can. Talk it over and let us know what you plan. Delegate everyone to take some responsibility. Work together to reduce expenses; but essential needs should be met."

Mr Zahn struggled on but could never hope to assume the respect of these insecure youngsters enjoyed by his predecessor.

What was involved in moving on

To acquire visas to travel abroad information about every child had to be scrutinised by several different consulates. Questions were raised where names and dates and birthplaces had been tampered with and documentary evidence was unavailable. Strategies for solving these problems led to long delays. Mrs Eppel built up sound relationships with officials in the consulates and persevered to answer every query that arose.

Every Visa application also required a Medical Certificate that showed the holder's current state of health. Dr Nurock, Delvin's GP, gave thorough examinations and certified that relevant vaccinations and inoculations had been administered but he baulked at arranging X-rays, oculist and dental inspections, demanded by Youth Aliyah. Mrs Eppel said the limited time available made this impossible. Rabbi Schonfeld wrote across her letter to Mr Pels: "You must get Youth Aliyah to waive this." And presumably he did. The USA made additional demands. All who had lived in a Communist country had to provide a full family history showing addresses of all their domiciles since birth. Those applying for student visas had to give proof that college places had been offered them and these visas were restricted to the period of study.

The original agreement with the Irish authorities limited the children's stay to twelve months. In April 1949, when remaining children's departures were delayed and their Irish Visas ran out, Mrs Eppel succeeded in renewing them at a cost of 12/6d each. Half a century later, **Alfred Leicht**, one of the boys from the Dublin Hostel, still felt that the Irish had made a mistake. He and his companions had deeply appreciated the year given them to recuperate in Ireland. Afterwards many of the refugees, like him, settled in North America and prospered there. But he would have preferred to stay and he and others could have contributed to the Irish economy.

It is one of the ironies of history that inward-looking Ireland offered us only conditional and temporary status in their land. Yet masses of their own poverty-stricken citizens had emigrated to America to seek a better life. Some of us might have opted to remain there.

Alfred Leicht

Aliyah

Many wanted to go to Israel, some to follow family already there, others to join schemes designed for young immigrants. Rabbi Schonfeld had reservations because of lax religious observance in the new state. Nevertheless he gave his blessing to those who made this decision. The services of Youth Aliyah were called upon to organise this. They set up an Israeli orientation course at the Castle over 5 weeks. They dealt with immigration formalities and made travel arrangements for group after group to leave over the following months. Eventually about a third of the Slovak children settled in Israel and more have followed since.

The first group of twenty-five boys and girls left on January 24th 1949. Their impending departure was fully reported in Dublin newspaper "The Times Pictorial", January 8th.

Rabbi Schonfeld came to see them off with a blessing at the airport.

We each had to decide where we wanted to go from Ireland. I opted for Israel. So together with my cousin and 23 other kids I flew from Dublin to Paris. From there we took a train to Marseilles where we stayed in Villa Gabi for about ten days while we waited for the ship "Eilath" which took us to Haifa.

Erich Bock

At the Dublin Hostel there were different problems to address. Mrs Eppel never ceased seeking work or training opportunities for the lads; but they had to observe the Jewish Sabbath and Irish firms required staff to work on Saturdays. Other employees would surely object if they were absent, she explained. **Ervin Schwarz** was fortunate. He had an apprenticeship in a leather workshop and this experience some years later led to his establishing his own handbag factory in London.

Over the following months one by one joined family members in Israel, in North America, or in Britain. A number of boys were found places in *yeshivot* or boarding schools in England. Rabbi Zahn admitted four lads to his *yeshiva* in Sunderland. A proviso was added by Rabbi Schonfeld, acting as their guardian, that in addition to religious studies, they were to receive a secular education in English, maths and geography – though this was not normally offered there. A further 14 or 15 young people were preparing to attend a week's introduction for *aliyah* in England and hoped to reach Israel before Passover.

Then, in February, out of the blue, rumours circulated in the Dublin Jewish community that horrified Mrs Eppel and her valiant committee. Members of the former Refugee Committee, all along hostile to the programme for the Slovakian children, had heard that the Central British Fund - for which they had raised money in the past - was to take over from Rabbi Schonfeld's committee (CRREC) responsibility for the Castle children. It was also being said that his scheme was in debt by five or six thousand pounds.

The Ladies were aghast. They wrote to London saying they would never get involved with the former Refugee Committee. Mr Pels wrote at once to allay their fears. Mrs Eppel reported to Rabbi Schonfeld that, so widespread were these rumours, Rabbi Jakobovitch, Chief Rabbi of Ireland, made an unannounced visit to see for himself how matters stood. Mrs Eppel welcomed this. And as can be imagined he found no basis for complaint.

Clonyn Castle "FOR SALE"

The CRREC had instructed Mrs Eppel to find a smaller property to house the remaining 41 children as well as those lads left in the Dublin Hostel. When these boys heard this they sent a vicious letter of complaint to Rabbi Schonfeld, to Mr Pels and to Mrs Goldwater, the Chair of the valiant Ladies' Committee. They made out there was insufficient food or heating and accused Mrs Eppel of pocketing the funds saved for her own use! It turned out that supplies of chicken were not available but there was ample meat, that the children were receiving their full ration of sugar and that it would have been extravagant to order more coal prior to vacating the Castle (the merchants would only deliver a minimum amount). Nor could the boys understand why a matron was required, and saw this as an unnecessary expense!

The Rabbi told the boys that everyone was doing their best, that expenditure was rising when it should be going down with smaller numbers to care for, that "regular and full control" was held over Mrs Eppel's expenditure that "we find hard to send to her". He told them they should submit to the discipline

VOL. 75 NO. 3,941 EVERY WEDNESDAY 2D.   OVERSEAS   WEEK ENDING JANUARY 8, 1949

TIMES PICTORIAL

PROMISED LAND AHEAD

More than 100 Jewish refugee children are living at Clonyn Castle, Co. Westmeath; while plans are made to enable them to go to Palestine, where they can begin a new life. Twenty of the children are setting off for the "promised land" this month. *ABOVE:* Judith Lowy, Judith Friedman and twin sisters, Ella and Rozie Schwarzhall, pack their suitcases. *BELOW:* A close-up of Judith Friedman, who seems to be having some difficulty in deciding what to take in the one suitcase which she will be allowed to bring.

This little boy's name could not be traced, so he is called Avrom Priseka, after the Czechoslovakian town in which he was born; he is being held by Leopold Zalm, of Nuremburg, one of the supervisors at Clonyn Castle. Avrom's story and the stories of other refugee children are in Page 5.

Mrs. Olga Eppel, head of the organisation which brought the children to Ireland and is sending them to Palestine, gives a talk on Israel to nineteen of the twenty young travellers; when this picture was taken the twentieth child was in hospital, but will be well enough to go with the others. *BELOW:* Young Avrom discovers the packing problem with Alexander Straus.

January 8th 1949. The Times Pictorial reports on the first group leaving for Israel © The Irish Times.

GLONYN CASTLE CHILDREN'S HOSTEL

Under the auspices of the Chief Rabbi's (Religious Emergency) Council.

================

Organising Secretary:
Mrs. OLGA EPPEL. Telephone No.
7, Garville Road, 93684.
Rathgar, Dublin.

London Office:
86, Amhurst Park. N.16.
STAMFORD HILL 1971/1646

28 FEB 1949

CLONYN CASTLE,
Nr. DELVIN,
Co. WEST MEATH, EIRE

24th February, 1949.

Rabbi Dr. S. Schonfeld,
London, N.16.

Dear Dr. Schonfeld,

I am having the under-mentioned children medically prepared for Israel, and should be glad if you would please contact Youth Aliyah and find out for me if that body are sending a transport in the near future.

Fleishmann.	Esther.
Wiesen children.	Two.
Steiner "	Three.
Grossman "	~~THREE~~ Two.

The undermentioned are anxious to go, and I should be glad to have your authority to have them prepared.

haven't consent? 2

Stasney children.	Three.
Binet "	Two.
Rosenfeld	One.

Esther Fleishmann is anxious of course to go to England, but imagines that if she cannot get an English visa, she should go to Israel. She will sign the necessary undertaking for Youth Aliyah, that she does not become a charge on them as she is over 16 years of age.

*Mr. Rds - check on parents
as far as I am
concerned, I agree.*

Please let me have your views.

yours sincerely,

Olga Eppel

P.S. I am enclosing a letter which I received to-day from Fitzsimons of Delvin, and should be glad if you would suitably reply to him. This letter gives the lie to the rumours in Dublin that the village have anti-semitic feelings. As I told you on many occasions, the friendship between the village and the Castle has been amazing, and I know the entire village will be dreadfully sorry when the childre go as they simply love them all.

February 24th, approval requested for another group of children to go to Israel. See the Rabbi's handwritten comment: parents' agreement also required.

133

necessary when they move to the new house near Dublin and try themselves to find suitable jobs. Mrs Goldwater wrote, too, to tell them that Mrs Eppel was held in the highest regard. She also told them that most Irish people lacked running hot water in their homes and that the boys should manage to wash themselves as they had always done.

Mrs Eppel found a suitable house at Dun Laoghaire, the port town seven miles from Dublin where the mail boat arrives "only a four-penny tram ride from the city and fifteen minutes by car". She recommended the property as a fine house in a good neighbourhood "so it would be essential to instill good discipline on the children and ensure they treat the neighbours with respect". The house overlooked a park, was fifteen minutes walk from the sea, in good order and admirably suitable at a very reasonable price: £4,000. Rates, taxes and interest would be about £4 per week. She negotiated a loan from the Bank based on a guarantee from the CRREC and a £5,000 deposit with the assistance of her brother-in-law, a surveyor and lawyer. To avoid 25% duty on the price for a foreign purchaser this amazing lady bought the property in her own name, as an Irish citizen. As a safeguard she made a will stating the CRREC was responsible for the property and any debts.

Mrs Eppel told Mr Pels she wanted to pay off some local debts before vacating the Castle and sent him, too, a summary of expenditure over the previous year.

In the first week of April the move was made. Rabbi Schonfeld called the new place Clonyn House and sent a telegram "May you all be happy in your new home!" **Israel Reich** recalls going to a Dublin school from there by train and finding it difficult to understand the Irish brogue. The headmaster complimented Mrs Eppel on the children. Mrs Eppel wrote that she was "very gratified" with his comments in contrast to some of the harsh criticism she continued to endure from within the Dublin Jewish community.

A tragic outcome

Mr Levy had to sell the Castle so Mrs Eppel was required to empty it. The only repairs needed were the replacement of two

CLONYN CASTLE CHILDREN'S HOSTEL

Under the auspices of the Chief Rabbi's (Religious Emergency) Council.

Organising Secretary:
Mrs. OLGA EPPEL,
7, Garville Road,
Rathgar, Dublin.

London Office:
86, Amhurst Park, N.16

CLONYN CASTLE,
Nr. DELVIN,
Co. WEST MEATH, EIRE

Friday. 11/2/49.

Rabbi Dr. Schonfeld,
London, N. 16.

Dear Dr. Schonfeld,

Further to my telephone call to you this morning, I immediately phoned Mrs. Goldwater, Rabbi Alony, but was disappointed that Bobby Briscoe is away until tonight. Having imparted all the information I had to these, I asked Rabbi Brodie for an interview and saw him at 2 p.m. today. I told Rabbi Brodie that I understood that the C.B.F. would take over the children, but not the liabilities and I showed him my books as made up to the end of December last. I am afraid that seemed rather like a bombshell to him. I showed him where I had roughly £4 in hand when the children started, but that since then I received over six thousand from you and nearly £2,000 from my committee. He was amazed. However, he said he had no answer to all that and I then informed him about the Rep. Council here, how they frustrated us from the beginning and how my committee got nothing but insults from them and in spite of those insults have carried on and successfully too. However, the Rabbi read a portion of a letter he received from Mr. Steffani and it said thus, but I am quoting from memory so although I have the gist of it, the words may not be correct:-

"I (Steffani) saw Prof. Abrahamson who informed me that
"he is prepared to take over the children and resuscitate
"the original refugee committee, and ensure that the
"Jewish public of Dublin will do all in their power to
"maintain the children".

The committee the Prof. refers to is the one that was in existence when Millisle was functioning and which collected monies (that £3,000) for Millisle. Since the closing down of Millisle, that committee ceased to function.

I am calling an emergency meeting of my committee for Monday night next and am asking Rabbi Alony and Mr. Briscoe to attend. Mrs. Goldwater is adamant that if the Rep. Council (Prof. Abrahamson) take over, she will resign. If she does, the whole committee collapses and I told Rabbi Brodie this. His final word to me was that I was to carry on until I heard further and my final word to him was, that it is impossible for anyone to reconcile Prof. Abrahamson's attitude to the children since

February 11th Mrs Eppel reports on rumours of a CBF take-over and her negotiations for a smaller property.

135

their arrival and his promise to Mr. Steffani.   Furthermore, I asked
Rabbi Brodie to be sure and consult with Rabbi Alony and Mr. Briscoe
before he leaves Dublin.   He has promised to do this.   He leaves
Monday morning.

       I told Rabbi Brodie that I was buying a house and in my name
but that I was expecting a guarantee against the outlay from London.
said the house is an asset which is correct, of course.

       Regarding the house, we offered £3,000 today, but were told
to forget it.   The trouble is that a house next door went for £3,900
and the person who bought it lives in one flat and' converted two other
floors into flats and is getting £4 each flat.   That is why the owner
of this house is reluctant to sell at a low figure.   My nephew is goi
to offer £3,300 and will probably have to give £3,500, but the lowest
figure which they will sell at is £3,600.   However, I will write you
about this again as nothing is settled yet.   I am reluctant to give
the £3,600 since there was no bid at the auction, but at the same time
know how difficult it is to get a house of this size and one that does n
need one penny to spend on decorations or repairs.   The house is
absolutely sound and clean.

       With kind regards.

              Yours sincerely,

              Olga Eppel

Forgive typing, am trying to get this off before Shabbos.

Rabbi Brodie says that if the C.B.F. takes over that the Rabbonim in
Dublin will have to take more interest in the children and that the
must be no interference in their religious practices.   I doubt very
much indeed if that will happen.   Can you imagine Prof. Abrahamson a
Blanca ?

When does Rabbi Pollak come back?   We must have some supervision at
the Castle.   There was a midnight film show in Dublin on Wed. night
last which Mizrachi gave.   7 of the older girls at the Castle hired
a taxi from Delvin to Dublin and back so that they could see the show.
They arrived back in Delvin at 3 a.m.   I am in full sympathy with th
girls who must have some recreation and certainly should see a Yiddish
film, but can you imagine the village talking about midnight trips to
Dublin, or the Dublin public for that matter?   Had I thought of it,
I could have arranged for them to come up and stay overnight with some
of the Committee, but I am afraid I did not think of it at all.

*February 11ᵗʰ (continued) Mrs Eppel reports on rumours of a CBF
take-over and her negotiations for a smaller property.*

CRC/HP/IS-

16th February, 1949.

Mrs. O. Eppel,
7, Batkill Road,
Rathgar, DUBLIN.

Dear Mrs. Eppel,

I am very much concerned to hear that rumours are being carelessly spread in the Dublin Community regarding negotiations between this Council and the Central British Fund regarding the financial position of this Council and our Children's Home at Clonyn Castle. Such rumours are bound to do considerable harm to our work and finally to the children in our charge and I am, therefore, writing this letter to you with the express desire that the information which it contains should be passed on not only to your co-workers but also to those who are so eager to spread the wrong information. Our Council is quite in a position to maintain its obligation and to carry on its activities of maintaining refugee children and others.

On the personal request of the Chief Rabbi who does not wish to be burdened with fund-raising activities this Council agreed to enter into negotiations with the Central British Fund with the view of the latter taking over the refugee work of the Chief Rabbi's Religious Emergency Council, including the maintenance of Jewish orphans whom we brought over from the Continent.

No financial considerations of any kind made us comply with the Chief Rabbi's desire, as the financial position of this Council is good and sound.

The conditions for such transfer, agreed to by the Chief Rabbi and laid down by the Council provide that the Council would hand over certain assets, avlued at approx. £25,000 over a few years to the Central British Fund, whereas the Central British Fund would take over maintenance obligations of the Council and certain financial responsibilities involved in this work.

It is libellous to suggest the Council is unable to settle its liabilities and unable to feed the Children at Clonyn Castle who would be starving, unless the C.B.F. takes over. We would advise you seriously to warn those who are so busy spreading such damaging rumours.
- II -

February 16th, Mr Pels' reply to damaging rumours circulating in Dublin.

<u>ctd. - letter to Mrs. Eppel, dated 16th February, 1949.</u>

      I am sending a copy of this letter to Chief Rabbi Brodie who is in possession of all relevant facts and will surely confirm these facts to anyone who really wishes to hear the truth.

      We sincerely hope that you and your co-workers, espec. Mrs. Goldwater, will not be discouraged in the holy work they are doing. So far nothing/regarding any transfer of responsibility and for the next months at least your Committee and we shall alone be responsible for feeding and maintaining the children. We shall keep you informed of any further developments in this matter.

      With kindest regards,

                      I remain,
                         Yours sincerely,

                         HENRY PELS
                     Secretary General.

February 16th, Mr Pels' reply (continued) to damaging rumours circulating in Dublin.

21st February 1949/5709

Mrs. O. Eppel
7, Gerville Road,
RATHGAR
Dublin

Dear Mrs. Eppel,

Thank you for your various letters explaining developments. I had a long talk with the Chief Rabbi on Thursday and among other matters he assured me that the purpose of his discussion with Professor Abrahamson was merely to get him and his Committee to raise funds for the Central British Fund, having regard to the possibility of the Central British Fund becoming financially responsible for the maintenance of the children.

The whole thing thus really boils down to an effort to get even more money out of Dublin Jewry.

As to the management of the hostel, we have no intention of handing it over to any other Committee in Dublin, even should the C.B.F. take over financially - which, as you know, is by no means certain.

The ultimate responsibility for the children rests with me, both towards the children and towards the Eire Government.

If and when I have any new arrangements to place before you, I shall place them in the first place before your Committee, which is the only body in Ireland responsible for the children. I earnestly beg you and your co-workers to continue your very devoted work and to redouble your efforts to raise funds for the maintenance and welfare of the children.

I shall make an effort to come over in the near future in order to meet your Committee.

Yours sincerely,

P.S. I am giving every attention to the English visas of the older girls and I hope for good results soon.

February 21st - Rabbi Schonfeld's reassurance.

panes of glass and a couple of door handles, and removal of a bit of scribbling. She organised the sale of all remaining contents. The lengthy inventory survives.

Mr Levy had great difficulty in finding a buyer. It had cost him very much more than he had expected; the expenses of adaptation and maintenance during the following year far exceeded original estimates and incurred severe financial pressure on the Levy family.

This meant that Mr Levy had continuing obligations for another twenty years adding to the huge contribution he had already made. The venture seriously impinged on his family's resources. One of his daughters told me that their father was no business man and had put nothing aside for his children. This led to his having to take out loans for a daughter's wedding and further family expenses. He was declared bankrupt. Despite this critical situation I was assured by Mrs Shula Jacobs, his wife's sister, who married Rabbi Louis Jacobs, that the whole family fully supported their parents' decision to provide the premises for the Slovakian survivors.

Only after 1969 did the Castle pass to the present owners.

The final months

"The Boys", as they signed themselves, wrote again at the end of March with more complaints: that from the new place "We can't make it in time for work in the mornings as the transport is very bad". In the end the four boys who had work in Dublin took lodgings there and paid their own way; but there were no chores at the new address to occupy those unemployed. So, as Mrs Eppel wrote to the Rabbi in March, she was giving them 5/- a week pocket money, that there were local amusements and it cost only 8d to go into Dublin. She also paid " for barbers and everything but I fear they will run wild if I gave them more and get themselves talked about". This situation no doubt added to the boys' frustration.

So when a matron was eventually found to manage the new house her task was no easy one. She proved a capable housekeeper and worked well with Mr and Mrs Margulies who managed the

FOR SALE BY PRIVATE TREATY
CLONYN CASTLE,
DELVIN, CO. WESTMEATH
DUBLIN (AIRPORT) 45 MILES

On 128 Acres of Pasture and Woodland

Magnificent Residence with oil-fired central heating. Lovely timbered parklands and old walled garden. Imposing Hall, Ballroom and 3 Reception Rooms; 17 Bedrooms; 7 Bathrooms; staff quarters and bathrooms. In excellent, unspoilt sporting country. Freehold.

Solicitors: Messrs JOHN J. McDONALD & CO.,
21 Earlsfort Terrace, Dublin 2.
Full details from the Auctioneers.

Clonyn Castle still for sale in 1969 © The Irish Times

"Clonyn House", 9 Vesey Place, Dun Laoghaire where the remaining children moved when Clonyn Castle was vacated. (JS)

R U L E S and R E G U L A T I O N S at Clonyn House.

1.   These rules are established only for the purpose of
     regulating our daily life,
     for keeping our house- that is our home -in good tidy order,
     to give its inhabitants(each of us)happiness and comfort.

2.   M E A L S are served :
     breakfast 8/30 to 9/00 a.m.;   dinner 12/30 to 1/00 p.m.;
     afternoon-tea 4/45 to 5/15 p.m.;
     supper children 6/30 p.m.;
                bigger children and others 8/00 to 8/30 p.m.;
     evening-tea 10/00 p.m.;
     meals are served only at the above mentioned times.

3.   L I G H T will be switched off at 11/00 p.m.; Friday and Saturday
          night according to season.
          Switch off the electric light when leaving any place or
          if nobody is in it.

4.   Keep our house clean and tidy. Don't throw paper anywhere and use
          the paper-baskets for collecting waste-paper.

5.   Clean your shoes before entering the house from the street or
          from the garden.

6.   In the gardens walk only on the roads. Don't cut or tear flowers
          or bushes but let everybody have his and her joy at them.

7.   It is strictly forbidden   t o   l o i t e r at any time :
          at the front-entrance,   at the front-stairs,
          in the front-garden,   on the side-walk in front of the
                                                         house.
          Open at once the main entrance-door, if you hear somebody
     XXXXXXXXXXXXXXXXXXXXXXXXXXXXXXXXXXXXXXXXX   knocking.

8.   This house is not a Hostel for Refugees but a private ▨▨▨▨▨▨▨
          House,and therefore we must all prevent making much noise.
          Otherwise neighbours might complain at the Police, who
          would cause us great difficulties.

9.   If you have any worries, wishes or suggestions entrust yourself
          in fullest confidence to one of the House Committee Mem-
          bers; they will be happy to help you.
     XXX
10. Take consideration to your comrades where ever and when ever you
          can. Mutual assistance makes their lifes and your own life
          happy and comfortable.

     Dun Laoghaire, the 17th day of April 1949.

Clonyn House, Rules and Regulations.

Clonyn free

CRC/HP/ML.

7th January, 1949.

Excerpts of the Minutes of a meeting of the Executive Committee
of the Chief Rabbi's Religious Emergency Council a6 86 Amhurst Pl
London, N.16., on the 14th February, 1949.

"The Secretary reported that on account of the reduced number
of children at Clonyn Castle, it had become necessary to move
from Clonyn Castle to a smaller house where the remaining
children could be accommodated.

The Council's representative in Dublin, Mrs. Olga Eppel, had
found a suitable house at 9, Vesey Place, Dun Laoghaire, near
Dublin, which could be purchased at a price of £3500. plus
fees, stamp duty and other expenses, amounting to another £500.

The Hibernian Bank Ltd., Thomas St., Dublin, were prepared to
advance £4000. on this house on the Council's guarantee.

The Executive Committee approved the purchase of the house and
authorised the Executive Director and the Secretary jointly to
sign the guarantee required by the Hibernian Bank".

This is to certify that the above is a true copy of part of
the minutes dealing with the acquisition of 9 Vesey Place,
Dun Laoghaire, near Dublin.

Secretary.   Executive Director.

*Mention in the Minutes of the purchase of Clonyn House (wrongly
dated) Note "Clonyn free" written across the page by the Rabbi.*

144

CLONYN CASTLE CHILDREN'S HOSTEL

Under the auspices of the Chief Rabbi's (Religious Emergency) Council.

Organising Secretary:
Mrs. OLGA EPPEL.
7, Garville Road,
Rathgar, Dublin.

Telephone No.
93684.

London Office:
86, Amhurst Park, N.16
STAMFORD HILL 1971/1646.

CLONYN CASTLE,
Nr. DELVIN,
Co. WEST MEATH, EIRE

29th March, 1949.

Mr. H. Pels,
London, N.16.

Dear Mr. Pels,

In regard to the £500. you sent me, I want to tell you that I have decided, as we are leaving Delvin this week, to pay up everybody there. Fitzsimons account as you know is a current account, and there is the milk account in Delvin, Chemist a/c, and so out of the £500. I had to pay £6.15.0. interest on it. Also last Friday's wages which came to £57. 9. 6. I am holding back £1. per week for some of the bigger boys. A few of them are in Dublin and have wired up the house were lights were lacking, and have papered the rooms, therefore, they will have to be paid, and I might add that they made a very good job of it.

In regard to the money from the sale of work, I doubt if I will get that for a few weeks yet, and we are determined to reduce some of the Dublin debts, so that when we get to Dublin, I will not have so much on my mind.

I shall be sending you another cash account in a day or t covering the £500 you sent me, but I would like you to let me have l weeks and this weeks cheque so that the whole £500 will not be used current expenses, but to pay off . If you do not send me last week this weeks cheques the £500 becomes £350. Please do your utmost to let me have the £150 as I have the final eages to meet at Delvin on Friday next when the Castle will be closed down.

I will show a refund on my cash account for whatever wage I am holding back from the boys and will show it as a refund in my later cash account.

In any case after I dispose of the £500 today for last week's wages and debts at Delvin, I have no money at all for this we wages and other accounts to be cleared at Delvin.

Yours sincerely,

Olga Eppel

March 29th. Note that the impression is given that debts were to be settled before leaving the Castle. Later information questions this.

145

<u>Meat supplied from Rubensteins, Lwr. Clanbrassil St., Dublin.</u>

28/2/49.   17 lbs. soup meat.
2/3/49.   2 hens, 13 lbs. mince; 15 lbs. soup meat.
March 3rd.   56 lbs. roast meat; 5 lbs. worsht; 1 stone of fat; 6 hens.
 to 6th.

Note:-   This works out at ¼ lb. per meat per adult person per day and
         6 ozs. meat for every child under 12 per day.   This is a weekly
         standing order.

<u>Supplies from Star Market, Lwr. Richmond St., Dublin:-</u>

1 case of oranges (averaging 220 in each case).
½ st. apples   "   200 "   "   "
10 to 15 lbs. Tomatoes.
4 doz. Bananas.
1 sack cabbage.
½ sack onions
½ sack carrots.
1 box dates or figs.
48 tins of fruit.

Note:-   You will see from this that each child gets an average of 1½
         oranges per day and approx. the same in apples.   This is a weekly
         standing order.

----

30 doz. eggs per week from Fitzsimons, Delvin.
Sardines; Tinned Tomatoes; corn flakes; fish for Shabbos (when possible).
Fish is difficult to get. Tea; coffee Cocoa.   Sweets; cake; Jam; 2
bottles wine; six gals. milk per day.

Regarding sugar:-   The ration is ½lb. per person per week, but they do not
manage and I have to buy black market at 7½ per lb, which is preposterous.

Butter on ration 6 ozs. per child per week.

The breakfasts consists of cornflakes plus an egg every morning if they
so wish.   We buy sweets wholesale at 1 stone per time and 48 pints of
milk per day.

Coal:-   13th May 1948   11 tons.
         9th June   9   "
         17th August   5   "
         24th Sept.   9   "
         16th Oct.   8   "
         24th Nov.   8   "
         16th Dec.   6   "   9 cwts.
         5th Jan 1949   6   "   2   "
         26th Jan.   3   6
         11th Feb.   6   4
         11th March   1
         18th "   1

                                        { Total cost
                                        { 90 numbers
                                        { £546.

In addition we have bought and paid for 4 tons locally in Delvin.
I am only buying 1 ton at a time now as we are moving.
You will see that we used 78 tons of coal up to now. If there were no
baths it is because they neglected to stoke the furnace.

146   *Page from Mrs Eppel's accounts. A summary of essential purchases.
      Note coal usage.*

kitchen. But she failed to achieve a reasonable relationship with the young people. She lacked skills in handling them and they reacted unkindly, making her life a misery. Eventually she gave up the struggle and returned to London.

Correspondence shows that Mrs Eppel made fresh efforts to sort out expenditure and deal with past debts.

Yet financial stress continued to plague her even with fewer children and a smaller house to manage. On top of that she sent a further list of outstanding debts that astounded Mr Pels.

Mrs Eppel eventually made a suprising deal with those patient local tradesmen! She wrote on June 28th, 1949 "I settled a lot of debts in Delvin, reducing them by about 20% in recognition of full settlement."

Efforts continued to sort out future plans for the remaining young people.

Then five of the older girls became terribly frustrated. They wrote to Mrs Eppel and to Rabbi Schonfeld.

Here is a translation of their letter (see page 157):

Clonyn House, 22nd June 1949

Dear Mrs Appel, [sic]
I am sure you will be surprised to receive this letter but we ask your help once more to expedite our return to London. We have written to Rabbi Schonfeld several times but he has not answered us. Maybe he does not see our letters. We do not know where the mistake is, whether it is with you, dear Mrs Appel, or with the English people.

We have been waiting here for more than a year now, aimless and without work. Being unemployed does not feel good or right. We long to become independent. We have received promises but that is not enough. Friends have told us that we need our permits within the next days. Now we have learned that they have still not arrived. How can that be? Is it not an awful situation?

We are really very grateful to Rabbi Schonfeld for getting us out of the fire, and also to you, dear Mrs Appel, for doing so much for us, but we are not happy - rather the opposite. How can we be when we are unemployed? One day here is as boring as a whole year. That's why we implore you to help us in any possible way so we can go back to London as soon as possible.

We are waiting for some good news,

Yours sincerely,
Chaja Kurz   [signatures]
Helena Fischer
Helen Adler
Klara Kalman
Ester Fleischman.

They did not know who to blame for the endless delays and probably did not understand the reasons. Mrs Eppel was exasperated. Her covering letter to Rabbi Schonfeld reiterates her concern for these girls.

Over the page is a p.s. with a typical problem: "I understand that you said Chaja Kurz has to be 18 years of age to get a permit to work in England. She has a birth certificate dated 9 August 1930 that makes her 19 years old this year."

Rabbi Schonfeld has added in ink: "Has Chaja's Irish Identity Card been made out for 1930? I hope not as it will cause difficulty and delay. If it is not, 1931 should be given. If it is already in hand the employer will have to write to the Ministry of Labour".

By July 5th, those British visas came through and Ester Fleischman and Klara Kalman left for London on July 12th.

Mrs Eppel's financial problems continued to the end.

Transfer

Those rumours that had spread through the Dublin community eventually came to the surface. Rabbi Schonfeld was indeed negotiating the transfer of responsibility for the last remaining children to the CBF. Those always adverse to the venture spread more tales of mismanagement and even a suggestion that the quiescent Immigration Committee would take over responsibility. These whispers badly damaged the morale of the capable and loyal Ladies' Committee. Local contributors began to lose interest and withhold their payments. Mr Pels reported that over the past year some £2,520 had been collected. The Ladies' bazaar in March had added £440. But by

CLONYN CASTLE CHILDREN'S HOSTEL

Under the auspices of the Chief Rabbi's (Religious Emergency) Council.

Organising Secretary :
Mrs. OLGA EPPEL,
7, Garville Road,   'Phone: 93584.
Rathgar, Dublin.

London Office :
86, Amhurst Park, N.16
STAMFORD HILL 1971/1846

CLONYN CASTLE.
X ~~NUCXPROWN.~~
~~CO. WEST. MEATH. EIRE.~~

6th April, 1949.

Mr. H. Pels,
London, N.16.

Dear Mr. Pels,

You will be pleased to hear that I have been successful in obtaining free Matzo, Meal and Wine for the children at Dun Laoghaire, and we have also been promised a quantity of eggs and fruit.

At a committee meeting of our executive, it was decided to audit a balance sheet, and they thought it advisable to do so in order to satisfy the usual doubting type of people amongst our Community.

As you know from my cash account, I bulk the money I receive from you together with what I receive from the committee, and pay out accordingly. Suppose we struck a balance sheet showing the amount of money received from you in the past, and from the committee, and then showed the itemised expenditure, would you have any objection to that? The Balance Sheet, when completed, would merely be a summary over almost a year of the cash accounts that I send you every week.

Yours sincerely,

Olga Eppel

April 6th. About a gift of kosher food supplies for Passover and an audit of her accounts.

149

CLONYN CASTLE CHILDREN'S HOSTEL

Under the auspices of the Chief Rabbi's (Religious Emergency) Council.

Organising Secretary:
Mrs. OLGA EPPEL.
7, Garville Road.
Rathgar, Dublin.

'PHONE: 93684.

London Office:
86, Amhurst Park. N.16
STAMFORD HILL 1971/1646

XXXXXXXXXXXXXX
XXXXXXXXXX
XXXXWESTXMEATHXXDREXX

10th June, 1949.

Mr. H. Pels,
London, N.16.

Dear Mr. Pels,

I wonder if you will agree to this suggestion of mine, in fact, I hope you will agree, as you will make things much easier for me over the summer months anyway.

As you know, we are continually being pressed for outstanding debts, and I must say the tradespeople here have been very generous and understanding, nevertheless, a time comes even with the good name of "Eppel" prevailing, when the pressing for monies becomes very hard.

During the summer months I anticipate a great falling off in the activities of the committee. In fact, I might say that it is now two weeks since I received any money from them, and this is due to the fact that practically the entire Jewish Community move out of Dublin to the Seasides for the Summer Season, and there are no card games or anything.

With the £75. you send me each week, the following are cash payments:-

Wages.	£28.	15. 0.
(Rations) Eggs & Butter	7.	5. 0.
Milk.	5.	0. 0.
Pocket money)		
and Petty cash at)		
Clonyn House)	£ 10.	0. 0.

Total. £51. 0. 0.

Then there are always extra expenses of another £5-£10 say, which leaves me very little money to discharge a debt, and I would suggest that for the summer months you send me £100. per week, and I shall make every endeavour to pay off £40. per week off our debts.

You see, we do not buy half as much as we used to, and the outstanding debts are big from previous buyings, so if I could reduce those accounts by £40. per week, what we incur would be far less than usual, and the accounts would then gradually come down.

Please do your utmost to co-operate with me, as you know I do my best not to ask you for money, but I have been playing a "staving-off" game for so long now that I feel it cannot go on much longer.

I know you understand and realise that if it is at all in my power to tell you to reduce the weekly allowance, I would hurriedly do so.

With kind regards.

Yours sincerely,

Olga Effel

June 10th. A suggestion for settling the rest of the debts. (Two pages)

Gas Co.,	Current a/c.	22.	14.	0.
American Window Clg. Co.,			15.	0.
Bacon Shops Ltd.,	" "	94.	4.	4.
Bailey Bros.	Repairs. new house.	192.	1.	3.
Clein's Bakery.	Current A/c.	48.	11.	0.
Dr. Cox.	March. 1949. *Delvin*	15.	10.	0.
Crowley. Dentist.	" " "	4.	4.	0.
Coleman. Chemist.	Oct.'48.	1.	5.	3.
Westmeath County Council. May '48-Mar '49.		23.	11.	9.
Dairy Engineering Co.,	April. '49.	22.	12.	5.
Elo Press.	" "	5.	0.	0.
Doherty's Coal Co.,	Current A/c.	101.	18.	10.
Drogheda Coal Co.	" "	136.	5.	0.
Dublin Laundry Ltd.,	" "	5.	9.	2.
Dunne. Delvin.	Mar. '49.	9.	17.	11.
Davis. Grocers.	Current A/c.	7.	19.	0.
Rubensteins.	" "	233.	14.	10.
Ryland. Mullingar.		4.	10.	6.
Smiley & Co.,	" "	14.	3.	9.
Scullions.	" "	132.	13.	11.
Star Market.	" "	192.	13.	11.
Skin & Cancer Hospital.	X-Ray. Oct. '48.	2.	2.	0.
Smyth. Trim.	Current. Closed at Mar. '49.	131.	2.	6.
Thrift Motor Co.,	Current.	39.	2.	8.
Terenure Laundry.	"	150.	12.	8.
Telephone. Delvin.	Closed. Mar. '49.	14.	18.	10.
Vigzol. Lubricant.		1.	13.	9.
Upholstery & Textiles.	June. '48.	7.	10.	0.
Dept. of Pathology.		2.	2.	0.
Vigoders.	Wallpaper. New house.	1.	17.	9.
Wertzberger.	Current A/c.	19.	10.	0.
Wallace Bros.	" "	12.	17.	0.
Walshe. Anne St.	Repairs.	2.	10.	6.
J. M. & O'Brien.	Current A/C. (Bread).	17.	3.	9.
Harry Jacobs.	Exam. engine. Oct. '48.	6.	17.	6.

Kearney. Transport. Current A/C.	16.	9.	0.
Kerrigan. Wireless. "	2.	18.	6.
Philip Lewis. Equipment Pesach. '49.	16.	16.	0.
S. Lapedus. Spectacles. Children. *(written)*	12.	12.	6.
Metropolitan Laundry. Current A/c.	12.	18.	10.
(crossed out) Garage "	12.	16.	6.
McManus. Chemist. "	5.	16.	1.
T & C. Martin. Stoves. Dec. '48.	36.	4.	4.
Motors Mullingar. Petrol. House petrol.	9.	6..	4.
McMullens. " Gas.	15.	7.	1.
Neville. Blinds etc.,	7.	16.	3.
O'Brien. Milk. May. '49.	6.	3.	0.
Purvey Dairy. Dec. '48.	22.	19.	6.
Pigott. Hire of Wireless.	6.	2.	6.
E.S.B.		17.	1.
Ettwein. Repairs.	3.	0.	0.
Eckford.	1.	19.	4.
Fitzsimons. Drapers. Mar. '49.	4.	11.	3.
Fay Bros. Cycle repairs.	1.	4.	0.
Freedman. Grocers. Jan. '49.	4.	5.	10.
H.C. Robinson. Current A/C.	6.	11.	6.
Glicks. " "	6.	11.	9.
Grafton Academy. Teaching girls' cutting etc.,	11.	3.	9.
G.N.Railway.	1.	1.	5.
Grosvenor Garage. Current A/c.	8.	2.	9.
Grantham Fish Stores. "	18.	8.	8.
Hely's. Stationery.	3.	6.	3.
Hendricks. "	3.	14.	4.

£1482. 19. 1

The list of outstanding debts that so shocked Mr Pels. (Two pages)

21st June 1949

Mrs. Olga Eppel
Dublin.

Dear Mrs. Eppel,
                  I acknowledge the receipt of your letter of the
15th inst and shall reply later to the various questions raised,
but first I have to tell you that your statement of outstanding
bills has given me a shock so terrible, I never have experienced
anything similar in all my life.

On the 9th of May, when you were here, you gave me the following
figures:
          unpaid bills approx. £ 1200
          Bank overdraft   1400

then we send you £300 to reduce the amount of the unpaid bills
and accordingly we reported on the 9th May to the CBF that unpaid
bills are 2900 approx. 900£ and bankoverdraft £1400.

Now your detailed statement says(if you deduct the £192 for ho
repair, unpaid bills are 1890 and overdarft £1652 therefore
within
      6 weeks your debts INCREASED by £ 1250   '

I am at a loss to understand and certainly I cannot even TRY to
explain that to the CBF.
I only hope, y o u w i l l b e   a b l e to tell me and
explain, how it is possible, as we sent you regularly the agree
weekly £75 and you got s o m e money(even if reduced scale)
from your committee.
It will be necessary for you to let me have a separate letter,
giving c l e a r and undisputable explanation(with a copy fo
our file) so that I can submit your Original letter to the CBF.
I wont be able to sleep, until I know what is going on, you kno
I dont like to be called with very bad names by the CBF people.
So I wait to have your reply BY RETURN of Mail.

   HOUSE: thanks for the copy of letter from your Solicitor.
          Let us hope that the Stamduty question will be settled
          with 5%.

   Claim Newman: thanks for the way you intend to settle this,le
          us hope the best.
The other content of your letter is noted.

Enclosed is our cheque for £100 for this week.

June 21st. Here is Mr Pels' reaction.

154

CLONYN CASTLE CHILDREN'S HOSTEL

Under the auspices of the Chief Rabbi's (Religious Emergency) Council.

Organising Secretary:
Mrs. OLGA EPPEL   PHONE: 97684.
7, Garville Road,
Rathgar, Dublin.

London Office:
86, Amhurst Park, N 16
STAMFORD HILL 1971/1646

CLONYN CASTLE,
DELVIN,
CO. WEST MEATH, EIRE.

Mr. A. Fels,
London, N.16.

Dear Mr. Fels,

I sent you on Chaya Kurz's birth certificate some weeks
ago by registered mail, showing her birth date, as shown on her
Identity Card.   I do hope you have this birth certificate, as that
will enable you to change the date at your end, and she would not
have to wait until August.

I also wrote you in connection with the Identity Cards
you sent me of the children studying in England, but you failed to
send me on Eva Haupt's.   I hope you have that safe, and I trust
you will let me know whether we ought to get them extended now, or
wait until later.

In case you did not understand my telegram, it was
this:-   I had a 'phone call from the representative in Ireland of
the British Ministry of Labour.   This gentleman is rather anxious
to help us in every way, and I found him very co-operative.   He
told me that there appears to be some misapprehension at your end that
labour permits are not required, even for children under 18 years,
and he asked me to send you a telegram saying that labour permits
are required in every case for children under and over 18 years old.
I myself do not quite understand his concern about this, and thought
you would know more about it.   However, I am very well in with
this representative, and if at any time you are finding difficulty
at your end getting labour permits, perhaps I could do something
with this Mr. Toms in Dublin.

Yours sincerely,

Olga Eppel

P.T.O.

P.T.O.

*Undated but soon after the move to Vesey Place. A glimpse at the
complexity faced in arranging every child's future.*

<u>P.S.</u>

       I had occasion to speak to the Headmaster of the School at which our children attend. He is non-Jewish, and congratulated me on the children, and stated they were the best dressed, ~~most~~ *best-*behaved children in the school, and very clean.

       I am very gratified about this, as you know how people here have talked that the children were ill-clad, starved and God knows what.

Olga Uffel

P.S. A welcome compliment from the children's new headmaster.

15th June 1949

Mrs.Olga Eppel
Dublin.

Dear Mrs. Eppel,

Dr.Schonfeld contemplates to apply
to the Home Office for permission to bring over to UK
for enrolment in Schools here the following children:

Vera Fischer
Eva Rubinstein
Gaspar and Robert Binet
David Rosenfeld
and the 2 Grossmann girls.

We would like to have your comment and what the news
are from parents who are on their way to Israel or about
to emigrate to Israel or USA, as we would prefer those
who have the least chance to emigrate and join their
parents in the near future,.

I would suggest not to let the children concerned know
as we want to avoid unrest amongst them or amongst others.
Actually have you got passports for a l l children?

What is the actually state of affairs regarding
the 4 candidates for Student visas to USA?

Enclosed is this weeks cheque for £100

We are waiting to have the figures for the House and the
accounts.

Yours sincerely

Secretary

June 15th. Future of the last group of children.

CLONYN CASTLE CHILDREN'S HOSTEL

(under the auspices of the Chief (Rabbi's Religious Emergency) Council.)

Organising Secretary:
MRS. OLGA EPPEL. PHONE 92-581.
3, Garville Road,
Rathgar, Dublin.

London Office:
86 Amhurst Park, N.16
STAMFORD HILL 1971/1846

XXONYNXXCASTLEXX
XXXDUBLINXX
XXXWESTXMEATHXEIRE

23rd June, 1949.

Rabbi Dr. S. Schonfeld,
London, N.16.

Dear Dr. Schonfeld,

I am enclosing herewith a letter I received this
morning from four of the girls at Clonyn House. Then there is
Leah Rubin who I am endeavouring to get to Canada, and I have
written to the Overseas Settlement in London about her and her
brother, but have had no reply from them. Perhaps you would
contact them about the Rubins. Helena Deutel and Blanka
Federweiss are candidates for America, and as I wrote you, there
is no doubt they will travel in the Fall.

It is quite true that the girls are very, very
unhappy, and when I called the other afternoon, all of them were
in tears, and as they say, they do not know whether London is to
blame, or me. I wish I had some information to give these girls,
as it is terrible for them to sit day after day doing nothing,
just waiting for "permits". They get various letters from friends
saying the permits are coming, and none come. Even if they do
come, is there any chance of them getting visas? We must bear
in mind that Klara Kalman and Esther Fleishmann got permits to work
in London last November, but no visas were forthcoming. I have now
applied for a visa for Helena Fischer, and I am wondering will the
same thing happen there as in the other cases.

Something must be done about these girls immediately, as I cannot get them jobs in Dublin,(and I doubt if they
want jobs here), owing to the fact that there are no firms that
close on the Sabbath, and the non-Jewish workers object to Jewish
workers getting the Sabbath off.

Will you, for Heaven's sake, send me a letter giving me information about the chances of these girls getting to
London quickly. It is impossible for me to face them day after
day with the never ending question of "what will be with me", and
it is heartbreaking not to have the answer for them.

Please let me hear from you by return, so that
I can give them some consolatory reply.
With kind regards.

Yours sincerely,

P.T.O

158   *June 23rd. Mrs Eppel's exasperation at further delays and concern for
the frustrated girls. The letter "enclosed herewith" is on page 159.*

file

Camp Jouve 1st VI.

Cl.

Hochgeehrter Rabbi Schönfeld 'Lor

Ihren l. Brief haben wir erhalten, für welchen wir Ihnen sehr dankbahr sind. Entschuldigen Sie uns das wir Ihnen wieder stören mit diese paar Zeilen, aber wir warten schon sehr ungeduldig auf dem Bericht das die Schriften welche gehören zum unseren zurückkehr sind schon erledigt. Aber wir hoffen das es wird schon wircklich nicht mehr lange dauern; denn es ist schon eben genug mehr wie einen Jahr so Zielles verbringen. Wir möchten schon gerne unser Ziel erreichen. Es ist vileicht von uns ein undankbarheit das wir Ihnen so schreiben, denn Sie haben wircklich geschätt das wir sich hier gut haben sollen, aber Sie mussen uns verstehen das junge Mädchens wie wir können nicht so arbeitslos und ohne Ziel leben.

Deshalb bitten wir Sie alle sehr, das Sie sollen haben alles mögliches in unseren angelegenheit und hoffentlich wir es auch mit erfolg sein.

Wir danken Ihnen vorhinein für Ihre groze bemühung, und erwartend wie am schnelsten gute Nachrichte verbleibe Ihre dankbahre

Wir wünschen Ihnen und für die g. Familie lustige Feiertage

Chaja Kurz
Helene Fischer
Helen Walter
Kalman Klara
Eszter Fleischman

Five of the older girls express their concern.

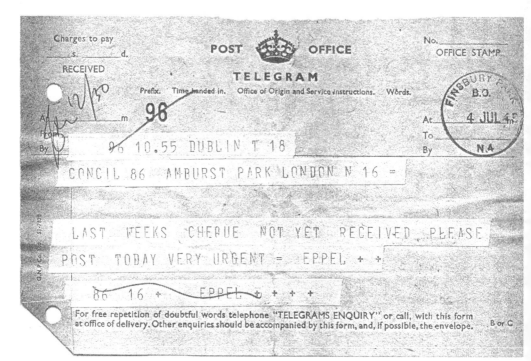

July 4th. Telegram typical of several from an exasperated Mrs Eppel.

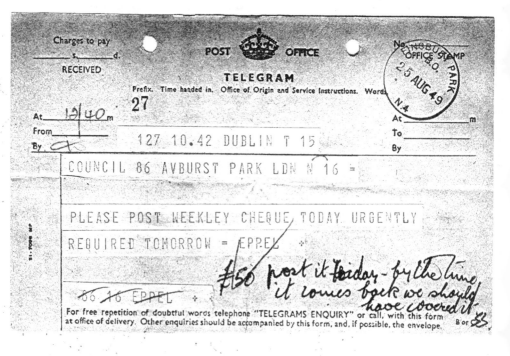

August 25th. Notice the Rabbi's comment.

May 1949 the average monthly donations had dropped by a half. On the 25th Mrs Eppel wrote to the Rabbi saying that something must be done to restore the community's confidence in her and in the CRREC. He replied that this was a rather difficult time "…. but you and your Committee still have a holy duty to see this task through".

The Archive for the final weeks seems incomplete.

One letter dated 25th July 1949 demonstrates Mrs Eppel's concern for Helena Deutel, aged 16, a Hungarian survivor of Auschwitz still awaiting a visa to Canada. Mrs Eppel asks Rabbi Schonfeld to allow her to visit her father in Antwerp for two weeks "as she may never see him again and this trip would boost her morale." Mrs Eppel and her sister offered to pay all her expenses and the Belgian Consul had promised to give her a visa "…Please buy her a ticket and ask Séndi Templer to meet her in London and see her on her way".

In a rare personal disclosure Mrs Eppel admits her own fatigue. On July 25th she wrote to Rabbi Schonfeld:

"My niece's wedding will be in Manchester in late August. Both parents are dead and we are very close so I want to be there. I am feeling a bit tired. I have not had a rest or a holiday since the children arrived. I would like a month off and return in early September. So I hope you will not disappoint me. The audit won't be attended to until after the Dublin Horse Show when there is virtually a national holiday; August is a dead month in Ireland".

Mrs Eppel expresses for the first time concern about her own future. She will have no choice but to resign if, when the CBF takes over, Prof Abrahamson is brought in to work with them. She asks Mr Pels if he can assist her to find work in the future of a similar sort. She goes on to discuss the audit mentioned before and the latest news on the remaining children. There were "… only twelve to worry about." And these she suggest should move to England.

The reply from Mr Pels is firm. Yes, she should attend the family wedding but to take a holiday during August would put in jeopardy arrangements for the last children's departure. And he tells her about a vacancy for a matron at the Hasmonean School.

27th July, 1949.

Mr. H. Pels,
London, N.16.

Dear Mr. Pels,

Thank you for your telephone call this afternoon, and there a one or two points I would like to discuss with you and please get Dr. Schonfelds immediate views.

The first thing is my selfishness in wanting to get away on the 10th August. It is very important that I get away on that date in time for my niece's wedding on the 14th. You see, my niece lost her mother, who was my sister, and her father, and believe me, it will not be a Simcha unless she has her Aunt Olga with her, and I have promised her faithfully that I will be at her only daughter's wedding. Then, as I wrote you, I want to go to my second home in Newcastle. My sister in Newcastle has given up a holiday in Italy in order to have me over there. I had to make these plans for August because I must be back here at the end of August as sometime in September I have to get 5 children away to America. Therefore, I cannot postpone my holiday to September on account of these 5 children; and then Rosh Hashonna sets in on the 25th which means I will not get a holiday at all, and believe me I very much need one.

Please consult with Dr. Schonfeld and perhaps he could come xt Monday and could return then before I leave on the 10th. Surely that could be arranged? Otherwise, I am afraid I am going to be more th disappointed.

I have your letter in regard to the audit. I have already spoken to the auditor here about a complete audit which I would prefer for the C.B.F. when they take over, but in Ireland August is a dead month. The first week we have the Horse Show which is virtually a National holiday for a whole week. In view of that most people go away and everything is a stand still. The auditor told me this moning that in no circumstances could he attempt the audit before Sept. 1st and would have it cimpleted by Oct. 1st. Therefore, I again want my holiday before Sept 1st so that I will be on hand all the time for the children to go to America, and for the auditor to answer all queries that my arise and see he gets all books, documents etc.,

Regarding the C.B.F. taking over. As I wrote you on several occasions, I doubt very much if I could function under Professo

July 27th. A holiday?

Abrahamson's committee, because I know in my own heart and soul that I will have endless trouble from the children, as they will look to me to keep them to their way of thinking, and I know perfectly well that Prof. Abrahamson will prevent me in every way helping the children towards their Spiritual goal. Furthermore, I doubt if there will be any tolerance at all for refugees from that quarter. These are, of course, my own personal views, but I think they are shared with me, by my committee. Therefore, I suggest that if the C.B.F. will allow my committee to function as hitherto, that I would remain on with the children until I can get them all away, and Chaya Steinmetz married, which should not take longer than a few months. The following children are earmarked for emigration, on these dates.

3 Steiners.	Aug. 10.	
6 children to London.	" "	
5 " U.S.A.	Sept.	approx.
4 boys working.		
Chaya Steinmetz.	Dec. '49.	marriage.
Chaya Kurz & Helena Adler.	London.	Sept.

That only leaves 12 children to worry for, and I feel that you could take these over to England. Therefore, it will only be a few months before all the children leave, and I beg of you to do all in your power that these children will not be disturbed in any way until they all leave here.

Regarding Chaya Steinmetz, I have given her and her young man my solemn promise that I will give them a nice wedding and trousseau and furniture to start their young lives in marriage, and I know they looke to me to carry this thing through. Believe me, the old cttee here will not tolerate the kind of wedding that these orthodox children demand.

Please treat this matter as urgent, and give me a few days warning before Dr. Schonfeld and the C.B.F. gentlemen arrive. Although I have everything up to date, I would like a couple of days to call in everything for their scrutiny.

What is going to happen about the house att Dun Laoghaire and will they take over this house for any length of time, or will they close down when the children go? As you know, the house is on my name, and even though I could sell it, I would like to know exactly how I stand.

Yours sincerely,

Olga Effel

July 27th, continued "… and when the last child leaves shall the house be sold?"

It is probable she attended the wedding but there is no further word of her taking any holiday. It appears that she worked from March 1948 until September or October 1949 without a break.

There follows a series of letters asking for clarification about the CBF take-over. Again concern was expressed over a suggestion that Professor Abramson's committee might get involved and if that happened the Dublin Ladies would resign. They must have been reassured. For Mrs Eppel next writes that the Ladies vow to continue their work till all the children have dispersed. "They are determined to keep their promise to **Chaja Steinmetz** and her fiancé - that they would provide her with a trousseau and furniture and a nice wedding as a start off - though it will not be till later in the year."

In July 1949, following many months of negotiation behind the scenes a contract was agreed. Mrs Eppel asks when to expect a visit from the Rabbi and the CBF representatives to finalise the matter. She reminds him it is essential that all debts be settled. And what about the house at Dun Laoghaire? Will the CBF take it over or is it to be closed? Should she sell it - as she could do as it is in her name? We are left guessing.

The Chief Rabbi of the United Synagogue – by then Dr Israel Brodie - confirmed future arrangements.

The final agreement was signed by Mr M. Stephany of the CBF and Rabbi Schonfeld on September 4th 1949. It confirmed that the maintenance and support of those remaining dependent children and young people was to be transferred to the CBF together with the transfer of covenants from individual contributors. It also provided for the cancelling of £4,000 debts that had accumulated in Ireland.

More letters exemplify Mrs Eppel's sincere concern for the last of her charges. "The six youngest children are to be sent to London; they can travel in a special carriage from Holyhead and be met at the other end. The three Steiner boys are to go on *aliyah* via London in early August." Later letters tell of an escort for them "... who understands our children". They left on 9th August 1949. Telegrams were exchanged. One advises the train left two hours late, and another that "all arrived safely". Soon afterwards the younger girls were found foster homes or hostel places in London and attended the Avigdor High School where they acquired fluent English and a sound education. The boys were placed in *yeshivot*. Some in London, others further afield.

OFFICE OF THE CHIEF RABBI

TELEPHONE:
MANSION HOUSE 0292/3

4, CREECHURCH PLACE, ALDGATE

LONDON, E.C.3 3rd Aug.1949,5709

My dear Dr. Schonfeld,

Following our conversation of this morning,
I agree that the Covenants at present held by the Chief
Rabbi's Religious Emergency Council for purposes other than
those connected with refugee children and pensioners, should
be transferred to the Jewish Secondary Schools Movement, instead
of being taken over by the Central British Fund as was originally
suggested. I have spoken to Dayan Grunfeld who concurs with
the proposal. I xx have also communicated with Mr. Stephany
of the Central British Fund, and I have no doubt that this will
also be acceptable to the Central British Fund. I now feel
that immediate steps can be taken by the C.B.F. to finalise
matters.

I expect that during the course of the next few
days, an announcement will be made in the press and a letter sent
to the subscribers intimating that the responsibility for
refugee children and pensioners has been assumed by the C.B.F.

With all good wishes,

I am,

Yours sincerely,

Chief Rabbi

Rabbi Dr.S.Schonfeld,

August 3rd. The Chief Rabbi, Dr Israel Brodie, approves the CBF take-over.

165

· CLONYN CASTLE CHILDREN'S · HOSTEL

Under the auspices of the Chief Rabbi's (Religious Emergency) Council.

Organising Secretary :
Mrs. OLGA EPPEL.
7, Garville Road,
Rathgar, Dublin.

London Office :
86, Amhurst Park. N.16
STAMFORD HILL 1971/1648

CLONYN CASTLE,
Nr. DELVIN,
Co. WEST MEATH, EIRE

3rd August, 1949.

Dear Mr. Fels,

I am sorry you had to send me a telegram yesterday about getting the children away and about having them accompanied. Actually, I could have re-assured you on that point, as, naturally, I am anxious for them to go and would not have allowed them to travel alone. Hitherto, I used to send Zahn so far as Holyhead, but as I have no-one at Vesey Place with a suitable travel permit to accompany them, I have made two contacts and will pick the best of the two to give the childre absolute safety from here to London. You can leave that to me to see that all will be well.

The traffic is simply enormous here and sailing tickets most difficult, but I have all in hand and don't anticipate any hold up. The children will leave on Tuesday morning next the 9th instant from Dunleary pier to Holyhead and will change from the boat at Holyhead to the awaiting train for Euston. The boat leaves Dunleary at 9.30 a.m., but I cannot find out the exact time of arrival of the train at Euston as on account of the traffic the times are changing, but please make enquiries at your end and please have them met at Euston. I will instruct whoever travels with them to hand them over to you or your representative. They will, of course, be accompanied by a Yiddishe person.

The following are the children travelling and remarks as to the state of their papers:—

Helena Deutel:— Has ticket to leave Harwich on Wednesday 10th August. Will require room for one night in London. Belgian visa not yet granted as the Belgian consul has to make enquiries as to whether she really has a father in Antwerp. He assured me that I will get her visa on Friday next in time t travel on Tuesday.

? Steins?, Awaiting Certificates of Identity from Youth Aliyah; also British visas. Was informed by Youth Aliyah that British visa were authorised by the British Home Office on the 25th July. U.K. Office here not

August 3rd. Concern over children's travel arrangements. Page 1

2 Binets!)   All visas in order and no hitch at all.
2 Grossmans))
1 Rosenfeld.)
1 Fischer.)

        I had a lot of trouble getting the children ready to go as there
are thousands of people over here and not a sailing ticket to be had.
However, all is set now and I even managed to get a permit for myself to go
on board with them and to get them through the customs without searching.
No-one is allowed on the boat at all these days, nor even on the pier.
I have engaged seats for them on the train from Holyhead to Euston. They
will all sit together.   I could not get a coach, as that train has
only got dining compartments. However, I have explained to the British
Railways' people here that the children will not be dining, but will have
their own food and will only need Russian tea and lemonade.

        I am sure the kiddies will be alright and in any case I have
an Irish Yidd to travel with them, so please do not worry about them. I am
confident now that I have all tied up for their safety, please God.

        Please give me 24 hours notice of when Dr. Schonfeld intends to
come here. I am well in with Aer Lingas and have no doubt I will manage a
seat for him from Northolt.

        I have cancelled my own holiday, but may have to go to London
for one day on the 18th August as I have an interview there for a public job.
I will try and put it off until after Sept. the 1st, but in case I cannot I
will go by the last plane on Aug. 17th and return by the first plane on Aug.
19th.

        I have been thinking about the change over. What a pity we
could not have dispersed the remainder of the children before the change over
But, of course, the debts have to be paid. I am very worried about Chaya
Steinmetz' wedding. I only hope the C.B.F. will make as wide an appeal
we would have done here and give her the same send off as to a trousseau and
money for furniture. We anticipated raising £400 for furniture for her as
Alec Richmond informed me that he could not get married without furniture
and a trousseau.   I gave him my promise I would endeavour to reach that
traget.   I hope there won't be a hitch there. He is a nice boy, but is
anxious to have a start off. He has asked me to choose a ring for £50 and
his family are helping him to put down a deposit to buy a house. The wedding
is to be in December,

        Please let me know who will meet the children at Euston so
that I could tell the accompanying traveller who to hand them over to. In
all probability I will send them with a Mr. Cyril Winters. He understands
our children and can converse with them and is very very kind, and understan
their "frum Keit".

                              Yours sincerely,

Please also write me safe arrival of chil dren.

August 3rd. Concern over children's travel arrangements. Page 2

There is no further information in the files about the winding up of the Irish scheme. So the Irish episode ended. The one hundred young people greatly strengthened, one can surmise, both in body and soul were enabled to move on to wherever they or their family had decided to settle. This was achieved by those dedicated personalities, Mrs Eppel and her ladies, Rabbi and Mrs Israel Cohen, and Mr Pels all of them sustained by the unrelenting determination of Rabbi Schonfeld. There was one final commitment. In December, true to their promise the Ladies organised the trousseau and wedding of **Chaya Steinmetz**.

How the children remember Clonyn Castle

Alfred Leicht was at 18, one of the oldest boys:

Moving to Ireland was a seminal point in our lives, moving from a closed to a free society, a liberating experience. And yet our inbred insecurities, the language barriers and having little control over our destinies inculcated a sense of paranoia about our future.

One of the youngest, **Emanuel Weinberger**, wrote:

The memories of Clonyn Castle are among the happiest of my childhood, with large green fields, visits to and from local Jewish families, sports competitions and "colour wars" which carried excitement and prizes (even for children who did not exactly win the races), plenty of attention from the older ones, especially the adolescent girls - in short: idyllic.

Ella Schwarzthal added:

Many years later I saw at my father's home the first letter Rozsi and I wrote to him in Czechoslovakia, from the Castle. It began: "Dear Father, We love you! The sun is shining and we are playing." It made me shiver to realise that it seemed so important to us, then nine years old, to state that the sun was shining, as though it had never shined before.

And for Ella the sun really had not shined before.

A treasured memento of Clonyn Castle from 1948; many of the Hide-and-Seek Children retained a copy of this photo.

Sonja Kummeldorfer was there with her brother Ervin when she was aged 8 and he was 10 years old. This is what she wrote in 2007:

I think of that year in Clonyn Castle as a unique episode: the Castle, with its large wooden gate and wicket, labyrinths and hidden corners, surrounded by huge lawns and wild roses. It seemed as if taken from a fairy tale - at least in the eyes of the very young girl I was. It had a lasting impact on my imagination. And of course there were those unforgettable rides at dawn with the horse and trap to fetch the milk. I remember impatiently awaiting my turn to join them again. There was also that exciting team game we played in the woods – Hide-and-Seek – in which they put numbers on our foreheads and we had to be very tricky and inventive to avoid being discovered by the opposing team. Our staff were devoted and caring and the atmosphere was cheerful although personally I missed my mother and my family very much. This was later the primary reason my brother and I decided to go to Israel instead of continuing our education in England. We were both very young and very homesick. We had family in Israel and knew that our mother would join us there a few months later. Looking back I am very happy with how things turned out because we both consider ourselves lucky and privileged to have been able to live and raise our families in an independent, sovereign Jewish state. Clonyn Castle was a singular experience. It was a pleasing interlude between the horrors of war and the traumatic loss of our father, and the difficulties we were to face in our first years in Israel.

Dezider Rosenfeld, then 10 years old said:
It was like paradise. I appreciated a bit of mothering by Blanka and Séndi. During the night we would make raids on each other, smearing our faces with black shoe polish, squirting toothpaste on the girls' hair while they slept.

Olga Grossman, also aged 10 at the time, wrote:
There at Clonyn Castle we learned to play games – Hide-and-Seek, for example. In the beginning we associated hiding with fear and running away meant for us escaping; but with the loving care of our leaders we learned to play— and to enjoy playing.

Some among the older children could not join in Hide-and-Seek. It was too reminiscent of their experiences with the Hlinka

Sonja and Ervin Kummeldorfer aged 8 and 10 at the Castle in 1948 (SK)

Gyorgy Prissegi with Lily Lowinger and another girl (JW)

Guards, the Arrow-Cross (the Hungarian equivalent of the Hlinka) and the Nazis.

Chaja Steinmetz said:
I could not play that game.

Judit Weisner was at least 16. She said:
It was like a beautiful big family with freedom and kindness and love after the horror that everybody had suffered.

Different messages come from some of older boys and girls. In her diary **Anna Katscher** wrote:
We had to live in a castle and I loved it. It was like a dream holiday—not a school.

But in a later diary entry she had different thoughts:
We left Prague six months ago. Just one word and I would not be here today.I could be going to school and should have stayed with my parents.

Eva Haupt says:
Life at Clonyn Castle was an unnatural one for a 15 year old. We had been promised we would go to school in Britain. I was desperate to study. But it was a long wait before we were granted British Visas.

Alfred Kahan was one of the older boys at the Dublin Hostel. At the age of 17 he managed - with much enterprise and to Mrs Eppel's horror - to briefly visit England, France and Switzerland. He wanted to talk to other survivors and find the right place, the best country, in which to start a new life. "… and I discussed our situation with many other refugees …"

All the Slovakian young people dispersed to begin new lives. Few kept in touch with each other until Anna Katscher, by then a grandmother living in London, suggested a Reunion after fifty years to pay homage to Rabbi Schonfeld and to meet each other again.

Chapter Five

The Reunion – Fifty Years On

Headed notepaper of the Jubilee Reunion Committee

It was **Anna Katscher** who suggested there be a Reunion of the Slovakian children to commemorate 50 years since they had arrived in Britain. It was her suggestion, too, that participants contribute their memoirs. It is so sad that she did not live to see the result. She died in 2006.

The Jubilee Reunion Committee was set up in 1996 by **Israel Reich, Tamáš Reif, Dezider Rosenfeld** and chaired by Jonathan Schonfeld, I was co-opted and **Eva Haupt** joined us later. Very few had stayed in touch so the initial task was to locate the rest of the 148 named on the Group Visa. By early 1998 addresses had been found for nearly half the original group. Then plans were devised and invitations circulated for a weekend packed with activities. Forty-nine people signed up frequently with their partners and sometimes with their children - the Second Generation.

We assembled in Golders Green, in North-West London where coaches awaited us. It was curious to watch people gather, look around at each other and then need to introduce themselves. The first destination was Silver Street Cemetery at Cheshunt, in Hertfordshire. There *Kadish* was recited at the grave of Rabbi Schonfeld. Rabbi Israel Cohen, who had come specially with his wife Trudi from Jerusalem, paid homage to him.

At the grave of Rabbi Schonfeld. Behind, Gertruda Muller with Eva Schwarz. In front Barbara Barnett, Judy - wife of Tamáš Reif - and Trudi, wife of Rabbi Israel Cohen. (TR)

The coaches drove on to Bournemouth, a pleasant and popular seaside resort on the south coast. During the journey conversation grew in intensity, reminiscences poured forth and continued to do so throughout the week-end. *Shabat* was celebrated in traditional style at the Normandy Hotel where we all stayed. At the close of each of the three Sabbath meals different speakers shared their thoughts, adding to the nostalgic atmosphere that characterised the whole event. Rabbi Brazil, the hotel owner, led the Sabbath morning service. Afterwards there was time to wander by the sea. People gathered in little groups and the women congregated around **Blanka Federweiss**, drawn to her as they had been fifty years before. Some were still chatting at midnight. It was a memorable Sabbath.

I put together a small exhibition in the billiard room. There were relevant documents and photos, maps and news cuttings. These provoked more memories. Trudi Cohen showed her photograph album from Clonyn Castle. A booklet was distributed of a dozen memoirs I had collected.

We returned to London next day for the presentation of a new *Sepher Torah* by **Anna Katscher** and Manfred Nussbaum, her husband. It was dedicated to Rabbi Schonfeld at the Adath Yisroel Synagogue. A large congregation attended the traditional consecration ceremony. They walked through the streets to the Old People's Home, in Schonfeld Square, carrying it under a wedding canopy, as though a bride.

That same evening a grand dinner was given at the community hall of Hendon United Synagogue.

One hundred and sixty people gathered from far and wide, filling the hall to capacity. Many owed their lives to Rabbi Schonfeld including the Chairman, Aba Dunner, as his father, an eminent Rabbi, was among those he brought to Britain before the war. He also brought our host, Isaac Tajtelbaum, after the war as a young boy. Aba Dunner spoke of the passion of the man, and of his call from "the Burning Bush" that inspired him to save as many Jewish souls as possible from the Nazi inferno and later from the Communists. He wondered when he ever slept since it was quite usual for him to have an appointment at 2 a.m. He commented, too, on the Rabbi's unusual and sometimes questionable strategies. Some saw these as irregular if not illegal. But his primary purpose was to save lives and for that

Rabbi Israel Cohen and Barbara Barnett at the Reunion. (JS)

כל המקיים נפש אחת מישראל כאילו קיים עולם מלא

Rabbi Dr. Solomon Schonfeld's Childrens Transport
Jubilee Reunion Committee
takes pleasure in inviting

Mrs. Barbara Barnett
_____

to a Celebration Dinner
on Sunday 26th April 1998 א׳ דראש חודש אייר תשנ״ח
at 7.30 p.m.
at the Hendon Synagogue, Raleigh Close, London NW4
Hosted by Mr & Mrs I. Tajtelbaum
Chairman: Mr Aba Dunner

£25 per person
RSVP before 9th April

Invitation to the Reunion Dinner April 26th 1998. (TR)

177

he considered any tactics were acceptable. He was our "Moshe Rabbenu".

Rabbi Israel Cohen said that the Dinner marked the climax of the Reunion. He mentioned that in the *Gemara* it is said that all offerings will be abolished but that thanksgiving was always needed, at the right time and at the right place. "It is appropriate today to remember the power of the man who saved us", he said. And on behalf of the 148 children in the 1948 transport, he presented to Jonathan Schonfeld a silver *Kiddush* cup on a tray.

Jonathan responded with warm thanks to the Jubilee Reunion Committee. He described its members as hard-working, always cheerful and very caring. Many present had known or worked with his father and with Judith Grunfeld. "We are only now learning what our father achieved", he said. He had had no use for committees or bureaucracy and in his many ventures he never took "no" for an answer. He had no wish for credit and turned away any thanks saying "they don't owe me anything".

Trudy Caplan, a daughter of Yankel Levy, was given a framed photo of the Castle in tribute to her father. The Jubilee Committee announced that a Memorial Fund was to be set up in the Rabbi's name for scholarships to be awarded to students in his schools. Everyone was presented with "A New-Old Rendering of the Psalms" [1] and a copy of the Brochure I produced commemorating the occasion. Most of the contents have been included in this book.

Next morning I joined a dozen of the group to fly to Dublin and make a sentimental visit to Clonyn Castle.

Anna Katscher had phoned the present owners to tell them about the Reunion and they had graciously agreed to this visit. They knew that the Castle had sheltered child survivors. Our hostess and her daughter welcomed their unusual guests and gave them the freedom to roam at will through their home. Excitement mounted as the group entered the Castle and were ushered into the great hall.

Soon the visitors were climbing the marble staircase and exploring in all directions. There were cries of pleasure as rooms were recognised and episodes recalled. There was the gracious room with fine views across gardens and rolling hills that had been used as a synagogue; and the fireplace that had held the scrolls of the law.

Solomon's children

It was April 1948 and 148 Jewish children and youngsters, survivors of the horrors of the Holocaust, left Bratislava and Prague by train and then by ferry for England. They were led by the legendary Rabbi Dr Solomon Schonfeld, the very last group he brought to freedom in the West before the Iron Curtain descended over Eastern Europe.

On reaching London they were able to celebrate Pesach, the festival of freedom, before moving on either to Clonwyn Castle or Dublin.

In the intervening half century the group's members have scattered across the globe, lost touch with one another and have never yet met together again. A number of the children have now formed a 'Rabbi Dr Solomon Schonfeld's Children's Transport Jubilee Reunion Committee' and are aiming to come together once more, to share memories and to exchange news. They also wish to recall Rabbi Schonfeld and pay due respect to his memory.

The reunion is planned to take place between 23rd and 26th April this year in London, with Shabbat spent in Bournemouth, and every single one of the children is being sought and invited to attend. To learn more, contact Issy Reich, 4 The Approach, London NW4 2HV. Tel: 0181 202 9784 Fax: 0181 203 8694. Please let him know if you wish to participate or if you know of someone who was among those 148 bewildered and lonely children given renewed hope and a new life.

□ *RDC*

From the Bulletin of the Association of Jewish Refugees, March 1998.

No 1429   Thursday 30th April 1998   4th Iyar 5758   45p

Mr M Nussbaum (left) and Mr C M Feldman carry Sifrei Torah at a ceremony on Sunday in North London's Schonfeld Square which was part of a special reunion weekend.

"Schonfeld children" hold reunion

By Elisha Horowitz

THE presentation of a Sefer Torah to the Schonfeld Square home and complex in North London on Sunday was one of the highlights of a moving reunion last weekend. The people being reunited, some for the first time in 50 years, had all been members of the last group of children personally saved from Nazi clutches by Rabbi Dr Solomon Schonfeld ztl in 1948. The occasion not only brought these survivors together again but also paid some long overdue tribute to this giant of *hatzoloh* activity in our generation.

The Sefer was presented by Family Mordechai Menachem (Manny) Nussbaum of North West London whose wife Anna had been one of the rescued group and had thought of the reunion idea. The final letters of the Sefer were completed at the Adass Yisroel Synagogue in Queen Elizabeth's Walk whereupon it was carried under a *chupah* to Schonfeld Square in bright sunshine – truly a blessing considering the unsettled period of weather London is presently experiencing. Tehillim were recited by Rabbi Yosef Dunner, Ravad of the Union who succeeded Rabbi Schonfeld as Rov of the Adass Yisroel; Mr I M Cymerman; Rabbi Yisroel Cohen, now living in Yerusholayim, who had been a *madrich* to Rabbi Schonfeld's children at their temporary haven in Clonyn Castle, Ireland when they reached these shores; and Mr Nussbaum.

The Consecration of a new Sepher Torah during Schonfeld Children's Reunion

Rabbi Dunner, in a voice ⸀eaking with emotion, spoke briefly of the event's significance, recalling Rabbi Schonfeld's ⸀nbelievableS heroism in one of ⸀lal Yisroel's darkest hours and ⸀ow his courageous activities ⸀elped to enable our people to ⸀rvive. Now 50 years later it is ⸀so appropriate that a Sefer Torah, symbolic of the Jewish people's continuing existence, is being pre⸀ented to this beautiful place dedi⸀ated to the memory of this great ⸀nan, declared Rabbi Dunner.

At the *seudah* honouring the Sefer, held at Hendon Synagogue, North West London the host, Mr Yitzchok Dovid Tajtelbaum – another survivor of the group – introduced the evening. He expressed his personal gratitude to Rabbi Schonfeld, pointing out that he lived exactly 72 years – he passed away on his birthday, 4th Adar – which is the *gematria* of *chessed*. Moshe Rabbeinu got his message to save Klal Yisroel from the burning bush; where exactly Rabbi Schonfeld got his similar message to act as he did is not clear but he sacrificed his many talents in order to save the precious *neshomos* of our people. A father could not have done more, declared Mr Tajtelbaum, who went on to relate several daring exploits carried out by Rabbi Schonfeld some of which showed amazing facets of his character.

Rabbi Yisroel Cohen spoke of the event as the climax of the reunion, quoting the words of Hallel... *moh oshiv*, how can I repay... thanks and praise are due forever. Rabbi Schonfeld, he said, was concerned with a higher ideal than simply saving life – he was rescuing the very *neshomoh* of Klal Yisroel. His efforts obligate every one of his children to safeguard the spiritual future of our people. All *korbonos* will in time be discontinued but the *korban todah* will remain, for thanksgiving is an eternal concept.

Mr Jonathan Schonfeld, son of Rabbi Schonfeld responded to a presentation made to him by Rabbi Cohen. He paid tribute to the hardworking committee members who had made the reunion possible – Mr I Reich, Mr H Rosenfield. the Nussbaum

Family, Mrs Barbara Barnett, Mr T Reif and others. He wished Dr Judith Grunfeld, a close associate of his father in those eventful years, a *refuoh sheleimoh*. He presented Mrs J Caplan of Gateshead, whose father Mr Jacob Levy zl owned Clonyn Castle and gave it over to Rabbi Schonfeld's use, a framed certificate/picture of the castle.

Mr Aba Dunner, in the chair, recalled that Rabbi Schonfeld had saved his father – and thereby himself. I was privileged to work for Rabbi Schonfeld and share many adventures with him, he

Rabbi Schonfeld

said, some of which he related. He welcomed Mrs Blanka Direnfeld of the USA who had been a "mother" in Clonyn Castle and had come to attend the reunion.

Mr Nussbaum spoke of growing up in Stamford Hill as a teenager under Rabbi Schonfeld's auspices. He also paid tribute to the committee and read out a moving letter from the Nitra Rov, Rabbi Shlomo Ungar of Mount Kisco, New York who described Rabbi Schonfeld as "an angel of salvation".

Shabbos in Bournemouth had been a wonderful experience for the reunion's participants. They had separate rooms of their own at the Normandie Hotel and were inspiringly addressed by Rabbi Cohen, Rabbi Mordechai Fisher, Rabbi Mordechai Miller of Gateshead and Mr J Schonfeld. The group went on to visit Clonyn Castle on Monday which is now a golf club.

From The Jewish Tribune, April 30ᵗʰ 1988.

*April 28th 1998. Istvan Stahler arrives at Dublin airport
followed by Chaja Steinmetz and her husband. (JS)*

Anna Katscher's husband Manfred Nussbaum points the way. (JS)

Friends reunited on the steps.
Left to Right: Eva Schwarz, Anna Katscher, Agi Weisner, Chaja
Steinmetz, Judit Weisner, Istvan Stahler. Behind Josef Ickovitc in cap,
Ervin Schwarz. Front: Franklina Wiesen, another, Vera Wiesen. (JS)

There was delight in finding the serving hatch again, the "dumb waiter". On the top floor, where the boys had slept, still evident were the impressions of *mezuzot* on doorposts.

The girls revisited their bedrooms in the towers, remembering the comfort of the fireplaces in winter and how difficult it had been to arrange furniture within the curved walls. And on the old bell board in the basement someone noticed one was still marked: "Headmaster's Study".

It was an extraordinary experience for the visitors to see through adult eyes the haven they had enjoyed in very different circumstances so long ago. The visit was an emotional pilgrimage and an appropriate closure to a very special Reunion.

Reactions

A fax reached me later from Isaac Pinkesz. He and his brother came to the Reunion from the United States with their mother and aunt, **Franklina** and **Vera Wiesen**, who had lived at Clonyn Castle.

> *"Dear Barbara,*
> *It was truly a remarkable experience to have attended at Shabbos at the Normandy Hotel. I felt it was incredible to see 55 to 65 year old people re-living this part of their childhood, to seeing the look of joy on their faces when they discovered themselves in the pictures and the smile on their faces when someone would recount a game they used to play. I think it was incredibly therapeutic for them to be able to recount and relive a part of their childhood that was joyous and allowed them to be children. As they were telling their tales you could see on their faces the little girls and boys in the pictures coming to life. I was amazed by the re-strengthening of memories when one person would be remembering a story and the others would feel the familiarity of wisps of memory that were pushed to the back of their minds and were fading but would come back stronger than ever.*
> *Then came the chilling words of Rabbi Aba Dunner when he was saying that after 120 years we will meet Rabbi Schonfeld and he will ask us "what have you done with the life I saved?" These words still ring in my ears.*

Dining Room used as the synagogue. (JS)

186   *Agi Wiesner, with her husband pointing to the mark left by a mezuzah. (JS)*

(Left) Doorpost on the top landing where the boys slept, showing where there had been another mezuzah. (JS)

(Below) Another clue to the past: Bell Board in the servants' basement, installed by the Manchester builders, still marked "Headmaster" (JS)

Jonathan Schonfeld shows the present owner the architect's plans of the building. Chaja Steinmetz's husband looks on. (JS)

It was amazing to hear the squeaks of joy upon the first sighting of Clonyn Castle. I feel so fortunate to have witnessed the flood of memories and stories that came pouring out as they walked through the Castle - from children climbing into the dumb waiter and being pulled up and down from the kitchen, to the trees swaying, to the sounds of the singing during prayers in the shul or on a cold night dragging their mattresses down the grand staircase to sleep next to the fireplace - or not sleeping too close to the window because they were afraid of the moon. The kinship among them, the ability to empathize with each other, the feeling of being one big family again was truly inspirational all the more so when considering that they have not kept in touch for fifty years.

The organizers are owed a tremendous debt of gratitude for all their hard work. On behalf of my entire family I would like to thank everyone involved. All the best – Isaac"

And this from **Blanka Federweiss**, the oldest of the girls:

I am so glad I came to the Reunion. It has been wonderful to see these children again.

Some surprises

Two years later "the Two Alfreds", **Kahan** and **Leicht,** made their own pilgrimage to the Castle. There they learned from local journalists of the Reunion they had missed and were put in touch with the group again. They had both stayed at the Dublin Hostel and then emigrated to the States. There they built up distinguished careers and remained firm friends.

In the following year **Alfred Leicht** and his wife came on a visit to London and **Israel Reich** invited them to meet some of the group. "The Two Alfreds" sent me their stories and were keen to urge others in North America to do so, too, but they had little success. So I called a halt to collecting more contributions and concentrated on preparing an introduction to those I already had.

There came a further surprise. An email arrived from California in 2002 and the sender introduced himself as the former **Gyorgy Prissegi.** This was the name given him by his

Reunion with the past–and what might have been

Two men who were taken into Ireland as refugees after the second World War have come back more than 50 years later to thank the Irish for giving them a second chance in life. **Roddy O'Sullivan** talked to them in Dublin yesterday

MURRAY LYNN was sent to Auschwitz with his family in 1944 when he was 13 years old. His three brothers and his parents were gassed in the Nazi concentration camp.

Murray survived and returned to Hungary on a freight train after being liberated in 1945. He spent almost a month in hospital, recovering from his time in the camp and moved to the Czech Republic shortly afterwards. From there he was evacuated to London and soon afterwards to Ireland.

There he met Alfred Kahan, who had fled from the Communist regime in Romania. The two boys formed a lifelong friendship, and this month they returned to Ireland more than 50 years later.

Murray and Alfred were evacuated by a Jewish organisation in the UK. "They wanted to take us to a neutral country that would be a springboard for us, for our dreams and aspirations wherever we wanted to go from there," Murray said in his hotel room in Dublin yesterday. "We came first to London but England could not absorb us. The Irish Government was good enough to give us temporary status as refugees."

Murray Lynn — then Alfred Murray Leicht — knew nothing at the time of the reluctance of the Government to let him into the State. A representative of the Jewish organisation, Religious Emergency Council, had contacted the Department of Justice in 1946, two years before the children arrived, asking the Department of Justice to admit 100 orphans who survived the concentration camps.

With the help of money from the UK, a Jewish organising group here had bought Clonyn Castle and 100 acres of land in Delvin, Co Westmeath. They promised the Government that if it wished, they would "undertake to make arrangements for [the children's] emigration after a specified period".

Nevertheless, the Department of Justice refused to let the holocaust survivors into the State in August 1946 on the instruction of the Minister at the time, Mr Gerald Boland. A Department of Justice memorandum noted that the Minister feared "any substantial increase in our Jewish population might give rise to an anti-Semitic problem".

Two months later, the then Taoiseach, Éamon de Valera, ordered that the children be let in on condition that there was a guarantee from a responsible organisation that their stay would be for a short period only. Then — a month before the children came to Ireland in May 1948 — a local person attempted to set fire to Clonyn Castle.

The Department of Justice noted that while "numbers of the local people do not like the proposal to house Jewish children in the castle", as far as the Garda was aware there was not "any local organised agitation against the admission of the children". The organising secretary of the project concluded

it must be "the work of some silly ass in the village".

Alfred Kahan learned of the Irish resistance to his arrival only earlier this year, when he read Dermot Keogh's *Jews in Twentieth Century Ireland*. He said the book was "an eye-opener" for him, but he doesn't feel any less grateful to the Irish.

"We have very happy memories of Ireland. It was different from the turmoil of Eastern Europe. It was a very beautiful country that was in peace. We were able to relax without fear of either Nazism or Communism. It was a turning point in our lives."

Alfred stayed in Ireland for 15 months, first living in Clonyn Castle with 100 other children from Eastern Europe, then moving to a house in Dún Laoghaire. He recalls getting up before dawn to watch the sun rising over Dun Laoghaire harbour, because he had never lived near the sea before. Fifty-one years later, he still drives for more than an hour from his home in Massachusetts to perform the same ritual at Cape Cod.

Alfred left Ireland for the United States, where he put himself through school in the evenings, eventually graduating from Harvard University with a postgraduate degree in physics. He went to work in the US Airforce's research laboratories.

He has not visited Ireland since he left in August 1949, but has always wanted to come back to as an act of remembrance. "I wanted to thank the Irish for providing us with a haven that helped us in the transition from a fearful past to a promising future."

He also wanted to explore what might have been. "If we had been allowed to stay here, I think we would have stayed. But the conditions obviously weren't very good at the time. Maybe Ireland lost out. There was a lot of initiative among the refugees. It could have been a very positive development for the country, both economically and educationally."

While he has read about the current controversy over immigration here in the newspapers, he is reluctant to comment on asylum policy here. Murray Lynn, who went on from his troubled childhood to become chief executive of a company in Atlanta, Georgia, has no such reticence.

"The policy should be more liberal. What has made the United States a great country is a relatively open door policy for immigrants from the world over. The US became a great nation because we have tapped into the resources of a lot of other countries' skills. The immigrants helped make America what it is. Ireland ought to prise the doors open a little bit and encourage skilled people in particular to come to this country," he said.

"But we didn't come here to campaign. We came here for a reunion. It's a sort of closure for us. As we get older, we get more and more sentimental about our time here. Ireland was our turning point and this visit has been our rendezvous with a fading past."
roddyosullivan@ireland.com

The Two Alfreds; a lifelong friendship. May 6th 2000 © The Irish Times

190

Alfred Kahn (left) and Murray Lynn, back in Ireland on a visit: "If we had been allowed to stay here, I think we would have stayed . . Maybe Ireland lost out.'
Photograph: Brenda Fitzsimmons

Slovak foster family. He was one of the youngest boys at Clonyn Castle who went on *aliyah* in January 1949. The impression given from sparse notes in the Archive was that his mother had survived but deserted him. I imagined he had been adopted. He now explained he had been reunited with his mother on arrival in Israel although Mrs Eppel had thought this unlikely to occur.

His mother who had last seen him as an infant in 1942 slowly and patiently built up a close relationship with him. She never spoke about their early history and he felt the subject too sensitive to probe. On a recent visit to Israel with his own sons she showed them some old photos. On the back of one was written "Clonyn Castle". He traced the Castle on the web and through local journalists he was put in touch with "The Two Alfreds". Through them he contacted me. His remarkable story is now added to the collection.

A further task was to obtain images of people and places and documents to illustrate my text and the contributors' memoirs. Jonathan Schonfeld has provided some splendid pictures from his extensive collection. Among them were several group pictures of the Hide-and-Seek Children but without any names. So I circulated copies by email asking people if they could put names to faces. That exercise was very successful and led to a final surprise!

Erich Bock forwarded the photo of the football team to **Richard Reich** who with his brother Oskar appear in the photo. The Reich brothers had not known about the Reunion or this book although Richard had made his own pilgrimage to the Castle as recently as 2008. He was able to identify almost everyone in the photo! An amazing achievement! Now the Reich brothers' story is added to the rest.

Some observations

It was astonishing to discover the resilience of these young survivors and how successfully they had re-invented themselves. It was evident that they were now fully at ease with the language and idiosyncrasies of their adopted country, whether the United States or Britain or Israel. Where had they found the strength and the skills to accomplish this metamorphosis? That they were not yet adults when their lives fell apart was to their advantage. It seems they had recovered enough to capture that natural urge of the healthy young, to look ahead and think positively, something far more difficult for survivors of a mature age to achieve.

It took exceptional determination and perseverance to adapt to a totally unfamiliar environment.[2] Yet they had been determined to establish themselves by their own efforts, to become financially independent as soon as possible and establish new families. They persisted against all odds in a competitive society impoverished by the war, a war the Allies had been near to losing. It was won at a heavy cost and the peace introduced a further period when life was tough for everyone. There was widespread austerity in Britain. Both there and in the United States survivors competed with returning servicemen and war workers in a massive search for jobs. Few were fortunate enough to enjoy the parental stimulation and encouragement that is expected in a normal family situation. The CBF in London and kindred organisations elsewhere gave what help they could but community resources were in heavy demand.

In Israel survivors found themselves in another war. It was a desperate fight to establish the new state which had so little infrastructure and that was over-stretched. Newly-arrived survivors often felt shunned by fellow Jews. When asked where they were during the war their replies were frequently turned away or greeted with disbelief. Similarly comments heard, but rarely written, tell how they met a coolness and a distancing from some Jewish families long settled in London,[3] and this also occurred in the States. Boris Cyrulnik has written about similar experiences in France.[4] There was even some suggestion among Israelis that European Jews had been cowards. They showed ignorance of Nazi tactics used to persecute and control their victims and lure them to disaster; how the study of human psychology was turned on its head and used to control and torture people. It was a lonely and painful experience and presented many of them with further profound tests of endurance.

Such barriers and the complexities faced by immigrants have been well expressed by some brilliant and discerning writers. George Mikes gives a vivid picture of his experience as a refugee in England in "How to be an Alien" and as a newcomer in Israel in "Milk and Honey" [5] and Kirschen's cartoons depict behaviour typical in Israel.[6] Amos Oz, on a more sombre note, recalls cruel reactions of children to Holocaust survivors, children born like him in Israel where they grew up with little knowledge and less understanding of the horrors experienced by these newcomers.[7] Only a few years ago I was shocked to hear a *Sabra* tell a Holocaust survivor "We had a hard time here, too". **Chaja Steinmetz** recounts how her British landlady reacted similarly. In New York new immigrants often faced animosity and a lack of sympathy but found much kindness in other quarters.

In the atmosphere of the Reunion participants shared with each other their success in building a new life. There was a further realisation: it became apparent that almost all those present still observe strictly traditional Orthodox Jewish practice; and so do their children. This is interesting because, while it was Rabbi Schonfeld's hope and intention, it is not typical of Holocaust survivors. Martin Gilbert referring to "The Boys" mentions that they are very strong in their involvement with living Judaism and show a firm commitment to Israel,but the terrible experiences in their earlier years have not strengthened their religious belief or the practice of the majority.[8]

The Slovakian children were brought up in families where traditional observance was deeply embedded; even those who had joined the Neolog movement were not far removed from an Orthodox past. They had imbibed from their parents a way of life taught by example, a heritage passed on from generation to generation. The principles of Jewish faith instructed their behaviour and attitudes and these deeply-rooted values stayed firm. But the Fascist onslaught had denied them freedom to practice during the war years and for long after liberation conditions did not allow a return to an Orthodox life style. Many of these youngsters had all but lost the memory and the rituals of their childhood.

It would appear that this firm commitment is at least partly due to the personal influence of Rabbi Schonfeld - and for the Clonyn Castle children the impact of Rabbi and Mrs Israel Cohen has endured. The intensely traditional Jewish life style they created at the Castle was readily absorbed by these needy children and intensified by the "mothering" and the example set by **Séndi Templer** and **Blanka Federweiss**. The opportunity provided space to begin to look back on the sudden and traumatic experiences that they had all endured to absorb the past in order to start to look towards the future. As their awareness and well-being grew so did an urgency in their demands. A newly-found resilience urged them forward. They were deprived of previously secure parental care and had missed extensive periods of education. Jews have been dubbed "The People of the Book" and the evidence was clear, specially among the older children. The urge to study and to learn was very strong indeed. These young people were determined to catch up with life. As they recovered strength they were impatient to move on. It is impressive that even when the Hide-and-Seek Children became immersed in study and occupational courses and then with the demands of a family life and earning a living, religious practice and studies were granted a high priority and continue to do so.

That is not to say their lives are trouble-free. None of them can be rid of the demonic experiences of the past. The smallest trigger is enough to revive them.

For years I never sat opposite one of the windows in my living room. Why? Because outside it was an old-fashioned lamp post that reminded me of those at Auschwitz. My son-in-law recently learned of this and asked the municipality to replace it with a modern one. And they have done so. Sights or circumstances can abruptly jolt me back to that ghastly past. Queues and vegetable peelings still bother me and I readily faint.

Olga Grossman

Fifty-five years later I freeze every time I hear hooting and whistling trains.

Alfred Leicht

Hetty Weiner-Fisch was afraid to go outdoors for at least six months after hostilities ceased. The impact of those grim times can never really disappear. For many nightmares persist.

I used to have very bad dreams till I was about 14. Since I turned fifty they have returned.

Gaspar Binet

Recording and Commemorating

There has been a massive transition in attitudes towards Holocaust survivors. When they first emerged so many, like **Olga Grossman,** were met with an absence of understanding. It has taken a long time before they have been shown the respect and recognition due for their extraordinary fortitude and valued for the testimony which only they can give about the darkest chapter in World War Two history.

Yad Vashem was established in 1953 as a memorial and repository for information on the Nazi Holocaust and collects personal testimonies.

But it was only in 1987 that Manfred Klafter established Amcha[9] in Israel. It is a support group specifically designed to serve survivors reaching retirement. It has centres in the main cities that offer wide-ranging social facilities and therapeutic services. These are well used today and much appreciated.

In 1989 Bertha Leverton organised the first reunion of the *Kindertransport* children. The occasion marked the 50th Anniversary of their arrival in Britain. One thousand *kinder* turned up. Bertha was amazed by the reaction. Up till then little had been known about them.[10] Bertha's sister followed that initiative in Israel where many of the *kinder* had settled.[11] There followed two films.[12] The bronze sculpture at Liverpool Street Station only appeared in 2006, a reminder of the British government's role in rescuing Jewish children from Nazi Europe.

In 1985 the French film director, Claude Lanzmann, made "Shoah", a remarkable investigation of previously unrecorded details about the impact of the Concentration Camps.[13] In England James and Stephen Smith and their family, who are devout Christians, were shocked to realise that there was no national memorial to the Nazi Holocaust in Britain. So In 1991 they established Beth Shalom in Nottinghamshire, in place of their Meditation Centre. It is a unique organisation to commemorate and inform on the Holocaust and pay homage to survivors. Their brave venture began very modestly but soon attracted wide backing among survivors and from the wider public. In 2000 they established the Aegis Trust. This works towards the prevention of crimes against humanity worldwide through research, policy development, education and raising awareness of genocide and mass atrocity.

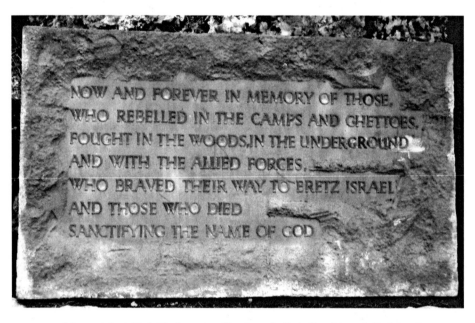

Memorial at Yad Vashem to all who rebelled, fought and died in the Holocaust. (HB).

In 1993 an international surge of interest followed Steven Spielberg's film "Schindler's List". From this emerged the Shoah Foundation that encouraged survivors worldwide to record their testimonies. In approximately six years, from 1994 to 2000, the Shoah Foundation gathered nearly 52,000 videotaped contributions from 56 countries and in 32 languages. In 2000 the Imperial War Museum in London, opened a permanent Holocaust Exhibition and also archived audio memoirs. In 2003 a documentary was produced on Hidden Children.

There have been some memorable national and international conferences and other relevant events. A national Holocaust Memorial Day has taken place in Israel since 1959 but it is only since 2001 that it became an annual event in Britain falling on 27th January. In 2005 it was adopted worldwide to commemorate all genocides. Also in July 2000 Elizabeth Maxwell chaired the Third International Conference in Oxford and London entitled "Remembering for the Future, the Holocaust in an Age of Genocide". It drew survivors and scholars from all over the world and for the first time "The Second and Third Generation" of survivors' children took part. They have founded their own international organisation to give mutual support and to carry on from their parents the responsibility for passing on the Torch of Remembrance and to teach and disseminate knowledge about the Holocaust. A stream of TV documentaries and studies on war and the Holocaust continues to flow. So do personal memoirs. "The Hide-and-Seek Children" is now among them.

Many people, like **Edit Katz,** recognise problems in recording personal accounts of past events. She suggests that people are apt to say what they think will be acceptable rather than what is accurate and also that children's perceptions will be different from those of adults. She also says that some think it inauspicious to mention the names of the dead – a reason others of the group gave me for not sharing their stories and that I found quoted, too, in wider sources.

Survivors' children have had differing experiences. Some have absorbed their parents' trauma and suffer, too, while others were never told directly about their parents' suffering for fear of the impact it may have. **Bertha Fischer** and her husband avoided the subject in their family. So did **Alfred Leicht.** Helen Epstein, an American journalist, only discovered that her parents were survivors when already an adult. She was curious to know how others had reacted. So she travelled across the United States interviewing survivors and recording their widely different ways of dealing with their past.[14]

Post Script

This book, I hope, fulfils **Olga Grossman's** ardent wish - shared by her former companions - that the saga of Rabbi Schonfeld's transport from Slovakia be recorded, and with it the personal stories from the Hide-and-Seek Children themselves as a monument to his endeavours.

Their memoirs illustrate how these young people emerged from a shattered childhood to build a new existence. More than sixty years on they continue to show that indomitable inner strength, and in their daily lives fulfill Rabbi Schonfeld's long-term aspirations and have brought them to fruition. They have displayed that promise, carried on their inheritance and passed on the tenets of Judaism to their children and grandchildren. Through these actions the Hide-and-Seek Children have demonstrated they have won and that the Final Solution failed. We are privileged to share their bitter-sweet memories and respect their inspiring achievements.

Part Two

Recollections

The personal impact of past experience varies widely. For some vivid memories persist, whether traumatic or triumphant, while for others these may be suppressed. Recollections are always selective and therefore unpredictable.

Contributions from the Staff

Here in their own words are reports by those responsible for the Irish venture. Rabbi Israel Cohen wrote specially for the Reunion.

The second article was written by the Irish Administrator, Mrs Olga Eppel, midway through the scheme and provides a lively picture of the situation at that time. Both convey in their own inimitable style their deep involvement but with no hint of the obstacles they faced.

I have added a note from conversations with Séndi Templer, the much-loved *metepelet*. She had herself endured horrendous wartime experiences and her parents had not survived. Yet she dedicated herself to give unstintingly to younger survivors. These three together created the ambience of care and security at Clonyn Castle that made it a haven for The Hide-and-Seek Children.

Rabbi and Mrs Israel Cohen

Memories of Clonyn Castle

"You are going to Ireland tomorrow." This was Rabbi Schonfeld's voice - a short, abrupt phone call. "But I'm teaching." I was teaching the Polish children at the Avigdor School. "No questions, no arguments. Pick up your tickets at the office" - which we did the same afternoon.

Miss Ruth Lunzer, Rabbi Schonfeld's ever loyal secretary, told us this was a result of our both having had experience with refugee children, my wife Trudi in Shefford and both of us in Windermere, a rehabilitation centre established by the Central British Fund. Anyway we went, or rather flew, to Dublin. We had a year old baby girl and number two was on the way. Mrs Eppel met us with her ancient car. It was a pretty awful drive to Clonyn Castle, Delvin. She told us Delvin was a small village about 40 miles from Dublin. The village boasted a massive cathedral, and the vicar had been urging the villagers not to accept our children, describing them as blood-thirsty and disease-ridden, etc. But the local inhabitants proved stubborn, fortunately for us as it turned out.

Mrs Eppel was a tartar - a tough nut with a golden heart. She organised the Dublin Jewish Community and raised funds for "her refugee children". She could be very demanding, and didn't always agree with our way of life, yet she always provided us with what we needed: bedding and particularly books, games, toys and writing materials.

The Castle itself wasn't all that old; there were more ancient ruins in the grounds. It had been empty for some time till bought by the late Mr Yankel Levy, a wine merchant from Manchester. It had no electricity so Mr Levy had imported an electric generator with a massive dynamo wheel fully two meters in diameter. I was told it came off a battleship from Northern Ireland. When we attempted to turn it on the whole Castle literally vibrated and it became imperative to make alternative arrangements; fortunately these were completed within 24 hours.

A big advantage that came with the Castle was Oliver. He'd been caretaker for many years, and would do anything for the

"Rabbi and his children". He was a mine of information on local people, many of whom, except for the priest, visited us at one time or another. Loyal Oliver provided for us a horse and trap. I learned to manage it but we rarely had time to use it. Another good friend was a local publican, Mr Fitzsimmons, and his daughter Norma, who arranged delivery of *kosher* milk, supplied eggs and gave much practical advice.

The Castle had four floors: the basement contained the huge kitchens, storage rooms and cellars. The dining room, classrooms, recreation room-cum-*shul* were on the ground floor. When the weather was good most activities including classes we held outdoors. On the first floor were the girls' dormitories and staff quarters, while the boys, mostly under *barmitzvah* age, and *madrichim*, occupied the second floor. All the older boys had a home in Dublin.

There were prayers three times daily and lessons mostly in the morning, given by the late Mr Bleier, a very gentle and popular rabbi, Ervin Schwarz, and myself. The little girls were cared for by the older girls under **Séndi Templer** (now Rebbitzen Pels in Jerusalem) and **Blanka Federweiss** (now in the USA). There were also two competent and popular English *madrichot* from London: Judith Sternbuch (now in Jerusalem) and Bertha Goodman (also in Jerusalem today). The atmosphere was tremendously uplifting especially on *Shabbos* and *Yom Tov*. It rained a lot but the children loved exploring in the grounds and the village. They made many friends there. There were several soccer matches with the local team. Somehow our boys moved faster. The locals wanted us to compete in their hurling matches - a kind of very rough hockey - but we politely refused. It was really wild and we were afraid our boys would get hurt.

Occasionally there were outings to the nearby lakes or "lochs" and once we were invited as guests of the Dublin community over *Shabbos*. In those days all Jewish-owned businesses were closed on *Shabbos* and there were four synagogues. Friday night we prayed in Adelaide Road and one of the youngest boys, Chaim Schnebalg, enthralled the congregation with *Divrei Toire* in Yiddish. I remember some of the families as being especially welcoming, such as the Yodanken, Green, Clyne and Steinberg families and Alony the *Dayan*. Others will remember more. Some of the girls became unofficial nannies in charge of Mrs Bleier's little boy and our Chanali. That left Mrs Bleier free to supervise the kitchen, ably assisted by Gellu (the late Klara Kalman) and my wife, to see to the ordering and general welfare of the Castle as well as acting as nurse. I am sure a lot went on of which I was not aware but overall affairs ran smoothly.

Sometimes Benjamin Pels (lately Rabbi of Lucerne and now retired in Jerusalem together with Séndi his wife) joined us and proved a tower of strength. When we left in late September '48 we took with us the first group that settled in Israel. Mr Moishe Lozor Zahn took over until all the children had left. Many will have their own memories and their own stories to tell. We were privileged to participate in a great humanitarian *mitzva*, the *zechut* of which rightly belongs to Rabbi Solomon Schonfeld.

Rabbi Schonfeld's letter of recommendation of Rabbi Israel Cohen:

> *TO WHOM IT MAY CONCERN*
> *Mr Israel Cohen has been - from May to December 1948 - Administrator and Headmaster of the Refugee Children's Hostel at "Clonyn Castle" Delvin, Westmeath, Eire. This hostel consisted of over eighty children, boys and girls, ages from 5-19. During these eight months, under very trying circumstances, Mr Cohen gained the full confidence and affection of the children and the sincere respect of his colleagues. By his personal dignity and charm he succeeded in commanding the implicit obedience and respect of the non-Jewish staff and in creating a good name for the Jewish hostel among the local inhabitants and traders. Conscientiously, Mr Cohen devoted his efforts to the comfort and welfare of the children, taking part in their work and play as well as in the daily routine. On the educational side he organised a system of schooling in Jewish and secular subjects, and played an important part himself in the teaching and lecturing. All in the castle enjoyed his rendering of religious services. His weekly moral talks did a great deal to foster a true spirit of Jewish home life and companionship in all spheres of life at the Castle.*
>
> *Signed by Solomon Schonfeld Ph.D., Executive Director.*

"What Will Be With Me?" by Olga Eppel

Olga Eppel, the Irish Administrator, wrote the following article for Nachlath Dublin, the bi-monthly magazine of the Jewish Community, in 1949.

A year has passed since Mr Robert Briscoe informed me that 100 Jewish Refugee Children were expected from the Concentration Camps of Europe and were to be housed at Clonyn Castle, Delvin, County Westmeath. He asked me if I would organise a home for the children and take care of their welfare. I agreed, and subsequently visited Rabbi Dr Schonfeld at the offices of the Chief Rabbi's Religious Emergency Council, London, in February, 1948. On my return to Dublin I drove down to see the future home of these children and was very impressed with the very beautiful building and with the alterations and modernising which were in progress by the owner. The children were expected in April. Equipment was to be sent from England but many kind people in Dublin gave me furniture, bedding, etc., to help equip this vast place for 100 children and staff.

About the end of April I received a phone call from London: the children would arrive on the 6th May. Up till then my activities were lone ones except for the good counsel of Rabbi Alony and Mr Briscoe. I made representation to the Dublin Jewish Ladies' Society to help me receive the children from the boat. I shall never forget the 6th May, 1948, that fine sunny morning when I drove down to the Liverpool boat accompanied by Rabbi Alony and Rabbi Lewis. When the boat berthed I was informed that every facility would be given to let the children off at once. Three buses awaited them on the dockside and there they all stood on the deck, accompanied by Rabbi Dr Schonfeld who had braved the Iron Curtain to rescue them. The older ones were clasping the hands of the younger ones, very tired after their long journey from London. Those little people stood and looked out on the dockside of Dublin. The question in their eyes was "what will be with me?"

Rabbi Lewis immediately got the children into the buses and to Greenville Hall where the kind Dublin Jewish Ladies' Society awaited them with a hot breakfast. There was not a dry eye amongst those ladies when the flotsam and jetsam of Nazidom entered the Hall. The buses took the children on to their new home at Clonyn Castle, arriving there for midday lunch. I arrived later with Dr Schonfeld. My heart filled with great joy, and tears of gladness came into my eyes when I turned into the drive and heard happy shrieks of laughter and saw youngsters playing in brilliant sunshine on the lawn. The children had arrived.

Some of them spoke only Hungarian, others spoke Czechoslovakian, a few spoke German, a few Yiddish. It was impossible to converse freely but we seemed to understand each other although our vocabulary was onomatopoeic. I then realised how much these children needed in comfort, food, clothing, personal attention, teaching etc., and although the Chief Rabbi's Religious Emergency Council were financially responsible for all these things, they had not realised the cost of living in Eire was much greater than in England nor had they foreseen what extra monies would be required to meet these children's essential needs. Amongst my friends were many who were willing to help by giving in cash or kind for the welfare of these children. One good friend was Mrs Erwin Goldwater. She formed the Dublin Jewish Ladies' Voluntary Aid Committee which has been tireless in its efforts to help our children. As one lady said to me "I have worked communally for years, but work for these children gives me great satisfaction; I can see the results of my efforts."

After a few weeks tuition in English, some of the older children came to me and said: "Mrs Eppel, what will be with me?" That question has stayed in my heart and on my mind. After months of great effort these children no longer asked "what will be with me?" Two boys, Gustav Lowy and **Alfred Leicht** were sponsored by Hebrew Universities and left for America. It was a complex process. Forms had to be filled in; searches made for birth certificates; police certificates obtained from abroad, copies to be submitted; X-rays, blood tests, vaccinations - but these two boys are now in America. The two **Wiesner** girls, beautiful young ladies from the Concentration Camp of Auschwitz, had been separated from their parents for several years. I remember the day I received a letter from their mother saying "My arms are aching to embrace my children." These girls were to go on a Hungarian quota that would have taken several years but through the kindness of the American Vice-Consul in Dublin, it was possible, after months of delay, for him to issue them with a second referee quota number. The **Wiesner** girls are happy now with their parents in New York.

Then came a letter from Rabbi Schonfeld that young **Gyorgy Prissegi**, whose age we could only guess as six because he still had his baby teeth, had to be initiated into the Covenant of Abraham [i.e. to be circumcised.] He entered Portobello Nursing Home as **Gyorgy Prissegi**, the name he got from his non-Jewish foster parents in Czechoslovakia. He came out of the Nursing Home as Avrom Dov, the name I gave him, after my late Father. Alice Feldman, who got separated from her sister, now a refugee in Canada, also cried "what will be with me?" Alice has now joined her sister in Canada, and Relly Bleier accompanied her. Several boys and girls have entered Rabbi Schonfeld's schools in London, a few at the Avigdor High School and a few at the Hasmonean Grammar School. Tommy Lehner is in London learning Dental Mechanics. Gertrude Mangel is taking a secretarial course. **Séndi Templer** is looking after a refugee hostel in London, assisted by Lily Lowinger. All are from Clonyn Castle.

One little boy is Chaim Schnebalg. His mother, sisters and brothers were murdered; but his father escaped and is in Manchester. This boy, although only 8, is a little genius. He is quite capable of delivering an address from the pulpit, and because of his learning and brains, was always addressed by his Clonyn Castle sisters and brothers, as "Reb Chaim". Reb Chaim is now united with his father, Rabbi Schnebalg in Manchester.

Still more children asked "Mrs Eppel, what will be with me?" Then Mr Arieh Handler arrived at the Castle and told the children that twenty-five of them could go to Israel. He was followed by Dr Lichtenstein, the European Director of Youth Aliyah, London. Then selections were made for Israel. Preparations became intense and Rabbi and Mrs Heinemann were sent to prepare those twenty-five children for *aliyah*. An emigration committee was formed under the kind leadership of Mr Maurice Wine and Mr Maurice Baum. To facilitate the journey they chartered a plane for the first stage, from Dublin to Paris. I look back on the 24th January, 1949, that cold frosty morning with brilliant sunshine when we saw the children off. The plane was silhouetted on the field. The children clasped their little satchels of food and night attire for a night in Paris, thence on to Marseilles to board a boat to Israel. Little Judith Lowy clasped her doll, and Avrom Dov had his picture books with him. Several members of the Dublin Jewish Community and members of the Dublin Jewish Ladies' Voluntary Aid Committee came to the airport to wish the children "God Speed". Mrs Goldwater and I, with Dr Schonfeld, stood at the plane as the children entered. The Aer Lingus management, too, came on the field to wish the children goodbye, and every child received a personal blessing from Rabbi Schonfeld. Mr O'Neill of Aer Lingus management said "Aer Lingus are doing what Moses did 4,000 years ago." and there was a sudden and spontaneous burst of the *Hatikvah*. Everyone stood to attention whilst Israel's National Anthem was sung and as the plane slowly taxied down the strip, I could just imagine someone saying "Mrs Eppel, what will be with me?"

There are plans for 12 more, all teenagers, to go on *aliyah*; they hope to receive some kind of industrial training before they leave. Clonyn Castle has become too big for the 45 children who remain. We hope to bring them closer to Dublin where it would be easier to find them schools and training. Thanks to the great help of the Dublin Jewish Ladies' Voluntary Aid Committee, the ever-sung question "What will be with me?" can now be answered.

Séndi Templer

This note I put together after we met in Jerusalem in 1998 and from conversations on the phone since then. Séndi was 15 years old when she joined Rabbi Schonfeld's transport. She is still affectionately remembered by staff and children alike.

In 1942 the Germans collected men aged between 16 and 42 and took them to work in Labour Camps. They took my father. My brother was only 15 but he told my mother "Where father goes, I go. Or else I shall jump out of the window". So they went together. Neither returned.

My mother cared for my younger brother and me. She worked so hard to keep us happy. In 1943 the Jewish community was collected together for deportation but my mother managed to escape with us to Hungary. She had to pay a lot to manage that. We travelled on foot a long way with a group of non-Jews to Budapest. I was put in an orphanage and mother had a small flat till 1944 when the Germans came. They came to remove all of us from the orphanage. My mother came to say good-bye but managed to take me away with her. I do not know how she achieved that. By then it was quieter in Bratislava. She sent me on alone saying it was too dangerous to travel together and that she would follow with my brother. But my mother, although she had non-Jewish papers, insisted on still wearing a *sheitl* - and she was caught.

Fifty years later someone recognised me walking in a Jerusalem street. This lady told me that she had searched for me all these years, that she and my mother had travelled together in the same truck to Auschwitz but were separated on arrival. She gave me this incredible message: "Your mother told me I would live through the war and be witness to her children and that I was to tell them when her *Yartzeit* was to be observed. She spoke like a prophetess".

In 1946, when I was sixteen and a half, I travelled with three orphan children to Novitak. There at midnight we crossed the Polish border into Czechoslovakia. We had no money. We eventually reached Bratislava but at one point found ourselves on the wrong train, on the way to Prague! It was chaos after we were liberated but it was an idealistic time in Bratislava after the war. I was prepared to undertake any sacrifices if I could work. I did not even want to be paid. In Bratislava the children and I had to keep eight days quarantine because they had lice and suffered from other diseases, too.

I spent six months in hospital. I had TB and water on the lungs. We were then sent to the Beis Ya'acov organization where I studied at the teachers' seminary. Bigger girls lived on the second floor and orphan children on the first. It was a wonderful experience to be there. We had a roof over our heads, a few clothes at last, and excellent teachers. (Later on in Ireland I realised we had not really learned very much). Twenty young girls, including me, became *madrichim* for seventy children rescued from a monastery. They were in a terrible state and severely undernourished. Some had rickets, many had lice. I visited the sick in hospital and people who had no visitors, and organised others to do so, too. **Tamáš Reif**'s mother was among the patients. We collected funds. Often I added my pocket money. My teacher said I would be sorry I did not study more. Yet even when I was so busy, I was listening to her lessons and I did all my homework. But though I studied to be a teacher, I preferred to be helping people.

Then Rabbi Schonfeld arrived. By then I was working with child survivors in Michelovsky, a small town outside Bratislava, the only Orthodox girl among them, and was enjoying the task. Then word came I was to return at once to Bratislava and join the group leaving for England with Rabbi Schonfeld. Plans were being made as a matter of urgency as the Communists were about to take over control of the country. I did not want to go because I was enjoying what I was doing. But as a recipient of training by the Beis Ya'acov Seminary I was obliged to go where they told me over the following two years. That is how I happened to leave Slovakia and travel across the Continent to London and then to Clonyn Castle where I spent some months looking after the younger children.

Later I was *madrich* at Woodberry Down Hostel in North London. Twenty-five religious girls lived there. They were all survivors. Some had come via Sweden. Four friends **Anna Katscher, Eva Haupt, Eva Schwarz** and Gertruda Muller who had shared a tower room at Clonyn Castle, insisted on coming

Vyplňte a obratom expres zašlite !

Dotazník evid.mládeže.

Meno a priezvisko : **Templer Séndi** ....

narodený/á/ *2. . VI. . . .*1932. v č. *Vrbovom* ....

sirota,polosirota,nesireta ? *sirota cel* ....

barva očí : *sivé* .... postava /výška/: *stredná* ....

barva vlasov : *hnedé* .... nos : *riadny* ....

zvláštne znamenie : ....

absolvoval školy : *5. ľudovej 3 meštianske 1 obchodnu* .....

absolv.školy náboženské : *Bét – Jokob Seminari* ....

učil/a/ sa remeslu : .... po dobu : ....

hodlá sa venovať:/ nábož.štúdiám – ješiva,Bet Jakob,–: *Bét Jakob*
 іným štúdiám : ....
vyučeniu remesla : ....

Meno otca : *Josua Templer* .... povolanie: *hotel "nlomed"*
meno matky: *Karolína* .... rodená : *Mendelsohnový*

presná adresa: ....
....

Rodičia /otec,matka/ zahynuli : v *Vaariedúrno* .... v roku : *1942-44*
Príbuzní v tuzemsku : *nikoho* ....
adresa : : ....
Príbuzní v cudzine : *Jakob Kolu Julius Templer*
adresa : *Tel-aviv Jeruzalejim*

Poznámky : ....
....
....

Séndi Templer's application form.

211

with me though Rabbi Schonfeld had expected them to go to Hendon. I did not admit I was only a little older than they were and very inexperienced. My teacher was Rabbi Dunner and I was baby-sitter to the Dunner children. I was proud to earn seven shillings and sixpence a week for this.

I was always interested in anything connected with medicine. For six months I was a volunteer in a hospital and was so proud of that. Then through Mrs Cohen I also helped at a laboratory. She ran a very good club where a small group of girls would visit lonely people. One old lady I visited turned out to come from the same place as my aunt and she had known my family.

Somehow I had the strength and felt I had a duty to look after others. There were no boundaries to my activities. I neglected myself and was very much on my own. **Blanka Federweiss** came with me, although her brother and sister had gone to New York. We had worked closely together in Ireland and she would not leave me till I had married and settled in Gateshead. Then Blanka joined her family in the States and married there. Her husband died young.

At Clonyn Castle I had met the man who was to be my husband. He had joined the staff there as a volunteer. That was such an amazing episode in my life. He had applied to study at Gateshead Yeshiva. Two of his friends were accepted but there was no place for him. Then Rabbi Schonfeld offered him three months work at the Castle which he accepted. Next day a telegram arrived saying that a place was available at Gateshead. He refused it because by then he had promised to help Rabbi Schonfeld. That was lucky for me!

My married life has taken me to live in many different countries where my husband has served as Rabbi. Early in our life together we spent a few years in Morocco. We were appalled by the utter poverty among many Jewish families. In 1951 we opened a Children's Hostel there. But I already had two small babies and conditions were not favourable for their health so we returned to Europe. Some of those Moroccan children settled later in Israel and one boy still keeps in touch with us. We went on to live in several different European countries where my husband served as Community Rabbi. When he eventually retired we settled in Jerusalem where many of our family have joined us.

Key to wedding photograph

Those identified:
1. *Lily Lowinger* 2. *Our Cook at Woodberry Down Hostel* 4.*Sonia* 5.
Judith Mannheimer 6. *Lenke Rubin* 9. *Chaya Kurtz* 10. *Vera Wiesen.*
13. *Séndi Templer, The Bride.* 14. *Rachel Grunfeld.* 15. *Franklina
Wiesen.* 16. *Vera Grossman.* 17. *Helena Sichermann.* 18. *Vera
Fischer.* 19. *Olga Grossman.* 20. *Anna Katscher* 21. *Eva Rubinstein.*
22. *Marianna Stahler.*

214

Séndi's wedding to Benjamin, son of Henry Pels, London, 1949 (JM)

Rabbi Schonfeld with the youngest wedding guests (JM, MN)
Rear Row: Olga Grossman, Judith Mannheimer, Eva Rubinstein, Vera Grossman.
Front Row: Anna Katscher, Vera Wiesen, Vera Fischer, Marianna Stahler, Franklina Wiesen.

Today my husband has a complicated heart problem. He is very courageous about it but this is a hard time for us. He is a wonderful man. I have to be strong. We have a lovely relationship. The older we get the closer we are.

"Let me recognise danger but not have a disaster."

Recollections from the Children

Personal reminiscences of The Hide-and-Seek Children follow; some include their siblings, representing almost half of those we traced. Since then many have Anglicised or Hebraised their family names and most girls have married so together with variations made by Rabbi Schonfeld in 1948, numerous changes have occurred. In deference to those who wish to preserve their privacy their names are given here as they appear on the original Group Visa.

The stories are grouped according to their wartime experience - hidden with or without an adult family member, in an institution or in a Concentration Camp. They are listed with the youngest first to draw attention to their age during the events they describe. There are memories from peace time, the war years and from the chaos that followed. Another group tells only of post-war events. All these stories are recounted here as they were written or told to me. I felt it inappropriate to interview, question or edit them. It was enough of an ordeal for any survivor to take part at all. Only four chose to edit my drafts, so any errors I have made remain, and for these I apologise.

Finally I have added a further six stories. In seeking more information about pre-war Jewish life in Slovakia I was led to four survivors who provided a much fuller picture of that time. Their own stories emerged from these encounters and were so remarkable I sought their permission to include them. They provide interesting links with the main collection. How then could I leave out the stories of my old friends, **Betty Fischer** and **Rachel Malmud**, who first introduced me to **Olga Grossman**? So here they are. Thanks to **Erika Stern** I was able to add an account of my privileged meeting with **Fela Maybaum**, an outstanding woman who rarely gave an interview.

Hidden Children

Children hidden with their mother and/or siblings

The impression I have is that many parents made frantic arrangements to save their children and themselves from deportation only at the last moment when the reality of the situation was thrust upon them. So no warnings, far less introductions, prepared children for a huge upheaval in their lives. Those that fled with their mothers, though they had the comfort of staying together, were suddenly engulfed in a climate of fear. Nowhere was safe. They moved frequently from hideout to hideout, fugitives reliant on the compassion and fortitude of non-Jewish acquaintances and a network of Partisans.

Susanna and Israel Reich

Israel Reich was born in 1939. He was a stalwart member of the Jubilee Reunion Committee. He left Bratislava with his sister Susanna who is three years older. Later she settled in Israel, he stayed in London.

My father was the Rabbi of Namesto in Bohemia, Czechoslovakia. My mother was one of nine children. She came from a line of Rabbis of Nitra; her father was the head of the *Beth Din* there. We lived openly as Jews during the earlier years of the war but in 1942 deportations began. We were all illegal residents and in danger of deportation if found out. I have very little recollection of that time. Conditions worsened and in 1944 Jews were rounded up into ghettos. My father stayed with his congregation and was deported with them to Majdanek Concentration Camp. Only after the war did we learn that he had died there.

Our mother fled with us. My father, with my mother's brothers, made an arrangement for payment to a non-Jew to take our mother, my sister and myself to Nitra to stay with our grandparents. There was a safe haven there they called "The Vatican". However when we reached there my mother's parents decided it would be safer for her and for us to proceed to Hungary where there had been no deportations. My sister and I were sent as illegal immigrants across the border. We escaped disguised as the children of a gentile lady. I was dressed as a girl. We went to stay with our great-grandfather, the Rabbi in Makó where two of our aunts looked after us. His pupils were angry at my disguise and cut short my hair. My mother was found a flat by one of her brothers in Budapest and she would visit us. But my sister and I had no papers. This situation could not continue.

Then, in the early summer deportations started in Hungary. In Makó, as in all other towns, the Nazis established a ghetto. So our mother came from Budapest and despite all the dangers succeeded in taking us back to Nitra, my sister and me, my grandparents and my aunts. We crossed the border again, this time by night and on foot and eventually reached her people again. To this day she cannot imagine how she managed it. She and us children received from our great-grandfather, the Rabbi of Makó, a blessing. He was a great and holy man. My mother says that this blessing was the reason that G-d saved her and us throughout the war years. Her brothers found bunkers for us, hiding places with non-Jews. Our grandparents, uncles and aunts were all together during those months when we were hiding.

The gentile woman who hid us was living alone; her husband was in the army. One day he came back on leave. He was fearful of the risk we were to his family and betrayed us. The Germans came to look for us. We were hidden behind a false wall. The police came. Shots were fired. Someone was hit in our hiding place. Their screams disclosed us. We were left in the cellars of the police station for several days. The place was infested with rats. From there we were taken to Sered, a collecting centre for deported Jews on the way to Auschwitz. It was a huge Camp. We found there the rest of the family from Nitra. My mother told me that when her parents and one of her sisters were transported away by train, her mother's parting words were: "And what is going to happen to you with these two small children?" They died in the Camps.

It was early December. Ours was the last, or one of the last, transports to leave Sered. We spent seven days on that awful train. It was scheduled to take us to Auschwitz. I do not remember it, but my mother tells me it was a horrendous experience. The battle front had come nearer. The Russians were advancing so instead of going to Auschwitz the train was turned back and took us to Theresienstadt instead. It was a divine deliverance.

Theresienstadt has been well documented. It was like a Jewish town. The Red Cross was allowed in but that was only a part of the story. I remember grim prison blocks where many atrocities were committed. Jewish doctors who were looking after the sick, befriended my mother and her friends. We lived in their compound. Our mother became ill and my sister too. My sister would share her food with her and they recovered.

Then, in the beginning of May, the Russians came. We were liberated. I recall those soldiers jumping off trains, playing football with us and giving us chocolates. Although we were now free to go where we wished, Jewish survivors were scared to go back to the smaller towns. Our mother arranged to take us with friends to Bratislava.

My mother had been looking after two sisters. It came about in Nitra during the summer of 1944 when we were preparing to go into hiding. These two Herzog girls were there, too, with their father. He had arranged to take them to hide in Verbove, his home town, but the opportunity had been lost. So he had asked our mother to look after them which she did. She looked after them in the Nitra bunker, then in Sered and in Theresienstadt, as her own children. At the time of our liberation they were in hospital. My mother would not leave them behind so she discharged them without permission and they came back to Bratislava with us. They were reunited with their father who survived the war. Their mother did not. We then lost touch. Very recently contact was regained by chance. We discovered one sister is settled in Australia, the other in the USA.

In Bratislava mother learned that our father had died. She received a state pension as a Rabbi's widow and was allotted a flat. There she made a home again for those of her brothers and sisters who had returned. There were no Jewish schools, so we went to a non-Jewish school and at night to *cheder*. Our mother and uncles brought us up in the old tradition of Jewish religious life as followed by their illustrious father and grandfather. We lived in Bratislava from 1945 to 1948.

I have a clear memory of how, when the Communists walked into Prague in 1948, we children were made to see Stalin as the greatest hero ever. We would cheer the Russian soldiers, going quite crazy when we saw them. The older generation were thankful to be liberated after the intense trauma of the Holocaust. Younger people were brainwashed by the Communists and offered no opposition. It was only later that another generation began to question Communist doctrines. My mother and uncles, though, recognised what was happening, and saw in Communism yet another great danger emerging for Jews.

That great and unique man, Rabbi Schonfeld, also recognised what was happening. He let it be known through various Jewish connections including my uncle, Rabbi Vorhand, the Chief Rabbi of Prague, that he was offering to take a group of children to Britain. There he would assure them a religious way of life, a good education and his personal care until such time as their families were in a better situation. We left Prague in February 1948. Rabbi Schonfeld travelled with us on the train to Ostende and then to England. I recall the Red Cross offering us bananas at Ostende. We had never seen any before and asked what blessing we should say on them.

We spent Pesach with an uncle and aunt who had already come to live in England. Then we re-joined the group and went on to Clonyn Castle in Ireland - a great, huge place in beautiful grounds with a wonderful atmosphere. I remember my time there as special - the football games and our favourite game: a sort of "Hide-and-Seek" where the other side had to spot numbers written on cards tied round our heads. You were out if your number was called. The teachers were very dedicated.

In February 1949 we returned to London. I spent six months at a *yeshiva* in Letchworth and then I went to the Gateshead Jewish Boarding School until 1954. My sister attended the Avigdor High School run by Rabbi Schonfeld and lived with the Schwab family in Lordship Park.

After we came to England my mother stayed behind in Czechoslovakia. She married again to Mr Alexander Schweid, an outstanding man. He had been a leading member of the Košice community before the war. He wrote his story, in German. He gives a detailed account of Nazi activities and his experience as a prisoner in Auschwitz. In his later years he was a well-known communal figure, active in helping Russian Jewry during the Communist era. In 1951 my mother and stepfather moved to London and we were re-united.

Oskar and Richard Reich

These two brothers (not related to Israel and Susanna) knew nothing about the Reunion till they saw photos I circulated just before this book went to press. I was seeking names for faces in group pictures and they recognised themselves and many others! In 2007 Richard re-visited Clonyn Castle. One of his photos is reproduced here. Oskar has retired as a senior officer of the Israel Defence Forces and Richard is a Master Mariner in the Israeli Merchant Navy, based in Eilat.

We two brothers, Aharon Oskar born in 1935 and Yehuda Richard born in 1938 arrived in Israel with Youth Aliyah to settle there in January 1949. We had been liberated by the British from Concentration Camp Bergen-Belsen with our mother, *blessed be her memory*. We decided while she was still alive to collect information about our family's past history and our roots in Slovakia. We searched for our house and our father's pharmacy and particularly recognised our moral obligation to locate the Mihalik family.

They were Slovak peasants who hid us to save us from the Germans.

In July 1999 we tried and failed to locate Helena Hodickova the oldest daughter of that family. We returned and eventually found her. We had an exciting reunion in a town called Holic and she told us details of our story that we had not known before.

Our parents lived in the village named Mocenok near the town of Nitra, Our father was the only pharmacist there. Mihal, the head of the family Mihalik, knew our family well as he frequently bought drugs from him. Just before the Germans came to our village in 1944 the Mihalik family provided a hiding place for us, all five of us: father, mother, grandmother and us two children, then aged six and nine years old. At first they hid us in a side room with a cupboard placed to hide the door. As the danger of German searches increased Mihal dug a pit in his yard as a bunker where we could hide. It was 2.5 x 2 meters and covered with planks. In it were two buckets – one for drinking water and another for sewage. Today the bunker is used as an ice box. It was Helena, then aged 22, who provided food for us and brought us information about what was going on in the village. She put her life in danger by going day by day to find out if the Germans were still looking for Jews, and what their fate was.

In wintertime guests would come every night to visit the Mihalik family and sit in their living room. If we had made any noise they would have discovered us and reported us to the Germans. Then we would have been caught and killed - us and all the Mihalik family, too. Knocking on the room was the sign of coming guests.

Later on we learned from our mother that the worst happened. We were caught by informants. That was in October 1944. The Mihalik family was ordered by the Germans to stand against the wall to be shot. But they informed their captors that our father was the pharmacist who had saved many lives by providing drugs throughout the war years. They begged them not to kill them. This argument persuaded the Germans to let the family go.

If the Mihalik family had not hidden us and we had been caught in September, after the Slovak Uprising when the Germans invaded Slovakia, we would have been sent directly to Auschwitz and to our certain destruction. The period the family hid us saved our lives. By the time we were caught in December 1944 ours was the first transport not to be sent to the Auschwitz gas chambers. That was because by then the railway lines had been so badly damaged by the Allies. When we were caught all five of us were taken to the deportation camp at Sered and from there to Bergen-Belsen. Our father was separated from us and sent to Buchenwald Concentration Camp. He never came back.

In our opinion the Mihalik family merited recognition as "Righteous among the Nations". They were a simple, honest peasant family who worked in the fields and loved to help others. They endangered their lives to help us and without any monetary reward. This honour we negotiated and it was presented to them in 2000 by Yad Vashem. Sadly it could not be given to the parents who were no longer alive but it was received by their daughter, Helena Hodickova, who cared for us with their full support and encouragement.

Aharon Reich's address at the President's Pálace in Bratislava, Slovakia on June 26th 2000 when the Mihalik family was presented with a medal proclaiming them as "Righteous Gentiles".

Our father, Artur Reich, blessed be his memory, was a pharmacist in our village of Mocenok. He provided your grandfather, Mihal Mihalik, with medicines he needed and they became friends. The Germans invaded Mocenok in 1944 and were searching for Jews. They were determined to annihilate any they found. So your grandfather and his family hid us in their courtyard putting their lives in mortal danger by doing so.

We were caught. Our father was taken to a Labour Camp and was never heard of again. We two brothers who are standing here with you

Jerusalem, 10 November 1999

Ref: MIHALIK MIHAL & WIFE & DAUGTER HELENA - SLOVAKIA (8666)

We are pleased to announce that the above persons were awarded
the title of "Righteous Among the Nations," for help rendered to
Jewish persons during the period of the Holocaust.

A medal and certificate of honor will be mailed to the Israeli
consulate/embassy listed below, which will organize a ceremony in
their honor. Their names will also soon be added on the
Righteous Honor Wall at Yad Vashem.

Copies of this letter are being mailed to the honorees, to
persons who have submitted testimonies, and other interested
parties.

Dr. Mordecai Paldiel
Director, Dept. for the Righteous

Yad Vashem Award of "Righteous among the Nations". (RR)

today were deported with our mother and our grandmother to Bergen-Belsen. We were eventually liberated by the British – and we survived.

Later we emigrated to Israel where we studied and worked and established our own families – and none of this would have been possible were it not for the courage and determination of your grandparents.

[Translated from the Slovak by Richard Reich].

My speech on Israel Independence Day May 12th 2006 when we also celebrated the 70th Birthday of my beloved brother, Aharon (Oskar) Reich

I want to look back at our childhood. The 15th of last month marked 60 years since our liberation from Bergen-Belsen when we were set free with our mother, blessed be her name. We returned to Slovakia and were looked after in a camp for orphan children who had survived the Concentration Camps. From there we were taken to a Children's Home in Ireland.

Just recently we received a booklet which contains a photo of the two of us in the football team at Clonyn Castle where we stayed. Recently Aharon told me he was the only child to have his barmitzvah in Clonyn Castle. While we were there our mother called us by phone every week from Slovakia and wrote letters to us every day. In 1949 we left Ireland for Israel. While we waited for a ship we stayed for ten days at Villa Gabi in Marseilles. Aharon I recall was in charge of the baguettes – a funny memory! We have lived in Israel ever since. We studied, joined the army and established our own families. You married Naomi and I married Penina. I pray for your good health and many blessings so you can fulfil all your hopes.

[Translated from the Hebrew by Richard Reich]

Oskar and Richard Reich at the Castle. (RR)

Hedviga and Judita Friedmann

Hedviga Friedmann was 15 years old and her sister Judita was 10 when they left for Prague. They were traced only after the Reunion. Hedviga told me their story and Judita added comments during a visit I paid to them in Haifa during 1999.

Our grandfather was Emmanuel Honig of Prešov. He was a timber merchant with large concerns in the forest. The Germans needed his expertise so they gave him exemption from deportation so he could work for them. Our mother had six brothers and two sisters. Our uncles were very active in the Partisans. One brother, in a responsible position, built a big bunker as a hiding place for his parents and all the family. We lived originally in a village, near the Polish border in Eastern Slovakia called Mely Litnip (meaning "Small Street"). Judita was born in Gnazdach in 1937. A year or two later our father was deported and he never returned. Mother took us to live with her parents. Grandfather had a good relationship with the local priest, so the villagers closed their eyes to our existence. Our mother hid in the attic; but by day, disguised as a man, she went to work for her brother in his protected business. In the evenings she would return to join us. The family thought we did not know about this. We used to whisper to each other a lot in German, our mother tongue. "What are you children chattering about?" they would ask. One day a young uncle hid under our bed and discovered that we knew, but although we were very young, we understood we had to keep it secret.

When conditions worsened, the priest obtained false papers for us as Christians, and we hid in the forest. It was a terribly cold winter. The snow was very deep and there was not enough to eat. Once we found some blackberries. Our mother occasionally gave us a special treat. She had filled a tiny nail-polish bottle with honey and would give us a taste, now and then, on the little brush.

Then we moved in with the priest's daughter, living as Christians. She was a beautiful young woman called Marianka, a teacher. Our mother worked in the fields and we would go with her. A little goat used to follow me around.

Then came the Uprising of the Partisans. I remember the shootings. The Germans arrested us and put us in a truck. A pretty young cousin was with us so perhaps that is why the soldiers let us escape. Next we were sent to live with a Christian family in Poprad. Our mother worked and paid them for our keep. They were butchers and we had steak. I remember the smell to this day!

One day our mother told us she was going to see the Christian chemist in another village. He knew we were Jews and received money for us from our grandfather. But she did not return. No news came from her. So we two children, aged nine and six years old, were left all alone. The woman of the house said she could not keep us any longer and would take us to a convent. I said no, I was sure our mother would return. Every evening we said our prayers. And they kept us. Was it because their son had been with the Partisans and was killed by the Germans?

Three months later the Russians arrived. They marched up the main street of Poprad. It was the end of the war and there was a big celebration. We were playing in the yard when the housewife called out "Someone is looking for you" and there in the shop was our Uncle Moishe. (He is now in Jerusalem). We screamed with joy! Now we could say again quite openly that we were Jews.

He had found us through the chemist who also told him when he last saw our mother. As she was about to leave with the money from our grandfather a young man had arrived saying: "I am your friend. Your brother was my best friend." That brother was a well-known Partisan. The police were seeking him, alive or dead. It seems that this man had recognised mother's likeness to his picture. The chemist told Uncle Moishe that Mother had denied any relationship and she showed the man her Christian papers where her name was Shandova and we were called Anna and Julia. Mother did not trust him but he forced her to go to the Gestapo. She was interrogated and then sent to Bergen-Belsen.

We returned with Uncle Moishe to our grandparents but Mother did not reappear and there was no news of her. Eventually she did reach us, terribly thin, her skin darkened. We hardly recognised her. She had suffered so very much.

A new life began. We moved back to Prešov with our grandparents. We attended the Jewish school. I recall falling on the icy street on the way there. Then came more bad news. The Communists threatened to take over Slovakia. We were sent to a big *Hasharah* in Košice called "Micha". We were there for more than a year but there were difficulties. There seemed to be no progress in reaching Palestine.

It was then in 1948 that my mother heard about Rabbi Schonfeld and accepted his invitation. She assured us she would follow. She had an affidavit from a man who wanted to marry her. We met the group in Prague and went to London for *Pesach*. The family we stayed with gave us horrid green food - was it cabbage? We spent some months at Clonyn Castle in Ireland. I took on a mother's role and every day plaited my little sister's hair and tucked Yossi's shirt into his trousers.

When a *shaliach* visited the castle I at once agreed we should go to Israel. I wrote to our mother saying we would meet her over there. In February 1949 we boarded an illegal ship, the "Eilat", at Ostende. It was a terrible journey. The overcrowded ship nearly sank. The weather was very stormy. Our *madrich* disappeared. He did not appear during the journey or at Haifa port. We heard later that he had gone off with his family to Tel Aviv.

We were taken first to a hospital. Then 20 of us went from Kiryat Shmuel to settle at Kfar Hanoah Hadat, a Children's Home near Haifa. Our mother arrived two weeks after us. We spent some weekends with her in Tel Aviv. She married again and encouraged me to join her. This I did a year later. I studied half the day and worked the other half until I was due for army service. I married an Auschwitz survivor from Transylvania, a relative of Elie Wiesel. Judita spent three and a half years at the Children's Home and was very happy there. She eventually decided to join mother and attend High School in Tel Aviv. In 1962 she married a *sabra* who was born in Tel Aviv. We both settled with our husbands in Haifa, starting from scratch with no resources.

When we were well-established we bought our mother a fridge and a simple oven. Much later we brought her and her husband to Haifa and we were able to support them financially and with much love. Her second marriage was a very happy one and they had 30 good years together. She was ill only in her final year.

We have no recollection or any information about our father, Aaron Friedmann - no pictures or even his birth date. Somehow we could never bring up the subject with our mother. Probably he was born in Dolny Kubin.

Gizella, Ella and Rozsi Schwarzthal

Ella Schwarzthal and her twin sister Rozsi were 9 years old when they left Ohel David Children's Home with their sister Gizella to come to Britain and Ireland. I was given Ella's phone number only after the Reunion. I told her about it and she sent me their story.

Me and my two sisters (one of which is my twin) were born and brought up in Topoľčany in Czechoslovakia. My twin sister and I were born only in 1939. Our big sister is five and a half years older than us. In March 1942 we were sent to Camp Nováky which started as a Labour Camp and ended up as a Concentration Camp. A few months earlier, our father had been taken there with the other men and they were forced to build the Camp. We were kept there until October 1944. At this point there was an uprising of the guards. Many of them fled and left the Camp unguarded, and this gave us a chance to run away. My family and some 30 others decided not to try to return to our homes but went to hide together in the forests near Banská Bystrica. And there we stayed until the war ended.

On the 19th of February 1945, so very near the end of the war, our dearly beloved mother succumbed to the terrible conditions and suffering we were going through and died there.

Our father survived the war with us three small children but we were all in a very bad state. Our father and Ruzena (Rozsi), my twin, were very ill indeed. After a short time of convalescence our father started working in order to support us. So we children were left very much alone and an easy target for harassment and beatings. Anti-Semitism did not stop at the end of the war.

Realising this, our father married again and we moved to Bratislava where his new wife lived - somebody who he hoped would look after us. But we could not stay there because the living conditions were too crowded and after a short time we three were sent to a Children's Home - the Villa Silvia in the Tatra Mountains. Later we were moved to the Ohel David Children's Home in Nové Mesto.

In 1948 we were among those who went from there with Rabbi Schonfeld to Clonyn Castle in Ireland where we arrived after Pesach. There, in Clonyn Castle, for the very first time, we felt happy and secure. Many years later after my father came to Israel I saw at his home the first letter Ruzena and I wrote to him in Czechoslovakia from the Castle. It began: "Dear Father, we love you! The sun is shining and we are playing".

It made me shiver to realise that it seemed important to us, then nine years old, to state that the sun was shining, as though it had never shone before. And, actually, for us it did not shine during all those black days of war. Even after the war had ended, we had always felt frightened and unsafe. Only after arriving at Clonyn Castle where we were accepted with so much love and understanding did we begin to see that the sun really was shining. We felt then, and during all the years since then, so very grateful to Rabbi Dr Schonfeld, to our teachers and all the other staff at Clonyn Castle. Their great hearts helped to put us on our feet again and gave us the strength to try to rebuild our demolished lives.

In February 1949 we left Ireland for Israel. Ruzena and I were sent to a Children's Home in B'nei B'rak and Grete (Gizella) went to a Children's Village near Kfar Chasidim. Later we all served in the army, I myself for five and a half years. Grete married early while she was still in the army. Now she is 65 years old. She is living in Tel Aviv and looking after her invalid husband. She has two daughters and four grandchildren. Ruzena was the first woman detective in Israel and a very successful one. She is a widow with two daughters and a son. Unfortunately she has been very sick for the last six years. She has Alzheimer's Disease and is in a nursing home. She and I of course are now 60 years old. I am single and also live in Tel Aviv. I retired a few months ago after working for El Al, the Israeli airline, for thirty-eight years.

Eva Schwarz

Eva was 13 years old when she joined Rabbi Schonfeld's transport; there is an error in the Visa date. She told me her story when we met in London after the Reunion.

I was born in Bratislava in 1936. My parents were secular Jews but they only ate *kosher* food. My father was a barrister. Before the war began my parents had a visa for us to go to the States; but my father was the eldest son and would not leave his elderly parents. My grandfather died at the age of 84 while I was reading a story to him; he just fell asleep next to me. That was in 1940-41. A week later my grandmother was taken away. My mother sewed some precious things into the lining of her fur coat.

Although my father was a lawyer and that was a reserved occupation, the authorities ordered him to go to work on the railway. That was early in 1942 when I was six years old. He would not complain. He said it was only fair he should work alongside the others and show he was not lazy. Then he twisted his ankle. I remember my mother taking him to the station. He was going to a Concentration Camp and believed that it was a Work Camp. My father said we were not to follow him and that he would come back to us if he possibly could. Lawyer friends tried to persuade him to appeal but he insisted "I am not going to be different from the rest". I heard later that a friend of his jumped off that train and escaped to the USA.

After he left Mother heard warnings that the Gestapo were rounding up more Jewish people. So we stayed overnight with friends in a mixed marriage. Next day she went back home to pack up a few things before hurrying away. Later she learned she had barely missed being deported: the SS had come looking for her.

Here are some of my recollections from that time: on a farm with my mother where we spent a week in a pigsty. I was half excited, half afraid - but I was with my mother so it was all right. We stayed with a Hungarian family. It was, though, very dangerous for us to be together as we were well-known in that town. There was lots of bombing - by the British, by the Germans, by the Russians. One day I was watching a plane and a German soldier passing by put his arm on mine and said "Don't worry, it is one of ours". And we saw the petrol station blow up.

I was an extravert and a friendly child. I used to chat with a German officer and his wife who lived in a cul-de-sac opposite to us, near a big

Cathedral. Priests lived next door to them and also a manicurist. My mother realised this was an impossible situation. It was then that Mrs Kurtansky, the manicurist, and her family took me in while, unbeknown to me, my mother tried to follow my father. I noticed she was collecting money and I said "If you are going, I am going". I was an inquisitive child.

I attended a state primary school with a son of the family I lived with. He was two years older than me. I am still in touch with his younger brother; he lives in Freiburg and has visited us here. My mother had to keep away; it was too risky for her to be seen. At one time she was hiding among flour sacks in a cellar when German soldiers came searching.

My mother had attended university before her marriage. Then she went to work in her parents' printing shop where she learned the business; she managed to continue to work in that line. It was considered essential work in wartime so she wore a "little star" - a smaller *Magen David* than the regular one Jews were required to wear.

It was during the last six months of the war that the Germans came to round up any remaining Jews. There was a great commotion. My foster family went to look for my mother; there was no reply at the house. In the evening they found her at work, hiding in a wall. She changed clothes with Mrs Kurtansky and escaped. During the final months of the war she hid in a pantry.

Then the Russians arrived. We heard fighting during the night; but in the morning there was silence. We had forgotten what that was like. The occupying forces were there. They liked children and were very kind to us; they gave us chocolate and sweets. We children had to pretend we were orphans because the Russian soldiers wanted women; so every woman was in danger. I remember seeing dead bodies on the streets. We were on the front line. I think children survived if they were accepting of situations they were in.

Once there was peace my first plea was "Please take me to find my Daddy". I was my Daddy's girl. Much later I heard he had been a victim of medical experiments. I never saw him again. My mother and I went to stay with her brother and his wife in Silesia. Their son was in the Free Czech Air Force. Somehow he met Rabbi Dr Schonfeld and heard about his offer to take children to Britain. My mother had to make a very quick decision: mine was the last name on the Group Visa.

27. The child's biography:

Als die grossen Deportationen im Jahre 1942 begannen, arbeitete der Vater der schon seidt dem Jahre 1939, seine Praxis als Advokat nicht mehr ausüben konnte als Bahnarbeiter an der Strecke.Er wurde am 23.Sept.1942 von der Arbeit in den Transport nač Polen genommen und ist nicht mehr zurückgekehrt.
Es gelang der Mutter,sich über ein paar Wochen mit dem Kinde zu verstecken so entkam sie der Deportationen,denn man war sie in der Wohnung abholen, fand sie aber nicht vor und versiegelte die Wohnung.Es gelang dann der Mutter sich die erforderlichen Papiere zu besorgen ,sie arbeitete als Einlegerin in einer Druckerei.Das Kind lebte bei einer arischen Familie mit arischen und ging auch regelmäsig zu Schule.
Der Mutter gelang es auch noch nach dem Slovakischen Aufstand im Jahre 1944 sich bei Ariern zu verstecken
Leider kann sich die Mutter dem Kinde nicht widmen, weil sie für das täg. Brot sorgen muss und auch in einem möblierten Zimmer wohnt.Das Kind beeisitzt Verwandte in London sowie auch in Manchester,letztere wünschen es zu sich zu nehmen und bitten wir Sie darum l.Gönner ihnen dies zu ermöglichen. Die Kleine ist sehr inteligent,lernt sehr gut und spricht einige Sprachen.

28. Was the child deported: nein   Where:

Give details:

29. Which occupation does it
    want to choose:

30. State of health: gut

31. Eventual special remarks:

32. The child's weight and measures:

   a. Weight: b. Height:

   c.   d. Size oi shoes:

Date: 13.IV.1948.

                    Marta Tochten Bratislava.Markovičovv
                    Parent's, trustee's, or guard's signature.

A page from Eva Schwarz's Application Form with her story in German.   235

Vyplňte a obratom expres zašlite !

Dotazník evid.mládeže.

IA- Č:............................

Predzn..........................

Meno a priezvisko : *EVA VERA SCHWARZOVÁ*

narodený/á/ *7./.5.*.........193*4* v ....*BRATISLAVE*

sirota,polosirota,nesirota ? ...*polosirota*

barva očí : .....*hnedá*...... postava /výška/: ...*160 cm*

barva vlasov : .....*hnedé*......, nos : .....*stredný*....

zvláštne znamenie : ....*nemá ni*............

absolvoval školy : т....*3.triedy strednej školy.*

absolv.školy náboženské : ....

učil/a/ sa remeslu : ....— .... na dobu : ....

hodlá sa venovať:/ nábož.štúdiám — ješiva,Bat Jakob, ...
                        iným štúdiám : ....
                        vyučeniu remesla : ....

Meno otca : .....*Julius Schwarz*......, povolanie: *advokát.*

meno matky: *Marta Schwarzová*........ rodená : *Mayerová*

presná adresa: ....*Uzka ul. 1. Bratislave.*

....

Rodičia /otec, ~~matka~~/ zahynuli : v....*Polsku*........ v roku : ...*1942*

Príbuzní v tuzemsku : ....

        adresa : ....

Príbuzní v cudzine : ...*LONDYNE A MANCHESTRU*

        adresa : ....

Poznámky : ....

....

Vyplní ústredňa !   Čl.č...........Registr................

                       Doporuč.skup.:........................

Zadel.:............... dňa: ....porad.č..........

Poznámky :...

Agudat Jisrael,ústredňa,Bratislava,Klariská č.16/I. — Telef.41 — 72.

Eva Schwarz's Application Form in Czech.

Translation of Eva's Application Form.

The father could not work in his solicitor's practice anymore. From 1939 he worked for the railways and was a railway worker when the deportations began in 1942. He was taken from work on September 23rd 1942 and deported to Poland from where he never returned.

The mother managed to hide with the child for a few weeks and so escaped deportation when they came to search her flat. They could not find her and sealed up the flat. She succeeded in organising the necessary papers and worked as a compositor for a printer. The child lived with an Aryan family, had Aryan papers and went to school regularly. The mother still managed to continue to hide her with an Aryan family after the Slovakian Revolt in 1944.

Unfortunately the mother is unable to look after the child now as she has to work to buy food and also has to live in a furnished room. The child has relatives in London and Manchester who would like to take her in, so we are asking, Dear Benefactor, to make this possible. The little one is very intelligent, a good learner and speaks several languages.

My airman cousin took me to Prague and saw me off. I was 12 years old.

At Clonyn Castle we ate very well and I put on weight. We drank fresh milk from the cows. We made cocoa mid-morning. I cut my hand on the bread machine; I still have the scar to remind me of that.

My mother stayed in Czechoslovakia and then spent about three years in Kiryat Bialyk in Israel. I had stayed on in London and so she came to Britain, first as housekeeper to a second cousin in Manchester. When we met after six years separation she did not recognise me. Then she moved to London and shared my flat in West Hampstead. We learned that because our landlord was emigrating he was selling the house and needed a quick sale. So we bought it - with a sitting tenant who later moved out. My mother found work till she broke her leg. That led to her spending eight months in hospital. She used that time to take a correspondence course in bookkeeping and came first in her class. She went on working till she was 75. She lived until the age of 89; that was only a few years ago.

I studied medicine for two years at University College until I got engaged. I then decided it would not be fair to my husband and children to follow such a demanding career. So I took a job at the Pharmaceutical

Society, opposite the British Museum, working on digitalis. Later I was a technician in the Psychology Department at University College. In more recent years I worked in insurance in the City for Atlas Life and for Guardian Royal Exchange.

In 1965 I had married. My husband is a gentile, born in Estonia. He escaped with his parents and sister to Sudetenland during the war. When peace came they moved to England. At first his father worked in a sausage factory while mother and son stayed in a hostel near Bath. His sister settled later in the USA. My husband is a sorter in an industrial diamond factory. He loves his work and does not want to retire.Our son went to Wessex Gardens School, and then to Haberdashers and to University College, London University. He had a healthy balance of interests; he played the piano and the violin, and he loved football. We encouraged this and took him abroad and on skiing holidays. When at primary school he was not sure whether he wanted to be a dentist in private practice or a concert pianist. Now he is a GP in a Dulwich group practice shared with two lady doctors - till one of them gave birth to a baby boy.

As for me - I like people. Always there is something to give and something to gain.

Tamáš Reif

Tamáš was 13 years old when he joined Rabbi Schonfeld's transport. He took a major role in organising the Jubilee Reunion and gave me lots of encouragement and suggestions while I was preparing this book. He told me his story at his home in London during 1998 and 1999 and was the first to introduce me to Slovakian history.

I was born in Bratislava at a time when we Jews were proud to live in Czechoslovakia, among enterprising and tolerant people with a rich culture. We were free to follow our own practices and Jews prospered there. That was why my parents named me Tamáš, in honour of President Masaryk. Ours was a well organised community, with Orthodox and Reform congregations, settled in a centuries-old area of the city built in Hapsburg times. It was near the bridge across the Danube by the great Cathedral and the Fish Market. When the war came and throughout the ghetto years the community centre remained active. The soup kitchen was open every day, *shabat* meals pre-paid. There was true charity above all else - until the Russians came. Today the "Street of the Jews" exists only in name, replaced by a dual carriageway. The Communists' hatred for the past was so great they pulled down the synagogues and bulldozed the whole area. They even lifted up the cobblestones.

I remember little about those pre-war years. I have a vague picture of my father as a big, jovial and lively man. I used to go around the shops with him. He provided wholesale supplies for the bakery trade: flour and yeast, poppy seeds, sugar and salt were delivered by boys pushing handcarts. Huge drums of cooking oil stood in the storerooms in the lower part of our house; it had big attics and cellars and a central courtyard. This is where we lived and there were tenants, too, and a concierge whose son was a Fascist. My father and my uncle managed the business until the Dictator, Father Tiso, took over the country. He was a rabid anti-Semite.

He made new regulations. Everyone had to hold an Identity Card and numerous rules were made that were continually altered to catch out people; any errors could lead to humiliation and death. My father had to sign over his business to a gentile who kept the profits while my father managed the place.

During the early years of the war I lived with my maternal grandparents.

When Jewish families were being rounded up and sent into the ghetto my mother and I went into hiding. We fled south to stay with an accountant, my uncle's gentile friend in a small village. But there were suspicions among the villagers and we had to move on. It was usually too dangerous to stay together. My mother would leave me in gentile families, paying them for my keep; but they were risking their lives as well as mine by taking me in. My mother moved me many times to different hiding places. In one I remember being covered with a *talet* they had come by somehow. At another my name was changed to Tomy Molnar (appropriately meaning Miller).

I realised we were being hunted. I was unruly, wild and lively; but only once do I recall being really frightened. My mother and I were hiding in an empty flat in a big block in Bratislava, a place found by my uncle. And there was a raid by the Gestapo. We heard shouts and screams, dogs barking, doors being splintered with axes. I wetted myself in fright. Then - a miracle - they walked away. G-d decides who should live and who should die. And we were chosen.

Meanwhile when the Russians approached Bratislava from the north my father, who looked typically Semitic, arranged with some non-Jewish customers to be hidden on their premises. But they stole his money and threw him out. He was captured and taken away. He did not come back.

I was an only child. My mother was a very young widow. She had lost her parents, too, and was wrapped up in herself. We were living on the streets. Lots of shooting was going on around us. She was shot in the back during the 1947 Russian invasion of Bratislava. The shot barely missed her heart. She was cared for in the Jewish Hospital and treated with leeches. There she met **Séndi**, now Mrs Pels; they became good friends. I was looked after at the *Hasharah* hostel and given training for *aliyah* to Israel.

The Communist take-over was horrifying. It was enough that the war had already ravaged the Jewish community. Now we were "jumping from the frying pan into the fire". It was then that my mother heard about Rabbi Solomon Schonfeld. She kitted me out to join his transport and saw me off on the train to meet him in Prague. I travelled with my school friend, George Gross. There was a border inspection when suddenly I was whacked across the face by a uniformed British Officer. Corporal punishment was nothing unusual in those days but what was the reason? **Ervin Schwarz** explained to me that it was because I was talking in Slovak. That was not allowed. Our Visa allowed us to cross Europe from Prague to England as Hungarians, not Czechs. That was my first encounter with Rabbi Dr Schonfeld.

On the Channel ferry we were served tea and offered slices of lemon and little jugs of milk. So we used both - that was our introduction to

English tea! In London I was taken to the Woodberry Down Hostel and spent *Pesach* there. Then we went on to Dublin. Initially I stayed with the Sternberg family; then seventeen of us, all teenage boys, most from a Prague *yeshiva*, moved into a family house in the city.

I had hardly any schooling and knew little English. A tall Irishman gave me a few lessons; he sat me in front of a mirror and told me to practise like that. And we had evening classes in English at the Zion School. **Chaja Steinmetz** was our cook. She gave us our first taste of sea fish although it was very expensive. That would have angered Mrs Eppel! Occasionally we would visit Clonyn Castle. I recall big rooms and wide passages, the cellars and the grounds.

I wrote to Rabbi Schonfeld to tell him I very much wanted to attend his school in London. Eventually I reached his office in Amhurst Park with Yossie (**Josef Ickovitc**). For a year I attended the Avigdor School and lived at a hostel run by Mr and Mrs Tischauer, German refugees. Then I took a job in Brimsdown, a chemical firm making a powder for TV tubes - a dangerous substance - at 30 shillings a week. My digs cost 20 shillings, yet I managed to own a bike - and I smoked. At evening classes I learned about organic chemistry. My next job was with a glue maker in Tottenham, an analytical chemist. He paid me 50 shillings a week and gave me more responsibility.

My mother wrote from Bratislava, urging me to return to the *yeshiva*. So I went off to Gateshead *Yeshiva* with a young Polish-Belgian friend who died tragically from Motor Neurone Disease. Rav Moshe Schwartz took an interest in my spiritual welfare.

Back in London I went into the garment industry; I learned shirt-cutting and pattern-making, attended night school and an extra-mural course in sociology at LSE. Then I was made manager of my firm. Having reached as far as I could go, I left there to become a door-to-door-salesman, and sold all sorts of goods: electrical appliances, hearing aids, insurance, mortgages, jewellery.

In 1956 came the Hungarian Revolution. Mrs Stella Epstein of the Central British Fund - with whom I had a love-hate relationship - had taken over responsibility for the last of the Schonfeld children to be settled. That was after Rabbi Schonfeld's Emergency Council closed down. Mrs Epstein applied for a Visa for my mother to come to England on my behalf as I was still stateless. My mother though had been persuaded by the Jewish Agency to apply to go to Israel. It was very difficult. I had not seen her since I was a boy in shorts in 1948. So I met her in Vienna, whisked her off to a hotel and tipped the concierge to keep her out of the clutches of the Agency while we awaited a British Visa.

Eventually it came and my mother arrived in Britain with a suitcase, $30 from her community but no English. She learned the language quickly and made friends while diligently earning her way by any manner of homework such as painting toy soldiers, and sticking envelopes. My mother was proudly independent. But there was no real bonding between us. I had grown up as an Englishman and had lost the Continental outlook; we had slowly drifted apart. We shared a home together till I married. She lived well into her 80s.

My wife is Judy Kupler. She was brought up in an Anglo-Jewish family in Stoke Newington. Both sets of her grandparents came from Russia. We have a daughter in Baltimore and two sons here, all married. Both our sons qualified as Rabbis and all the adults in our family work in the field of education. We have more than twenty grandchildren.

Robert Bock

Robert was 13 years old when he joined Rabbi Schonfeld's transport. When I traced him he apologised for not contributing as he does not speak English. However I found some information about him in the Schonfeld Archive.

Robert was born in Skadany, in Slovakia. In 1941 while he was at school in Topoľčany, his father who was described as a windmill worker, was sent to Nováky to build the Deportation Camp for Auschwitz. In the following year Robert, his mother and his brother, who was three years older, and his grandmother were sent to join him there. During the Uprising in 1944 they escaped and fled with hundreds of others. Their mother took them and their grandmother into the forests of Banská Bystrica and they hid among the Partisans. They were followed by German troops and many Jews lost their lives. Conditions were terrible. They lost their mother in the forest and no trace of her or their 18 month old brother was ever found. Robert's older brother was wounded in the foot. A family in Banská Bystrica took them in. Their father who had suffered greatly, both emotionally and physically, found them after the war and they returned to Topoľčany where they were reunited with their grandmother. She was penniless. They were all destitute till their father found a job and a school for the boys. In 1948 Robert came to Britain and then to Clonyn Castle with his cousin Erich. Later they went on *aliyah* together. Robert now lives in Jerusalem.

Erich Bock

Erich is a cousin of Robert Bock. He was 14 years old when they left Slovakia. He settled in the USA. These are excerpts from a letter that I received from him in 2001.

Before the war, we had little social contact with our non-Jewish neighbors. There were, of course, business contacts and these were cordial. In the early 1940s the government of Slovakia became more and more anti-Semitic and that rubbed off on the general population. During that time I was in the Detention Camp in Nováky. The Slovak guards and soldiers were tough in the beginning but became more relaxed during 1943 and 1944. There was a revolt at the Nováky Camp in 1944 at the time of the Partisan's Uprising and the Camp was opened up. We escaped and had to go into hiding.

In April 1945 when we returned to the village we lived in, our apartment was occupied. We managed to find a room to rent. The Slovak population was mostly indifferent to returning survivors but some were sympathetic and helpful. Our former landlady returned to us all the furniture and other items that we had asked her to hold for us when we had to leave for the Camp. We received help from relatives in the United States, mostly clothing, which we used to barter in exchange for food from the nearby farms. Later UNRRA, a United Nations organisation, and the Jewish organization, The Joint, helped us with food and clothing.

Clonyn Castle

It was a long journey to Clonyn Castle. We traveled by train from Prague to Ostende, Belgium via Germany, then by boat to Dover, England. We stayed about ten days in the Primrose Club in London during Passover. We toured the city by the Underground and it was fascinating. It was also the first time I ever saw an escalator; this was in a London department store (probably Selfridges).

We traveled by bus to Liverpool. There were about 100 children. We sang songs and had a good time. Then we took an overnight ship to Dublin and from Dublin we took a bus to Delvin where we arrived at Clonyn Castle. The Castle was huge. Our daily routine began with praying and breakfast. This was the first time I had cornflakes, and I was fascinated and thrilled by the fact that I could put all the sugar and milk I wanted on the cereal. We got the milk from a nearby farm. To assure that it was 100% *kosher*, one *madrich* and one child rode in a horse and buggy to make sure that the milk went straight from the cow to our pail.

The manager of the Castle was a young rabbi - Rabbi Cohen. He lived in the Castle with his family. Several of the older children were *madrichim* or teachers and some of the others helped us with chores like laundry and cleaning. My room was on the third floor, just before the entry to one of the turrets. I shared the room with Mordechai Hirsh who ended up in Australia and Victor Mangel, now a rabbi in Brooklyn, New York. When we woke up, we always yelled, in Slovak, "I'm taking the first turn in the shower."

The mornings were devoted to studying - mostly *Torah* and *Gemara*, but also English and Math. I remember Rabbi Cohen taught us the song "Row, Row, Row Your Boat" and translated the words for us. After lunch, it was game time which was the highlight of the day. Football (soccer) was our main preoccupation. We had tournaments, and it was a most serious matter for us. We had little contact with the local villagers though on *Shabbat* we took strolls to the village. We could not communicate with them because we did not speak English but we managed to invite the locals to a soccer match. It turned out that they played rugby and we played soccer. Rugby was a more aggressive game. We managed to teach them our game, and next time it was okay.

Mordechai Hirsh had his *barmitzvah* in the Castle, and Blanka, a *madricha*, organized a big party with plenty of food, songs and lots of fun.

In January 1949, we each had to decide where we wanted to go from Ireland. I opted for Israel since my sister and stepmother who were still in Czechoslovakia, were also going there. So together with my cousin Robert (Zvi) and 23 other kids, I flew from Dublin to Paris. From there we took a train to Marseilles where we stayed in "Villa Gabi" for about ten days while we waited for the ship "Eilath" which took us to Haifa. The last leg of our trip took one week.

P.S. Thank you for the information about the Primrose Club and Clonyn Castle. We have written a letter to the present owner of Clonyn Castle and hope her answer will be positive - that she will let us visit the Castle.

Sincerely, Erich Bock,
June 13th 2001.

Alfred Kahan

*Alfred was over 16 years old when he joined Rabbi Schonfeld's transport though the Visa made him younger. He only heard about the Reunion a few years after the event, during a "pilgrimage" to Clonyn Castle with his friend **Alfred Leicht**. The following memoir is drawn from three sources: a biographical sketch in a college scholarship application from 1951, his remarks at the unveiling of Peter Goldring's tombstone in January 1988 and a speech at his retirement party, January 1999.*

Mrs Eppel always considered Alfred Kahan to be "naughty" and was very worried by his escapades, particularly his visits to Europe. She could not understand how he had raised enough money for these and doubted his integrity. The other boys were becoming restless, too, and she feared that his initiative was a bad influence. However I feel sure that she would have been completely mollified if she had lived to read his memoir.

I was born in March 1931 in Sighet, in Transylvania - at times part of Hungary and other times of Romania - but first I want to describe my mother's background. In the late 1800s my maternal grandparents, Yehuda Yaakov Goldring Halevi and Chaia Surah Weiss, lived in Munkach when part of the Austrian-Hungarian Empire. At the turn of the 20th century they moved to a town in Transylvania, known by three names: Grosswardein in German, Nagyvarad in Hungarian, and Oradea in Romanian. My grandparents had eight living children (two others died young). Peter was the youngest. My grandfather was a fish merchant. He owned an apartment house that became known as the "Goldring House".

My mother, Nechi, Nellie, or Cornelia Goldring - depending on whether you prefer Yiddish, Hungarian, or Romanian - married my father, Shlomo Kahan from Sighet. Sighet was a well known town even before Elie Wiesel or David Weiss/Halivni put it on the map. My uncle Peter told me that when my mother was expecting me, he was sent to Sighet to assist her. I questioned his functions: a 17-year-old lad assisting at childbirth? He said that his responsibilities included boiling water, summoning the mid-wife, and escorting my older brother to the *cheder*. So my handsome uncle's wonderful record in helping people in life also extended to bringing them to life. He played a central role in our family's survival and remained an inspiration to me and many others during the rest of his life.

In the mid 1930s when I was 4 years old, we moved from Sighet to join the family in Oradea. We lived in one of the Goldring House apartments.

My grandparents, their eight children and their families all lived within a radius of several hundred yards. It was an extended family, but my recollection of it is of an extended community. There was no shortage of poor people, or *yeshiva* boys or "*teg*". There were guests at every meal, on weekdays and on *Shabbos*. At the Goldring House hospitality to strangers as commanded in the Bible was not an empty phrase.

In 1940, Hungary annexed Transylvania, the area where we lived. The official language, including that used in schools, was changed from Romanian to Hungarian. Otherwise the Second World War did not affect me until the second half of 1941. Then Hungary entered the war against Soviet Russia and German control over Hungary became stronger. Under German influence persecution of Jews increased. We hoped for victory and liberation by the Allies. My father owned a textile store. Business until this time was flourishing and we lived in prosperity. Then we started hearing reports from German and Polish refugees about the horrors of Concentration Camps, mass executions, and Nazi barbarism.

In March 1944, when I was 13, just after my *barmitzvah*, the Germans took complete control of Hungary. Ghettos were established, Jewish properties confiscated and a reign of terror began. My formal education terminated and did not re-start for six years. In May and June 1944 the ghetto was evacuated. Some individuals tried to escape to Romania where German control was incomplete but most of them were caught. My parents decided to employ every possible means to avoid deportation. We built a hiding place in the ghetto with a secret entrance. We hoped for the best. We stayed in the bunker for four weeks after the last transport was deported. We were able to establish connections with a trustworthy person who specialized in smuggling people across the border to Romania.

This was the superintendent of the Goldring House, Micklosh Bacsi (uncle) He was actively involved with the smuggling of human traffic to Romania. So was my uncle Peter and the Zionist organizations. The goal was to get people, especially the Zionist youth, to Romania and thence to Palestine. The route was through the Goldring House - a "safe house". I recall people arriving at night, and disappearing during the next night.

I believe the story of Micklosh is part of a deposition Peter gave to one of the *Shoah* agencies. Peter told me that several times after the War he sent money to Micklosh who qualified as a "Righteous Gentile."

I do not want to dwell upon the history of the Oradea ghetto, about the life and persecution that went on there and the subsequent deportations to Auschwitz. These are well described in the *Shoah* literature. Similarly I do not want to describe the efforts and exploits of Peter in saving the

Wishnizer Rebbe, their escape, and Peter taking the Rebbe to Romania. I do remember, though, being in the ghetto and I did witness the loading of the deportation trains. I also recall hearing discussions relative to the morality of escape. Even if one did believe the tales of the refugees - that these deportations were to Concentration Camps, rather than Work Camps in Western Hungary - does a leader have a right to escape? Does the principle "my place is with my people" [1] apply?

Then a message was smuggled into the ghetto from Peter: "*ki yesh shever b'mitzraim*".[2] In other words this implied "there is hope in Romania and one should do everything possible not to get deported". This message reinforced the efforts of my father and other Goldring family members to build or find bunkers, go into hiding, avoid deportation, get in touch with Micklosh and escape to Romania. But two of my uncles were caught and with their wives and children died in Auschwitz. Another one boarded a boat bound for Palestine with his family but a German torpedo sunk the ship and they all perished. Yet somehow five of the eight Goldring families did survive and without entering Auschwitz.

The Romanian police eventually arrested my father and brother. They were sentenced to death for illegally crossing the border. The death sentences were not carried out but my father was imprisoned in Timishora and my brother sent to a Camp with political prisoners. There they stayed until September 1944 when the victorious Red Army swept through Romania.

In March 1944, a Nazi Hungarian government had come to power. The German army presence increased. In retrospect, we now know that Eichmann was sent to Hungary with the mission of exterminating Hungarian Jewry. The situation deteriorated at a very fast pace. According to the Polish refugees the persecutions followed the Polish model but at an accelerated pace. Years of persecutions were telescoped into weeks. Comparatively the situation in Romania was peaceful and the Polish refugees began to smuggle themselves into Romania. Thus as a young teenager, in 1944, I came under Nazi German occupation and the threat of deportation. Yet in large part due to the stubbornness of my father, *blessed be his name*, our entire family survived. We descend from a long line of stiff-necked people.

In early 1945 Transylvania was restored to Romania, and Oradea once again became Romanian. We returned there from Bucharest. We did not find any relatives or friends. Later on some survivors of the Concentration Camps returned and Jewish life revived there. The number of survivors of Oradea was estimated as 2,500 out of a population of 30,000.

My father had insisted that both my brother and I should be trained in a trade that could not be taken away from us. This was to ensure for us an income whether we wound up in the West, or in Palestine. I was apprenticed to a watchmaker, my brother to a goldsmith. My fascination with timing devices - and in later life my involvement in the development of precise timing and frequency standards for military systems at the US Air Force Research Laboratory - may have their origin in this apprenticeship. My brother ended up in the early 1950s in New York, worked as a goldsmith, established a jewelry factory, and became fairly prosperous. My father's ideas worked well for both his sons.

In 1946 a Communist government took over Romania. There was great confusion and we were faced with a great dilemma. Should we remain at the scene of our destruction? It was a major moral question. There was also the problem of Communism. We heard about horrors in Russia from prisoners returning from Russia and from Jewish Red Army officers who awaited their first opportunity to escape to the West. We also saw the behaviour of the glorious Red Army and this alone was sufficient to convince us of the undesirability of staying in Romania.

A general exodus of the surviving Jewish population began from Romania to Western Europe and Palestine. My father, being a religious Orthodox man, refused to raise his children aged 19 and 16 to be Communists so he decided to send us into the West as soon as possible. My parents planned to follow us as soon as they could convert our properties into cash. I was more than eager to go. I did not see my parents for 10 years when they too ended up in the US. (I apologise for this short historical capsule; I owe it to myself and my family to expand each of these sentences into chapters.) During the spring of 1947 I was smuggled through Hungary to Prague, Czechoslovakia. I was supposed to wait for my parents in Prague.

I joined a *yeshiva*, in Marienbad (Mariansky Lazne), near Prague. One day we were visited by Rabbi Kalmanowitz, President of the world famous Mirer *Yeshiva* in Brooklyn, New York. He was surveying surviving *yeshiva* boys. He gave me a thorough examination and said that for my age I was very advanced. He offered me a full scholarship if I was willing to come to the United States. But I did not get that scholarship.

Meanwhile two events occurred which had a great influence on my future: the lowering of the Iron Curtain over Romania, and, in February 1948, the Communist *coup d'état* in Czechoslovakia. My parents were still in Romania, hoping to emigrate to Israel, which they did in 1950. In 1949 my brother reached Austria by a flight through the Iron Curtain from

Romania to Hungary to Austria. Eventually he reached the United States in the early 1950s.

I did not want to be trapped again under a Communist regime, and once again took flight. In May 1948, when I was 16, I left with other boys of the *yeshiva* and other orphan children from Eastern Europe and landed in Ireland. In Ireland I concentrated on learning a new language, English. Again, the same question was raised: what to do next? It took me several months to get acquainted with the situation in Ireland. I concluded that it did not hold any future for me. I visited England, France, and Switzerland. It was the first time that I was exposed to the social, economic, and political structure of Western Europe. I discussed our situation with many other refugees. I visited cultural and historical sites and gained tremendous experience and education in a very short time. London made the strongest impression on me. My US Visa became entangled in legal obstacles. I made steps towards entering England on a permanent basis.

Then in July 1949 my US Visa was granted, and on August 29th I was admitted to the United States as a student in a Rabbinical Seminary. Even though I did not pay any tuition fees in 1951 the *yeshiva* provided shelter, food, and 10 dollars a week in pocket money. I was not unique. They provided a home for many Eastern European kids. I am more than grateful to them. The last few years the *Mesivta* has sent a *shaliach* to Boston to collect money and I respond gratefully. I am glad that I can partially repay that debt.

I always had a desire for higher education and a lively interest in mathematics and in technical subjects and sought professional status. After two years I realized that advancement for a refugee boy in a new country could be made only through perseverance and education. I felt depressed that I only began college at the age of 21, rather than the usual 18. Three years made a lot of difference then but I consoled myself that later on it will not matter. Also I considered myself more realistic and better able to face the problems of life than an average American boy of the same age. I missed formal education from the age of 13 to 19, so I took schooling more seriously and with a more mature attitude. Nobody forced me to do this. I realized the importance of education, had the will to learn and only asked for the opportunity to do so. I find this topic, the pent-up energy and talent of Eastern European youth who survived the Second World War, to be very interesting and worth discussing some other time. They, we, were avid in our search for knowledge, whether religious, secular, or both.

I earnestly started to learn a new language. I am still learning it. I attended the *yeshiva* by day, the Washington Irving Evening High - a mecca for new immigrants - between 6 and 10 pm and did homework from 11pm until 2 or 3 in the morning. So my schedule was simple. It paid off. I graduated from high school in record time, was the number one graduate, and received a medal in American History. What next? A friend was studying engineering at Brooklyn Polytechnic Institute so I, too, decided to become an engineer. With the generous support of my uncle Peter Goldring, *blessed be his memory*, I enrolled at the Polytechnic - and protested when they raised the tuition from $250 to $275 per semester.

The best thing that ever happened to me, thanks to the *yeshiva* again, is that they ran a summer camp in the Catskills. They took me on as a counselor - though properly classified as a "freeloader"! One day I was offered a vacancy at another camp. I packed in after 10 minutes and went to Camp Ahava. There I met another counselor, a most attractive 16½ year old girl, and for the first time in my life I fell in love. After 4 years of tumultuous courtship I married that counselor, and our marriage is now in its 44th year. When Nadia was 1 year old, we moved to Brooklyn. Four years later, after David's arrival, we moved two blocks away. In 1976 we moved another two blocks to our current house so, for the last 40 years, we have been living within a radius of 200 yards. We must like the neighborhood! We made friends, and this relationship was cemented when one of our sons married a woman within 100 yards of our residence. We have 3 children of whom we are very proud, and 10 wonderful grandchildren. All this did not happen in a vacuum. A lot is due to the influence of our families, our friends and neighbors and the community at large. What else can one ask for?

I graduated from Brooklyn Polytechnic Institute in 1956, with a degree in Aeronautical Engineering. My first job was with the Curtiss-Wright Corporation in New Jersey as a jet engine design engineer. I also worked for General Electric before I settled for work at the US Air Force Cambridge Research Laboratory. I stayed there for 37 years.

The two youthful traumas, Nazi persecution and living under Communist rule, crystallized in me two guiding principles: the crucial importance of adherence to human rights and civil liberties, and the critical value of democratic regimes. My decision to stay with the Air Force was related to these principles. The Air Force was very good to me, but at the same time, in all modesty, I do believe that during these years I did make contributions to the strengthening of United States defenses.

Children hidden in "bunkers" without parent or sibling

Adults who acquired forged papers could not move around with small children in tow - a situation particularly dangerous when any of the family had distinctive Jewish features. So many distraught parents in desperation sought "bunkers" for their children. This usually referred to structures above or under ground turned into places of safety. Rabbi Schonfeld stretched the term also to cover placement with gentile families. Amongst his papers are lists of children he rescued with notes about them. To denote where they were during the war years he has written "in Bratislava Bunker", "in Košice Bunker" and so forth.

	NAME		GEBOREN	ELTERN	IN KRIEG
39	MARIANNA	STAHLER	MICHALOVCE	FATHER	NOVE MESTO BUNKER
47	ZUZA	REICH	NITRA	MATHER	BRATISLAVA
2	VIERA	FISCHER	BRATISLAVA	MATHER	PRAHA BUNKER
52	GYÖRY	FRISCHGI	BRATISLAVA	MATHER	NOVE MESTO BUNKER
66	SANDI	TEMPLER	~~KE~~ VRBOVE	NO	BRATISLAVA MAUTHAUSEN AUCHWITZ

BUNKER = hidden of gentile

An unusual definition used by Rabbi Schonfeld.

Emanuel Weinberger

*Emanuel was probably the youngest child to join the Schonfeld transport. He is the younger brother of **Artur** who accompanied him. He wrote this for the Reunion Brochure but he did not attend the occasion.*

I was born in Cracow, Nazi-occupied Poland, in August 1943, the youngest of three children. My family was fortunate to be able to continue living outside the Ghetto although in increasingly difficult physical conditions. This was as a result of my father having had papers attesting to a foreign (Hungarian) nationality. Until about mid-1943 these papers and status afforded us a measure of protection from the deportations going on all over Poland. As the situation became more precarious and untenable by the day, with immediate danger lurking ominously, my family managed, only after several attempts, to flee Poland by illegally crossing the border into Hungary. There we lived under a false, non-Jewish identity in Budapest. I was then called Andrish, a gentile Hungarian name which stuck to me until I was about 20 years old.

After several months, as the Jewish situation in Hungary quickly deteriorated, my father took precautions to safeguard us children in case our false identity be discovered and we be deported. I was "deposited" with a non-Jewish woman caretaker, under the pretext of being the product of a romantic liaison out of wedlock and urgently in need of a foster home. My siblings too were "parcelled" out just in the nick of time, barely before my parents were arrested in a dragnet by the new regime in Budapest. Several days later my father and mother were deported to Auschwitz.

It is one of the marvels of my life that despite such terrible odds, all of my immediate family survived the Holocaust intact. My mother survived almost a year in one of the Slave Labour Camps of the Auschwitz Concentration Camp complex in the shadows of the ceaselessly smoking stacks of the crematoria. My father was able to escape the "pleasure" of a stay in Auschwitz by jumping off the cattle wagon in the transport train deporting him to Auschwitz and then hiding in Slovakian towns. After several months he again escaped across the border to Hungary, just ahead of the ever-threatening Nazi round-ups and deportations. He spent the rest of the war hiding in Budapest. My sister was one of those thousands of Jews in Budapest saved by Raoul Wallenberg's protective "diplomatic" shield over Jewish "safe-houses" [3], while my brother survived in a non-

Jewish boy's institution. Each of them had been given non-Jewish names by then, Bashu for my sister Judy, and Yantshi for my brother Jacob.

I was too young then to remember much but apparently I thrived under the care of my caretaker whom I know only as Aunt Sibi. So strong was my bond with her so that I am told that I wanted to stay with her when my estranged family came to collect me after the war. Of my more distant family, only one first cousin survived the inferno. Of my grandparents, uncles and aunts not one survived.

After my parents found one another and their three children, itself a miraculous tale against tremendous odds, they tried to pick up the pieces and re-establish their home in Košice, Czechoslovakia, where my grandfather had lived before and during the Holocaust period. The rebuilding and rehabilitation progressed reasonably well, despite the hardships of war-ravaged Eastern Europe, including an exceptionally severe outbreak of typhus which threatened the lives of my siblings and myself. I was finally circumcised and shortly thereafter began attending a *cheder*.

But the peace and quiet, such as it was, proved very short-lived. In 1948, a Communist putsch was engineered in Czechoslovakia, democracy ended abruptly, and with it my family's hope to rebuild their lives and livelihood in a relatively familiar environment. Taught by bitter experience to sense impending danger, my parents' primary goal now became "saving the children", getting us out of reach from what they perceived as a potential danger to our physical existence and a more immediate danger to our Jewish existence.

It was at this point that Rabbi Schonfeld and the transport he organised in 1948 for orphan children out of post-Holocaust Eastern Europe, came to the rescue. Although fortunately not orphans, my siblings and I were allowed to join this transport and leave the Communist paradise which had quickly closed its borders to other Jewish emigration to become yet another prison for its Jews. At the age of five and a half I was the youngest child in the transport. For my parents this was the second separation from their children, and break-up of their family, within six years and was to last some five years this time.

I recall the train-side scene before we left, with a bearded, uniformed military officer in charge: Rabbi Schonfeld in his Chaplain's uniform. I have several other recollections of the journey out of Czechoslovakia, including a most frightening experience on the boat ferrying us to Ireland. [*When I queried this Emanuel told me that there was a trapdoor in the floor and he had been terrified it would open and wash him into the sea.*]

But the memories of Clonyn Castle near Dublin are among the happiest of my childhood, with large green fields, visits from and to local

Jewish families, sports' competitions and "colour wars" which carried excitement and prizes (even for children who didn't exactly win the races), plenty of attention from the older ones, especially the adolescent girls - in short: idyllic.

My next stop was the Ahavas Torah *Yeshiva* Boarding School in Stamford Hill, London, where I spent some four years after leaving Ireland.

Meanwhile, in 1950 my parents were able to get out of Czechoslovakia, and became refugees in Vienna. During 1952 I was reunited with them there but it required my sister's help to even recognise them. I had totally lost any memory of my parents by then. Now I, too, joined the ranks of the Jewish post-war refugees moving slowly westward, living in various transient DP (Displaced Persons) Camps in very difficult, primitive and crowded conditions, a ward of the Joint Distribution Organisation charity. My family's efforts to re-establish a semblance of normal life proceeded with great difficulty but by 1955 we were able to afford the rental of two rooms in an apartment in the city. I was enrolled in the public-school system, a drastic change from the *yeshiva* environment in London where no secular subjects were taught, not even the alphabet.

By 1957 my parents were able to obtain an immigration visa to the US and with much trepidation we set out for the New World. My sister, who had meanwhile married in Vienna, joined us a year later in New York and so did my brother who had stayed in London all this time. Thus, just about 10 years after the separation in 1948, my family was reunited once more though having to start all over again from scratch in a completely new environment and another language.

I was quickly enrolled in Yeshiva Torah Vodaas High School in Brooklyn. One of my most precious recollections is the scene when my father brought me to be enrolled there. To his question how much it would cost, Rabbi Rivlin, the Administrative Director, responded that it would not cost anything until we could afford it. On the contrary, he asked whether my family might need some help to tide us over. I was given boarding facilities, and even the luxury of a seven week vacation at the Torah Vodaas summer camp, almost entirely free of charge. After graduating in 1960, I enrolled in the evening studies program of Brooklyn College, and continued to learn by day at Yeshiva Netzath Israel. In 1964 I graduated with a BS in physics and math, and went on to NY University to obtain a MS degree in 1966, also in physics. In 1967 I married Esther Rosenbaum and within a few years became the father of three children. I worked at several large American aerospace companies specialising in the field of optical systems design. After some five years of this we decided to realise in practice the ancient hope and pledge "*next year in Jerusalem*" – a wish that is repeated every year round the Passover table - by moving on *aliyah* to Israel in 1972.

After spending almost a year in an immigrants' hostel in Bet Yam we settled in Rehovot. In 1975 due to employment considerations we soon moved again, this time to Haifa where we have been living ever since. I work on Research and Development in the field of optics and electro-optics for the Rafael Organisation, an advanced facility of the Israel government.

My brother Jacob came on *aliyah* several weeks before I did, and he, too, has established his home in Israel. My mother came several years ago, at the young age of 95 and she too has established her home here. *May she live till 120!* My sister, Judy, is still resident in Brooklyn NY but spends considerable time in Israel. *G-d willing*, the day is not far off when she, too, establishes her residence here. That would again reunite the family in our own Promised Land for many good years of peace and quiet.

Issued for Emigration

I.B.113.

No. W.32547

CERTIFICATE OF IDENTITY.
CERTIFICAT D'IDENTITÉ.

E J

This Certificate is issued by the HOME OFFICE, LONDON, and expires on ___ 9 AUG 1952 unless its validity is extended or renewed.

Ce Certificat est delivré par le HOME OFFICE, LONDON, et expire le ___ sauf prorogation de validité.

The present Certificate is issued for the sole purpose of providing the holder with identity papers in lieu of a national passport. It is without prejudice to and in no way affects the national status of the holder. If the holder obtains a national passport this Certificate ceases to be valid and must be surrendered to the issuing authority.

Le présent certificat est délivré à seule fin de fournir au titulaire une pièce d'identité pouvant tenir lieu de passeport national. Il ne préjuge pas la nationalité du titulaire et est sans effet sur celle-ci. Au cas où le titulaire obtiendrait un passeport national, ce certificat cessera d'être valable et devra être renvoyé à l'autorité qui l'a délivré.

Surname / Nom de Famille } *Weinberger*

Forenames / Prénoms } *Emanuel*

Accompanied by / Accompagné de } child (children) / enfant (enfants)

Remarks / Observations }

This Certificate must be Vised by a British Authority for return to the United Kingdom.

Place and date of birth / Lieu et date de naissance } KRAKOW 6.5.42

Occupation / Profession } Student

Present residence / Résidence actuelle } 193 Stamford Hill N16

*Maiden name and forename(s) of wife / Nom (avant le mariage) et prénom(s) de l'épouse }

*Name and forename(s) of husband / Nom et prénom(s) du mari }

DESCRIPTION   **SIGNALEMENT**

Height / Taille } 4'2

Hair / Cheveux } Brown

Colour of eyes / Couleur des yeux } Blue

Nose / Nez } normal

Shape of face / Forme du visage } oval

Complexion / Teint } medium

Special peculiarities / Signes particuliers }

The undersigned certifies that the photograph and signature hereon are those of the bearer of the present document.

Le soussigné certifie que la photographie et la signature apposées ci-contre sont bien celles du porteur du présent document.

Issued at / Delivré à / Date   LONDON

Signature and stamp of authority issuing the document. / Signature et cachet de l'autorité qui délivre le titre.

(21) — 7 AUG 1951 / CHIEF INSPECTOR IMMIGRATION BRANCH / HOME OFFICE

CHILDREN / ENFANTS			
Name / Nom	Forename(s) / Prénom(s)	Place and date of birth / Lieu et date de naissance	Sex / Sexe

*Strike out whichever does not apply.

Emanuel Weinberger's British Certificate of Identity. (EW)   257

Istvan and Gyury Stahler and their sister

Istvan was nearly 10 years old, his brother a year younger and his little sister only five years old when they travelled together to Clonyn Castle. They were too traumatised and too young to remember or understand much of the terrible things that had happened to them during the war. Then in 1957 they received an extraordinary letter from an uncle, their mother's brother. He wrote at length recounting their lost family history, before and during the war. He wrote especially movingly about their mother's great courage and resolute determination to protect her children. He described how they survived while in hiding, moving from place to place and then how their mother was finally sent to her death. This account is based on conversations I had with Istvan and his sister.

My mother and her five brothers were all born in Vylok, then in Hungary. Our grandmother had been widowed suddenly when young and pregnant, and struggled to cope with very limited resources. Yet all her sons acquired higher education abroad. Our mother attended a Catholic High School where she gained top marks, and an enthusiasm for literature, philosophy and music. They all returned home to a failing economy. In 1937, our mother, ever resourceful, found a husband through advertising in a newspaper. The two of them used the loan for a honeymoon to set themselves up in a textile business – a business that soon flourished under their determined hands. I was born in 1938, my brother in 1939.

When Hitler walked into Austria the family was shocked and like so many others, our parents sought an escape route. We received an affidavit from an American aunt but failed to obtain places on the very limited quota. One uncle managed to enter Palestine illegally. And then the pressures began. Our parents with both grandmothers continued to manage their shop in Michalovce; that was made possible by an honest *"arisator"*. Another uncle was a railway engineer, a reserved occupation, and managed to procure some risky protection for the rest of the family. In 1942 further deportations began. He learned of dates through information confidential to his employers as they were responsible for arranging train transport.

The family devised various strategies to avoid deportation. They sought false papers with the help of Christian friends and of their *arisator*. For as long as possible they held out on the grounds of our uncle's occupation but that soon proved too dangerous. My brother and I were taken with our grandmother to Bratislava to stay with non-Jewish friends but our mother, heavily pregnant, only barely succeeded in fooling the guards. Then, after our sister was born, she went into hiding moving around with the baby, always at grave risk. She managed to find shelter with another uncle in Budapest where conditions for Jews were less severe but conditions were poor, the baby often ill. I was placed in a family where the Christian wife became very fond me. She did not charge for my keep. My brother stayed with our paternal grandmother.

Somehow our determined mother escaped with the baby back to cousins in Sátoraljaújhely in Hungary. But conditions rapidly worsened when the Germans invaded. Ghettos were set up everywhere. Our mother entreated her cousins to make an escape before it was too late but they absorbed the propaganda and believed that going to a Labour Camp would provide them with work and protection. There were fierce quarrels. So our mother with our baby sister fled the ghetto and bribed a peasant to take them across the border back to Slovakia. Tragically our cousins met their fate in Auschwitz.

Our mother with the baby managed to reach Michalovce again after a hazardous journey. There with the help of an acquaintance she contacted our father. They arranged for an uncle to bring them back to hide in Bratislava with the rest of the family – only we two boys were missing. So our valiant mother collected donations from house to house to pay for an escort to bring us back to join them. A huge sum was involved and more was demanded before we boys were handed over. We had been separated for two years and now enjoyed lots of attention but tragically, only briefly. It was July 1944. It looked as though the war would soon end. The British bombed daily. The Russians were nearing Warsaw.

Our mother feared the worst. She arranged that we boys stay with a caring gentile family outside Bratislava while our grandmother and our little sister stayed in Ivanka with the kindly Zahradnik family. They were the ones who had brought us boys home. Our uncle visited us every week.

Our mother had false Aryan papers and took a job as a maid in a German family and worked hard to please them. But on November 3rd 1944, so near the end of hostilities, someone denounced her. She tried desperately to escape but failed. We never heard from her again. She was imprisoned in Sered and then deported to Ravensbrück Concentration Camp. Later we discovered that she was sent from there to Bergen-Belsen where she died.

All of us were utterly broken. We boys returned to the family but the Gestapo heard we were with our uncle's Aryan wife. She was beaten mercilessly by Gestapo thugs until they found us. We spent several months in Thereisenstadt Concentration Camp.

When peace came, our devoted uncle brought grandmother back with the baby to his wife in Bratislava. For us boys he arranged places with Baptist sisters in a convent and as before he visited us every week. We were too young to recall much detail but I do remember being singled out to act as ministrant or altar boy, and leading a procession in the church. When a Jewish organisation turned up we were taken with our grandmother and our sister to convalesce at Villa Silvia in the High Tatras with other Jewish child survivors until we were all moved to Nové Mesto. That was where we were when our father heard of Rabbi Schonfeld's invitation.

By the time liberation came, our father had lost his house and his livelihood as a pharmacist. He was in no position to look after three young children. When he first heard about Rabbi Schonfeld's transport all the places had been filled. But so keen was he for us to join the group that he took us along anyhow and, as he hoped, at the last moment a family of three failed to turn up and we were accepted instead. That was how Rabbi Schonfeld came to alter our names by changing them to those of the missing family shown on the Visa. Years later, after I married, I reverted to our original family name in place of the Slovak name that our father had used when he was in hiding.

Our father, despite his extremely limited resources, made an immense effort to provide us with full outfits of clothes. He collected so very carefully everything he could find for the three of us. He wanted to be sure we had what we needed. He knew he would not see us again for a long time and that strangers would be looking after us. So he added mementos, too, and my stamp collection. But our luggage was lost on the journey and all our cherished possessions disappeared. They were probably stolen. I remember the embarrassment of my having no cap; so I borrowed my little sister's red beret and wore it for some months till I was given a *kipa*.

In the early days at Clonyn Castle there was consternation when the local police came to visit us. Some of the children were petrified to see men in uniform. The reason was explained to them and so when they came again they wore civvies until we children learned to trust them.

Many of us were lined up to have our tonsils removed. It was the practice at that time, one not followed today; but I had no ill-effects from the experience. The operation was performed at Mullingar Hospital. I remember Mrs Eppel bringing us ice cream to soothe our sore and angry throats. Oliver was the handyman. Lots of us knew him. He would do anything for us. We had rides in his pony trap.

When most of the children had dispersed to relatives or friends Clonyn Castle was closed down and the few of us who were left moved to No.9

At Villa Silvia: Amiel Lucknar leading Gyury Stahler, second from front, his brother Istvan fourth, Tamáš Krausz at the back. (IS)

Vesey Place in Dun Laoghaire. There we each had a small garden plot. I grew spring onions in mine.

Our father married again to a nice lady. They have two children. The first time we met our half-sister was in 1967 when she was 17. She visited us in London, stayed on and married here. Her husband is a taxi driver, their son is a musician. They live in Ilford. Her brother has remained in Slovakia. Sadly our brother Gyury died of cancer in 1995 leaving a large family. Our father continued to live in Slovakia, in a small town near Bratislava where we used to visit him. He kept a large garden where he grew all his own vegetables until late in life. We used to visit him there until died in 2002 aged 91.

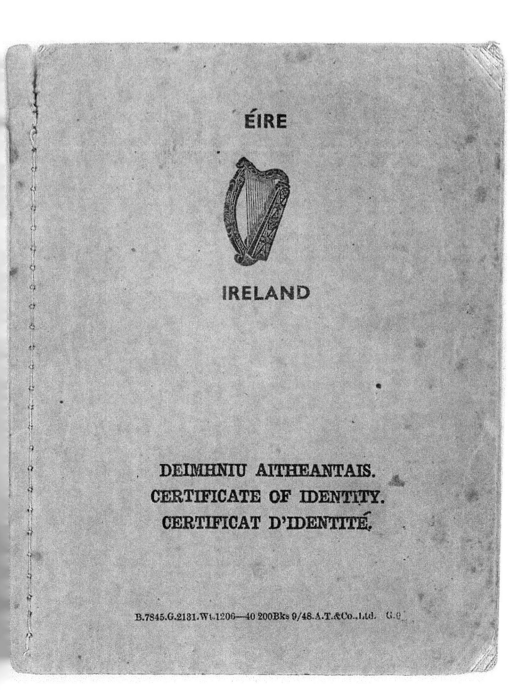

ÉIRE

IRELAND

DEIMHNIU AITHEANTAIS.
CERTIFICATE OF IDENTITY.
CERTIFICAT D'IDENTITÉ.

B.7845.G.2131.Wt.1206—40 200Bks 9/48.A.T.&Co.,Ltd. G.6

Cover of Istvan Stahler's Certificate of Identity for the newly established Republic of Ireland. (IS)

2

An dáta ar a rughadh / Date of Birth / Date de naissance	6. 5. 1938
An áit in a rugadh / Place of birth / Lieu de naissance	Michalovce, Czechoslovakia
Náisiúntacht bhunaidh / Nationality of origin / Nationalité d'origine	UNCERTAIN.
Sloinneadh agus ainmneacha a athar / Surname and forenames of father / Nom de famille et prénoms du père	Stasting-Stahler, Josef.
Sloinneadh agus ainmneacha a mhathar / Surname and forenames of mother / Nom de famille et prénoms de la mère	hot known
Ainm a mhná (fir) chéile / Name of wife (husband) / Nom de la femme (mari)	
Ainmneacha clainne / Names of children / Noms des enfants	

Comhnaí i gcoigrich roimhe seo / Former residence abroad / Ancien domicile à l'étranger	Czechoslovakia
Comhnaí fé láthair in Éirinn / Present residence in Ireland / Résidence actuelle dans l'Irlande	Clonyn Castle, Delvin, Co. Westmeath.
Deimhniú clárathachta / Police Registration Certificate / Certificat d'enregistrement délivré par la Police	nil

COMHARTHAI.
DESCRIPTION.
SIGNALEMENT.

Aoirde / Height / Taille	4 ft. 10 ins.	Aghaidh / Face / Visage	Oval

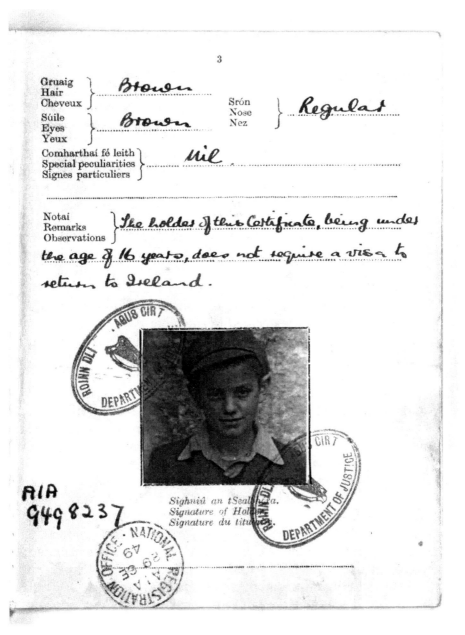

Gruaig Hair Cheveux }	*Brown*	
Súile Eyes Yeux }	*Brown*	Srón Nose Nez } *Regular*

Comhartaí fé leith
Special peculiarities
Signes particuliers } *nil*

Notaí
Remarks
Observations } *The holder of this Certificate, being under the age of 16 years, does not require a visa to return to Ireland.*

AIA
9498237

Sighniú an tSealbhóra.
Signature of Holder.
Signature du titulaire.

The details inside the Certificate, stamped on his departure

Gyorgy Prissegi

Gyorgy Prissegi's birth date is missing on the Collective Visa. In January 1949 he went on aliyah with the first group to leave the castle and I lost track of him. Then in 2003 an email reached me beginning "You will not know my name" and signed "Jerry". It was a great delight to learn that he was the young boy who had been called Gyorgy Prissegi by the Slovak family who had cared for him. Jerry's plan was to visit Britain and Ireland and fill in some of the details of his story but sudden illness in the family obliged him to cancel that trip and no more news came. In August 2005, I phoned the family in California and learned further details from his wife.

Gyorgy was born in Tešín on September 6th 1941 when anti-Semitic measures were very severe. Eva, his mother, was living as a gentile with false papers. The following year all young Jewish women were being rounded up for deportation. Eva became anxious because the Hlinka Guard had doubts about her papers so one night she decided to leave her baby in the care of a local Evangelical priest. That same night she was deported to Auschwitz. The priest placed the baby with a non-Jewish family. Some time later Eva's Catholic neighbours, the Prissegi's, found out where he was and went to visit him. They were so shocked by the poor state he was in that they took him home with them. They looked after him with their daughter, caring for him as their own child, at tremendous risk to themselves and their family. Gyorgy's birth certificate names Mrs Prissegi as godmother so it is evident she had already been a close friend of Eva.

The Engel family, who were Jewish and lived nearby, were also good friends. They managed to keep in touch with the Prissegis after they had fled to join the Partisans and even after the Prissegi family had moved to Bratislava. And they contributed to Gyorgy's keep.

Thanks to the Engel family an astonishing relic has survived the war and is now a treasured possession of Gyorgy and his family. And here it is: a postcard sent by Eva from Birkenau in which she gives no indication of her horrendous situation

Eva's postcard is reproduced on page 270. Here is a translation:

May 15, 1943 Birkenau

Dearest Engl Family,

I have already written to you once but even though I have received no answer. I am once again writing to you. You are the only people that I still have. How are you? Hopefully you are all well.

How is my beloved child? Do you have any news of my Hanri? I am well and often think of the nice times that I spent when I was with you. How is Laci? How come he doesn't write to me? Has he forgotten me completely? Please write about everything and I will write back promptly. I will be very happy. All of you at home – stay healthy.

Many regards and hand-blown kisses. Write me everything about my beloved Hanri and kiss him for me.

Eva Gisela Pomeranz

Nr. 7747 Block 11.

Gyorgy's mother miraculously survived. She must have been a very strong young woman, both mentally and physically. After liberation she was sent by the Red Cross to Sweden and she wrote to the Engels. They were able to tell her that Gyorgy was safe with the Prissegi family in Bratislava. They sent Eva a photo showing the boy wearing a sailor suit she had sent him.

Eva left Sweden to join her cousin in Palestine but her ship was impounded by the British. At the time of Rabbi Schonfeld's arrival in Bratislava she was being held in a camp for illegal immigrants in Cyprus. Gyorgy learned years later that she remained there until the end of the British Mandate which finally occurred some four weeks after he had arrived in England. Some time later the Engel family also settled in Israel. Gyorgy is still in touch with their son.

One of the Jewish relief organisations insisted on moving Gyorgy to Rabbi Frieder's centre, Ohel David. Considerable pressure was put on the Prissegi family to let him go. This was a severe shock for them all. Gyorgy suddenly lost the only family he knew. He recalls a few incidents from that time: that two men came to fetch him and that he had a little suitcase and was afraid to let it go. A letter in the Archives shows he was at Ohel David Children's Home when Rabbi Schonfeld came and arranged to take him with others to Eire. Gyorgy still remembers that at the

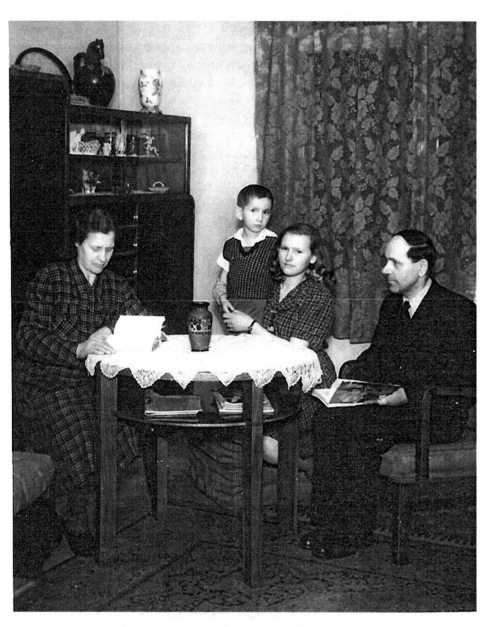

Gyorgy with the Prissegi family in 1946. (GP)

Gyorgy on a rocking horse. (GP)

Abs:

Rückantwort nur über die Reichsvereinigung der Juden in Deutschland Berlin-Charlottenburg 2, ...str. 158

Pomeranz Gizela
Nr. 7747
Block 11

Lager-Birkenau
O.S. bei Neu-Berün.

Schreibt mir bitte alles über meinen l. Hansi, und Küssi Ihm ab von mir. Ews.

Postkarte

Jedweder Postverkehr mit der Slowakei ... lich durch Vermittlung Judezentrale in Pressburg, gestattet!

Herrn

Michal Bučko
für Engl.
Firma „Eco"

Bratislava

Rečna 2.

Slowakei

Birkenau, 15.V.43.

Liebste Familie Engl!

Ich habe schon einmahl an Euch geschrieben, habe aber keine Antwort bekommen, trotzdem schreibe ich noch einmal an Euch. Ihr seit doch die einzigen mir naheschtehenden menschen, die ich noch habe. Wie geht es Euch? Hoffentlich seit Ihr alle gesund. Wie geht es meinem l. Kind? Habt Ihr welche Nachricht von meinem Hansi?

Ich bin gesund, und denke sehr oft an die schöne Zeiten, die ich bei Euch verlebt habe.

Wie geht es dem Laci? Warum schreibt er mir nicht? Hat er schon ganz auf mich vergessen? Schreibt mir bitte alles ausführlich u. gebt Antwort. Ich werde mich sehr, sehr freuen. Bleibet alle zu Hause gesund.

---

270   The postcard from Gyorgy's mother in Birkenau Concentration Camp,
       May 15th, 1943. (GP)

Castle he slept on the second floor overlooking a big grassy area. He has a recollection of an older girl looking after him who was quite strict! That was Lily Lowinger, now living in Jerusalem.

Mrs Eppel arranged for Gyorgy to be circumcised and gave him her father's name. He still has the prayer book given him on that occasion inscribed "Avrom Dov".

He went with the first contingent to leave the Castle on *aliyah* in January 1949. He remembers being seasick on the voyage. When he arrived in Israel a man in uniform picked him up and introduced himself as his Dad, his new step-father. Finally he was reunited with the mother he had lost in infancy. She patiently built up a strong and lasting bond with him - but she told him nothing at all about his early life or about what she had endured during the war years.

I learned more details from an article the family sent to me written by Michael, Gyorgy's son, for the "Los Angeles Times" on Holocaust Memorial Day in April 2002. It was entitled "Honor Heroes Past and Present". Michael said that his grandmother was captured by the Nazis and sent to Auschwitz. For three years she endured horrors impossible to imagine until the liberation in 1945. Before she was deported she had made an agreement with the Prissegi family to take care of her only son, his father, then only nine months old.

The Prissegis risked their property, their peace of mind, and their very lives. Yet despite these tremendous perils, his father was welcomed as an integral part of their household amid the chaos engulfing Europe. To this day he has some fond, if somewhat faded, memories of picking cherries off a tree, carrying beer mugs to friends and family visiting the house, and of Santa Claus coming to his kindergarten. While other Jewish children were being slaughtered by the thousands, his father enjoyed a happy and safe early childhood thanks to this his adoptive family.

Shortly after the war the Jewish Agency came to take him to a camp for the reunification of families. The family who raised him as their own lost him in a matter of days. He will never forget the valour of those heroes.

Some twenty-three years later, at his father's wedding, a rather unusual gift arrived: a pair of gold rings, the wedding bands of the couple that saved his father's life. They and their daughter were poverty-stricken, living by then behind the Iron Curtain.

Gyorgy with Mrs. Prissegi wearing the sailor suit sent by his mother.
(GP)

Soon after the war ended the Prissegi and Engel families together again relaxing in their garden with Gyorgy. (GP)

Gyorgy at Clonyn Castle. (GP)

Gyorgy with "big sister" Lily Lowinger and two other girls at Clonyn Castle. (GP)

They could have sold the rings to buy a little comfort but instead they passed them on to the son they briefly had, could not keep but could never forget. They were simple, unadorned ordinary rings, but the people who had worn them were anything but and those rings are a reminder of those righteous people.

Gyorgy's mother kept in touch with the Prissegi family until her death in 2007 and his wife Rita continues to write to Magda, the Prissegi's daughter. Gyorgy and Rita visited her in 2009 "and I show our boys the rings and tell them what we know about their father's early life".

Gyorgy and Rita had a joyful reunion with foster sister Magda Pichler, née Prissegen in Bratislava in 2009. (GP)

Anna Katscher

Anna Katscher was born in 1936 her brother Ivan in 1934. The Reunion of the Slovak children was Anna's idea. It was also her idea that people write up their memoirs to exchange on that occasion; and it was Anna who persuaded the present owner of Clonyn Castle to allow us to visit there following the Reunion.

This volume would never have appeared without her initiative. To my great regret she died in 2006 before it could be published, and her brother died before her. At the stone-setting at her grave a great crowd turned up to honour her memory. People there said they had never seen so large a gathering for such an occasion. She was respected for her initiative, her determination and the many skills that she demonstrated – in business, in charity work, as a skilled dressmaker, a devoted mother and grandmother. Here is what she wrote for the Reunion Brochure.

Is it a coincidence or was it *bescher* (predestined) that my grandaughter is six today and my story starts in 1942 when I was six? I got a watch for my birthday, but I did not have it for long; for when it broke I gave it to our watchmaker (a Jewish one) to have it repaired. The next thing I remember was that suddenly we were fleeing at night by foot. We stole over the border from Nitra in Slovakia to Komaron in Hungary where some relatives put us up for a few days; and then my late brother and I went to Békéscsaba to my grandparents (maternal) and my parents went into hiding for three years in Budapest.

However, two years later, when Hitler occupied Hungary, my grandparents could not keep us any longer. By some miracle we were found places in families of Righteous Gentiles. I have been in touch with mine to this very day. Mr Howarth died some time ago but Mrs Howarth died only late last year. They knew the danger of having me, especially as I used to get up to all sorts of mischief. My brother did not have such a happy time in Yugoslavia whereas I called my family mother and father. I was 8 at the time. I started off in Szeged where I put my Christian family in danger a few times. Once I happened to meet my real mother in the street and of course I stopped my pretence for a moment to be with her. That was the only contact I had with my family till after we were liberated.

When the Russians invaded from the south, my family fled to the north with me, with the Germans, as "my father" was a journalist. They settled in Sopron and I stayed with Mrs Howarth's sister in Kophaza from time to time as they had a daughter a bit older than myself. There I learnt another language, Croat. In this village I saw Jewish transports passing through on foot. Sometimes they stayed in the big barns at the back of the houses overnight - or even longer. "My family" used to invite groups of 6 or 7 in the evening and feed them and this is something that always stays in my mind. There was a watchmaker amongst them to whom the whole village brought their clocks to be repaired. I was taken to Sopron for holidays then, and when I came back to the village the watchmaker was gone.

We were very lucky to survive the war. I was only liberated in May 1945. On June 10th I was reunited in Békéscsaba with my parents and grandparents and my late brother and other family members. It was the day of a cousin's birthday. My parents went back to Slovakia. My brother and I stayed another year in Hungary with our grandparents. How my parents survived is another story.

We then moved in with our paternal grandparents in Slovakia in the town of Nitra. Everybody had to start from scratch. Some members of our family, who had survived but lost their families, also came to live with us. The *parnose* side (the business of earning a living) lay all on the shoulders of my father. In 1947 my paternal grandfather died; then my grandmother packed up and emigrated to America to join her daughter and family who were fortunate to get there before the war.

My brother and I joined our parents. By then I was 10 years old. I went to school and remember mainly the language problems. I had forgotten my Slovak completely and in addition we had to learn Russian. My first trip in Nitra was to the Jewish watchmaker to ask for my watch which I had given him four years earlier. He said he never had it! However who did I meet there repairing watches, but the man from Kophaza. I had to tell him how I happened to know him as he took no notice of me at the time.

My father went to Prague, a long journey from Nitra, in order to get permission to emigrate to Canada. He was refused on the grounds of being a "communist". Today this is easier to understand after what had happened to the Russian Refuseniks. Naturally he was very disappointed. He walked the streets for a while and met someone he recognised. Picture that - two young men, who went to *yeshiva* together almost 20 years earlier, meeting by chance in Prague! It was Dr Schonfeld. That was how it happened that we were on the Kindertransport that Dr Schonfeld put together of 150 children (85% were orphans). It was the last one that he ever organised and it was lucky for us that my brother, my cousin **Judith Mannheimer** and I were all on it.

We spent *Pesach* in London then we had to go to Ireland because the British authorities would not let us stay here. We lived in a castle and

I loved it. It was like a dream holiday, not a school. I was again lucky to come back to England after 6 months as most of the others had to stay there for longer. In London, Dr Schonfeld arranged for me to stay in a girls' hostel for two years in the house that is now the Beis Ya'acov seminary. I remember we had no hot water and I used to mend electric fuses. I attended the Avigdor School and this time had to struggle with four new languages, English, Hebrew, French and Latin. On top of this our schoolmates at first looked down on us as refugees but later on I became the best of friends with most of them.

The other girls in the hostel were all much older. I was the youngest and all the girls were very close friends. This was the only family most of them had and **Séndi** was in charge. Now she is Rebbitzin Pels; then she was a girl of 18. I went to school while others, much older, went to work and some got married. Everybody was busy telling their stories of survival and when I told mine, especially about the watchmaker, one girl, Hani, exclaimed, "That is my brother!" It turned out that he went to America, so I never met him again, although Hani was going to arrange it. (I hope to see Hani again, at the Reunion).

Some of the girls got married and others left England and the hostel had to close. Again it was Dr Schonfeld who found me a family with whom to stay. They were his best friends and they were very special. How did I deserve them? I ask myself often. The family was that of Dayan and Dr Grunfeld. She was my headmistress at the time in school and also taught me Jewish Studies. They had five children of their own and I was number six. I can tell you that it was the only time in my childhood that I received real parental love. I lived with them for three years altogether and I saw quite a lot of Dr Schonfeld as he was always popping in to the Grunfelds, most often at two in the morning!

My parents left Slovakia in 1949 for Vienna, Austria and my brother and I used to visit them in the summer holidays. When I finished my O-Levels my brother and I returned to live with them in Vienna. But that is not the end of my story - as you can see I have lived here now for almost 34 years - since I got married. How come? Again thanks to Dr Schonfeld.

In 1958 on my way back from the States I was again invited to stay with the Grunfelds. I felt it was also my home. I came before *Yom Kippur* and during the middle days of the festival of *Succoth* I got a phone call - of course, late at night. Who could know I was in London, I thought? It was Dr Schonfeld and he had a *shidduch* for me! The rest is history. Dr Schonfeld always kept in touch with us, every year a *Rosh Hashanah* card arrived and he came to all our *simches* and made us feel very special.

Can you imagine what would have happened to all the children he rescued before and after the war had he not looked after us? He was the Principal of the Avigdor and Hasmonean Schools and that task occupied most of his time. He was also the Rabbi of the Adath synagogues. He walked every *Shabbos* from his Highgate home to Stamford Hill until he suffered a stroke and then he was not the same man any more. No one else achieved what he did. To me he was the greatest human being I have ever known and I continue to thank him all the days of my life.

Anna Katscher with her cousin Judith Mannheimer on the left. (JM)

Judith Mannheimer

Judith was a cousin of Anna Katscher. Older members of their family were closely involved with Nitra Yeshiva and had long known the Schonfeld family. Rabbi Schonfeld showed a special interest in Judith that she greatly appreciated. She did not go to Ireland. Her visa allowed her to stay in London.

When the war broke out I was a little girl in Slovakia, the youngest of six children. I was born in 1937. We lived with our parents, Eugene (Yona) and Dora Mannheimer in Piestany, a spa then and now, famous for treating rheumatism and arthritis. My father was a business man; he owned a dry goods store. My mother stayed at home and provided for us a beautiful, warm and loving environment.

Over the course of time the Nazis infiltrated our peaceful life with edicts, restrictions and anti-Semitic overtures. In 1942 we were rounded up and sent to Zilina with few belongings. It was a deportation centre from where many people were sent to Auschwitz. I was too young to remember it very clearly. Luckily my parents could afford to buy us our freedom and we left to live as non-Jews with fake passports. But of course that was a difficult thing for Jews to do. My father had no beard but my mother covered her hair and we observed the Sabbath in secret. We children went to school but otherwise we lived very withdrawn lives. Perhaps this is what made the neighbours suspicious because one morning there was a knock on our door. It was the Hlinka Guards. I was at home with my parents; my brothers and sisters were at school. The Guards wanted to see our passports. They said there was something wrong with them and took them to their offices. My brother Robi and sister Rena came home for lunch and soon thereafter I went to nursery. During that afternoon the Guards returned. They took away my parents and older brother and sister.

Word quickly spread that the officials were searching for the four remaining children. The Jewish community hid us through their underground network. I was in hiding with my brother Bubi. In the meantime word got round that if we wanted to see our parents we should go to the railroad station where they would be on a train going to Auschwitz. So early one morning the two of us went there and saw my parents and my two older siblings board the last cattle car of the transport. Of course I became hysterical. I screamed for my parents until a Gestapo soldier, with a gun in hand, said if I kept on screaming and yelling I, too, would board that train. My instinct for survival overcame my hysteria and I stopped crying. In silence, terror and fear, we watched the train pull away taking with it my youth, my security, my foundation. I never saw my parents again.

My aunt, my father's oldest sister, lived near Nitra. Her name was Giselle Katscher, *née* Mannheimer. She was **Anna Katscher's** grandmother. She was a founder of Nitra *Yeshiva* and survived the war to become a mainstay of its post-war establishment at Mount Kisco, in upstate New York. Her family had been friends of Rabbi Schonfeld for years. She employed many peasants to work the farm that she and my uncle owned. When she heard what had happened to our parents she made arrangements with local peasants to pick us up and bring us to her home. Plans would be made to escort us across the border to another uncle and aunt in Budapest, Hungary which was still a neutral country.

I remember how my brother Bubi and I were dressed like peasant children to cross the border. Peasants hired by my aunt escorted us. We slowly worked our way in the cold and snow. We stayed over night at a peasant's house. He was to take us into Hungary next day but I overheard him say that he would take only my brother. They wanted to keep me with them. I was petrified. I could not sleep. As the morning rays peered through I grasped my brother's hand and would not let go for a second. I cried and begged that they take me, too. Finally, in the freezing cold and deep snow we crossed the border and made our way to our aunt and uncle's apartment in Budapest. But when we arrived there we were rudely disillusioned. Our aunt refused to take us in! She said that anyone who took in illegal immigrants was subject to the death penalty. We children spoke no Hungarian, only Czech and German. Neighbours would soon discover this and report us to the authorities. The peasants said they had been paid only to take us to this address and promptly left us alone in the street. The police picked us up and I remember that our heads were shaved and we were thrown into a prison cell. It was the same cell where later I learned Hanna Szenes[4] was shot. We were terrified.

But there were some Jews in Budapest who were not afraid of helping bereft Jewish children. A watchmaker called Tannebaum, active in the Jewish underground, heard about us and succeeded in freeing us and took us to his home for a few hours. It was *Chanukah*, we lit candles, had wonderful homemade food and most importantly - they promised that they would work to get us released from the prison. Soon thereafter, we were indeed freed and placed in the care of Marci and Ilonka Stern, the owner of a famous *kosher* restaurant in Budapest. Everyone knew Stern Bacsi's (basci means uncle) *cholent*. He had very good connections in high circles and was said to be on friendly terms with Admiral Horthy, the

"My mother with her six children. I am the youngest." (JM).

Bella, Moshe (Morris), Asher (Arthur), Rena (Renka), Robi   *283*
(Robert) and Judith the youngest. (JM)

Regent of Hungary. The result was that Stern and his wife adopted me and I immediately called them Anyu and Apu (Mother and Father). Their only child had died many years before. I asked them to take in my brother, too, as I could still never let go of Bubi. So connected was I to him that I would even follow him into the bathroom. He was my security blanket.

Then we heard that Budapest's largest synagogue, the Dohany Ucca, had become an emergency centre for refugees. There we found my brother Turi and my sister Bella and all four of us came to live with the Stern couple. I remember the big commotion made when the Belzer Rebbe stayed at the Stern's house. He, too, had taken refuge in Budapest. People queued in the street to see him. He only stayed a night or two and the Sterns gave a big dinner in his honour. I was allowed to stay up because they wanted me to drink from the Rebbe's *kiddush* cup. The Rabbi told *bacsi* Stern that my big brother Bubi, who was then about 9 or 10 years old, should go to Israel before the war reached Hungary. It was arranged for Bubi to be sent but it was a perilous and difficult journey. Eventually both my brothers did end up in Israel. My sister Bella was sent to live with another aunt, Mella Itzkowitz in Békéscsaba, Hungary.

When the Nazis entered Budapest in 1944 I went into hiding with the Sterns into a property protected by the Swiss Red Cross known as "The Glass House". It was a glass factory, turned into a safe house. As long as we stayed there we could come to no harm, although there were many close calls. Quarters were tight and depressing. We lived underground in a basement which resembled a tunnel, long and cave like, and full of dampness, cold and moisture. That is how I contracted lung disease - but also survived the war.

Unfortunately, after the war was over Stern *bacsi*'s wife was diagnosed with cancer and passed away. Soon after he married again but his new wife did not want me, his adopted daughter. Mr Stern made arrangements for me to go to a sanatorium, Villa Sylvia, in the Tatra Mountains in Czechoslovakia to recover. After that, I was sent to Ohel David, Rabbi Frieder's Children's Home at Nové Mesto Nad Váhom. While there we got our education at the convent, a Catholic elementary school. The nuns tried to persuade Jewish children to accept Christianity but if a child refused the nuns respected that decision. It was at that point that Rabbi Dr Schonfeld entered my life.

The Katschers had learned that Dr Schonfeld had come to Czechoslovakia and was offering to take war orphans back with him to England. My relatives told him about me and arranged for me and two of my cousins to be included in his group. I met Dr Schonfeld at the

The four who survived – Bella, Morris, Arthur and Judith (JM)

Children's Home and was immediately taken with him. I travelled to London with my cousin Anna, the **Krauz** brothers, **Tom** and **Pál**, and my friend Eva Steiner. And from then on Dr Schonfeld assumed responsibility for me. I was sent to live in a hostel for orphans in Stamford Hill while those with surviving parents went to Ireland. For school, I was enrolled at the Avigdor High School run by Dr Schonfeld, where our headmistress was Dr Judith Grunwald. Dr Schonfeld continued to fascinate me. He reminded me of Stern *bacsi* who also had that indefinable something we call charisma. But Stern *bacsi* was a much older man and his beard was white. Dr Schonfeld had a little red Van Dyke beard; his eyes sparkled and he had a warm smile. He would put his hand on my shoulder and somehow I felt as though there was some invisible tie between us – there was something very special about it. He said: "What is your name?" I said "Judith Mannheimer". And he said: "Judith, from now on you will be very well taken care of."

And from that moment and throughout the years ahead he never forgot my name. I felt as if I had become one of his favourite little girls. He had a way of noticing me among a whole group of children in the auditorium at the roll call taken every day before school began. Whenever he entered the room we would all rise out of respect for him and as he passed he would wink at me and say "And how are you this morning, Judith?" making me feel I was one of the most important children in the group. Once there was some special occasion at Covent Garden. I was selected to go on stage as an example of an orphan girl and I presented flowers to the guest-of-honour.

Later I was transferred to live with the Warhaftig family in Golders Green and went to the Hasmonean Grammar School, founded by Dr Schonfeld. The headmistress was Mrs Herman, a kindly woman whom I liked very much. Dr Schonfeld often came there. Every time he saw me he would say "Ah, Judith Mannheimer, how are you today? Any problems"? I was so impressed by this. To me, a child, sensitive and insecure, he was the most beautiful person. My world had collapsed but Dr Schonfeld made me feel ten feet tall and someone very special. It is thanks to him that I grew up feeling good about myself. He gave me confidence when I needed it so badly.

Years later I came back to London from America on a visit. One of my Katscher cousins took me to see Dr Schonfeld again and said to him: "Would you remember this young lady?" And Dr Schonfeld said: "How could I forget? It's Judith Mannheimer". Just like that! I was by then a married woman with children of my own. Some years later on I met him by chance in a street in Israel where I hardly expected he would recognise me. I stopped and said: "Dr. Schonfeld, how are you?" and he said: "Let me see who this is. I know that face. Of course, it's Judith Mannheimer!"

I owe more than just my physical survival to Dr Solomon Schonfeld. Had I stayed on in Slovakia I do not know whether I would have been able to hold on to my Judaism or even to life itself. I was in desperate need for someone to uphold me and to show me the way ahead. Dr Schonfeld came into my life just when I was most needing support. He gave me that kindness, that love which no one else was giving me at that point. All the people who had meant the most to me were gone. I felt totally alone and I think Dr Schonfeld sensed it. He gave me the feeling he was glad to know me. Whenever he said "Why, it's Judith Mannheimer!" I felt as if the sun had begun to shine on me again and that after all, God had been very good to me. If today I am a mature woman, a proud Jewess, the mother of three beautiful children who love their Judaism, I owe it all to Rabbi Dr Solomon Schonfeld.

My last encounter with Dr Schonfeld was after he had become very ill and it was not to be face to face. I came as a representative of those children from his transports who had settled in the United States and Canada. In his absence, I presented a book, lovingly written for him in his honour. How I wanted to tell him that I had become a grandmother and that there were now two generations of my descendants who were growing up hearing tales of my survival and about my gratitude to him! His memory will live with me for ever.

Judith at the Hasmonean School. (JM)

Judith with her foster sister Helen Warhaftig in London. (JM)   289

Judith on holiday with Eva Steiner also from the Bratislava group,
who was placed with a family in Cardiff. (JM)

Judith with Moses Schonfeld in the USA. He was an international journalist at the UN and a brother of Rabbi Schonfeld. (JM)

Dezider Rosenfeld

Dezider was a member of the Jubilee Reunion Committee and has written his own story. In 2007 he told me of his great joy that not only had he children and grandchildren but he had become a great-grandfather!

I was only four-and-a-half in 1942 so there is not a great deal I can remember from those times and what I recall now may not be accurate. It was necessary then to take careful measures to avoid being caught and deported by the Nazis and taken onwards to Concentration Camps. I do remember my father took every step possible to avoid our being interred in the local ghetto. That was in Dobšiná where we were residing at the time. To enhance my chances of survival he placed me with a peasant and his family just outside the town and close to the Hungarian border. I remember going with him in his horse-drawn wagon to the fields and having cheese and corn bread for lunch. He was not unkind but he did not have a bed for me to sleep in so when the Gestapo was combing the area to catch evaders I was hidden in the oven of some defunct brickworks. Indeed it was from that factory that I was liberated by the Russian Army. The advancing troops gave me real bread that I had not tasted for years. It was such a delight although it was tainted with paraffin!

Those years of the war, 1942-45, were like hell for me but I was very fortunate to have remained both alive and sane. The terrible atrocities, the shelling, the shooting, the bombing and above all the constant fear of the dreaded Gestapo are hard to describe. For thirty years after these experiences I kept getting nightmares, awakening covered in sweat. It is this fear of war that keeps me putting off the idea of residing in Israel.

When the war was over my father came to fetch me. He apparently escaped *en route* to Auschwitz and managed to join the Partisans. Although he was wounded in some daring action he remained with the resistance movement.

Some time late in 1945 we moved north-west to Cheb near Karlsbad (Karlovy Vary) on the German border. My father found employment there and we had a decent house on Skolska Ulica [street]. I attended a local Czech school for a while; my mother tongue was Slovak and I knew some German but I managed with the local language. During 1947 a local man, Dr Weisz, persuaded my parents to send me to Bratislava where I could benefit from Jewish studies in addition to secular schooling. It took me a long time to come to terms with being alone once more and I felt very homesick. I lived at the Jewish Internat and attended a local Slovak school; in addition on Sundays and some evenings I went to *cheder*. Although oranges and bananas I only imagined in dreams - and an apple was a luxury - basic foods were provided by "The Joint".

It was in Bratislava that I met Rabbi Dr Schonfeld. He offered me a place on his transport of children to Eire via London. I was included only because a boy from Zlati Mikolas had dropped out. I told him my parents lived 12 hours train journey away and were hard to contact. He reassured me he had already obtained my father's consent and all that was needed was my "yes". This I gladly gave. We must have spoken in Hungarian or German because as far as I am aware Dr Schonfeld did not speak either Czech or Slovak. I am truly grateful to Dr Schonfeld. If he had not accepted me, I would most probably have landed up in some *kibbutz* in Israel and become a secular Jew. So the continuity of Jewish practice in our family today and in the future is due to this decision by Dr Schonfeld.

It was during the week before Passover in 1948 that we boarded the night train from Bratislava to Prague. There some more children, including the Fischers, joined the group. I possessed no passport. The only document I had was an identity card and this was torn from my grasp by a terrific draught in the train corridor. I was almost certain I would be taken off the train by the police when we reached Cheb. I was not too concerned; for if that happened I would at least be home again. When we reached there my parents were waiting on the platform to see me off. They had been told exactly which train I was on.

During the journey from Prague Dr Schonfeld told me to remember that I was born in Trnava and not, as was the truth, in Trenčín. This was, I suppose, the place named on the papers of the boy I had replaced and why he also gave me another date of birth. When we reached Cheb the police boarded the train. Two armed officers came into our compartment. One was inspecting our meagre possessions, the other checking passports. After I had opened my suitcase, I sat there in the corner dreading being asked to show my passport; but *by the grace of G-d* I was overlooked and the officer moved on. I felt a great relief.

The journey was an eye-opener for me: the vastness of the sea - not being able to see the farther shore. The widest waterway I had ever seen had been the Danube River. Then there was the first sight of a red double-decker London bus. We arrived there just before *Pesach*. Some of our group were sent to spend the week of the Festival in Brighton. I stayed with others at Woodberry Down Hostel, Manor House, run by Rabbi Schonfeld's community. We had a happy *Yom Tov* there and I enjoyed the

Seder nights led by some personality - he may have been a brother of Dr Schonfeld. I recall the sheer size of Finsbury Park and the streets and the tidy shops were most impressive.

After *Pesach* we travelled by coaches to Holyhead and from there took a boat to Dublin. I remember when we arrived in Dublin being served cornflakes and tea with milk and finding it very strange. I liked milk in coffee and cocoa but never had had it in tea. Clonyn Castle was most impressive. The grounds and the fields around it and the racecourse were to me like paradise. I was very happy at the Castle. I appreciated a bit of mothering by **Blanka** and **Séndi**; and I very much enjoyed the activities and outings arranged by Rabbi Cohen. He was my favourite *madrich* and I always think of him fondly. Schooling there was very limited. There were difficulties for the staff because so many different languages were spoken by us children; but they did their utmost to make us happy and care for our needs. *Shabat* and *Yom Tov* services were beautiful and Rabbi Cohen had a very pleasant and melodious voice.

Obviously girls and boys had separate dorms but often during the night we would make raids on each other, smearing our faces with black shoe polish and squirting toothpaste on to the girls' hair while they were asleep. Then there was the trick of turning back the top sheet so that when the exhausted occupant tried to climb into bed they found themselves stuck there.

Dr Schonfeld came over to see us a couple of times and on one occasion I had the privilege of playing a game of table tennis with him. We had plenty of football and running and jumping. The older boys made up a football team and beat the local village team from Delvin. I remember our goalkeeper; he was a real acrobat and he stopped almost any ball. On the whole it was like being at a holiday camp.

A year later, in the spring of 1949 most of the group had dispersed. Those of us who were left were moved to Dun Laoghaire just before *Pesach*. We used to go by train to school in Dublin but found the lingo incomprehensible. We had to learn some kind of rhyme or poetry by heart but I could not understand it at all.

In the late summer Dr Schonfeld arranged for some of us to return to London. There I was enrolled in the Ahavat Torah Jewish Boarding School, now defunct. In the three and a half years I spent there, I caught up with some of the basic education I had missed, both Hebrew and secular. When I was about fourteen and a half, I moved on to join the Schneider *Yeshiva* in Clapton. There I studied *Gemara* and the *Shulchan Aruch* for about four and a half years till 1951 when I left to begin making a living and fend for myself.

294

I applied for British nationality as I had no desire to return to Czechoslovakia and wanted to make the United Kingdom my permanent home. I was interviewed and asked about my journey to these shores. I told them about all the countries we had travelled through until we reached Ostende in Belgium and how we had taken the ferry to cross to Dover. They heard me out then suddenly asked: "But where are your identity papers?" I told them the whole story: how I had met Rabbi Dr Schonfeld, that he had a mission to save children from further hardship under the Communists, children who had already survived the terrible sufferings inflicted on them by the Germans. I explained that I was offered a place on his transport at the last moment, there was no time to obtain a passport, that I had only had an identity card and that it had flown out of my hand on the way. They found my story quite incredible but duly accepted it and granted my application.

Artur Weinberger

Artur Weinberger was 11 in 1948. He was the Israeli co-ordinator for the Reunion which he attended. He contributed his story for that event and so did Emanuel, his younger brother.

There are several events of the Holocaust years that stand out in my memory. I was born in Cracow in 1937 to a Jewish religious family of the upper middle class. Our grandfathers were both industrialists. One had a sizeable refinery producing gasoline, paraffin and other fuels for heating and lighting; these were pre-electricity days in many parts of Europe. My other grandfather had a factory producing bricks, tiles and iron products for the building industry. These people, their children and grandchildren, all of a sudden became like hunted animals and had to learn to survive in the wilds of unfriendly countries. During that critical period, from 1942 till 1945, I was 5 to 8 years old.

My earliest traumatic experience came when the Gestapo barged into our luxurious home in Cracow. They interrogated me about my large collection of keys; collecting keys was my hobby. They ordered us to move within 48 hours and took my father for further questioning. My father was a Hungarian citizen and as such we could continue living outside the Ghetto. Our parents knew what the Concentration Camps were all about and so we moved to a small village and lived as non-Jews on forged papers. Within eyesight and earshot lived a high-ranking German officer. When drunk he used his Jewish servants for target practice, and when we heard him we rolled under our beds.

As the German searches became more thorough we succeeded after several dangerous failures to steal across the border to Budapest to join my father's family. There we lived as Polish war refugees. My father, being very much aware of future dangers, sought and found a family to adopt me. He wanted to be sure that some scion of the family would survive. The Christian household he chose was that of a very attractive widow who had been married to a Jewish relative of ours.

This woman owned a typewriter repair business and had blond hair. Being a "Merry Widow" she had several highly-placed boyfriends who would visit her and sometimes bring me candies and toys. I was seven years old at this time. Going to school was out of the question as my identity would be discovered; so I just played all day and developed into a rather skilled street boy. I played with the local children and went to church regularly. The Ghetto was not far from where we lived, but I was smart enough to keep a goodly distance from it and avoided all contact with Jews. Toward the end of the war we went scavenging and I chanced to come close to the Ghetto. A group of Jewish children there spotted me; one called "Look, there is a Jewish boy. Why are you outside?" And I moved out of sight very quickly.

What I can say about non-Jews we met during our wanderings is quite trite. There were good people and there were rotten people; the same goes for Jews, of course. One thing was certain: you kept your identity and money secret and did not trust anyone. More specifically the woman I hid with in Hungary, and her servants, knew my identity and my religion but kept it secret; but the people we stayed with in Poland robbed us - especially their sons - but for some reason did not give us away. It helped that at this time we had permission to live out of the Ghetto as Hungarian citizens. In Hungary itself, after the Nazi take-over, I once made the mistake of asking a neighbor for a dairy dish towel. They called the Gestapo right away. Some robbed us while others supported us with food, money etc, when we were in real need.

My family moved to a secluded area but was soon caught by the Gestapo. My mother spent a year in Auschwitz; my father escaped from a Camp train and wandered like a hunted animal all over Slovakia and Hungary never knowing where he would find his next bed or his next meal. I have to emphasize we were a middle-class family and hardly equipped to cope with these ordeals. My sister roamed around Budapest, hiding in Wallenberg's houses.[3] My little brother Emanuel was also hidden by non-Jews.

After the war my immediate family was miraculously reunited. We settled in Košice. Schools resumed and we returned to a more civilized existence, I had only two years of schooling in the years 1946 and 1947, up to the age of eleven and hardly any after that. Most of my tuition was accomplished with the help of private tutors whom my parents could barely afford. I cannot fathom to this day where we all found the energies to survive and to rebuild our lives.

Then in 1948 came another parting from our parents when we had barely come together again. Normal life was interrupted this time to escape from the Communist menace. The German horror had been defeated. Now we fled in the guise of war orphans with the transport organized by Rabbi Dr Schonfeld of *Blessed Memory*. We headed for England and then to Ireland, that blessed isle where we could behave like regular children and human beings. After about a year at Clonyn Castle, a period well described by my brother and others, I was placed in the Schneider School (*yeshiva*) in London. There we learned to read and write English, a little arithmetic, and a bare minimum of secular studies. After three years - I was by then 15 - I grew tired of all the religious study. So I went to work by day and studied for the GCE by self-study in all sorts of night and correspondence courses.

My parents at about this time were allowed to leave Czechoslovakia and they lived as refugees in Vienna as Displaced Persons or "DPs" as they were called in those days. I came to visit them and had little to occupy my time except for some private lessons in German grammar and general knowledge.

After completing the GCE exams I studied at a Polytechnic in London for several months. By this time I was an experienced jeweler. I worked in this trade for more than five years in London's Hatton Garden. During all that time I was also studying and had to support myself, or at least contribute to expenses. My parents had by then migrated from Vienna to the US. When I received an entrance visa I joined them in New York where they had arrived a year earlier.

I studied at Brooklyn and NYC colleges. My physics instructor was describing his other, more advanced class and he was praising the better students in that class especially a girl called Libby. By 1962 I was an upward-mobile computer programmer. A year later I met this Libby on a date set up by a family friend and soon we were married. That was in 1964. Thirty-six years on I can certainly attest to her cleverness as well as some other great attributes. She is the best wife any man can have. Two children later and with some savings we moved to Israel. Now we have five children, six grandchildren and a peaceful life in Israel.

Now I look back at all that studying. It took me over five years of mostly night school. I had to work as well to pay my way and help with the household expenses. I didn't fully appreciate then what they call a well-rounded education. Now I appreciate the analytical mind and the fighting spirit I received there, and the ability to discern tyrants under any guise.

Hetty Weiner-Fisch

Hetty Fisch was nearly 16 when she reached London. David Steiner introduced me to her in Jerusalem. We met several times between 1998 and 2007 where I gradually recorded her story. Since then she has provided some remarkable photos and documents to illustrate it and written the captions.

My mother died when I was 3 days old. Gisi Fleischman, a wartime heroine, one of the Committee of Six[5] and a great lady, spoke at her funeral and wrote a condolence letter to my father.

Translation from the original German:

> *On behalf of the Women's International Zionist Organisation: I have the sad task of finding some words to remember an unforgettable Jewish woman. I only want to say just a few words as that is what she would have wished. We proud Jewish women have lost a faithful and tireless fighter who devoted her considerable intellectual abilities, her noble Jewish heart and her free time to serve the Jewish people. We want to follow in her footsteps, to remember her with love and loyalty. Her name will be inscribed in the temple of the glory of the Jewish people. Jeanette Fisch! Rest in Peace! We will continue working on your behalf, to continue your work for the welfare of our people and for the whole of humanity. May this bring some comfort to your husband whom you loved so dearly.*

My mother knew she would die, and wrote letters for me to read when I was old enough. Her sister came to Bratislava to look after me. She was born in Berlin, read law at university and worked as an aide to a government minister. It was most unusual for a good Jewish girl - whose father wore a beard and her mother a *sheitl* - to take a job and work outside the Jewish community. She was a true "Women's Libber". Yet she gave up her career for my sake. It is due to her that I grew up with a healthy attitude towards life. She always gave me good advice.

When I was 6 or 7 years old she married. I do not know why my father did not marry her for she lived for his child - and for Zionism. My father was an oculist, an eye surgeon in private practice. He had beds in two hospitals, one of them a Jewish one. He knew numerous languages and enjoyed studying new ones using the Berlitz method. He was a cultured man with wide interests. To relax prior to a difficult operation he would untangle the sewing threads in my aunt's workbox. His hair was in a crew-cut.

After the war I found these old photos and papers in our totally demolished flat in an old couch that had been hacked to splinters.

My father was a religious man. He kept a *kosher* house and did not travel on the Sabbath or use power. I argued that using electricity did not involve work. There were not many Jewish families around us; we had no contact with the ultra-Orthodox but we observed all the laws of Jewish life. We met little anti-Semitism. There were many non-Jews among my father's patients, friends and colleagues. My aunt had coffee afternoons every Tuesday in aid of WIZO and made a collection in the blue-and-white box. She baked cakes and everyone contributed what they wished for planting trees and to help Zionist causes. I can remember being bought chestnuts in the street in the winter and keeping them warm in my muff and eating an ice cream during the summer in a promenade café. One day I saw a notice at the coffee place we frequented: "Jews and dogs not wanted here". After that we met our friends at home.

When the Fascists took over in Slovakia they were quick to institute anti-Semitic regulations. They followed the Nuremberg Laws introduced by the Nazis. Many Jews were deported from Bratislava including all young people over 16 but my father was in a reserved occupation so we stayed. That was between 1942 and 1943.

After that there was a lull; some sort of agreement was reached between Jewish community leaders and the Gestapo; this led to some people being accused of collaboration. Then came the cry "*Judenrein*, cleanse the country of Jews!" And suddenly our lives changed. There was no more protection. We were scapegoats, blamed for every ill. There was a curfew at 6 pm. During that time all Jews had to wear the yellow star on their chest except priority people like my father who wore a smaller star and could stay out later. When shopping in the market we would cover it up with a parcel. We were not allowed in many areas of the town and had to crowd into small flats. There had been no ghetto in Bratislava but the poorest streets were used to house any Jews found in the city; we were crammed in but only briefly. All those rounded up there were soon deported.

My father and I had been sent there, too. We were thrown out of our big, comfortable home. After that my father's loyal non-Jewish patients felt uncomfortable about visiting him in the densely overcrowded and dilapidated Jewish quarter so they made a petition to the authorities. The result was they gave us two tiny rooms at the top of the building that contained our old home. Our apartment was now used as offices for the Gardista, the Hlinka Guards' newspaper.

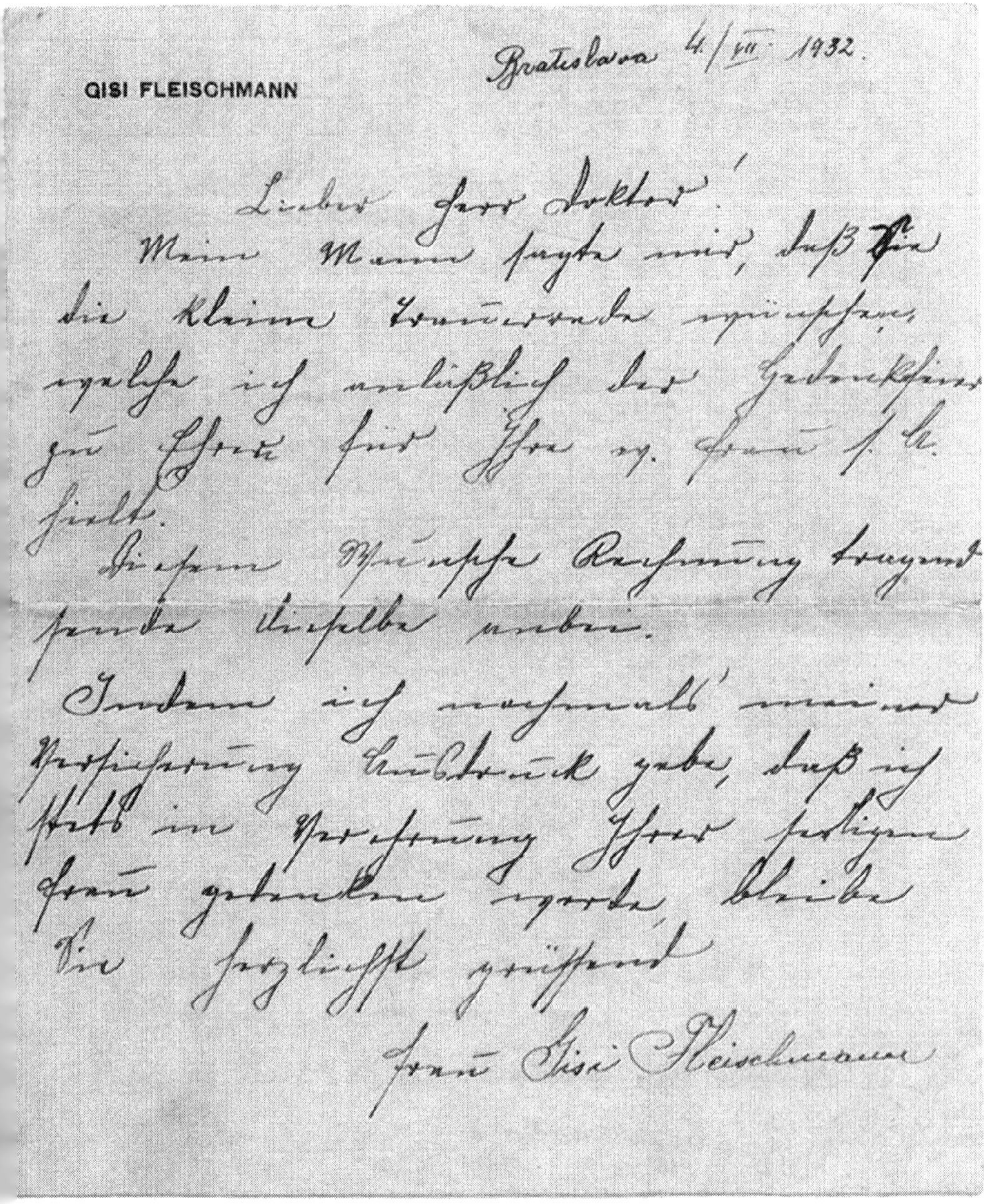

Bratislava 4/VII 1932.

[handwritten letter in German cursive]

Lieber Herr Doktor!

Mein Mann sagte mir, daß Sie die kleine Trauerrede wünschen, welche ich anläßlich der Gedenkfeier zu Ehren für Ihre sel. Frau p. b. hielt.

Diesem Wunsche Rechnung tragend sende dieselbe anbei.

Indem ich nochmals meiner Versicherung Ausdruck gebe, daß ich stets in Verehrung Ihrer seligen Frau gedenken werde, bleibe ich herzlichst grüßend

Ihre Frau Gisi Fleischmann

"Condolence letter from Gisi Fleischman to my father after my mother died in 1932. She was my parents' friend and partner in their Zionist organization and social activities." (Three pages)

Es wurde mir die schmerzliche Aufgabe
zuteil, im Namen der Wizo, der
unvergesslichen Frau und Jüdin Frau
J. F. Worte des Gedenkens zu widmen.
Ich will mit wenige, schlichte Worte
sagen, so wie sie es immer gerne hatte.

Wir bewusst jüdischen Frauen, haben
in ihr eine treue, unermüdliche
Kämpferin verloren, welche ihre hoch-
wertigen geistigen Fähigkeiten, ihr gutes,
edles jüdisches Herz, ihre freie Zeit
dem Dienste ihres Volkes weihte.

Wir wollen uns bemühen in
ihren Fußstapfen zu wandeln, ihrer
in Liebe und Treue gedenken.
Ihr Name wird im Ehrentempel
des jüdischen Volkes stehen, das ihr
gleichfalls ein treues Andenken
bewahren wird.

Jeanette Fisch! Ruhe in
Frieden!
Wir aber wollen es versuchen

"On one side she writes that she is sorry and that she is sending him
a copy of what she intends to say at my mother's grave. On the other
side is the actual speech which she plans to give at the unveiling of the
gravestone." {HF}

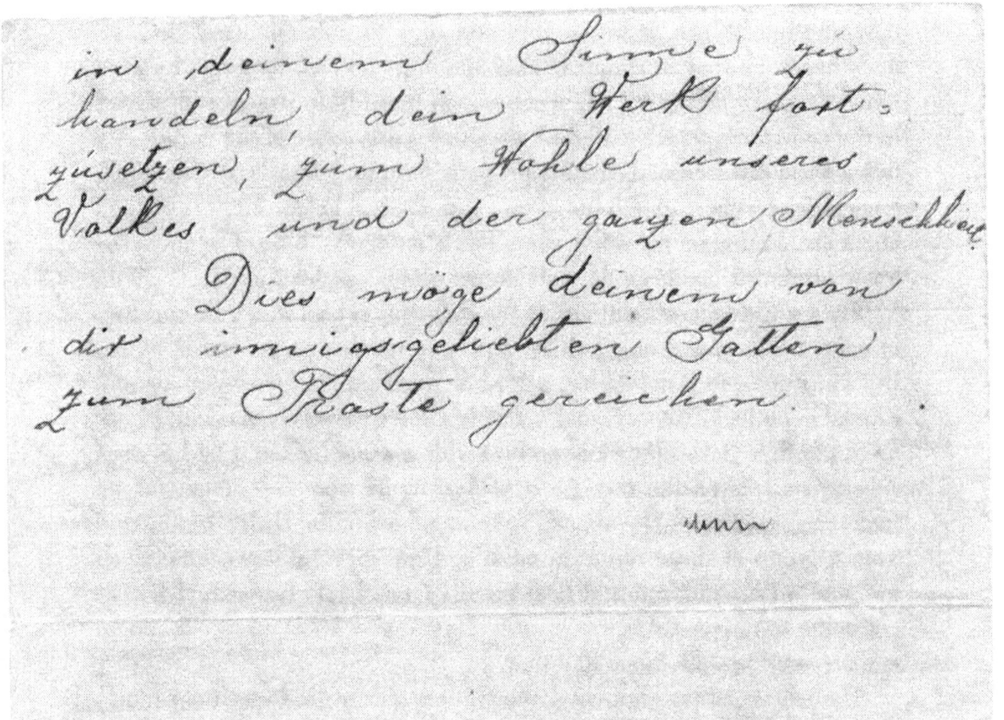

in deinem Sinne zu
handeln, dein Werk fort-
zusetzen, zum Wohle unseres
Volkes und der ganzen Menschheit.

Dies möge deinem von
dir innigstgeliebten Gatten
zum Troste gereichen.

We had to manage in that little place. It was so crowded that I kept bumping into things. It was a very odd time for me. Our cook and the maid had to be sent away; our weekly laundress had left long ago. I was so lonely because all my friends were now in those little streets and played in the courtyards together while I was confined because of the curfew. My father was fully occupied, visiting his patients at their homes or in hospital. Sometimes I went with him but often I was alone at home. He was worried about me, fearing for my safety when I went outdoors. When I went to visit my old friends I had to go through streets where non-Jews lived.

For a while I was still attending the Orthodox school where 78 children remained. Later, and only briefly, a private teacher taught me at home. But I still went to B'nei Akiva, a Jewish Youth group, both religious and Zionist in outlook. We were making a big effort to carry on as usual. I wore my uniform, a dark blue skirt and tie with a white blouse. I had to pass several schools on the way. Most of the pupils were German-speaking Sudetens; some were Slovaks, all were members of the Hitler Youth. One time a group of these children assaulted me. Several boys jumped on me, tore off my uniform and beat me till I was badly bruised. I had to get home in my pants. It was a nasty experience. I felt mortified and so embarrassed to walk home like that.

Then the bombing happened: the refineries were hit. I was in the house alone and among gentiles. I was very frightened. So my father decided to send me to live with my aunt and her husband in Zilina. It was a town with a population of 40,000 some three or four hours from Bratislava.

My aunt was secretary to the Jewish community; her husband was in business. Zilina was on a big railway junction and Jews were rounded up there for deportation. In September 1942 deportations were halted. Jews were set free. Some were working in building teams. My uncle joined one of these known as "The Betonnari" (men of the concrete). They were involved in building a Sports Stadium. Most were living in the Labour Camp. My uncle was a strong and charming man and the Camp Commandant took a liking to him. So in return for payment he allowed him to live outside the Camp. I shared their small room in a flat with another Jewish family. We were allowed to go outside only between 6am and 7am. I met some good people at that time.

Opposite where we lived was a small Jewish cemetery some 2km from a military camp. So we would run there when the air raid warning sounded, hoping the cemetery would not be bombed. I can remember sitting in the funeral hall where a body was on the table ready to be washed in preparation for burial.

"My parents Dr Geza and Jeanette Fisch (Hartvig) in the late 1920s." (HF)

"With my grandparents Jakob and Thekla Hartvig in Berlin, 1933". (HF)

"Daddy and I in 1933." (HF)

"A visit to my cousins Egon and Ursel Hartvig in Berlin, 1934" (HF)

By August 1944 the Uprising had began. Many Slovaks were organising anti-German activities. We heard shots, then people running. Slovak soldiers shouted at us to go home. The revolution had begun. "We are going to throw the Germans out". But the Uprising was defeated. All remaining Slovak Jews were deported. Of the original 20,000 only some thirty managed to stay behind.

My uncle had prepared a mountain hide-out in the woods and stocked it with food and bedding. It was an outhouse belonging to a poor family two or three hours trek away. We shared it with another family. It was in the vicinity of the Partisans. Three days after we reached there a message was brought by a friend. The manager of the Sports Stadium promised to protect all his workers for as long as work continued. So back we went and slept on the floor there. One day the Hlinka arrived, one of them was in uniform. They had come to deport the Jewish workers from the Stadium. The Manager was very apologetic and told us they had lied to him. My uncle told the guards "This child is not on the list". And he urged me to run away - no one would notice my absence in the present confusion. But I refused and said I wanted to go with him and my aunt wherever they went.

The guards escorted us back to our flat to be interrogated. But as we climbed the stairs a stranger appeared. He told the guards I did not belong with my uncle, and pulled me through a door into his flat, putting his hand over my mouth - all in a second. Once we were inside, he asked me where my father was and said he would take me to him next morning. He explained that he and his wife and two children had moved there the previous day and the building belonged to his elderly mother. His name was Dr Michal Majercik, a pleasant-looking man. He and his wife only knew that I was the daughter of a doctor in Bratislava.

My uncle and aunt were deported.

Only twenty years later I learned from Dr Majercik that my uncle had asked him to save me although they had never met before. To this day I still cannot quite understand how this came about and all in a few precious moments.

That same night someone warned my benefactors that the Hlinka were searching the building. There came a knock at the door "Open up!" Dr Majercik quickly took their three-month old baby from his cot, hid me under the mattress, and replaced the screaming child with his bedding on top of me. The Hlinka said they were searching for a 12 year old girl seen to have arrived the previous night. Dr Majercik explained he and his family had moved in only yesterday and there was no one else there. The two rooms were pulled apart. Everything was turned upside down -

except the baby's cot. And there I was shaking with fright, and only just out of sight.

The guards left. The family put their home in order again. Then towards midnight, the guards returned, this time with a warrant. I was hurriedly pushed back under the baby's bedding. I heard everything. "Do you know what the punishment is for harbouring Jews?" they asked. I was terrified. The baby was screaming again and again they failed to find me.

Early next morning they dressed me in Slovak style with a kerchief to cover my dark hair. The plan was to take me back to Bratislava. But at 6 am that morning it was announced on the radio that no one may travel without a permit. As I had no papers, not even a ration book, there was no way out of this. The family were stuck with me. What could they do with this extra child, who looked Jewish, and obviously was not theirs? Next door lived a grocer who was the President's cousin. The President was violently anti-Semitic. The Majercik family bought their rations there. Only after the war did I learn that it was the grocer's wife who had seen me arrive and reported this to the Hlinka.

Dr Majercik was studying law, doing his *staj*, his articles. His wife was a teacher of English and French. They had a three-year-old and the baby of a few months. This is what they did: they dismissed the village girl who was looking after the children, giving her a week's wages so she would make no complaint. And Mrs Majercik gave up her job to look after them - and me - herself. What a sacrifice! What a risk!

I was put in the maid's room. I could not put on a light as the grocer lived over the shop and their window was opposite my small room. I recall the cabin trunk in there with a pretty cover. They hid me in it whenever visitors came. Usually these were members of the family. While I was alone there I invented an imaginary friend, a girl who would come to call for me to come and play. My foster parents' daughter had a doll called Helinka so I called my friend Helinka.

I had come with only the clothes I was wearing, a summer dress and sandals with no socks. I was a quiet child but I felt so guilty in this situation. I helped by playing with the children and washing up. I loved looking after the baby. My foster mother cooked for me, washed my clothes and my long hair and plaited it with pretty things. In the cold winter when we had no heating she bought me stockings and knitted a pullover for me. It was light blue with a pattern on it; I only threw it out recently. She made me wear a headscarf and a shawl on the rare occasions I went out, to hide my dark hair. And she would put stuffing in my cheeks. "Say you are off to the dentist if anyone asks". At Christmas time I had more presents than

Dr and Mrs Majercik, newly-weds. (HF)

their own children, largely warm clothes, winter pyjamas and slippers.

Dr. Majercik looked after my soul. He found books for me to read and set sums for me to solve. He did his best to reassure me. He would discuss with me what I had read during the day and would tell me what news he had heard from the BBC on their secret hidden radio. It was 1944. He assured me the Germans were finished, that I should not worry. He also told me there was a boy hiding in the cellar who had a Jewish mother and a Christian father. He brought school books for him, too.

It was wonderful how he would stimulate my mind and raise my morale; for there were times when I was very forlorn. Yet I was so lucky. He had as powerful an impact on me as had my father and my aunt throughout my earlier, happier years. In those days children were expected to be seen and not heard in adult company but that was not the way in this household.

One stormy night word came that the Hlinka were making a search of the area and were due at any moment. I was bundled out of the house in a great rush and told to wheel the baby in her pram towards the slaughterhouse. "Wait for us by the wall! If anyone asks say you are taking baby home from his grandmother. We will come to find you when the Hlinka have gone!" It was bitterly cold weather and pitch dark in the blackout. I did not even know where the slaughterhouse was. I did not know the town at all. There was a wild snowstorm blowing. The baby yelled and I had no bottle to soothe her. I did not meet a soul. Numb from cold I walked on and on till exhausted and totally lost. I fell asleep sitting under a tree. My hand was still holding the pram and I had closed the hood when hours later a terribly worried foster father found us and took us home. I have no idea how many hours this took. It seemed an eternity. They put baby and me in a tub of warm water to revive us. I slept for days. I heard later that we had left just in time. The police had come at once. It had been yet another narrow escape.

When my foster mother took her children to call on one or other of their grandmothers I would be left alone in the house. On one of these occasions I watched from a window as a tender pulled up outside the Jewish cemetery opposite and some men entered the gates. There were people in casual clothes and others in uniform. Then I heard shots. Only those in uniform came back and drove away. When I told this to my foster father he thought I was hallucinating, that I had not enough stimulation and was imagining all this. But then another day I saw the same scene again and the same vehicle. When I told my foster father this time he said I should take down the car's registration number next time. I failed to manage that.

It was during that same harsh winter when there was heavy snow and severe gales, that someone reported seeing a light in the garden shed. The seven Jews hiding there were found by the Hlinka. It was Dr Majercik's mother who had hidden them there. She was a very old lady. It was near the end of the war by then. She was punished and fined. She had lived there all her life. It was awful for her.

Peace came at last on May 8^{th,} 1945.

My foster father took me to the police station to report what I had seen in the cemetery. Investigations were made and graves of Partisans were found there. And he took me to visit his mother next door, the lady who had saved me when I had first arrived. She had recognised the danger I was in, knew the police were coming and alerted my foster parents just in time. Until then I had never been aware of her concern for me.

When the war ended I returned to Bratislava. This is how I found my family again. Providence would laugh! I came across my uncle on a crowded train. Both of us were travelling back to Bratislava. I told him that my foster family wanted to adopt me but he said no, to await the return of my father and my aunt. We reached Bratislava where survivors were flocking to seek any relatives, anyone from their past. Schools were turned into hostels with mattresses on the floor. The general situation was chaotic. Despite this the Russian authorities insisted travellers must have a permit. My uncle had no identity papers and was put in jail. He was a redhead with green eyes and a snub nose. They thought he was a German. 24 hours later I went to the prison to identify him and gave his address. He tore off the strip stuck on his forehead, branding him a prisoner, and off we went to search for my aunt.

In the street we met **David Steiner** who was out looking for me. He was the father of my best friend. His mother had been a great friend of my mother and he even recalled pushing me in my pram. He told us he had seen my aunt the previous night. My poor aunt was crawling like a baby, searching for me. He had taken her to be looked after by the nuns while he went off to look for me. So I left my uncle, who could barely walk, and ran off to trace her. I rushed to the convent only to learn she had just disappeared despite being very ill.

I was 13 years old, frantic, desperate. I still have nightmares about this. The information centre had no address for her. Then I bumped into the man who had been my father's tailor, a non-Jew. He used to bring us treats in hard times earlier in the war as did many of my father's patients. He was so well-loved. He did not recognise me until I stopped crying. "Hetty!" he exclaimed. "Your aunt is in my house". Later he told me how

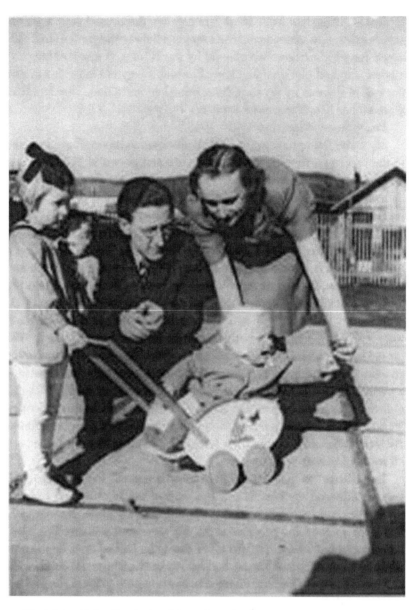

The Majercik family during May 1945. (HF)

"This picture was taken on about May 10th, 1945, two or three days after my liberation, when I left the room - and the trunk I had been hiding in for the last nine months - for the first time. I am standing on the left, Mrs Majercik is on the right, her daughter Miroslava and son Michal-Mito between us. They had this splash in an old laundry tub made of wood in their tiny back-yard." (HF)

she had recognised him, and how perplexed he was at first to be addressed by name by this unfamiliar and pathetic old woman, collapsed in the street. I tore away, running faster than him. His wife opened the door.

I rushed in and there she was, "The Lady of the Box" that I had always known as so elegant with her black hair carefully tinted, her skin smoothed with almond oil. But now she was lying on a couch, her skin yellow, her hair white. She had on a green smock (though she had never worn green) and one red wooden shoe. Her breasts were like empty sacks. She weighed no more than 27 kilos and smelt of vomit and sweat. Then she saw me. She was in shock but so HAPPY. I froze before going near her.

A medical friend of my father took her into his clinic but he told us we must not bring her any food. She had water in her lungs causing pleurisy and a severe infection. American friends sent us a supply of the first antibiotics. A cousin on a mission to Prague delivered it. We were so lucky!

I learned that my father and my aunt had found each other in the same transport on the way to Auschwitz. So he had learned from her that I was safe. I had been writing to him in code as if I was a patient of his saying the "operation was successful". But he never returned from the Concentration Camp. I found out that he died there in October 1944.

We moved back into our old home and there I found something precious: the letters that my mother had written to me before I was born. Another pleasant surprise came from one of my father's patients, the flower man. He presented me with a bag of gold ducats that he had saved until my return. We had a good summer recuperating with our surviving relatives including my maternal grandfather. It took a full year for my aunt to recover; and I continued to be frightened to go outside for at least nine months.

We settled down again. My uncle became a buyer for the Russian Army, a task that took him all over Europe. Then he opened a big shop in Prague. My foster family still wanted to adopt me. So I would stay with them during term time and spend holidays with my family in Bratislava. A year or two after the war Dr Majercik was made Czech Ambassador to Poland. He suggested I work towards joining the Diplomatic Corps with a view to becoming his secretary. This sounded quite attractive. I imagined enjoying coffee and cake in Warsaw. This led to their sending me to the Mefice School, a boarding school near Prague that prepared girls for this sort of career.

I was the only Jewish girl admitted there apart from a half-Jewish girl I met again later in Nahariah in Northern Israel. I recall one nasty incident. We were studying "David Copperfield". Another girl wanted to copy my essay. I said no, although I was willing to help her. She retorted "What a pity Hitler did not burn you."

In April 1948 suddenly my aunt arrived at the school and without explanation took me back to Prague. She had met Rabbi Dr Schonfeld the previous day. He had persuaded her that it is the right of children to lead a normal Jewish life and that was to be impossible under the Communists. She had accepted his offer to take me to Britain the very next day. It all happened extremely abruptly.

It was the eve of *Pesach* when I was met in London by a cousin, Judith Rosenfeld, who was newly-married and very religious. I am still in touch with her. For a year and a half I slept in their kitchen in a tiny flat in Green Lanes. Her father, a brother of my father, was old and ill and bitter. He had been a dentist but the British did not recognise his qualifications. I studied at the Berlitz Secretarial College in Seven Sisters Road. The Jewish Refugee Committee at Bloomsbury House allowed me £2 for my board and lodgings and 3 shillings pocket money a week. Then in late 1949 I went on *aliyah* as a *madrich* with Aliyat Hanoah. My only continuing contact with the Schonfeld group has been with Trudy Mangel who attended the same secretarial course, and the Kaiser sisters. They have all settled in the United States.

To tell about our *aliyah* requires an earlier tale to be told. My handsome and clever uncle had sent by ship to Palestine, prior to 1938, two containers addressed to the care of Mr X, a friend in Tel Aviv. In the end my uncle had failed to obtain travel documents. So he wrote to Mr X, telling him to set up shop as a men's outfitter with the contents of the containers and share the proceeds with him 50/50. Mr X was to bank his share until he or his sons claimed it. They kept in touch. The shop on Ben Yehuda Street in Tel Aviv was very successful.

In 1948 my uncle and aunt went to Israel via Haifa. They found the shop on Ben Yehuda Street but it was empty. They learned that Mr X had left two days earlier for Vienna in order to evade my uncle. So they found themselves penniless and with no means of support. They went to WIZO and asked them to find them work. This led to the *Soknut* sending them to work at a house in Bak'aa, Jerusalem, with elderly new immigrants. Some were demented. They told me of a Yemenite woman there who was afraid of running water, ate eggshells and slept on the floor under her bed.

My enterprising uncle tried to start up a tailoring repair service with another man from Bratislava. My aunt was dismissed through some *protexia* so a man could be put in her place. He was later thrown out for dishonesty. Around the same time my uncle and aunt lost the two roomed flat they had found. It was all too much. My uncle became ill. Then his business collapsed. When I joined them in 1949 we shared one room. I slept in the hallway until I joined the army. My aunt was working in a toothpaste factory although she had a degree in law. "I know who I am" she would say, "a walking lexicon." Then she was found to have cancer; but she always welcomed me with a cup of coffee whenever I came.

My uncle was very angry. He had no money to care for her or to provide what she needed. So he borrowed enough to chase that Mr X. But he escaped again and there was no money left. Local people lent a bit here and there for my aunt - brought her an orange, perhaps - but there was minimal care and no treatment. Yet she went on making coffee for me even when she could no longer carry the cup. The weather was so very hot that summer in 1953. It was 31°C the day before she died so I cut her hair short. **David Steiner** came to see her that last day. He was very fond of her. My boyfriend came to see her, too. "When is the doctor coming?" he kept asking. She was in such awful pain. She just needed a shot of morphine to relieve her suffering. A cousin visited and advised me to take a nurse for the night but I could not afford it. Then friends found a nurse and paid her 10 *lirot*. All that last night I sat by her with my boyfriend. At 2am I went to a doctor and begged him to come to give her medication for the terrible pain. "But she is dying", he said and made all sorts of excuses then shut the door in my face. It was very hard.

The army had given me leave to nurse my aunt. I slept in her bed with her until she died. When the doctor had said she had only a few more days to live I wrote to tell my uncle even though she had told me not to. She died and he never came back to that flat. I was 19 years old. I was left with all their debts. I sent what there was to my uncle, to my handsome warm-hearted uncle who had adored her and was so grateful for her love. She was so gifted, had such wide interests, was such a wonderful human being and had so many good friends.

My husband was also a Czech. His mother had died while they were living in the woods amongst the Partisans. He had buried her and was the only one to know where. The Germans had attacked them. He was shot in the leg and had to spend a year in hospital before he could walk again. Only after that could he help his father find her grave. As they disinterred her body from the frozen earth to wrap her in an army blanket her head rolled away, a ghastly experience.

My husband studied engineering at the University in Prague after the war. He financed this by working as a night watchman and even cleaning toilets without any shame. In 1948 he went on *aliyah*. At first he did labouring work for Jerusalem Municipality. Now he has a business of his own producing special gifts for presentation to VIPs. For this he collects antiquities, old maps, Roman glass, and fossils and sets them in a frame usually of olive wood. [6]

Today I am a grandmother and I am a volunteer with Amcha. We adopted a granny who had lost all her children in the *Shoah*. She lived with us until she died of cancer aged 91. A few years ago relatives of my husband who had settled in Sydney, Australia came to visit us. I discovered that their grandmother, then 85, had been among those hidden next door to us in Zilina. She was their relative and was alive and well in Australia. And she had known all about me.

I met with my foster parents again when I was the mother of a five year old. "How could you do so much for me?" I asked them. "We only thought to save you" was their reply. Their son is a pathologist today. Mira, his sister, married an Englishman, a Communist. They met when he was a student at St Charles University in Prague. Later they lived in London. She worked for the BBC at Bush House. Then they divorced.

Mira had no family in London and little money, so she went back to Slovakia. She was teaching philosophy. When she was on a school teachers' outing to Germany she managed to slip away from the group. She had a British passport and so she was able to stay in Germany but she earned very little. She was highly intelligent but her qualifications were not recognised. She lived in awful conditions in Munich. I would not visit her there, so we would sometimes meet in London. After a year or two her parents obtained permission to visit her. For the first and only time, they asked if I could lend them some money. They were to stay ten days but were allowed only five dollars each. I turned to my husband. What else could we do?

He had a better idea. He suggested we go ourselves and meet with them in Germany. I had always vowed I would never go to that country. But these circumstances were exceptional. And I enjoyed that visit so very much, an enjoyment mixed with some guilt. I was once again steeped in the culture in which I had been brought up and heard my mother-tongue all around me.

In 1995 Mira came to Jerusalem to receive recognition on her parents' behalf as Righteous Gentiles and to plant a tree in their name. Her parents had been refused an exit visa. I tried to ask her again how they could have risked taking me in. She would have none of it. "You would have done the same thing in their position", she insisted. My own daughter wrote a letter to her, a letter which is now shown in the Yad Vashem Museum.

"The exhibit at Yad Vashem honouring Dr and Mrs Majercik. With me are three of my five children, Amital, Eva and Michal - the last named after Dr Michal Majercik. Under the glass exhibits there are some drawers in which you find part of my story in Hebrew and in English." (HF)

"Four of my children and nine grandchildren with Dr Majercik, son of Dr Michal and Anna Majercik, my benefactors, in front of the house where they hid me for nine months. The smaller house on the right side of this picture was the home of the woman who called the Hlinka Guards saying that she had seen me enter the house but had not seen me leave it." (HF)

Hetty's daughter's letter to Mira Majercik

Dear Mira,

I am writing to you to thank you for accepting Hetty who appeared so suddenly in your home, and for agreeing to share your parents' attention with her. Did they ever explain to you why she was staying with you? Were you hurt by her presence or were you glad to have a big sister? What did you think when someone knocked at the door and she disappeared? You did a good deed that made Hetty feel safe and warm after a long period of fear. You behaved like human beings at a time when there were so few like that, and if it had not been for your parents' good deed you would not be reading this letter now.

With tears of gratitude I sign this letter
Michal, Hetty's daughter.

Another time I got a special permit for a 24-hour visit, thanks to Greville Janner (later Lord Janner, QC). It all happened because he had occasion to meet the Czechoslovak ambassador in London at diplomatic functions. The ambassador often boasted of the democracy practised in his country. So next time he saw him Mr Janner told him that he knew someone in Jerusalem who wanted very much to visit her mother's grave in Bratislava. Some months later I was informed that a visa awaited me in Vienna, good for collection within the next six months.

Unfortunately my great benefactor, Dr Majercik, had died a few days before I reached there. I wanted to visit his grave, but he had been cremated. Since then the borders have opened and I have twice visited the family again.

Children placed in institutions

Some were absorbed into Christian boarding schools, convents or monasteries amongst gentile children. Often they were baptised in the hope that this would protect them. It did not. For boys circumcision would give away their identity which was why **Israel Reich** was disguised as a girl when escaping across the Hungarian border and **Gyorgy Prissegi** was not circumcised as an infant. These institutions were often short of food. They were always liable to inspection by the Fascist authorities and yet some took the risk of harbouring Jewish children.

Several mentions are made by contributors of the Jewish Orphanage in Budapest. An orphanage for girls was opened there by the Jewish community in 1867, the first of its kind, and one for boys two years later. The establishment operating during the Second World War must have been its successor. It appears to have remained open and fully used until the German invasion in August 1944 when all its occupants were removed and most probably deported.

Pál and Tamáš Krausz

*The Krausz brothers are now settled in England. Pál was born in 1934,
Tamáš in 1936. Both contributed to this account. They have provided some
interesting photos to illustrate their story, one of which is exceptionally rare.*

We were living with our family in Bratislava when in 1942 the Gestapo
came for us but the same night we went into hiding with non-Jewish
friends on the outskirts of Bratislava.

Shortly after this, arrangements were made for us two boys to transfer
to an Evangelical Orphanage in Modra, a small town about one hour's
drive away. Our mother remained in hiding with her sister in Bratislava.
We were very fortunate to have found refuge in this place. It was run by
a group of kind and devoted nuns who knew that they were risking their
lives by hiding us. We were well looked after. We never suffered from
hunger or cold or any form of abuse. Besides us there were a handful of
other Jewish children in this home.

Among our most precious possessions is a photo of the two of us with
Zofia, the Mother Superior. This was taken at great risk by Mr Gerafy, our
aunt's gentile fiancé. This photo was to show our mother that we were well
and in good hands.

When liberation came in the spring of 1945 we were given the news
that our mother and her sister, together with the photographer, had been
deported only a few months earlier to Auschwitz where all three were
murdered.

In the autumn of 1944 the Slovaks had initiated The National
Uprising against the Germans who were by now losing the war on all
fronts. In reprisal they restarted the deportations of any remaining Jews
to the Camps.

The Russian liberators requisitioned the buildings of our orphanage,
and so we were transferred to an orphanage in Piešťany. It was run by the
Catholic Church and conditions there were very grim. We were cold and
hungry. We survived by stealing raw sugar beet and carrots from a hole
in the wall of a nearby warehouse.

Things changed again when the American Joint and World Jewish
Congress collected surviving Jewish children and placed us in Villa
Silvia in the High Tatras. There better conditions enabled us to
recuperate physically and spiritually. At last life was beginning to feel
normal. We spent just over a year there. It was a happy time and all of

The Krausz brothers with Sister Zofia, who protected them in her convent. This is a precious photo. It was taken at great risk to show their mother that they were safe and well. Late in 1944 she, her sister and her gentile fiancé who took the photo were all murdered in Auschwitz. (TK)

us children felt gratitude to these organisations for what they had done for us. Pál, who was a little older than the rest of us, each day made the one hour journey to the gymnasium high school in Kežmarok. The train passed through Huncovce, (formerly called Unsdorf). In the pre-Holocaust period, Kežmarok and Unsdorf contained important Jewish communities with famous *Yeshivot*. Pál celebrated his *barmitzvah* in the community of Kežmarok.

From the High Tatras we were transferred to another Jewish Children's home in Nové Mesto Nad Váhom. It had previously been the Old Age Home, Ohel David, where Rabbi Armin Frieder, the Rabbi of the local Neolog congregation saved a number of Jewish children by hiding them from the Nazis. He had been co-opted on to the Committee of Six[5] who negotiated with the Fascists and with the Nazi Wisliceny in trying to save Slovak Jewry.

At this Children's Home all of us were waiting for places on ships to sail on illegal *aliyah* to Palestine. Every week or two, one or two of the children departed quietly in the middle of the night. It is difficult to believe, but young as we were, the home was run on military lines. We were taught to use weapons and dance the *hora*. They told us this was in preparation for life in Palestine!

It was here in Nové Mesto that Rabbi Schonfeld came dressed in a British Army Officer's uniform and chose a number of us to accompany him to England. This was in the spring of 1948. The train journey through Europe - and particularly through Germany - was eerie as we travelled through landscapes of total war devastation. On the journey we all had fictitious identities, and we two had to say we had originated from Kluj, Romania. At Dover we were met by well-wishers who instructed us on how to peel and eat oranges and bananas. Eventually we reached 32 Woodberry Down, a Victorian mansion in Stoke Newington, North London. It was *Erev Pesach* and we were immediately told to clear any *chametz* from our bags. The *seder* was conducted by Rabbi Schonfeld's brother, Andrew, but as we were unable to read Hebrew or understand English and this was the first *seder* that we had ever experienced, we did not know what was going on.

After some ten months in Stoke Newington my brother and I moved to Gateshead, in the cold North of England, and stayed there for ten years, living at the Jewish Boarding School and studying at the *yeshiva*. In the space of two years, 1946-48, we made the transition from a Catholic setting to Orthodox Jewish Gateshead, a spiritual leap which only the young can be expected to handle.

In 1958 Pál married and Rabbi Schonfeld conducted the ceremony in the grounds of the Avigdor High School in Lordship Road. At the wedding dinner in Lea Bridge Road he spoke *in loco parentis*. He considered himself as the father to every child he brought to England.

It was an unconventional childhood but today we realise how fortunate we were that we were able to pick up the pieces and make the best of what life has to offer.

Tamáš Krausz returns to the High Tatras in 2008. (TK)

Alexander Mastbaum

Alexander was 11 years old when he joined Rabbi Schonfeld's transport. He talked to me about his life in August 1998 in Jerusalem. We knew each other before but I had no idea then that Alex was a survivor or that he had spent some time in Britain. I was on the staff of the Paul Baerwald School of Social Work, at the Hebrew University of Jerusalem and so was he. He was responsible for the stationery stores and he also managed the increasingly complex audio-visual equipment. He was always available to assist any of us working in the School. We bothered him with all sorts of problems yet he always greeted everyone with a cheery word and a warm smile. He was a very popular member of staff and his experience was highly valued. He came with his wife to the Reunion. In 2007 I was sad to learn that he had recently died.

My name is Alexander Mastbaum. I was born in 1936. As far as I can remember it was in 1943 or 1944 that I was sent by my parents with some other people to Hungary. We were caught on the border and put in a Camp from where they were sending people in transports to Germany. I was just a little boy and no one really looked after me but one evening someone came up to the fence and said they would rescue me from there. "Tomorrow evening we shall be here again to fetch you". And so they did.

Who were these people? Friends of ours - or family - who had non-Jewish papers. I think they were the reason I was sent to Hungary, but I am not sure. I walked out of the Camp and as I was only about seven years old the Guards paid no attention. The people waiting outside took me to a village and we lived there for a while. Whether it was months or weeks I cannot say. Later they placed me in a monastery and I stayed there till after the war.

Were they kind to you? Oh yes. They were very, very kind to me and looked after me well. There were two or three other Jewish boys and we felt very safe. I do not know what happened to the others. I used to collect pictures of the saints and after the war I very much wanted a bicycle. So I tried to exchange all my pictures for one. The priests did not like my doing this and said "A Jew is always a Jew".

My mother told me how she found me. She came to Hungary knowing she had sent me there but had no idea where to begin. She set about searching for me but she could not find any clue. One day she was sitting on a bus and a priest asked her "Why are you so nervous?" She said "I have been looking for two full weeks for my son without finding him". He asked her what his name was. She said "Alex Mastbaum" and he replied "He is with us!" So my mother came and took me away from the monastery.

We went to Czechoslovakia, to Bratislava. That was in 1946 or 1947. Stalin had occupied the country and people were fleeing from the Communists. It was Rabbi Schonfeld who organised a transport of children to go to England. I was amongst them. I don't know how many there were. They took us to England. There was some problem with our papers on reaching there and so first of all we were sent to Clonyn Castle in Ireland then later came to London. I was sent to the Schneider *Yeshiva*, a very Orthodox boarding school.

In 1955 I left the *Yeshiva*, found a room and shared it with **Artur Weinberger.** We went to work in the jewellery trade in Hatton Garden. The following year I started studying for GCEs at Westminster College.

In 1958 I received an invitation from my relatives in South America. I joined them and stayed there six years. In 1948 my mother had married again and came to Israel where conditions were very difficult. So she decided it was better for me to stay at school in England. My father never came back from the Camps. I don't remember him. I came to visit my mother in Jerusalem in 1964 and she insisted I stay. I started looking for a job. I tried several things then found a place as technician at the School of Social Work at the Hebrew University. I stayed there for over 30 years.

In the meantime I had married an Israeli girl. We have three children, two boys and a girl. I went on pension earlier this year and now I am studying at the Kolel, something I wanted to do for many years. My mother, now aged 87, lives in an old age home. She never wanted to be bothered with questions about the past and now it is too late.

Have you been in contact with other members of the group? No, we did not keep in touch with each other. There were occasional contacts, an exchange of news but no continuity. I decided I would like to participate in the Reunion in England next year. So I sent a fax immediately. I think I was the first to reply to the invitation.

Judit, Olga and Alfred Ziegler

Some years after the Reunion I met Judit in a Jerusalem hotel and she told me their story. Two of her poems follow, translated from Hebrew by her son, Moshe.

The three of us were all born in Bardejov. I am the eldest, born in 1936. Olga was 18 months younger, Alfred two years younger than her. I recall being called "The Princess" by my grandparents; I behaved differently from others. I always liked to have paper and pencil available. I always felt a lot of responsibility for my little sister and brother and this made me a very serious child. We were very close as children. They have only the vaguest memories of their early years; I wish mine were less vivid - they are so painful. All the family were in the forestry business. My father owned tracts of land and sold wood. His brother was a cattle exporter, dealing with Austria and Hungary. Both had papers that showed they were needed for the war effort, papers that were continually being altered. So we were protected from deportation. Our income was above average. We were very lucky.

Our mother tongue was German but outside our home we picked up Slovak. When the troubles began German was banned. That was very confusing for small children. If I used a German word the parents would say "you will destroy us" and hit us on our hands. As the eldest I had to see that the younger ones did not speak German. We found it best to keep silent. We lived in a Catholic area and had an honourable position among the gentiles. But when anti-Semitic regulations were introduced their attitude to us changed abruptly, something I could never understand.

From 1942 we began to run from place to place, in the snow, in the mountains - we were never safe. Later we children were sent to an orphanage in Budapest. On the journey I had a little suitcase and wore several dresses on top of each other, including a *Shabat* dress. We had an aunt and uncle there with a son 18 months older than me. But we were told not to relate to them. Hungarian Jews, at first unharassed, were afraid to associate with Slovak refugees. Our aunt promised to visit us but she never did. That family were deported later and never came back.

The Germans were coming. An uncle from Košice fetched us from the orphanage. He had brought his family there from Bardejov, the village where we were born. On the train a priest was sitting eating. He gave us apples. He told my uncle "Don't let them be caught like birds in a cage". Years later my uncle often reminded me of those words. That was in Israel where he died in 1986. In Košice we found his wife, my aunt. I was very sick and had earache. I was never strong. It was mumps. They took me to hospital.

Meanwhile our father had been in contact and said he would send for us. So my aunt dressed me in layers of clothes and smuggled me out of the hospital. He gave photos of us three children to a Slovak farmer who lived on the Hungarian-Slovak border and arranged for him to return us to our parents. But he brought the wrong children! Our father was furious. He wanted us. So he travelled with the farmer, and dressed like him, came on a second journey to find us. We climbed onto the cart and nestled down with the animals to keep warm. Father stayed withdrawn till we were over the border. Then he gave us food. "We know you," we said "you are our father!"

I had tried to persuade our uncle and aunt to come back, too, without success. They had been thrown out of their modern home and my uncle had lost his office. Later all their remaining possessions were stolen and they were taken away on a truck. They survived Auschwitz but their baby girl was killed there. They had given their little daughter, another Judith, then three years old, to a well-to-do children's doctor. But the Germans came and killed all the Jewish patients, children as well.

In Prešov mother was waiting for us but she looked different, strange. We were puzzled. She was pregnant but we did not realise it or understand what that meant. The Rabbi was with her but he no longer had a beard. No Jews were left in the town. In 1944 there was the Partisans' Uprising and during that time my mother gave birth to our baby sister. That was after *Pesach*. We tried to appear like gentiles. We had false papers and moved around between different bunkers. I was called Julie. I felt I no longer belonged. It was so unjust. We had been useful to our country. We had been good citizens but now the locals had turned against us.

By the time the war ended food was very scarce and precious. My mother would say "Drink milk - you are so thin". I would persuade my brother to drink it so as not to upset our mother. She wanted to feed us well, and we hated to upset her. She never got over the loss of her parents. The family had been in Slovakia for four hundred years, yet the neighbours allowed them to die.

In April 1948 we joined Rabbi Schonfeld's transport to Britain. The departure from Prague was very scary. I still remember how I felt at the time. I was eight-and-a half years old.

We arrived in London a few days before *Pesach*, 1948. Our rucksacks were packed with cookies and cakes that our mother baked for us, Judita (me), my sister Olga and my brother Buby (Alfred). We had to part with our rucksacks because they contained *chametz* food. This was not as easy as it may sound since we were very hungry.

I remember a very festive *Seder* that Rabbi Dr Schonfeld led for all of us. I planned to steal the *afikomen* for only one reason - I wanted to ask Rabbi Schonfeld for a really important reward. He had these friendly good eyes, an important-looking beard and a noble and authoritative appearance which led me to believe that I could ask anything of him and that he could fulfil my wishes. My plan was to return the *afikomen* in exchange for being reunited with my parents and my sister, Vierucka, who were still in Czechoslovakia. Alas, after prolonged singing - most of the songs new to me - we reached the song *"Dy Dyenu"*. At this point, all the children under 12 years old were asked to leave the dining room. That was long before the *afikomen* was discussed.

Clonyn Castle was a nice place especially for children with imagination. There was this long boulevard-like path (*shdeira*) where the branches of the trees formed a canopy over the path and were thick enough to hide the sky. Weather permitting, we walked this mysterious path almost every shabat. My sister, Olga (Tzipora), myself and two friends shared a perfectly round room in the tower. It was a challenge to arrange and fit the beds and suitcases in such a round room.

Blanka used to wake us up ever so gently, with a jug of water and a bowl, to wash our hands before getting out of bed. She taught us that to be pure you must not take more than three steps when you get up before washing. Every morning too, the *madrichim* would choose three or four children to go by horse and cart to fetch the milk. As a privilege we were given fresh warm milk (though I never liked milk from an early age - I do not know why). There was no shortage of food.

We were thirsty to study after spending so many years in the bunkers and other places where we had missed school. I fondly remember the *shiurim* our *madrichot* delivered with love and talent. We were taught to take religion very seriously. From the age of twelve we girls had to wear stockings. I remember **Séndi**, who taught us *Pirkei Avot* and *Parashat Shavu'a*. I identified with her so much that I even wanted to emulate her handwriting. I also remember Judy's *shiurim* which included a lot of humour and laughter, as well as the talks by Rabbi Cohen who gave us a lot of credit and treated us as mature students. I remember a simple *Batmitzvah* party my friends arranged for me, and a pack of six embroidered handkerchiefs I received from Susie Reich that I treasured for a long time.

I cannot forget the prayer which **Blanka** prayed with us every evening, and told us we could not talk after it. So we kept silent; but it was difficult to resist talking so we invented a secret sign language.

Mrs Eppel was so kind. She would come to see us frequently in her car. It had wood on it. Lots of us had sore throats so we had our tonsils and adenoids removed. The anaesthetic was very frightening. A mask was put on your face. And as we came round there would be Mrs Eppel with her smiling face offering us an ice cream cone. She did this for all the children. We were lucky to have met all these good people in one place at such a crucial time in our lives. Still today Mrs Eppel is my role model for volunteering. I was so devout that year; I did everything with real devotion.

On January 3rd 1949 our parents sent a cable to Rabbi Schonfeld saying we should be sent to "the best possible" Children's Home in Israel and on January 24th we left with a group from the Castle on *aliyah*. On arrival we were taken to a B'nei Akiva Children's Home till our parents arrived with our baby sister, Rachel. Our family was finally reunited at last.

Later on I studied at the Hebrew University, covering the fees by working as a typist for the Post Office for 8 hours a day - a job I hated. So when I saw an advert for a secretary at the Ben Zvi Institute I applied for it. I was a secretary for the President. When he came on Fridays it was as though he was a king. I used to say a special blessing and he liked that. It was a good time. I was young and excited.

My uncle took his family to the United States where they lead a peaceful life, unlike ours in Israel where we are always under stress. He used to send us parcels when such things were in short supply - salami, chocolates, yellow cheese.

I married Zvi Feintuch, a Romanian survivor, an intellectual. He had been a top student at a *yeshiva* in Transylvania when it was closed. Older Jews were taken to Labour Camps but he was too young. He continued to live in familiar surroundings though he was often hungry. Many Jewish refugees fled there from Poland and Hungary on their way to Bucharest. Though he was only a young boy he would be sent to meet them, find them shelter and prepare false papers for them. He forged these on a typewriter and bribed the police to stamp them. He was very skilled, quick and bright to recognise danger and he saved many people.

He was 17 years old when he went on *aliyah* with a youth group after the war. He stayed at Kibbutz Yavneh where he is still remembered. He was always very friendly and a natural leader. He taught *Talmud* for many years at Bar Ilan University. Our first son was born in 1968, one year after the 1967 war. In this tiny country all our friends were soldiers. I was always too concerned for my two wonderful sons. We brought them up to be flexible and tolerant. I used to over-protect them but now they are protective of me. Moshe lives in New York and Uri in Jerusalem. Since my husband died, I spend my time staying with one or the other.

I am a teacher by profession. Who knows if it were not for that period of almost a year in Clonyn Castle that I devoted my life to education? My teaching was mostly at Amit High School for Girls in Jerusalem and at Ramaz and Frisch *Yeshiva* in New York. I have taught literature, Jewish History and Jewish Studies for 34 years. Whenever a student comes and tells me "You see, *Mora*, (Teacher) I am following your example", I feel that I am a role model in the same way my teachers and *madrichot* were role models for me, those teachers and friends in Ireland.

We lost contact with the Clonyn Castle group but in 1997 we visited the Castle again. There were builders working there. After an hour the owner allowed us inside. We took some pictures of the grounds while we waited. She introduced us to her son-in-law, a scientist, with his three year old boy. He chatted with my son. We did not see the daughter but heard she had worked on an archaeological dig in Israel. I remembered the elevator to the kitchen, the greenhouse had been taken down and the beautiful arbour was no longer there. I invited the owner to visit us in Jerusalem but warned her we did not live in a castle.

Two Poems

Judit Ziegler wrote these poems in Hebrew in 1963. They were translated by her son, Moshe Feintuch.

The Girl From the Bunker

Oh God, your world is so white, white, white,
Why did you create a world so white, so cold?
We sit here in graves. How will we stay alive?
Just yesterday, my mom refused forbidden food.
And so we did the same. What shall we eat today?

You know we have among us a couple in love.
They love silently; in silence and in love.
The cold reaches to my toenails and pinches
At my heart. How long will it last?
And when did it start? We were not born here.

But my baby sister - have you heard of her?
The baby that doesn't cry? She was born here.
If you only knew what they wanted to do;
They wanted to kill her. That man wanted
To throw her to the bottom of the hill.

And you know why? Because she cried.
You know it isn't right to risk us all for one.
And they say that for her redemption will come
By her merit and the merit of old grandma.

My grandma and grandpa have already gone.
I have asked them all about it. When will they return?
Grandpa had a white beard, as white as this snow.
And You, God, have You seen them?

Who are You?

Who are you to sing? Who are you to sing your feelings?
This line is long, so very long. You are neither the first,
Nor the last one.

Look backwards: there in the distance
They have known suffering. Look at the black dots.
Those are silent eyes whose lights were dimmed
The eyes of babies and their mothers, sacrifice in their hands,
The eyes of raped virgins and vengeful fathers,
The eyes of the granny on whose lap you heard
Stories of the Messiah and of the Patriarchs.

This grandma of yours was whipped before your eyes.
She did not weep, she covered her head as she went
To the gas chamber.

And you sing songs about yourself?
Beg forgiveness from the eyes that have no tombstone.
Look around you and observe the wrinkled faces
Calloused hands struggling for a loaf of bread.

And there on a hill a boy-soldier was shot, one of many,
Shot dead on his guard. Who will erect him a monument?
And you sing of yourself?

In Auschwitz

Many others have written about their experiences in this hell on earth but few as young as those in the next two stories. It is beyond our imagination to consider what these children suffered in Block 10 - the site of Mengele's atrocities. In Appendix A Jona Laks, representing surviving Mengele Twins today, expresses their feelings half a century later.

Gaspar and Robert Binet and their sister Miriam

Gaspar was just 10 years old and his brother Robert a year younger when they joined Rabbi Schonfeld's group. Their little sister, Miriam, was only 5 and stayed behind with their parents. This account was given to me by Gaspar during 2001 when I visited him in Israel, with contributions from his brother and from his sister.

*Robert introduced me to Miriam, their little sister who did not come to England. He has little English but hers is fluent. She pointed to the number on her arm, tattooed there when she was just two years old. She is surely the youngest to have emerged alive from Auschwitz. She told me that some years ago an Israeli journalist begged them to tell their story. He would write it and publish it and share the proceeds. They were angry and refused. No one who was not there, they told him, could explain or forget the horror of it. And the idea of making money from it was abhorrent. So when I appeared they were suspicious at first. But I persevered and they started to trust me. I would call in to the little shop lined up to the ceiling with shelves of clothes. They gradually provided these recollections and arranged for me to visit their brother, Gaspar. All three spoke of their devoted parents, how wisely and well they coped and how amazing it was that all five of them survived the ordeals of the war. Extraordinary was it, too, that they managed to meet up again afterwards and successfully re-establish themselves in Israel. **Erika Stern**, who knew the Binet family through the clothing business, told me how successful they were before the war and afterwards how hard they worked to start afresh. Today, though retired, both Erica and Miriam still work part-time.*

Our father was very rich before the war. He owned a five-storey house with 28 rooms. When we heard that the Germans were coming to deport us our parents decided to bury some valuables - gold sovereigns and jewellery - in the garden. Our wise mother advised it was better to spread it. So they hid one half of it in a box deep in the forest - a decision that proved of great value to our family after the war was over.

We were three children, me and Asher (Robert) and Miriam. We were born in Nové Zámky in Hungary and moved with our parents to Nové Mesto near Bratislava in 1944. Father was taken away to a forced Labour Camp and disappeared. When all remaining Jews were being rounded up, Mother hid with us; but we were caught and taken to a big yard. There people were ordered to register with their name, age and address. Mother refused to do so, and the result was that our deportation was delayed by several weeks. Eventually we were sent off in cattle trucks.

We reached Auschwitz and were so very frightened. We boys were dressed alike. Robert was not yet five years old. I was six and two months. A huge man asked our mother if we were twins. Another officer, standing behind him, winked at our mother, urging her to say yes - which she did. That decision saved our lives. We were taken away by the scruff of our necks. Robert remembered vividly the number being burnt on to his arm, and that it took eight needles to make the figure eight. It hurt like mad; and two men had to hold him down. He recalled a garden for the children but no toys. At 3 am every night there was a roll call - by numbers. He remembered how some of the twins were sent to a big lab in Berlin for tests but they were not among them. Once they took an older boy for examination but the younger one began to cry. He wanted to go with him. So another boy was taken instead. No one survived from that group.

Our mother meanwhile was held in a barrack block in Birkenau with a friend, Mrs Rosie, who did not survive. She said to her "My children will stay alive." Mrs Rosie told her she was crazy, that no one comes back, "Look at the chimney". But Mother quoted a famous Hungarian Rabbi's words: "The sheep are crying. They want their father. Don't worry. I'll bring you back." Our mother was sent to work with 800 other women in 12 hour shifts in an ammunition factory in Lipstadt, Germany. She was 30 years old. She put all her faith in the belief that her children would survive.

I felt that all the responsibility for my little brother and sister lay on my shoulders. Miriam, aged two and a half years old, was in a different Block. She was just skin and bones. I took scraps to her twice a day - a bit of bread or parsnip wrapped in snow to soften it. She would cling to my shirt. One day she was not there. Then I saw a wagon of dead bodies. She was on the top of it - and alive. I climbed up over those bodies and brought her down. She was so weak she did not even know her name.

On Christmas Eve, before dusk, I saw a whole crowd of prisoners running. So I told Robert to wait for me and I ran, too. Some couple of hundred men and women and some children were running towards a small door in the electric fence. They were breaking it down. The guards had gone to have a drink. I watched and then rushed through the doorway with the rest. We were in the German stores. It was amazing to see masses of food, tins galore. Everyone was grasping stuff for themselves. Salamis were hanging from the roof on strings. I was too small to reach them so I climbed on to a wooden box, grabbed two salamis, hid them in my shirt and ran back.

Then I heard shooting. Everyone around me was shot dead. As far as I know I was the only one to survive. My brother was waiting for me. He was crying. "I thought you were dead", he said. I tore off a bit of sausage with my teeth, softened it in the snow and shared it with my brother. Every evening we ate a bit. It lasted for four or five weeks.

The gas chambers were no longer operating. They had run out of fuel. Eventually the Russians liberated us. We jumped for joy and sang. The Red Cross wrote our names on a list and our cousins saw this and came searching for us. Lists of survivors were posted all over Europe, wherever there were emergency centres set up for those liberated. Miriam was taken to a children's hospital. She was very, very ill. She remembers nothing about these, her early years. My brother and I were taken to a children's camp near Budapest and then to a Christian house in Košice.

Our father returned from the Labour Camp at Dachau and our mother returned from Lipstadt in Germany where she was liberated by the British. All five of us had amazingly survived. We were reunited in our village. The valuables hidden in the garden had been stolen but those in the forest we found intact. Thanks to our mother's wisdom, our father was able to start building a business again. We went to the local secular school where we were called "dirty Jews". There were only ten young Jewish boys, not enough to open a Jewish school. And the Communists were taking over the country. So father sent my brother and me to London with Rabbi Schonfeld and contributed to the cost. Our little sister stayed with our parents. Father travelled with us as far as Belgium; he cried when he left us there. I was ten years old. I remember that we were given bananas and had no idea what they were. So we ate them skin and all!

In London we were met by our cousin, George Klein. He was born in Hungary but his father had brought the family to England before the war. His wife, Renee, comes from Cardiff. They lived in St John's Wood, in London. At his *Seder* I found the *afikomen* and asked for a football and my uncle bought me one from Selfridges.

After *Pesach* we re-joined Rabbi Schonfeld's transport and travelled to Ireland. It was raining when we reached Devlin and I was delighted with the beautiful green grass, the tiny lanes and the big gate over the bridge. We made a synagogue in the Castle and prayed there morning and evening. We slept with six or eight other boys in a big room on army beds made from wood and iron. We boys had meals in the dining room sometimes with the girls, sometimes separately. I went to school in Dublin by train every day - an hour's journey.[7] Many of us had our tonsils and adenoids removed. That meant staying a night in hospital. We agreed to go when we heard we would be given ice cream. We could not speak for a few days but soon recovered. I had never had tonsillitis but my mother approved of our having the operation.

We enjoyed games at the Castle. There was a weekly prize that the bigger boys always won. I was so ambitious. I so much wanted to win. There was a wheelbarrow race. I prayed hard "G-d, let me win" and I said the *shema* - and I won a torch! We had 100 meter races. We went on treks through the woods for two hours at a time carrying walking sticks and water. We went to beautiful places. Every group of twelve or thirteen of us was led by a teacher or an older boy. We would sing Hebrew songs and tell stories about Israel. We spoke Hungarian or Czech. It was fun. In the summer we wore shorts and climbed fences - and sent the girls running. Food was good. I tasted cornflakes and peanut butter for the first time. We had lots of small apples and yellow pears. They wanted us to be happy.

After the Irish Children's Home closed down we spent some months living with a family in Stamford Hill in London. Our parents went on *aliyah* in 1949 with Miriam and six months later we followed them. My father used his savings to open a wholesale clothing business. He was a very good business man and very honest. He worked ten hours a day for the rest of his life, making money for his children and for others. He was much loved and laughed a lot - like Robert does today. He died suddenly on *Shabat* aged 84. He was such a modest man, so good with people; but he never relaxed. I hope to learn from that. Mother also lived to a good old age. She died in 1992 after a fall. She was aged 79.

What matters to me now is to reach pension age and then work less so that I can read and learn. My closest friend is my brother but I trust only myself. I am a bit less wary these days but I am not scared of anyone, nor even of death. I was an officer in the Israel Defence Force. I could cope with dead bodies. I had seen so many in the Concentration Camp. I never cried - I could not, until recent years. I used to have very bad dreams - I would be falling down from very high places and wake up just as I was about to reach the ground. I had these every night till I was about 14. Since I turned 50 years old they have returned.

Like my father I am in the clothing business. So was Robert. He had a clothing store in central Jerusalem just off Zion Square. Our sister Miriam worked there with him till he died of cancer in 2001. He had seven children, all of them married. I have five married children, and lots of grandchildren. I tell my children to remember that their father began with nothing. I used to tell them about the war and about Auschwitz, how we slept in bunks in 3 or 4 tiers like you see in movies and our sister slept in a corner. I advise them not to show off, to keep a low profile and not to waste any food: that it can cost a diamond.

Olga and Vera Grossman

*Olga and her twin sister, Vera, are survivors of Block 10 in Auschwitz where they were victims of Josef Mengele. When in 1948 their mother arranged for them to join Rabbi Schonfeld's transport to Britain they were just 10 years old. Many years later, in 1996, Olga met **Rachel Malmud**, another Slovakian survivor, at Amcha in Haifa. She told her she hoped to visit London again. Rachel knew I would be interested to meet her so gave her my details. I was working then in Jerusalem. Olga introduced herself over the phone. She told me how she and others were brought to London by Rabbi Schonfeld in 1948 - a group I had never heard about before - and that there was a plan for a Reunion in 1998. She had been asked to write up her story for that occasion.*

Olga had always wanted to write about the great debt she owed to Rabbi Schonfeld and about her wartime childhood but found this extremely difficult. It was a long and painful struggle for her to do so - though there were precious memories, too. So she accepted my offer to help her and we have stayed in close touch ever since. She bravely explored the nightmares of long ago and their impact since then during numerous telephone calls to me in London or in Jerusalem. Eventually she found it a therapeutic experience.

I have put together here what she has told me. A large part is drawn from her own writings and letters. A shorter version appeared in the Reunion Brochure although she did not manage to make the journey for that occasion. Olga chose some precious photos to illustrate her story but on her way to post them to me her handbag was stolen - a tragic loss.

Until now I have been running away from my past but I had always intended to write about it. I was always shy, the sick one, not so stable. For years I was dependent on others for support and encouragement. I lived on tranquillisers, sleeping my life away. Since my husband's death in 1995 I had a choice: to let go or go on. I now realise I had been over-protected by my wonderful husband and by the devoted Dr Stern but now I am moving forward, making decisions for myself, proving my capabilities. I have discovered the strength to do so hidden inside me.

Although I have been surrounded by some loving people none of them really knew what I have been through. When I came to Israel I started to express my gratitude to Rabbi Schonfeld. I wanted to put on record how every day he used to take assembly with us at school, how he inspired us all, how he built up my faith. My strength, evident today, stems from that faith. We looked up to him as a father as most of us had lost our fathers during the war.

When I heard that Rabbi Schonfeld had passed away I collapsed. His sister, Osnat Petry, then living in Jerusalem, phoned me. Her voice was so much like his. I broke down. She realised the state I was in and sent me to Dr Dreyfus, a psychiatrist she knew. He understood why I felt so utterly devastated. "And what would you like to do for him?" the psychiatrist asked me. "I want to be his *shaliach*" I told him, "to put on record Rabbi Schonfeld's achievements as some return for all he did for me and so many others". But my psychiatrist in Haifa stopped me writing.

Then in 1996 Barbara entered my life and offered to help me to continue writing my story. Another incident also persuaded me to return to the task. That was a question from my grandson at the age of six "What does the number on your arm mean, Savta Olga?" To my surprise I answered him right away "My little David, when you are old enough you will understand the meaning of our struggle to keep going. Only then will you find out how brave Saba (Grandpa) Rafael and Savta (Grandma) Olga have been in continuing to live for a new generation to come."

With all the hardships I had to go through I have lots of good memories to cherish as well as grim ones. We must give to life as much as we receive from it. So here is my story, sixty years on.

My sister and I were born on April 22nd, 1938 in the little village of Turiani, near Košice, Slovakia. Twins were a real attraction in those days. Long after the war I learned more about our parents from our cousin, Rosie. She is now living in Netanya in Israel. She was born in Braunhorf to a religious family, the sole survivor of five children. She survived three months in Ravensbrück and three years in Auschwitz-Birkenau but she does not talk about it. She had to sort clothes there and she came across our father's fur coat with his monogram embroidered in the lining, certain evidence that he had been killed.

His name was Yitzhak, or Izo, but his nickname was "Abati Nicolas" (Santa Claus in Czech) because he loved to give presents to everyone - as I do today. He was born in Bžany, Slovakia in 1888. He and his three brothers were builders and he owned a lot of property, farms and forests. He was very devout and attended *mincha* every afternoon. He was a lot older than our mother. He had noticed her as a young girl, crossing the street. She was a beautiful woman with raven black hair and bright blue eyes. We inherited our father's dark eyes - a fact that was of interest later to the monster Mengele. Our father was so taken with her that he decided on the spot she should become his wife and, without a *shidduk*, he married her late in his life. Our mother was Shari Shendl, Shendl appropriately meaning beauty in Yiddish. She was born on January 11th, 1913 in Medzilaborce near Michalovce in East Slovakia.

At the age of five we were suddenly taken from our home with our mother. They took us first to Sered, then to Birkenau and then to Auschwitz. At Auschwitz our arms were tattooed: mother as A26944, Olga A26945, Vera A26946. My sister and I were held in Dr Mengele's experimental block. There were about 1500 imprisoned there. We were among the last to arrive. Today we are among the 183 who survived. We were separated from the rest and kept in a cage with another pair of twins, Hannah and Susan. Hannah did not survive the ordeals but her sister Susan is living today in Cleveland, Ohio. At Yad Vashem there is a photo of her as a little child, pointing to the number on her arm.

We were injected several times a day and taken to the lab for blood tests. Often we were left naked in freezing cold, sick and weak with rashes, boils and blisters. At one stage those boils were injected and we were kept in quarantine for two months with 120 other children and gypsies in some sort of experiment. We had fevers, our skin was itchy, our bodies swollen. We dozed and slept a lot. One girl was beaten with a rubber instrument and died. Once we heard screams at night and the cry of a newborn infant. We wanted to find out what was going on and saw the baby thrown into an oven. We experienced inhuman cruelty and violence. We saw and heard others suffering appalling treatment. One surviving twin had to watch his brother being tortured. The impact of those experiences has remained within me as everlasting wounds. Mundane events can still take me back to those horrors and ever since I have been readily prone to fainting. My sister Vera has coped better than I have.

We were separated from our mother. She was working and not allowed to visit us but sometimes she would peep through our door at night and smuggle us scraps of food she had found, a bit of bread or raw potato. She was faint with exhaustion and she was beaten by the guards if they saw her. It must have been unbearable for her to see her children suffering.

The Russians liberated us on January 27th 1945. Our huts were set on fire and there were bullets flying around. We hid under our mother's skirt. We struggled through deep snow not knowing where we were. Our mother would carry each of us in turn, urging the other one to run, to move on. The Nazi guards were shooting stragglers indiscriminately. I remember German soldiers rushing by on motorcycles, fleeing from the Russians.

We returned to Stropkov in East Slovakia. Our mother kept geese and bought a cow so we could have fresh milk to strengthen us. Post-war conditions were very bad. It was there she met Yakir Sinsovitz. He was also a Camp survivor. He was Polish. He had lost his wife and all his six children. He and my mother decided to get together and so I acquired a second father. He dedicated himself to our welfare. My earliest memory was that he provided us with a bath. I remember, too, during that time that I fainted at the sight of the baker's oven and again at the butcher's shop.

In 1946 we moved to Košice where some Jewish survivors had returned and were re-organising community services. I recall an outing to a park outside the town and realising there was a pleasant world out there that had been obliterated by our Auschwitz experiences. My sister and I attended the Beis Ya'acov School which had been re-established. Mrs Matilde Schwartz was our teacher. She had bright blue eyes and always wore a turban. She inspired us at a difficult time. Today she lives in Netanya.

In 1948 a British Rabbi arrived in Košice. He offered care and education in England for child survivors till their parents were settled. Vera and I were sent off with him. I do not know how our mother decided to separate from us again. It was very hard. We had our tenth birthday on the journey and spent the next five years in the care of Rabbi Schonfeld.

For the first year we were at Clonyn Castle in Ireland. It was a real castle. We had special tutors and leaders there who taught us all subjects. What we liked most were religious studies. **Séndi** was our special *madrich*. We could listen for hours to her tales about our ancestors. There at Clonyn Castle we learned for the first time in our lives to play games - "Hide and Seek", for instance. In the beginning we associated "hiding" with fear, and "running" meant for us, escaping. But with the loving care of our leaders we learned to play - and enjoy playing.

In 1949 the last of the children left Ireland. Most had joined their families but we were among the final twenty taken to London. There my sister and I were fostered by Dayan and Mrs Posen in Stamford Hill. In 1999 I met a daughter of the Posen family again. She said her parents had fostered children throughout the war. She remembered us, the Grossman twins, as happy little girls who were always hungry.

We had an excellent Jewish education at the Avigdor High School. Rabbi Schonfeld was the Principal, Dr Judith Grunfeld the Headmistress of the girls' school. These people and the Posen family had a profound influence on us. They provided us with love and security and a fine Jewish value system which we have retained ever since. I also owe a lot to my school friend, Miriam, and her parents who treated us as their own. My friendship with Miriam continues to this day. She reminded me that Vera and I were the best at sports. In netball my sister was always attack and I was defence just as we are now. And we won swimming certificates at Clissold Road Baths.

Meanwhile my mother and stepfather had emigrated to Israel where they had four more children, all girls. We could not understand why they had not arranged for us to join them there. So we wrote to ask with the help of a dictionary as by then we had forgotten our mother tongue. Our mother replied that life was hard in Israel and we would do best to come with a British education. So we stayed on at the Avigdor High School till 1953. We were among the last of the Slovakian group to leave for Israel. Rabbi Schonfeld said it had been for our own good to stay and he was right.

We arrived on the ship *SS Negba* on January 6th 1953 and we met our mother again after living apart for six years. I was tongue-tied. Our bonding had faded. It had been such a long separation. Yet this was another miracle. I was so thankful and grateful to our dear G-d for bringing us together again.

We found that the family income was meagre. As the eldest I felt very responsible and went out to work for long hours in a beauty salon. At first my sister worked as a seamstress. Our stepfather, Yakir, had invested what money he had in Skoda, a cousin's car firm, but the venture failed. He was a good man and took full responsibility and loving care of us alongside his own four girls, our step-sisters. But his efforts were impeded by bad luck in business and poor health. He was such a very kind man but he lost his money and broke down. We were devoted to him. Vera and I called him *Abba* (Father) and that speaks for itself. In later years he became the cantor at our local synagogue and people flocked there to hear him sing. He had a fine voice.

Soon after we joined them our mother, too, became ill and there were the four young children. So my sister stayed at home to help look after the family but as the eldest I saw it as my duty to bring in some money. Really I had wanted to study. I love things that speak to me, like visiting art galleries, but that was out of the question. They discovered I had good hands and a talent for styling hair and making women look prettier. I was on my feet sometimes 18 hours a day and on the Fast of *Yom Kippur* I fainted in synagogue. Probably it was not so much from hunger as sheer fatigue. My mother panicked and asked for some water. A soldier in uniform came and brought me some. His name was Rafael. He was the only person in the entire congregation who bothered to come to my aid. When I woke up I saw him as if in a dream. He was so handsome. This was how I met my future husband.

We got to know each other when I went to thank him. I was very shy. But I realised then that he had everything I needed. He was my guardian angel. I called him "my angel Rafael". His family name, Solomon or

Samech, has the happy meaning "to rely on". It turned out that we had similar backgrounds for he, too, was a survivor of Auschwitz. He was the sole survivor of his family. He lost his parents there, his two brothers and his sister. He reached Israel on the ill-fated *SS Altalena*.[8] When it was bombed he jumped into the sea and swam ashore. He went to live with his uncle, Zvi, and his wife, Esther, in Haifa. He was very happy with them and their daughter, Sonia, was a great help to me later on. Another uncle, Nicolas in London, sent him to Prague. Then he joined the Israeli Air Force and became a Colonel, a *Sgan-Aluf*.

There was an instant kinship between Rafael and me but he did not propose immediately. I was only seventeen. He was ten years older and a professional soldier, very tough. I liked that. It gave me courage seeing him in uniform. An old friend recalled him years later as jolly, kind and a very pleasant man. We were married the following year. Vera, meanwhile, also married and had two children. They live in the south of Israel. Since then we have gone our separate ways. Vera's reactions to our past are very different from mine. She believes in using every opportunity to express her recollections. She sees this as a duty though she often assumes my reactions, too. That was how my husband first heard what I had been through, from the papers.

I had to share my husband with the Israeli Air Force where he had a very successful career and was highly respected. He was immensely popular with his men. They affectionately called him *Abba*. He took a parental interest in their welfare and great pride in the base he commanded. He called it his "empire" and worked long hours but he always remembered his other responsibility - his depressed wife at home.

The birth of our first child should have been a wonderful event. But I was terrified. Those episodes in Auschwitz came flooding back. The images rushed back into my vision. I was terrified my child would not live and that I would never see her again. I was hospitalised. My baby daughter was only two months old.

Two sisters, neighbours in Haifa, came to my rescue, both married with children of their own. They took devoted care of my Leah then and have continued ever since to support and help us in numerous ways. Both families have settled in Montreal, Canada but they stay in touch with us and are like the best of grandparents.

Five years later it happened again with the birth of my son, my second child: "Let me see my babies! Why could they not be brought to visit me?" I was sure that meant they were dead. They drugged me. They shut me off from them. They kept me in hospital. "You are not well enough to take care of your children." That broke my heart. It was *Pesach*. I collapsed. I starved myself. "I'll eat only *matzot*." They insisted, forced-fed me. I struggled. I fought like a lioness.

Only my husband understood. All this was too painful to speak about but we spoke with our eyes. One *Shabat* he came with bags of treats to take me home for the day. On the way the car broke down. We continued on a train, on a train again. I passed out. They had to take me back to hospital. I tried to throw myself out of the cab. I could not bear it any more. My husband restrained me. A nurse said "Just be obedient then they'll let you go home". But I thought I'd never be free.

I did not see the children that time. When I did visit them at first I could not cope but eventually I was allowed home every day. My husband had to work very long hours so my mother and Bella, an older woman, looked after my children and household. It was unbearable. I was so hurt inside. It was a sort of imprisonment yet home was the safest place. I slept a lot because I was on medication. Some injections made me sleep for days. My head stopped working and I chose not to mix with others.

There was only one social occasion that I attended during that time. My husband was determined I should attend the **Barmitzvah** with him of his Commander's son. I do not drive on *Shabat* so my husband booked a hotel room for us. I was worried about how I was going to keep awake and avoid disgracing him. As I was taking large doses of sedatives I was afraid I looked different from other people but he assured me I looked great! I could not let him down.

My Rafael was not a big talker, just the opposite of me. He would often phone me during the day. And I would stay at home where I felt safest, waiting for him to come back from work, guilty for being the sick and demanding wife. He never showed me pity. He accepted me as I was.

The doctors never asked about my history and they told my husband never to let me talk about my past. My husband kept me alive but as talk of the past was taboo he knew nothing about my wartime existence. I only wanted to look after my family and myself, to meet their needs and please other people but the medication forced me to sleep my life away.

Later on a psychiatrist who was also born in Košice looked after me. She had worked with the Partisans during the war. She treated me like the daughter she never had but she also prescribed sedatives. I became too dependant on her and my husband. Nevertheless they succeeded in bringing me back to real life and encouraged me to start going out again.

In 1979, after we had been to our daughter's wedding in Winnipeg, Canada, we went to visit Dr Schonfeld in London. To my surprise, he recognised me right away saying: "My child, you are Olga! Your eyes always spoke for you and expressed your gratitude." He took a little book, wrote down the date of our visit and then asked for our birth dates. Then he said "You chose well. Rafael is your match." I shed happy tears and said "Rabbi Schonfeld I want you to know that you were a father to me." He answered "No, my child, I was not your father, only G-d's messenger."

I was privileged to have been married to Rafael for forty years. He worried about me, supported me and gave me back my strength. When he was very tired he could depend on me for a change. During his final illness a good friend, a brother officer, came every day to help me to look after him. He spoke proudly of "a mission accomplished." He died at the age of 65 in 1993.

What gave me the greatest pleasure was to see Rafael's happy face when our children were born and later our wonderful grandchildren. It was especially meaningful for me when my daughter married a second time into the family of Sarah Schenirer, the founder of the Beis Ya'acov Schools. She was the inspiration of my teachers, Mrs Matilde Schwartz in Košice and Dr Judith Grunfeld in London.[9] My grandson, David, when aged seven, left a secret prayer in the Western Wall. Soon after, on my birthday, he confided his wish to me: "Savta Olga should be with us when I celebrate my *Barmitzvah*" - and I was! After he had been to Yad Vashem he told me "Now I know what happened to you. You did not have a childhood like ours. So now you can play with us." One day he asked if I would talk to his class about my wartime experiences. How could I refuse? I stood there, beside my daughter and my grandsons and spoke as if only to them. It was the first time I had ever spoken about the Holocaust in public. This was a turning point. Instead of relying on drugs I was learning to live my own life in my own way. I still struggle to prove I can cope on my own.

My children often find me difficult to understand. They say I am too emotional but my greatest joy is when I can be of help to them and to others in need. That is why I chose to stay in Israel even when a good friend tried hard to persuade me to move to the States.

Now my kind doctor is old and ill in a nursing home and we have reversed roles. I offer her loving care, visit her, feed her, and I arranged for her to have a night nurse.

In 1994 I attended the group led by Sara at Amcha in Haifa. Sara said that I must try to avoid being dependent on other people. Then in 1999 I went to Amcha again, looking my best. And what did I find? I was much the youngest there. Those elderly people obviously thought I had come to the wrong address!

It is very lonely to be a child survivor, and since 1993 a widow, but there are bright moments. In 1995 a stranger stared at me on a local bus and it was my turn to think she had made a mistake. "Aren't you a twin?" she said. She had recognised me. She was Bracha. We had met soon after Auschwitz-Birkenau was liberated. She had lost her sister. My beautiful mother gave her a place near us in the old barracks. "Your mother invited me to travel with you back to Slovakia. But I was still hoping to find my sister or someone from my family. So I refused. But I have never forgotten her kindness in those dark days". It was wonderful to hear Bracha talk about my heroine of a mother. Now we keep in touch. She, too, encouraged me to open up the past and that agonising process has freed me.

I live today with joy and concern for my children who are very successful and for my grandchildren who I dearly love. They give me huge pleasure. In 2006 Leah surprised everyone by producing twins, a boy and a girl; and, to my great joy, the boy is named Rafael after his grandfather.

I am a miracle. We are all heroes and heroines. But I do not think of myself or call any of us SURVIVORS. That word conveys the notion that we merely want to exist. The truth is we are STRUGGLERS, determined to overcome whatever stands in our way despite the hell we went through and despite all the trials and tribulations that we have had to face since then. We want recognition and we deserve it, not for any personal publicity but so that others, especially the medical profession, realise and understand what we went through. We won the war against those who wanted to destroy us at immeasurable personal cost. We are living evidence of that victory.

Rabbi Schonfeld said "It does not matter how long you live but only how you live." Among my most precious possessions is a letter he gave me when I was finally leaving his care. This clear statement has sustained me and given me strength throughout my life:

> ## TO WHOM IT MAY CONCERN
> *Miss Olga Grossman, born 22nd April 1938, has been known to me for about five years. She comes from a strictly Orthodox home in Czechoslovakia and has been brought up here in London in the same orthodoxy both at school and at home. She is determined to make Torah the guiding principle of her life. I am confident that Olga, who is now joining her parents in Israel, will always keep up the teachings of Orthodox Judaism.*
> *Rabbi Dr S. Schonfeld Ph.D.*
> *Presiding Rabbi, Union of Orthodox Hebrew Congregations.*

In 2001 Olga received an invitation to a Symposium at the Max Planck Institute in Berlin where Mengele's wartime activities were being investigated. She decided not to attend it but her sister Vera did. Olga introduced me to Jona Laks who represents today the remaining Mengele Twins. Jona spoke on their behalf to that gathering. Appendix A contains her powerful address.

Blanka Federweiss

*Blanka was probably the oldest girl to come from Bratislava. The Visa indicates that she was just 16 but she was in fact 20 years old. At Clonyn Castle she was valued almost as a member of staff. She became a close friend of **Séndi Templer** and, like her, left a lasting impact on the younger children. Here is what she told me during the 1998 Reunion.*

I was born in Dunaszerdahely, Czechoslovakia, in 1927, one of six children. It was a happy life. We were not rich. Father was a teacher at the local *cheder*. Mother ran a small "take away" service providing good Hungarian food. She was the youngest of seven children. Her mother, too, was a cook and had a big restaurant in Bratislava before I was born.

We had beautiful *Shabbos* that I often think about today. And we heard - but did not believe - rumours of what was to come. Then, suddenly, we were in the ghetto. We were allowed to take very little with us. We were there for three weeks in the school and the yard around it. Conditions were very bad. Then we were taken to Auschwitz in cattle trucks. I was 17 years old. There we were separated; the elderly and the young children went one way. I, with my two older sisters and a cousin went another.

It meant so much to know someone cared about you in that awful place. When one of my sisters and my cousin were terribly ill with typhus we helped look after them and gave them the most important thing we had: our bread and our soup. And when I was sick, or my other sister, the others gave us their bread, too. I remember one mother and daughter who fought over their bread. We worked all day, outdoors, and had to walk many miles in wooden shoes and with bare legs. It was bitterly cold at night. Every day was so long; and we suffered such hunger. Some of us were taken to Cracow. We had a five days' task to clear heavy stones. One group had to carry them uphill and convey them to another group who passed them hand to hand.

On the Ninth of Ab somehow our Jewish hearts woke up. The Almighty gave us the strength to rebel. Some of us decided to keep the Fast, refused our meagre rations and took on the lighter work. I was wearing a red scarf. It rained and the colour ran so it looked as though I was bleeding. This hard labour lasted till January 1st 1945. Then we were sent to Bergen-Belsen where there was no work and all we could do was lie on the floor, packed together like sardines, covered with lice, itching like mad. It was horrible.

In May or June the Americans came. They did not believe we would survive. But slowly, very slowly, we recovered though there was no room in the hospitals. They only had beds for people in a worse state than we were. Yet all my sisters survived and one brother. Although he was very weak he eventually reached Israel illegally. He had a dreadful journey. He stayed there but wrote to his sisters that it was no life for Jewish girls and told us not to come. My two older sisters married and obtained student papers that allowed them entry to the USA. I wanted to go, too. We knew the Russians were coming and that we would be hemmed in. We were very afraid. Then Rabbi Schonfeld came.

At that time I was attending the Beis Ya'acov Boarding School in Bratislava with the **Wiesner** sisters. It was there that I first met **Séndi Templer**. Séndi has become my very best friend though I am older than her. I love her dearly. She is still a great carer. Rabbi Schonfeld sent us with a hundred children from the group that he gathered from Bratislava and Prague and took us to London in April 1948.

Séndi and I went to Clonyn Castle. She became the main carer of the younger children and I helped her. I love children. It was so pitiful to realise that these little ones had no parents to look after them. We dressed them, washed their clothes and their hair and plaited it. There was plenty of food. I used to *kosher* the meat with another girl. Rabbi Schonfeld sent teachers from London. The boys had their own leaders and teachers. One of them was Benjamin Pels who later married Séndi.

We had not yet obtained papers to go to England. These were only acquired some months later. Then I went to live at Woodberry Down Hostel in North London. [10]

In London I learned English and worked as a machinist in a shirt factory. After a time I asked Rabbi Schonfeld if he could obtain for me a visa to the United States. Nine months later I arrived in Brooklyn.

I am settled well there. My husband was Hungarian and he was also a Holocaust survivor. He lost most of his family, all except for one brother who went to Israel. He was a good and very special man. He loved people and was himself a much-respected figure. He was an electrician. We did not want our children to know Hungarian so we talked Yiddish at home. We had eleven children, eight boys and three girls, now all married. There are lots of grandchildren. I have lost track of how many! The Almighty has helped us!

I am so glad I came to the Reunion. It has been wonderful to see these "children" again.

In 2007 I heard that Blanka had died. Her daughter said that attending the Reunion had been a wonderful closure to her life.

Ervin Schwarz

Ervin was 15 when he joined Rabbi Schonfeld's transport. I recorded this account of his experiences at his home in Jerusalem during August 1997 and included it in the Reunion Brochure.

I was born in Mala Torona, six kilometers from Satoralja Ujhel. It is a small place in Czechoslovakia on the borders of Hungary in the Tokai District noted for its vineyards. My father was in the wine business and had a grocery shop. We were kings of the place, one of about thirty-five Jewish families living there. Jewish families were spread in many similar villages locally and shared a synagogue. My parents were very religious.

I was the second child. I had an older sister and two younger ones. For two or three years I attended school in our village. After Hungary occupied Slovakia I went to one of the two Jewish schools and to *cheder* in the town of Satorlsa Ushel. Then in 1944 came the war and on the day after *Pesach* we were herded into the ghetto in Satorlsa Ushel. Two or three families were crowded into every room. Six weeks later we were taken in cattle trucks to Auschwitz of which we knew nothing at that time. Our family was in the third truck.

I remember how any jewellery, anything of value, had to be given up with the threat that otherwise the whole family would be shot. So when the train stopped on the way at Košice and the guards demanded any hidden valuables there were none left. We reached Auschwitz before dawn. Everyone was busy marking their luggage with no notion of what was to come. A Polish Jew came up to me. He had been in the Camp for the past several years. His job was to take baggage from the train for sorting. He asked me in Yiddish how old I was. I told him, 15. "Tell the German officer you are 18 and that you are a farm worker". I asked him why and he replied: "Don't ask! Just remember you are a worker and not a schoolboy. I'm not allowed to talk to you." And he went off.

Then men and women were separated. My sisters went with our mother, I went with my father. He was aged 38 or 39 then. We had to pass Mengele one by one. Anyone elderly or very ill was sent to the left - to the crematorium. My father was selected for work and sent to the right. When my turn came he asked my age and I answered as I had been advised and was sent to follow my father. Thousands of us were marshalled into rows then inspected again. This time the officer sent me off and told the others to move up but as he went rapidly on my father pulled me back, stopping others from filling my place. My mother and sisters were sent to the gas chamber.

Our heads were shaved and we were put through all the other procedures. Three weeks later about a thousand of us were sent to a Concentration Camp in Warsaw. Our task was to collect bricks from the bombed ruins of the ghetto to be sent to Germany. It was three months of very hard work.

I developed a high fever and was hospitalised. It was measles. You could hear shooting and bombing. The Russians were near us. Everyone rushed into the yard and we were told that if they could not march for four days to fall out and await transport to the next Camp. Though I was still very weak my father insisted I stay with him. We walked five in a row, SS men on either side, in very hot weather with no food, no water, on the go all day. At night we lay in fields in our thousands. If anyone got up he was shot. In the morning off we went again. Next we were packed into cattle trucks, standing, a hundred people crushed into a truck where thirty would have been enough. Anyone moving was shot on the spot. We were each given a spoonful of salty meat. That increased our thirst. By the time we reached Dachau my hands were badly swollen. I was too weak to recall much. I fell down, could no longer walk and was carried to the hospital, the youngest patient there. A Dutch Christian minister, a political prisoner, looked after me. He was allowed to receive food parcels and shared them with me. He would force up the reading on the thermometer so the doctors would keep me longer in the hospital. He bandaged me up to appear in a worse state than I was - until I was stronger. Then it became too dangerous to go on fooling the SS.

I worked in a cement factory for eight months near Alach Concentration Camp some 6km from Dachau. The war was ending. Himmler ordered that Dachau and all the other Camps were to be cleared. We were sent off in open trucks, closed in with wire netting. Our train was fleeing from the Allies as they approached nearer and nearer. The plan was for us to be gassed in the Tyrol. The German soldiers were very scared. Their Commandant tried to ingratiate himself - to make out he had our welfare at heart. "You'll be liberated. Don't stand on the main road where you'll be shot. If you have the strength, hide in the woods. I'm trying to save you." The war had still not ended. Americans were shooting at our train. They thought we were soldiers so we tore off our striped jackets and waved them so they could see we were not armed. And at last the Germans surrendered. The German Commandant saluted the US officers and handed us over, reporting so many were present, so many had died and trying to make out how efficient he was. Jewish American soldiers spoke to us in Yiddish and gave us something to eat. Everyone was running around everywhere searching for food. The Americans were very concerned about diseases and illness amongst us. They took us to army barracks in Landsberg where "The Joint" organised food and care for us. They asked where our homes had been and advised us how we could reach them. I did not think that my father was still alive but I was not sure. I wanted to go back to our village.

Only years later did my cousins who had escaped to Israel admit to me that my father had died in Dachau. I learned, too, how my mother and two younger sisters had been taken straight to the crematorium at Auschwitz and that my older sister had died two weeks before liberation.

A big US lorry took me into Czechoslovakia. They let me stay a few days in the barracks at Pilsen. We could travel free but trains were so packed we lay in peril on the roof. Some were killed by overhead wires. I reached Prague. Further on there were long detours as many bridges had been bombed. In Bratislava and in Budapest "The Joint" helped us on our way. A week later I reached the nearest town to my village. Not one Jew remained. A few had returned briefly. Two Christian families were living in our house. Another let me have a room. But I had no money. What was I to do?

By some lucky chance a letter came from my mother's sister in the United States in the hope of finding us. Enclosed was $5. So I crept by night over the fields and crossed into Hungary. As cigarettes were cheaper there than in Slovakia I bought some and sold them at a small profit and so slowly built up some savings. A non-Jewish lad began coming with me. We would walk along the main road, he with the parcel, while I went ahead with a torch. When I signalled any danger he fled into the fields. So we worked together and increased our income.

One day I met old friends of my parents in nearby Košice. They wanted me to stay with them. Meanwhile I had bought fine leather boots and a smart suit. This made the neighbours jealous. People started to tease me: "Where can I meet you and relieve you of your boots?" Others tried reporting me to the police for illegal activities but I was protected because they bought my cigarettes. My situation was worsening and I was galled to see our family furniture and other things brazenly displayed in neighbours' houses with never a word to me. I told the police about this. My newly-married cousin, living 25 km away, was badly off. I wanted her to have some of the family possessions. The police made a pact with me: they would assist me to reclaim what was mine if I took the stuff and left the village immediately. I agreed.

We went in a wagon from house to house where I identified what belonged to my family. The police asked each household if they had anything not theirs obtained during the war. They tried to say the Germans had given them the things I pointed out. We took them back. The last house we called at, two doors from my family home, was that of the Municipal Information Officer. I had been to school with his sons. On the sideboard were crystal bowls I knew had belonged to my family but they would not admit it. This man swore at me and said "Hitler should have burnt you with your parents and the rest of them. Why did you come back?" I don't know what got into me but I dragged the cloth off the laden table and smashed everything in sight with my new boots - and ran.

The next year I spent at a Mizrachi Community on the Sudeten border where boys and girls were prepared for *aliyah*. The Czechs sold ammunition to Israel so relations were friendly. Then I moved to a *yeshiva* run by Rabbi Shtern in Marienbad, studying with sixty other boys and trained for the electrical trade. It was 1948. The Communists had recently occupied Czechoslovakia. I returned from spending *Shabat* with relatives to be told by Rabbi Shtern that Rabbi Dr Schonfeld had an exit visa for 150 youngsters to return with him to England and had agreed to take a few from the *yeshiva*. Rabbi Shtern explained that this was an opportunity to escape the Communists. He wanted me to go to England to continue my Jewish studies rather than to Israel where he feared I would lose my faith. He sent me off to pack.

I first met Dr Schonfeld in his British Army uniform in his hotel room in Prague. He put my photo on a new ID card telling me that my name must from now on be changed from Eugene, a Czech name, to Ervin. I was to forget my Czech origins and tell the authorities at the border I was a war orphan born in Hungary. We were to speak no Czech, only Hungarian and Yiddish. The next day I joined the group of children leaving for Britain. We older boys were in charge of younger ones. According to the Visa we were all under 16 but in fact some of us were 18 or 19 - and we were told to make ourselves appear as short as possible. The Rabbi explained these lads looked older as they had been under-nourished in the camps and had now made up for it. But he was very nervous till we were safely over the German border and crossed into Belgium to take the ferry from Ostende. It was the day before *Pesach* when we reached London and we were dispersed among families in Stamford Hill for the week of the Feast.

Rabbi Schonfeld had persuaded the British authorities to allow him to take full financial responsibility for 50 children. They stayed in London. The Irish government had agreed to allow entry for 100. So after *Pesach* we travelled by bus to Holyhead, and by boat to Ireland. A great welcome was given to us by the Dublin community. They gave us a big breakfast at Greenville Hall Synagogue. Some of the older boys were taken in large cars to live with families in the city. The rest of us went to Clonyn Castle - a fine place owned by a Manchester wine merchant. Rabbi Cohen and his wife were in charge of us. One of our girls, **Séndi**, looked after the smallest children as she had already been doing as a young teenager before we left Prague. Rabbi Pels, another teacher on the staff, later married her. Marguiles - now an established caterer - was our cook. I had been persuaded to look after a group of 18 young children in return for pocket money. I taught them for six months; then I joined the older boys in Dublin where we lived in a big house with Rabbi Pollak in charge. I worked in a factory making ladies' handbags.

During 1949 the CBF (Central British Fund for Jewish Relief and Rehabilitation) found us rooms in private families in London and covered our rent till we became self-supporting. I managed that two years later and continued to work in the manufacture of ladies' handbags. It took me two years to learn the trade and then I opened my own business. At the start I employed two half-timers, a woman machinist and a bus conductor between his shifts, for cutting leather. Slowly the business developed until eventually we moved from the East End to Kilburn where I had 130 employees. During the 1970s imports built up and we could not compete with foreign competition. So reluctantly I sold up to big importers in Leicester on the understanding I continue to manage the business for a further 5 years. I did not enjoy that period. I retired in 1985.

Meanwhile I had met on holiday in Knocke, Belgium, a girl from Strasbourg. She had been hidden with other small children on a farm in France, near Limoges, where a number of Alsace Jews sat out the war under the Vichy government. Some of these managed to avoid being taken to Auschwitz. It was a near miss for my wife's parents. Her uncle and all his children were taken away by the Nazis but they failed to find my in-laws. Her father was interned but somehow was freed.

We married in Strasbourg in 1956 and I brought her to London. She knew a little English before she came and soon picked up the language. We had three sons. Two live in London and one is married with four children and lives in Israel. We lived first in Clapton then moved to Golders Green. After I retired from business we emigrated to Israel and settled in Jerusalem, something I had talked of doing many years before. My wife's mother and her brother were already living there. My wife died in 1996.

People ask how I occupy myself now. Three times a week I play bowls and we have competitions. It is an international game these days. I meet very pleasant people. We have a club in a beautiful place in the Jerusalem

Forest. In the mornings I attend a *shiur* for retired people; interesting subjects are discussed. I had dropped religious practice after the war when none of my family came back but slowly I returned to it. And I am a volunteer at Bikur Cholim Hospital.

We shall be ever grateful to Dr Schonfeld who with his own hands saved so many thousands both before the war and afterwards. Without him I would not have been here to tell my story. It was an extraordinary fact that when meeting us by chance in later years he still remembered our names.

In 2007 I learned that Ervin had married again. His new wife had reached England on a pre-war Schonfeld transport.

Alfred Leicht

*Alfred was nearly 18 when he joined Rabbi Schonfeld's transport though the Visa shows him as 15. Alfred only learned of the Reunion in 2001 when he made a private visit to Clonyn Castle with his friend **Alfred Kahan**. Later we met at a gathering at Israel Reich's home in London. He sent me three separate documents about his life story that I have combined into a single account. These were talks he had given to young audiences at the Jewish Museum in Atlanta.*

I was born in Hungary in 1930 in a town called Bilke. It is roughly 150 miles east of Budapest, the capital of Hungary. Hungary is the size of Maine, with a similar climate. Because it is a small country and surrounded by Austria, Yugoslavia, the Czech Republic, Romania and Ukraine, we spoke several languages. At home and at school we spoke Hungarian and Ukrainian and a little Czech. In our community of 30,000, about 25 to 30 families were of the Jewish faith.

Life was very primitive and harsh. We had no automobiles, no electricity and no indoor toilet facilities. It was like living in rural Georgia 100 years ago. Our life expectancy was 42 to 43 years. Medicine and the treatment of sick people were even more primitive. Health workers used leeches on the body to suck out the "bad blood" as a cure for most illnesses.

My parents were middle-class people. Abraham, my father, owned a clothing store and a farm where we often worked after school. My mother, Rose, was a model and a Hungarian beauty queen, highly admired in our community. I was the oldest of four brothers spaced two years apart. Our friends were mostly in the Jewish community. Because we were shunned and rejected as infidels we didn't socialize much with our Christian neighbors. We went to the public school, where our classmates had been taught at church and at home to dislike us. We were often treated contemptuously and taunted as Christ killers, accused of being in league with the devil.

The Hungarian government acted in concert with Nazi ideology from 1933 but the Nazis did not occupy the country until early 1944. It was a Fascist and totalitarian dictatorship, collaborating with Hitler and the Nazi agenda. There was no freedom of speech or press or assembly. Any dissenting views were treated harshly and without mercy. Jews had no civil rights, could not vote or hold public office and quotas were placed on higher education. We were isolated from the rest of the community; and as

Hitler expanded his power and aggression, it emboldened the Hungarian collaborators to threaten, persecute and even murder Jews. Only when the Hungarian government faltered in supporting mass murder did Hitler move in his forces to take charge of the liquidation of the last intact Jewish community on the Continent.

In 1942, when I was 12 years old, we were awakened in the night by a forceful knock on the door and the dreaded secret police burst into the house. They ordered my dad to go with them, barely giving him time to get dressed. We thought he would be questioned and released. We never dreamed that he would not return. My mother was left with four young children and very little money to support us. The trauma, grief and fear were devastating. This soul-scaring episode was a precursor to our deportation and the shadow of impending doom. Almost immediately we started to hear rumors about what had happened to my dad and the other Jewish leaders who were arrested that night. We later found out that they were taken on a death march into the mountains, ordered to dig their own mass grave, gunned down in the most savage and inhumane manner and disposed of as utterly worthless creatures.

In April 1944 when I was 14, my life as I knew it changed forever. One early morning, the Arrow Cross Fascist soldiers, the Hungarian equivalent of the Gestapo and of the Slovak Hlinka Guards, surrounded all the Jewish homes in Bilke. They gave us one hour to pack our bags and follow them to the train station. My mother, brothers and I, along with all the remaining Jews of our town, were to be sent to an unknown destination. The panic, hysteria and terror were so overwhelming that it still haunts me. Images of this experience are seared in my heart and will forever smolder in my memory. It left us gasping for comprehension. But the trauma and anxiety was a mere prelude to an even bigger nightmare. It was our turn to experience the Nazi Final Solution - the systematic extermination of the Jews of Europe.

We were initially taken to a ghetto, a central collection Camp for our region. From there a week later we were loaded onto a train. We didn't know it but we were headed for the Death Camp at Auschwitz. The train ride was an experience that defies description, civility and imagination. Roughly 100 people were herded into each box or cattle car. The doors were sealed and we were deprived of food, water and sanitation facilities for over two days. Hundreds died on route. The sense of impending doom drove countless others into insanity, hysteria and paralysis. People were praying and pleading for mercy to an unresponsive heaven. It was a surreal scene only approached in Dante's "Inferno" - his poem about hell.

Our transport had a rendezvous with a gruesome and ghoulish fate. As the clunking, hooting and smoke-belching train arrived at the notorious gates of Auschwitz with its sick, terrified, starving and unsanitary cargo, we were met by the terrorizing Gestapo with menacing dogs and dozens of prisoners called *sonderkommandos*. The fateful separation process started promptly. We saw the towering and ominous crematoriums belching out smoke and ashes. The stench of burning human flesh immediately permeated our nostrils. We were stripped of our possessions and dignity in a process that was so swift and brutal that most of us did not suspect the impending doom. Roughly 80% of our transport - the elderly, women with children, the infirm and sick - were herded into a deceptively arid lethal shower room. The murderers then unleashed the deadly Zyklon-B gas as the huddled victims gasped for air and frantically pleaded for mercy. Their contorted and disfigured bodies were then hauled away and dispatched to the crematoriums. They were reduced to ashes leaving only haunting images of their dreadful fate. Their remains were dishonored and dehumanized in a massive open pit and immortalized as a symbol of visceral hate, a monument to Hitler's madness.

My mother, clutching my three brothers, was forcefully separated from me and consigned to the gas chambers. The last words my mother uttered, with anguish and terror in her eyes, were "I love you." Within an hour, their precious lives and unrealized hopes and dreams were snuffed out. Their cruel fate became a traumatic memory that continues to haunt me over a half-century later. My mother was 36 and my brothers were 8, 10 and 12 years of age. Their only crime was their religious faith and commitment to the biblical injunction to honor our God "with all thy heart and with all thy soul" (a quote from the *Shema*). Fifty-five years later I still freeze every time I hear hooting and whistling trains chugging away with their clanking noises and squeaky brakes.

History has carved no sterner moments to its propensity for monstrous evil than Auschwitz. Auschwitz was the world's largest cemetery with two efficient killing machines: the gas chamber and starvation and disease. According to recovered archives, 1.3 million people had been shipped to Auschwitz and at least 1.1 million had perished in this single Death Camp. It was slaughter on a massive scale. For the 20-25% of us who were spared in the initial selection it was death in slow motion from the moment we were assigned the striped suits. Auschwitz was a brutal and savage slave Labour Camp with endless privations, endless beatings, endless cruelty, endless starvation and endless killings. Life was very fragile and fraught with hourly existential concerns. A third of the inmates died of starvation, dysentery, and disease during the first six months. The death rate accelerated during the second six months as our bodies weakened and our immune systems were destroyed.

We worked at various construction sites in twelve-hour shifts. Our daily ration of one slice of bread and black coffee in the morning and one cup of foul tasting turnip or potato soup at night made life unbearable. You could hear at night the persistent cries and moans that starving, diseased, wounded and freezing people make. In the mornings we would take out the emaciated bodies of the dead. These were removed daily by a crew of prisoners and dumped in large pits or burned when the ovens were not overloaded. Living under these conditions was a fate worse than death. Our barracks were running rivers of filth, vomit and excrement. They were lice-infested pits. We slept in three-tier wooden bunks, on bare wood without a mattress and most of the time without blankets. We used the lice-infested blankets during the winter to give us some protection at work sites against the brutal cold. I wore a striped, tattered and filthy jacket, trousers and shirt for a solid year without underwear and without ever washing them. Our clothes and hair were infested with lice and vermin. It was like wearing clothes pulled out of a cesspool. It was grotesquely dehumanizing and sucked away our souls and spirits.

As the Allied Forces entered German soil early in 1945, we were evacuated from Auschwitz to avoid our being saved. That Death March lasted for many weeks. It involved meandering from one place to the next and from one abyss to another. The carnage and savage treatment, death from exhaustion, starvation and programmed murders gained new heights in savagery. Over half of those who left Auschwitz with me perished along the way. Our final destination was another and more remote Death Camp in Germany. Our morale was at its lowest ebb.

Americans liberated us from Buchenwald in April, 1945. I was 15 years old, sick and disoriented, skeletal and in a semi-comatose condition. I spent over three weeks recovering in hospital before facing a stark choice: to stay in a Displaced Persons' Camp providing shelter and regular meals at last or return to my native country and face an uncertain future. While I knew my entire family had perished part of me hoped for a miracle. There had been no funerals or memorial services to honor the memories of my beloved family whose very presence on earth was begrudged them. So I reluctantly chose to go home for closure and to look for remnants of my past. What I found was silent testimony to man's inhumanity to man and only painful and evocative memories.

My first priority was to dispose of my tattered and filthy striped suit and get some clean clothes. In the Displaced Persons' Camp we were informed that the Hebrew Immigration Aid Society (HIAS) in Bucharest, Romania would provide us with food, shelter, clothes and $100 as seed money for resettlement. That journey from Munich, Germany to Bucharest found me amid a tidal wave of human migration: homebound soldiers criss-crossing the European continent and thousands of liberated and bewildered prisoners from every country in Europe. This mass of humanity created inconceivable stampedes and chaos at train stations - an exodus of titanic proportions. All freight and passenger trains were packed to the brim with anxious people clamoring to reach their homes and reclaim their lives. To find a train from Munich direct to Bucharest was "mission impossible". It took three days on three or four trains to reach there. I slept at stations and begged for food during the entire trip and had several brushes with bandits demanding money. Yet compared to Auschwitz and Buchenwald this adventurous journey was a "piece of cake". I was free at last and no hardship was going to derail my goals.

The HIAS had improvised dozens of barracks in a Bucharest suburb to house the flood of survivors coming to claim the bounty offered there: a new or second-hand suit, a shirt and shoes plus $100. The clothes may have been ill-fitting but were a vast improvement over our ragged and filthy striped prison clothes! Thus was finally severed any physical connection with our traumatic past and we gained new identities back in the fold of civil life. Our sole regret was that we had lost the striped suits that granted us free tickets to any European destination.

A majority of survivors opted to return to Camps for Displaced Persons. There Jewish rescue agencies from all over the world were engaged in sorting, assigning and resettling people. But I just wanted to go home, erase all vestiges of Camp life from my mind and never set foot again on German or Polish soil. At the young age of 15 I had decided to take charge of my life and my destiny.

The last leg of my journey from Budapest to my hometown, Bilke, took several more days. As the clunking, squeaking and smoke-belching train came to a screeching stop at our train station, I was gripped with a surge of anxiety, a profound sadness and fear of the unknown. I was hit by the sudden realization that I was alone, left to fend for myself and unprepared. I was just a boy with no practical experience and no financial resources. A second surge of horror hit me almost simultaneously: haunting flashbacks of our deportation from this very station just fifteen months earlier and the ensuing nightmares.

The Bilke train station was about a mile and a half from my house. I recall vividly that poignant and seemingly endless walk. It was between

7.00 and 9.00 on a balmy June evening in 1945. The rural road was eerily quiet and all I could hear was a symphony of melodic echoes from interacting frogs and the deafening noise of crickets - a scenario evocative of my childhood days when we used to play hide-and-seek in the dark of night. As I came closer to our house I saw shadows and lights and started hyperventilating. Could it be, I thought wistfully, that someone had survived? I knew the answer yet clung to hope in spite of that.

When I knocked at the door it was opened by a former neighbor, a gentile. He was startled and aghast at my appearance. "I thought you were all dead!" he exclaimed. "I am a ghost," I said instinctively. He slammed the door in my face only to open it a few seconds later to verify the validity of my claim. As I had not vanished into the darkness and while he was still overwhelmed, he invited me into the house. Our furniture and belongings were still in place. I was choked with emotion. For a while I was not sure who was the intruder - he or I. After a few weeks of an uneasy relationship, he and his family moved out.

Left alone in the house to fend for myself in an inhospitable environment heightened my loneliness and anxiety about my safety and my future. Much to my delight an uncle who had survived the ordeal moved in with me a few weeks later. He had joined a Jewish Partisan group in 1943 and fled into the mountains where he fought the Germans and Hungarian Fascists. It was an overwhelming joy and great relief to see him. He gave me some temporary peace and security.

My first act was to visit our only synagogue. It had been the soul and conscience of our community for nearly one hundred years. There my father and grandfather celebrated their *Barmitzvah*. What I found was emotionally devastating and heart wrenching. Racist epithets were scribbled all over the walls, inside and out. All doors had been removed, windows broken, benches removed, the reading desk and the ark (that stored the scrolls of the Law) had been destroyed. To compound my pain, stray dogs, goats and chickens were roaming in and out of the building. It was a grotesque desecration of our identity. I could not bear this reminder of the boiling rage and pathological hate of the Nazis and of *Kristallnacht* in Germany. This experience was a defining moment in my life. It left me with an unswerving resolve to flee this systemic and abysmal hatred and to erase it from my memory. My uncle was horrified at losing me.

Soon after I had returned home Russia had staked an ethnic, cultural, and historic claim to Carpathia. So by the fall of 1945 the impenetrable Iron Curtain descended. Our region officially became an integral part of the Ukraine Republic in the Soviet Union. All traffic across the border came to a dead halt. Anyone found crossing the border faced a five-year sentence of hard labor.

The Jewish underground developed a network of contacts whereby farmers near the border collaborated with border guards to organize an escape route for a fee. I contacted them for advice. They said it was safer to escape to Romania than Hungary. The nearest border town was approximately seventy-five miles from our town, an eight-hour journey by horse and wagon. Roads were primitive and meandered across rugged and steep mountain ranges. Snow would make the journey even more risky. Late in the fall of 1945 I negotiated a $50 package deal, to be paid in advance. It included day long transportation to the border town, my disguise as a farmer and the crossing with a guide over the Romanian border. The rendezvous was a barn. I was to be met there at midnight by a local farmer who would lead me on the two-hour journey over the treacherous rugged and jagged Carpathian Mountains to a Romanian village. There I was to be met by a local collaborator, transported to a larger community and turned loose.

There was an ironic twist to this dramatic odyssey. At midnight two men with dogs appeared at the barn. Their powerful searchlights beamed on me and they identified themselves as border police. The guide and the farmer had double-crossed me, royally. Angry and frightened, I was arrested and placed in a makeshift jail and in the morning was to be transferred to a regional prison. But I resolved not to be taken alive to yet another prison. The border police underestimated this skinny and undernourished lad's steely resolve. In the jail I turned the metal bed into a ladder, climbed through the ceiling and onto the roof, jumped into a haystack and fled the scene. It took me three or four days to return home. During the spring of 1946 I made a second and successful attempt.

But getting to Romania was merely a stepping-stone to my final destination: the United States. Alone in a strange land, without money and with language barriers, I faced endless hurdles and daunting challenges just to reach Budapest. My constant, nagging concern was the fear of being caught as an illegal alien and deported back to Carpathia. I contacted the Jewish community in Szatmar for guidance and assistance in reaching Budapest. I explored a web of networking and seemingly endless contacts before I was able to map out a solid game plan and a clear blueprint. To avoid the snares of border police and booby traps and after several tense and trying days I reached Budapest, overwhelmed and hungry, frightened and baffled. I searched for some Jewish connections. I needed a temporary "home" and springboard to reach the USA, my unswerving focal point.

I summoned all my survival instincts and used *chutzpah* and guile to get shelter at a **Kibbutz**, its members destined for Israel. My abundant youthful bravado and uncommon resilience, my clarity of purpose and vision, along with the defining spiritual forces of my dispossessed teenage years, had a far-reaching and decisive impact on my life and destiny.

After approximately six months at the *Kibbutz* in Budapest, it was obvious that unless I moved swiftly I would end up in Israel. The Iron Curtain was rapidly descending and I resolved not to be stuck there. Rumors had it that the Czech Republic had a more liberal emigration policy. The Soviets had not yet tightened their grip there. Bratislava, I was advised, would be my best bet. It was near and had a renowned modern *yeshiva* where I would most likely be found a place. It was early in 1947 and relatively easy to reach. Within weeks I was a student at the Bratislava *Yeshiva* among many other survivors. Most aspired to move on but few had sufficient financial resources or a strategic game plan to do so. For many Israel offered redemption and catharsis for pent-up insecurities and anger, saving them from self-destructive rage. For others, tired of the vicissitudes of life, nagging insecurity, poverty and despair the lure of economic security was more appealing. We were all oscillating between pragmatism and passion for Israel, that timeless yearning for our homeland. We had lively debates about this. I struggled with a confluence of passion and zeal, vision and patriotism, and the allure of greater economic security.

Just when we could no longer see through the mist of our doubts and fears an angel from heaven descended to rescue and lead us out of a cursed continent and to give us a new lease on life. This was Dr Solomon Schonfeld. I resolved to put the past behind me and look only to the future. In 1948 I left the Jewish graveyard of Europe for Dublin, Ireland.

Moving from a Third World continent to Ireland was a seminal point in our lives. It was a startling transition, politically and economically, a move from a closed to a free society. It was a spiritual and liberating experience. Yet our inbred insecurities, the language barriers and an absence of much control over our destinies inculcated a sense of paranoia about our future. While we suspected that Ireland was merely a transitory point, a way station to a final destination, the nagging question often surfaced: "When, where and how" would we go from there. As the drama of our arrival unfolded in Dublin and beyond we became objects of the curious and the dubious, the sympathetic and the indifferent.

Thanks to the late Mrs Eppel and Dr Schonfeld they set the stage for our arrival by enlisting the unconditional support of the local Jewish community. Their benevolence and warm hospitality touched us to the core. Mrs Eppel was deeply committed to our welfare. She wanted to ensure that all of us had the necessary and appropriate clothing for the damp spring and autumn weather as well as the medical and dental treatment when we needed it. I still recall my first experience of a dentist's office and being petrified by the sight of a white coat and an electric drill. Worse still, I was unable to understand what the dentist said and this compounded my anxiety. It was a seismic event in my new life, an abrupt transition from the 18th to the 20th century without any warning and not even any seat belts!

For reasons unexplained to us, ten to twelve of the older children were initially scheduled to remain in Dublin, at 143 Kimmage Road, while the rest moved on to Clonyn Castle. I was among those left in Dublin. Soon after our arrival Dr Schonfeld visited us at Kimmage and selected me as a counselor for the children at the Castle. I was reluctant to leave my friends and urged them in Hungarian to convince Dr Schonfeld that I was unqualified for the job. Much to my surprise and embarrassment it became clear that Dr Schonfeld understood Hungarian and with a broad smile he commented that in his judgment I was well suited to the task. So the dye was cast and I was soon on my way to the Castle.

It was a remarkable experience to live alongside one hundred children ranging in ages from six to seventeen, from different countries, with varying degrees of religious commitment, differing customs and endless stories of trials and tribulations. You could say we were an abstract tapestry, woven together yet unique, in color and contrast, symmetry and contradiction, too varied to fully comprehend. Our personalities and demeanor reflected the vagaries of an utterly confused past and a lost childhood. We wore our misery on our faces.

It is one of history's mocking ironies that inward-looking Ireland offered us, one hundred dispossessed and displaced orphans from war-torn Europe, only conditional and temporary status in their land. Yet masses of their own poverty-stricken citizens had emigrated to America during the 19th and the 20th centuries to seek a better life. Some of us might have opted to remain there had we been allowed to do so. But their restrictions were sadly emblematic of the antipathy and apathy that have so often spawned ugly misconceptions and inciting myths about Jews. Despite this our time in Ireland was a flare in the night for all of us and a dramatic crossroad in our formative years.

Today I look back at the years gone by and wonder at the faith and resilience, the gallantry and wit we encountered in a battle against those inscrutable and formidable forces of evil. It is a testament to an indomitable spirit within us that we were determined to win a reprieve against all odds and enjoy a second chance in life. In this struggle Dr Solomon Schonfeld epitomized the noble among mankind. He appeared at a critical moment in our lives. He will always be my hero, a larger-than-life legend. He was committed to rescuing Jews who were floundering in powerlessness and despair and gave us fresh hope and a new lease in life.

Dr. Solomon Schonfeld should be immortalized as a legend and saint for his undaunted and unwavering resolve to rescue countless souls, mired in powerlessness, from the jaws of tyranny and death. Regretfully, I never saw him again after I left Ireland. I wish I could have embraced this noble man and uttered my eternal gratitude for his wisdom, kindness, and humanity in saving us and countless others. He enabled us all to raise further generations. His memory will continue to be enshrined in our hearts and of those who succeed us.

It was in Ireland that I met **Alfred Kahan**, a native of Romania. We developed a long, warm and enduring friendship. We were separated for a year as I was among the first to leave Ireland for the United States. That was in 1949. I left Europe for New York as a student. Fate reunited us when we met again at school in New York and our friendship resumed. Then we moved in different directions. Alfred got married and moved to Boston to work for an advanced degree at Harvard. I sought a more relaxed life style and in 1956 settled in Atlanta where I met my "southern belle" and built a successful business career as a corporate executive. Our friendship continues today.

For me America was the culmination of unremitting dreams, an odyssey of hope, aspirations, travails and adventure. And yet the first ten years were less than idyllic. They were a slippery slope. Again I faced many barriers. There were language, social and financial problems - and while trying to assimilate into the strange and diverse New York society I was haunted always by memories of a horrendous past. From 1949 until 1956 I attended high school and several universities by day and by night. I was determined to achieve a higher level of education, realizing this was vital for a successful career. Those years were liberating as well as enslaving, demanding unconditional faith amid commitment, vision and patience.

For people without money New York was not hospitable. The heavy influx of refugees after the war was resented and we were often treated as an underclass, our motivation, education, our Holocaust experience ignored - a mere abstraction removed from their lives. It was hard, inconceivable, for the Jewish community to understand our traumatized past. It was equally

Westmeath Examiner

INCE 1882   SATURDAY, 13th MAY, 2000   £1 (UK £1.15)

Emotional return to Clonyn Castle for Holocaust survivors

By Ronan Casey

Alfred Kahan, on left and Murray Lynn

Clonyn Castle, Delvin, was the scene of an historic and emotional reunion for two World War II refugees last Thursday, the 4th of May. Mr Murray A. Lynn and Mr Alfred Kahan were two of over 100 stateless, homeless and dispossessed Jewish children who were allowed to enter Ireland in early 1948. They had spent several months situated in Clonyn Castle, Delvin before moving onto America and, as they put it themselves, a complete "rebirth".

Alfred Kahan has many memories of his days at Clonyn Castle. "At first, we felt that Ireland did not want us, we were scared and lonely but once we got here we were made to feel very welcome by the locals. They were very friendly," he told the *Westmeath Examiner.*

"We arrived in the spring, it was very cold but we soon settled in, the castle was a magical place. Ireland for me was a rebirth. I was free from the war, I was safe. I had lost some of my family but we managed to escape before it got too bad."

His colleague Murray Lynn wasn't so fortunate. Murray lost his entire family at Auschwitz. A Hungarian Jew, he arrived at Clonyn Castle after the liberation of the death camps. Obviously, talking about the past is still hard to do for Murray but he remembers his days at

Clonyn fondly. "I have wonderful memories of the castle. I arrived as spring was creating new and renewed life all around, so it was a rebirth not only in nature, but for me too. I was traumatised by the war, sure I have a nostalgia for where I was born but the war has numbed that feeling, I'll never forget

those days here in Delvin, it was a transitory point to a new life for me. A rebirth."

After Clonyn Castle, Murray and Alfred went their separate ways. Alfred left for New York in 1949. Aged 19 years of age he started school there. He studied engineering, science and physics at college and went on to join the US Air

Force. Now living in Boston he said: "I was very satisfied to be able to contribute towards a democratic world, a free world if you like. To play a part in any peace around the world is to the US to do this work."

Alfred has recently retired after 37 years of service. He plans to visit

Ireland, and in particular Westmeath more often but he wonders how it might have been. "I wonder what might have happened if I'd stayed in Ireland? It is a beautiful country and I hope to return soon."

For Murray it was an emotional visit on many

Continued on page 5

The Two Alfreds visit the Castle again. They were interviewed by the Westmeath Examiner. Photograph © John Mulvihill.

difficult for me to adapt to a harsh, callous and cynical lifestyle. So in 1956, after nearly seven years in New York City, I decided to move south to a more hospitable and more relaxed part of America - Atlanta, Georgia. This move produced a metamorphosis that shaped my future and gave it form and substance. It provided a launching pad to a successful business career and renewed my personal life. I married a girl from Nashville, Tennessee. We have three children, all born and raised in Atlanta.

I never spoke much to my wife or children about my experiences during the Holocaust. I feared that unleashing my pent-up traumas could open wounds and destabilize my new life. So I locked the door on my ghoulish past and became a captive of doubt in search of my soul and identity. I have recently retired as a corporate executive. As the curtain slowly descends on my life I have decided to unlock the door and talk about my past. My story reflects the life and fate of thousands of Holocaust survivors and six million voiceless victims who were not spared to bear witness to the world about the savage thirsting for Jewish blood. After the war I entertained the naive and utopian notion that the Allied victory over Nazidom would sink all evil forces into an abyss from which they would never re-emerge. When I see the other horrors of the 20th century and the growth of Holocaust denial I know this was a delusion. I feel it is a civic duty to share my childhood experiences with the next generation as a warning that they should never take freedom and democracy for granted.

If there is an epitaph to my story and my life it can be summed up like this: The Holocaust left us a terrifying and indelible legacy. Silence betrayed our faith and sealed our people's destiny.

"To sin by silence when we should protest", wrote Abraham Lincoln, "makes cowards of men."

Protesting voices are weapons of the spirit far more powerful than the mightiest guns. Do not remain silent when the pit bulldogs' hate is unleashed against anyone. Hatred is a pathology of the mind with no boundaries or limits for evil. To protect and preserve our way of life, I urge you to remember that freedom and justice for all must be our highest aspiration in life.

But there is a silver lining to this horror story. It is a testament to the power of the human spirit to renew life, to dig up what was cast off, to mend what was broken, to renew hope in the face of hopelessness and make life's journey a wellspring of challenging adventures. Destiny catapulted us into the vortex of history and a lifetime of nagging flashbacks and emptiness. No amount of rigorous training or conditioning could have adequately prepared anyone to deal with the scope and depth of our wartime experiences. As I wistfully reflect on the triumphs and the tragedies during the war, the exhilarating and life-renewing experiences in Ireland, the struggles that followed, I often wonder what life might have been like in Hungary had the 20ᵗʰ century monster not unleashed on us his rage and fury.

Metaphorically speaking the children of the Holocaust era will always remain children, frozen in time, because we were robbed of a formative, precious childhood and deprived of the emotional nourishment only loving parents can provide. Our losses and our pain have an enduring impact on our psyche and on our bedrock values. But in spite of this legacy we have not allowed our onward journey to become a scorched wasteland. We have integrated into our local communities, raised successful families and became leaders and activists, achievers - even overachievers - in various business and professional endeavors. Most importantly we have become passionate witnesses to validate and record the horrors of the 20th century. We stand firm to discredit any pariahs and our sworn enemies, Holocaust dealers and Hitler's apologists. It must be our eternal mission to be in the vanguard against hate and bigotry and speak out against social injustice. Our noblest aspiration is to defend and protect future generations from the scourges of evil and tyranny wherever these may reoccur.

Erika Stern

Erika was 16 years old, two years older than given on the Visa, when she joined Rabbi Schonfeld's transport. I located her thanks to Bertha Goodman who was a volunteer at Clonyn Castle. Erika did not go to the Castle. She stayed in London for a year until she went on aliyah. Her relative, Freddy Greenwood, had reached there earlier on another of Rabbi Schonfeld's post-war transports. She told her story to me at her Jerusalem home in 2001.

I was brought up in Galanta, a small town in Hungary where Rabbi Buchvarm was the head of the big local *yeshiva*. He was deported with his community to Auschwitz.

I was the youngest girl in a family of two boys and three girls. I was born on 7th August 1931. My father was a builders' merchant. We had a German nanny and spoke only German till 1939 when all Hungarians were sent back over the border. Family holidays were sometimes spent at Karlsbad. In 1940 we attended a music festival on Lake Balata. Our life had been pleasant enough but it suddenly became harder. Gradually my father lost his business and by March 1944 the Germans had taken everything we owned.

We were rounded up and taken to the ghetto. We were led through the town and everyone was looking at us. We held our heads high. When they hit us and shoved us into cattle trucks we had no idea where we were going. For a week or two we were left in a large brick factory in Nové Zámky – where the **Binet** family had lived. There everyone was treated alike. I recall queuing for soup. Then we were crushed into another cattle truck. We tried to see where we were going through the tiny window. Some people recognised we were in Western Germany. At one stop a German soldier who was guarding us cut his finger. He ordered my sister to give him a clean handkerchief "or I'll kill you". At that moment the train began to move on and that incident closed.

We knew neither day nor night until the train reached Auschwitz on 14th June. There we were confronted with screaming SS guards. It all happened so quickly. We were separated by that handsome Mengele: Mother and me to the left, my two older sisters to the right. Mother saw immediately I had been put with the elderly and she pushed me across to join my sisters. The next thing I remember we were all naked, our heads shaved and the kapos were laughing at us. "If you are ashamed to be naked leave your embarrassment at home. Here there is no such thing". They threw us dresses - not the striped uniform garments. Then they called out "Who is under 16? We'll take you to your parents." I was aged ten and a half. Of course that is not where we went but to Camp C where 1,000 children were housed. My sisters were in Camp B. Our Block Leader was **Fela Maybaum,** a genuinely kind and caring Jewish kapo, rare indeed among the rest who were notorious for their cruelty. She lives in Israel today. At roll call we had to kneel on the ground with our hands up. It was very cold at night, very hot in the day. One day the SS ordered us to take off our dresses so they could be washed and we were left naked and crying all night. Next day I got back my dress.

Then I developed a high fever and swollen glands. Fela kept me going, warning me that Mengele would take me if I did not keep working. I wanted to live so somehow I continued to carry stones from one place to another. Among the others I recognised Bobby, a friend of my sister (she is now in New York) but I did not recognise one of my own sisters. My sisters worked in Mengele's office because they knew German very well. Fela managed to arrange for me to join them. At some point I was hidden under a table, covered with a cloth. That was in October 1944.

Girls with good hands were wanted to work as slave labourers in the Horneburg Philips Factory near Hamburg. Mengele chose 200 girls from all of us. I stood with my sisters among the usual lines of five, naked, our dresses on the ground. I was sent to the left - probably due to my appendix scar and eczema. But I managed to run into the barracks, pull on a dress and pick up a bowl so as to appear busy, and run back. The SS man on duty at the door was reading a paper and I succeeded in slipping by him and re-joined my sisters. We were sent to wash in the showers prior to the journey and slept there overnight. Then there was another roll call. My sisters and Bobby, all big girls, squeezed me in between them. Nobody noticed we were 201.

During the final months of the war we were taken to a factory at Porpa. It was inside a mountain and there we worked and slept until hostilities ceased. Once a day we were taken to sit outside and breathe some fresh air but we were warned not to look at the sun. The sparse food they gave us was appalling. They wanted to shoot us but decided instead to send us away. We were on a train for days without food, moving back and forth. Eventually sixty or seventy of us were led off to Hamburg again with a group of Dutch prostitutes and political prisoners. They made us work hard in rain and cold. We ate grass. I wanted to die. But my sisters said we would soon be free.

On May 1st 1945 we were liberated by the Swedish diplomat, Count Folke Bernadotte and the Red Cross. It was my second sister's birthday.

She was always an optimist while my other sister, who was eight years older than me, and I were pessimists. We were taken to Denmark. There were still German Wermacht soldiers about and heavy bombing by the Allies lasted till May 5th. And then the war ended. My big sister heard through the Red Cross that her fiancé had survived so she went to join him in Slovakia. For a year I stayed with my other sister in Stockholm, in the care of Rabbi Jacobson.

We had a well-to-do aunt in Montreux where she had settled before the war. She sent us tickets and temporary visas to come there. I was first in a sanatorium and then spent three years, when aged 14 to 17, at Dr Asher's Jewish Boarding School at Box-les-Bain. (He was Bertha Goodman's cousin.) Every three months I had to report to the Swiss police until in 1947 I joined my younger sister again in Bratislava. I found work making ladies' handbags. Then the Russians came. It was at that time word reached us from Rabbi Vorhand, the Chief Rabbi of Prague, of the invitation from Rabbi Dr Schonfeld.

So I came to London with Rabbi Schonfeld and travelled with **Ervin Schwarz**. On the way I met my elder sister very briefly. I lived for the following year at the Woodberry Down Hostel in North London. I was the youngest there. Rita Mayer was our Housemother. She now lives, like me, in Jerusalem. The Katz and the Benedict families used to invite us and so did my relatives, the Greenwood family in Golders Green. My grandmother was Freddy Greenwood's paternal aunt. Rabbi Schonfeld had brought Freddy to Britain in a previous group. I learned English quickly. I already knew French and German was my mother tongue. Then I worked for a Jewish clothing factory behind D.H. Evans, the big store in Oxford Street, hemming and sewing on buttons. My employer was very helpful. I had an opportunity to go to Canada or to Israel where I had cousins. My older sister had settled in the USA where we had more cousins. In the end I went with Eva Steinberger on *aliyah* and had a very hard time there. I found my cousins in Haifa and slept on an open balcony. That was a culture shock!

The man I married also came from Galanta but he had reached Palestine in 1939. He owned a factory for ladies' dresses off Jaffa Road in Jerusalem where I joined him in running the business. He died 25 years ago. I retired in 1997 but still help out at a local boutique. We had two children and I now have 14 grandchildren. One of them asked me to speak about my life to the children at her school and I have now done so several times.

In the year 2000 the Horneburg Factory asked some of us to come on a five-day visit with all expenses covered. My older sister had died four years before but I attended. They showed us a model of the wartime camp and the SS barracks. I met a lady from the town. She told me how every morning she heard us going by and wanted to give us stockings. But she dared not do so. Another resident said "I remember as a little child myself seeing you arrive. My parents said I must not say a word. We were very frightened. Today's Mayor and the people here feel ashamed. I still feel ashamed that it happened." They asked us to excuse them and said they would never forget what was done. I spoke to the gathering at a service in a local church and told them they have to ensure nothing like it ever happens again.

Erika in 2007 beside an antique Czech cupboard in a Jerusalem café. (BB)

Following our meeting Erika told **Fela Maybaum** *that I was collecting stories for this book. Fela had chosen to withdraw from any association with her wartime experiences but* **Erika** *persuaded her to let me visit her – a privilege she very rarely granted.*

376

Fela Cajtak Maybaum

Fela Cajtak Maybaum was a Jewish Kapo in Auschwitz. She was in charge of 1,000 Hungarian girls aged between two and sixteen years old. Kapos were notorious for their cruelty and were generally hated but Fela was uniquely supportive. Though she had been obliged to enforce discipline on behalf of the SS she managed to imbue numerous young girls with the will and strength that enabled them to survive.

Fela invited me to her home in Jerusalem on 27th June 2001. I felt quite daunted. The door was opened by a tiny lady with snow-white hair and shining, bright blue eyes. We sat in the kitchen and while she smoked cigarillos she told me something of her life story.

My sister and I were born and brought up by devoted parents in Marava, near Danzig, on the Polish side of the German border. My father owned a business. He had a BA. I attended the Roman Catholic Franken Sisters School where students came from all over Poland. Our parents were Zionists. They visited Palestine just before the war. By then I was training as a nurse at the Polish Government Hospital in Vasovi. It was quiet there till 1942 or 1943.

Then the Germans sent the Jewish community of Marava into the ghetto and I chose to join my parents there. Marava was heavily bombed. For a year I worked as a Sister at the Frankenhaus Hospital inside the ghetto. All the patients were very seriously ill. I nearly died myself from typhus. I saw three or four groups of a thousand people at a time rounded up and deported to Auschwitz and Treblinka. My parents and I were deported on the last transport in December 1942 in very cold weather. We did not know where we were going. My mother was young but was taken straight to the crematorium. My father was sent to a Labour Camp. It was too hard for him and he died a month later.

I was put to work in a dental unit. It was in a special block next to the hospital and all kinds of prisoners were treated there. One of the female dentists was Daniella Casanova from Corsica. She came with a French Communist contingent. Another, Maria Handy, was Bulgarian and there was an elderly Jewish assistant from Germany. They were good people in a protected environment. Our situation was better than others in the Camp. But we could hear on the other side of the wall men who had been sterilised crying and vomiting.

Many prisoners brought us gifts from where they worked. Some brought clothes from "Canada", the infamous storehouse. Someone gave me a nightdress. I hid it but it was found and as a punishment Mengele sent me back to the main Camp, to Block 8. There I had to look after 1000 Hungarian girls aged between two and sixteen years. I learned to cope amongst people tougher than me and somehow survived to the end. I do not know how. I only stayed positive for those children. The SS were terrible, truly terrible. I persuaded those girls that there was no point in crying, that there was no one there to hear them. "The smoke from the chimneys is all that is left of your family. Any little mistake can cost you your life." But not everyone understood. Some were angry with me. During the final months of the war, there was no room left in the crematorium.

On January 18th 1945 the Nazis evacuated Auschwitz very rapidly. We were all marched out on what became known as the Death March. Few survived it. I was liberated by the US army near Hamburg and found my way to Belgium. I was imprisoned there as a German spy but soon released and the Jewish Brigade[11] smuggled me to Marseilles. I reached Palestine on a certificate provided by my sister. We married twin brothers and both of us worked at Hadassah Hospital as nurses. I worked in the Pain Clinic and more recently in the Ultra Sound Clinic.

My husband was a lovely person, so good and kind. He was Dutch. He passed his matriculation in Palestine and then went to university in the States where he studied agriculture. He returned to Palestine during the war. He travelled a lot on business for Labour organisations.

They had three children. Fela's elder son is a tour guide. He and his wife called during our interview. He came to bid farewell to his mother before leaving with a group for India. They have three children. Her daughter lives in the Judean hills and also has three children; the eldest is in the Army. Their younger son died of Multiple Sclerosis leaving a widow with four young children.

When she gave her testimony at Yad Vashem Fela said: "I did not want to lie or exaggerate but the real truth one cannot tell." Fela's last words to me were "There have been good things, too, in my life but never enough of them."

She handed me the following articles as I left her:

From Kol Ha'ir, a local Jerusalem newspaper, 2nd December, 1988. Translation from the Hebrew

Fela Maybaum has received historical recognition almost against her will and several decades late. Even now she avoids

giving details about the time she was Block leader for No.8 Lager in Auschwitz. But the girls that were there are doing that for her, girls whose life she saved. They will always remember her.

Fela was invited to Yad Vashem to receive the greatest honour they bestow, one till now presented only to Righteous Gentiles. This was something extraordinary. No one knew what had happened to her after the war till an announcement appeared in the press. Forty survivors from Block 8 turned up at the ceremony. They owed her their lives. Fela was the first to receive the Six-Branched Candelabrum which was specially designed to commemorate the six million who died in the Holocaust. There were many tears among those who gathered that day and in Fela's eyes, too, as she stood there quietly, nodding her head

It was Leah Smat, a journalist, who found her in 1967. Leah was among the first to visit Jerusalem following the Six Day War. She was walking near the *yeshiva* in Bet Hakerem when her eyes caught those of someone passing by, eyes she could not fail to recognise, those same bright eyes she remembered so well. After a long moment she managed to utter: "Fela! Block 8!" and Fela murmured "My little girl!"

Leah Smat wrote:

When we arrived in Auschwitz we did not touch food for several weeks. It was only fit for animals. Our ears ached, there was blood and mucous, our lips were cracked, we had high fevers. We knew where we would end up if we were ill. We did not care. We lay on the cold floor. We were apathetic, letting anything happen for the pain to stop. Then two eyes looked at me, pitifully. 'Go out on the parade! You are not allowed to be in here'. And two strong and brave hands pulled us up. This was Fela, the Elder of the Block. She was a veteran of Auschwitz.

We returned from the parade freezing cold. Fela took me to her little niche by the door, laid me on her bed and brought me hot tea. She gently began to clear my ears, her hand on my shaven head. Before we fell asleep on our palettes Fela kissed us on the forehead 'You girls must stay alive'. She looked after me and numerous others day after day. She was as dedicated as a mother. There were fewer girls every day yet she injected us with the will to live.

Leah and her husband are strictly Orthodox. When they visited Fela, who is secular, she said: "I can only offer you tea in a glass." And the husband replied "In your home even pork would be *kosher*." There is something in the very presence of this woman that ties you to her. She even looks angelic. Rachel Kramer was also in Block 8 with her two sisters and described how very carefully Fela looked after them and made sure they stayed together. The two of them attended the ceremony. Rachel dedicated a poem to her saying how with her bravery and courage Fela gave them life.

After Fela's public recognition her phone rang incessantly. The messages carried the same refrain "You saved me, I am so happy to have found you again." but Fela does not reply. She chooses to stay quiet and keeps away from events connected with that sobering past.

אחרי מות / אודי דרומי

"אל תבכו. אין טעם. אף אחד לא מאזין"

פלה מייבום, הצילה ילדות באושוויץ, 1919-2005

פלה צייטג נולדה במלאווה שבפולין, למדה בגימנסיה היהו־דית בעיר וסיימה בוורשה בית ספר לאחיות בריוק כשבפרצה מלחמת העולם השנייה. מלאווה, עיר על גבול גרמניה, הופצצה קשות, וזמן קצר אחרי שפלה הצליחה לחזור אליה, הוקם בה גטו. היא שימשה אחות ראשית בבית חולים למחלות מידבקות, ובעצמה כמעט שמתה מטיפוס הבהרות. כבר שם ניסתה פלה להציל יהודים, אך הגרמנים שלמו מבית החולים יהודי שהר־סוה כחולה ותלו אותו לעיני כל יהודי הגטו, בהם אמו. בדצמ־בר 1942 היא שולחה לאושוויץ בטרנספורט האחרון ממלאווה. כשירדה עם משפחתה מהרכבת, לא רצתה שאמה תצעד ברגל בקור המקפיא והובילה אותה בתמימותה למשאית, בלי לדעת שזו תיקח אותה מיד למשרפה. אביה מת חודש אחד כך.

כשנתה שירתה פלה כא־חות במרפאת השיניים בביר־קנאו, שומעת מבעד למחיצה את קולות הבכי וההתקאה של הגברים שעברו עיקור בחדר השני. יום אחד תפס אצלה ר"ד מנגלה כותנות לילה שהחביאה כדי לשמר את השומרים, וכער־נש שלח אותה לאושוויץ לשמש אחראית בלוק (או "זקנת בלוק", בלוקאלטרסטה) בבלוק 8 שבו שהו כאלף ילדים בני 12 עד 16 מהטרנספורטים מהונגריה.

בלומה אברמוביץ', שפלה הצילה את חייה כשהברירחה אר־תה מסלקציה של מנגלה, מספרת איך ניצבה ביום הראשון, אחת מהבורות ילדות ההמומות עטוות

פלה מייבום

שמלות דקות, שזה עתה איבדו את כל יקירזהן, כשדרבריה של פלה הולמות בה ללא חום: "אין טעם לבכות. כאן אין מי שמא־זין לבכי. העשן בחוץ הוא כל מה שנתר ממשפחותיכם. ציתו, כי כל שגיאה תעלה לכן בחייכן". אברמוביץ' אומרת כי לא כל הבנות הבינו שזו עצה לחיים וחלקן פרקו על פלה את הזעם שלא יכלו לפרוק על הגרמנים.

רבות בארץ ובחו"ל חבות לה את חייהן. לאה שנף זוכרת איך בייאושה נשארה בצדיף בעת המיפקד, מיחלת לסוף הגאל, כשלפתע הרימה שתי ידיים חזקות. פלה הביטה בה ב"עיניים טובות, רחמניות" וציוותה עליה לצאת למיפקד, "כי כאן אסור לך להיות חולה". אחר כך היא טיפלה במסירות בפצעי הקור ובמוגלה שהשקתה אותה תה חם. רחל קרמר הקדישה לה שיר ("היית אור בעגני חושך"), שבו תיארה כיצד עודרה פלה את הילדות לעמוד זקופות ולהתא־מץ להיראות בריאות, כדי שיי־

שלחו לטרנספורט לעבודה ולא להשמדה.

ב-18 בינואר 1945 פינו הנ־אצים את אושוויץ בחיפזון ופלה יצאה ל"צעדת המוות" שממנה שרדו מעטים. היא שוחחרה על ידי הצבא האמריקאי ליד המבו־רג ואחר כך התגלגלה לבלגיה, שם נאסרה כמרגלת גרמניה, אך שוחחרה. באמצעות הברייגרה היהודית היא הוברחה למרסיי ומשם הגיעה לארץ בסרטיפיקט ששלחה לה אחותה אסתר. שתי האחיות נישאו לאחים התאומים אברהם ושאול מייבום, ושתיהן עברו מאחיות בהדסה. לפלה וא־ברהם נולדו עוזי, מיכל וחב.

בתש"ח היא חיכתה לשוא על הר הצופים לשיירת הדסה, עד שנודע כי 78 מאנשיה, בהם מנהל בית החולים ד"ר חיים יסקי, נרצחו על ידי הערבים. אחרי שפרשה התנדבה לעבוד במרפאת כאב בהדסה, ועד לא־חרונה - במרפאת אולטרסאונד. היא מיעטה לדבר על תקופת השואה. "לא רציתי לשקר, לא רציתי להגזים, ואת האמת הא־מיתית אי אפשר לספר", אמרה בעדותה ביד ושם. בפני ד"ר אהרון לב מארגון "עמך", בעצ־מו ניצול שואה, פתחה את סגור לבה לדבריו, בעיניה היה ברק של שמחה, אך בלבה נשאה את הכאב הגדוא יום יום.

ב-1988 העניק לה "יד ושם" מנורה לאות הערכה על "פוע־לה. רבות מ"ילדותיה" הנד"ג־שות הקיפוה. לרחל מהגר מ"כל העיר" אמרה אז, כי "הילדות היו קטנות מאוד, ואני עשיתי את מה שיכולתי".

Fela Maybaum's obituary in Ha'aretz, a daily Israeli newspaper, 2005.

Post-War Recollections

This group of survivors has chosen to tell something about their experiences only after peace was declared. Perhaps it was too painful for them to write about what happened to them during the war. They offer some vivid details about the chaotic times that followed and how they persevered to re-build their lives.

The Wiesen Sisters

Vera Wiesen was born in 1939. Her sister Franklina was born in 1942, during the war. A note in the records says these two little girls were hidden in a Košice bunker. They both came with Vera's sons to the 1998 Reunion and contributed their stories to the Reunion Brochure.

Vera Wiesen

The war was over. My mother, a widow with two little girls - me, eight years old, and my sister, five years old - had to begin restructuring our lives. We had returned to a Czechoslovakia we did not recognize. The Communists were controlling more every day. Life for Jews was difficult. I went to a public school where we had to attend on *Shabbos* and where we were bullied and scorned as Jews. When my mother heard of Rabbi Schonfeld's transport she realized it was the best solution. Her children would be in a safe, Jewish environment and, also, possibly this would ensure her a way out of a Communist country.

Consequently we spent one year in Ireland getting the best spiritual and physical care possible until it was our time to leave. We stayed in England for another year. My sister and I and four other girls lived at Rabbi Posen's home in London. So many devoted people, so many sacrifices – how can we show them the appreciation they deserve?

By now, my mother and my new father had moved to Israel. We sailed, therefore, to Haifa, my sister and I, older than our years, in crowded uncomfortable conditions with little supervision save that of *Hashem*. After we docked we were put on a bus headed for Petach Tikvah: two foreign children who knew not a word of Hebrew and had only a slip of paper with an address. Nobody met us at the port or the bus stop.

In our English uniforms, that were quite unsuitable in the Israeli heat, we trekked down the long streets. These, we were told, would bring us to our final destination. We arrived at the wrong entrance but a kind neighbour asked our names and rushed to get our mother. The letter to tell of our coming had failed to reach her. Needless to say, she was shocked but overjoyed to see us. At this point my life in Israel began.

It was in Israel that I went to school and grew up. My family moved several times and changed jobs and I, too, went through many changes. The greatest change, however, took place when I left Israel for the United

States. My aunt suggested that I come to live with her until I got engaged and married.

Soon after I arrived I began working as a fifth grade teacher in Beth Jacob of Williamsburg. Divine Providence was soon realized when a fellow teacher suggested I meet a cousin she felt would suit. She was right. Barely a year after my coming to the United States, I was married to my husband, Pinches Pinkesz. (*May he live until 120!*)

Franklina Wiesen

Vera's sister, who was born in 1942, added the following account of her post-war life.

My family moved several times, changed livelihoods a few times and I, too, went through many changes. After I graduated from high school I taught in Meron for a year in a newly-established government school. After this I attended Bar-Ilan University for five years and majored in Hebrew and world literature. I received a licence to teach high school. Then I came to the United States and lived with my married sister for two years, studying English and teaching. I left for Israel one summer for a visit and met my husband, Reuben, *blessed be his memory*. We moved to Philadelphia where my husband taught. He was a professor of economics. In the five years living there I gave birth to three sons. We then moved to San Francisco where my husband worked for the city. We had plans to move to Israel when the children were bigger. However, shortly after we reached San Francisco my husband was diagnosed with a rare rheumatic disease. After nine and a half years this claimed his life. My three sons cared for their father with devotion and love.

Following his death we moved to New York where my sons attended *yeshiva*. They dedicated their lives to *Torah* study at a young age and this has kept them strong through rough times. All are excellent students. One studied in a New York *yeshiva*, another in Montreal. The eldest married five years ago, the middle one two years ago, both of them to wonderful girls from honourable families. The youngest is following his brothers' example.

Eventually I went back to my teaching career and am presently at a Sephardi Hebrew-speaking pre-school. I recently became engaged to Rabbi Mordecai. Our wedding will take place in July (1998), *please G-d*. May we all be worthy of greeting the Messiah in our days. *Amen*!

Josef Ickovitc

*These are excerpts from a letter Josef wrote to **Tamáš Reif** before the
Reunion which he attended with his wife.*

I was born in Romania in 1934. In 1947 we relocated to Czechoslovakia.
There was no *yeshiva* there so I was sent to Pressburg (Bratislava) for
several months. There I remained till Rabbi Schonfeld transported us to
England in time for *Pesach* 1948. I, along with 20 others, stayed in Brighton
for *Pesach*. From there I went to Ireland's Clonyn Castle where teachers
were hired and classes began. Not only did I have to learn English but also
Czechoslovak since everyone beside myself, was from Czechoslovakia.

Eventually, all of us boys were settled in various *yeshivas*. I went to a
yeshiva in Staines in England. The Rosh *Yeshiva* was the Lezsher Rav who
treated me kindly, even giving me pocket money to make my life easier.
During that time I met Rabbi Aryeh Reichman who gave me his personal
help. From there I went to a very *Chasidishe Mesivta* in London. *Yeshiva*
life was not very structured. I felt uncomfortable there. Subsequently I
went to Sunderland where I became a better student and tried to achieve
the status of a *Masmid*. My teacher was Rabbi Chaim Shmuel Lapian.

My parents had immigrated to the United States. In 1951 they sent
for me to join them in New York City. I enrolled in various *yeshivas*;
their ways of life were not what I had become accustomed to so I moved
to Yeshiva Torah Vodaas in New York City. I learned there until 1953.
Then I mistakenly thought I should seek my own livelihood. Since the
yeshiva did not allow part-time attendance, I was drafted into the US
Army. I served two years there. Despite the hardships of life in the army
among non-Jews, I did keep all the *Mitzvahs*, eating only *kosher* food, kept
Shabbos, and even lit *Chanukah* candles in the barracks.

Om my release I went for training in the field of optics and eventually
specialized in contact lenses. In 1959, with *Hashem*'s help, I went into
business for myself, opening a lab that manufactured contact lenses.
Over the years I became proficient in fitting lenses to the extent that I
became an instructor for ophthalmologic interns, teaching them how to
fit contact lenses.

My daughter married a nice and *choshuv* young man. Now I have two
grandchildren attending *yeshivas*. I have arrived at this point entirely
with the help of Rabbi Dr Schonfeld and I pray for myself and the Jewish
people for continued help from the Almighty. *May the righteous Redeemer
come speedily in our days, Amen!*

Eva and Ernst Rubinstein

Eva was 10 and Ernst was nearly 13 years old when Rabbi Schonfeld brought them from Czechoslovakia. Their contributions were among those in the Reunion Brochure.

Eva

It is with gratitude to the Almighty that I am able to write this for the Jubilee Reunion. Having survived the Second World War, thankfully with the immediate family intact, it must have been most difficult for my parents to send my brother Ernest and me on the transport to England and Ireland.

My memories of the years spent in Clonyn Castle and London are not very clear. However overall I remember the experience positively. The huge downstairs area where we ran around - the turret in which we slept - a *Chanuca* party - **Séndi, Blanka** and Judy who took such wonderful care of us - Blanka saying the *shema* to us every evening, Judy teaching us English and the *Chumash*.

In London I stayed with the Posen family and I attended the Avigdor School. I vividly recall the very foggy bus rides in the early morning. It was here that we became proficient in the English language and started using it as the language of choice.

I was reunited with my parents in the United States and we started life as a family once again. There I was able to have a Jewish and a secular education and to meet my husband who comes from Mexico. He in no way shared the hard life of my past but very much shares my present life. We have a wonderful son, David, and are very grateful that he is following in our traditions.

I thank G-d each day for having spared me and allowed me to grow up, to have a family and to be able to live a Jewish life.

Ernst

I was born in Nitra, Czechoslovakia. The war years I spent in Hungary and Bergen-Belsen. Our immediate family was reunited after liberation. I was sent to Bratislava to obtain a Jewish education. It was there that I heard about a transport of children leaving for England and added my name to the list as well as my sister's. It was led by the late Dr Schonfeld. We travelled by train to Ostende for two days, took the ferry to Dover and then a train to London. A week later we went to Brighton for *Pesach*. Our next stop was Clonyn Castle in Ireland. A few weeks later I celebrated my *Barmitzvah* in Dublin.

The time spent at Clonyn Castle was pleasant. We had classes in Jewish studies and some other subjects as well. Rabbi Cohen was in charge of us. He was a jolly fellow and liked by us all. As a youngster of 13 I had a pretty good time, enjoying pranks like any youngster would. I think we were isolated from the world except for the rare occasions when we walked to the village. I stayed in Clonyn Castle through the fall of 1948. My next stop was Sunderland Yeshiva.

I left for New York in 1950 to be reunited once again with my family. I finally began my secular education in addition to Jewish studies. I attended college and at the age of 21 began my own business. I met a lovely girl who became my wife 38 years ago. We have two wonderful children and this year we will celebrate the *Barmitzvah* of our first grandson.

Eva Haupt

Eva was 15 years old when she left Prague with Rabbi Schonfeld. She served as I did on the Reunion Committee. She told me her story over the telephone, I think during 1998. Her husband reached England in 1946 in the first group Rabbi Schonfeld brought from Poland.

It was my uncle, my father's brother, who heard about Rabbi Schonfeld's 1948 transport and put down my name and my sister's. He worked in the Agudath offices in Bratislava, a very devout man, and wanted to do something for us. We had survived the ghetto in Filakovo. Our father had been taken away and our mother was struggling hard to make a living and look after my little sister Agi and me in very difficult conditions. Our uncle feared we would lose our religion and this was a chance to escape the Communist regime.

My mother saw this as an opportunity for me to study abroad as others did. She was unaware of the grim impact of Communist rule and expected me to return after a short while. She was, though, devastated at the thought of separating from us. My sister was only 9 years old. I was 15 and a very quiet, happy-go-lucky girl. She feared I would die of hunger because I would never complain or ask for anything. In the end I went alone.

Sixteen years were to pass before I saw my mother and sister again. It was a traumatic wrench for my mother. We wrote to each other all the time. These were difficult times for me, too. Perhaps the most shattering moment for me was when I learned that my mother was re-marrying. I was deeply upset and wrote to tell her so.

Life at Clonyn Castle was an unnatural one for a teenager. We had been promised we would go to school in Britain. I was desperate to study and make up for those war years when I had received little education. It was a long wait before we were granted British Visas.

At Clonyn Castle our leader, **Séndi**, gave us religious instruction and taught us a lot. We were from a wide mix of backgrounds. Séndi was very beautiful and she had a wonderful influence on us all. She could be strict when necessary and we learned manners, too, from her example. An old man, Mr Mundheis, gave us English lessons. We knew hardly any.

In London I stayed at the Woodberry Down Hostel with **Anna Katscher**, Grete Muller and **Eva Schwarz**. And I attended the Hasmonean School. Later I lived with a family in Stamford Hill. They were very good to me. During that time my friend Eva's brother introduced me to a young man. He had just returned from serving as a mechanic in the Israeli Air Force, a volunteer during the War of Independence. He had survived the world war in Siberia, living on garlic and watermelon amidst epidemics of typhoid and malaria. He lost his parents there. Now he was 23. "What are you doing? Why aren't you married?"

We started going out together. There was nowhere we could meet, nowhere to sit down and talk except on buses and at the pictures. Yet in three weeks we were engaged! I was so young, still under age to be married, so I needed my mother's permission. She was horrified and refused to give it. She wrote that a decision based on "falling in love" was not to be trusted. It was unbearable to hurt my mother like this but I so very much wanted a home of my own. Eventually my London "family" persuaded her to allow us to marry. It was anguish for her to miss her daughter's wedding. We had no money - nothing. I remember buying two spoons and two forks. My foster family helped us in so many ways. They arranged the Town Hall legalities - even bribing an attendant with a bottle of whisky, to act as a witness. We were married by Rabbi Dr Schonfeld with a proper Jewish wedding but I had no one from my family there. Later on my foster parents put a deposit on a house for us that we repaid later.

Meanwhile my sister, cut off in Communist Europe, watched my mother suffer, devastated by the long, long separation. My sister eventually went to university. My mother sought a husband for her but found no eligible Jewish boys, no chance of marriage for her over there. So my sister obtained a visa to come to England to learn English but my mother was not permitted to leave and Agi had to return.

Only after my husband and I were naturalised was I able to visit my mother and twice a year I took my children to see her. During our first reunion after sixteen years my mother and I talked day and night. It was still difficult and dangerous for her. No one was supposed to leave the country. Neighbours were suspicious of my frequent visits. Her passport was taken from her till I persuaded the authorities that she had no reason to leave her home, her job and her pension rights.

At last, after my step-father died my mother wanted to be in England with Agi and me. Agi had married a Hungarian boy and was living in Southgate, North London with their two children. So my mother, then in her sixties, left her home. To sell it would have aroused suspicions. She gave up the pension acquired from working all her life and came with no knowledge of English and no rights to any pension here so as to be with us. It was hard for her and sad for us. We did all we could to make her as happy as possible. She died last year.

Despite having so little experience I found a marvelous husband. We have three children. My son lives in London, one daughter is in Manchester and the other in the States with a young child.

Judit and Agi Wiesner

Judit was 16 years old and her sister Agi was 14 when Rabbi Schonfeld took them to Britain. They both attended the Reunion and visited the Castle again with their husbands.

After the war my sister and I left Budapest and came to Bratislava where we stayed at the Agudath Home from 1947 till April 1948. Then we heard that Rabbi Schonfeld planned to take children who survived the horror of the Holocaust to England. I was happy with the news and so were a lot of others.

We woke up one morning and who did we see but this distinguished, beautiful person. I owe him so much. I shall never forget how he handled us like a father. He organized 150 children and brought us all to London. The older girls, like myself, looked after the younger ones on the long journey from Czechoslovakia to England. Rabbi Schonfeld arranged everything, our welcome, where we should stay, etc. It was the eve of *Pesach* and he sent us to Brighton near the ocean, a beautiful place. We had an unforgettable festival.

Afterwards we went to Ireland with 100 children on a ship. He rented a Castle for us with a cook and rabbis for the boys. Teachers for the younger girls taught them *yidishkeit*. It was like a beautiful big family with freedom and kindness and love after the horrors that everybody had suffered. I remember those days as if it all happened yesterday. What a wonderful and loving person was Rabbi Schonfeld! I cannot adequately express the kindness and devotion he showed to each and every one of us.

Judit Wiesner with sixteen grandchildren in 1996. (JW)

Chaja Steinmetz

Chaja was 15 years old when she came with Rabbi Schonfeld from Prague. She attended the 1998 Reunion with her husband. She contributed to the collection of stories circulated then and I have added a little more from conversations we had on an Irish coach on the way to visit Clonyn Castle.

Chaja comes from Romania near the Hungarian border. Her parents were shopkeepers, selling food and household provisions. Other relatives were in the textile business. They were a well-respected family and took their communal responsibilities seriously. Both parents died in Auschwitz. When she was around 16 years old a professor offered to write up her experiences but she could not face it then. "I was afraid I'd snap!" Now she recognises that she must pass on her experiences to her children and grandchildren. Chaja was in touch with the Shoah Foundation about recording her story.

I remember fetching mail from Delvin post office and how amazed the staff were to receive letters from all over the world for the children at the Castle. When uniformed police knocked at the Castle door the children were frightened. Their wartime fears were roused again. So when they understood this those police came next time in 'civvies'.

I could not play "Hide-and-Seek".

We older girls helped **Séndi** and **Blanka** look after the little ones. We cheered them up. The older boys lived in a house in Dublin. I went there to cook for them. I like preparing food for people. It gives me much happiness. Though money was short I once bought fresh fish as a treat for the boys. Mrs Eppel would not have approved! Now I won't let my grandchildren waste anything. They ask "Why are you so fussy?" and I explain what I went through during the war and how I was always hungry.

In Dublin I lived with the Wolfson family. Mr Wolfson was a big man, a coalman. One time I was alone in the house and a small man I had never seen before - and without a *kipa* - came to the door. He said he was Mr Wolfson's brother. I refused him entry and was praised for my vigilance by the family on their return.

I was married from the Wolfsons' home in December 1949. The Ladies Committee from the Dublin Synagogue had introduced me to my young man. He was working as a *shochet* in Belfast. There was lots of excitement about this. Some people said my handsome young man looked very much like Rabbi Schonfeld. Certainly their beards were similar! Mrs Eppel and the Ladies Committee were determined to provide well for me and they did so. They put together a trousseau and arranged the wedding celebrations after all the Castle children had dispersed.

My husband is the youngest of a big Manchester family. We, too, settled in Manchester. The first of our four children was born within the year. Our landlady was very active in *Mizrachim*. She once said to me: "Is it true you were in Auschwitz? You know we also had a hard time here - no maid, blackout. I had to wear the same coat for several years".

We were very poor but always managed by keeping a positive outlook. I did not go out to work but looked after my children. People used to ask us how we coped. You can always hear a laugh and a joke in our house and I always keep busy and energetic. Somehow I do not show depression. After liberation I spent some time in a sanatorium in Europe. The good food and the fresh air brought back my strength and my periods returned - unlike the experience of my survivor friend in Canada. Her periods never recommenced. She has had no children and is very embittered. She says "I'm not a woman" and she is no longer religious.

Chaja's son and his wife work with computers and live in Hendon. Another son has an American wife who is a lawyer. One daughter has four children and drove from Gateshead to attend the Reunion Dinner. Two other daughters live in London. The one in Ilford is involved in adult education; the other in Stamford Hill is married to Mrs Brazil's brother. Mrs Brazil is the manager of the Normandy Hotel, Bournemouth where Shabat was spent and celebrated during the 1998 Reunion.

Some Other Survivors

As this volume is dedicated to the stories of The Hide-and-Seek Children I wanted to learn more about their background, about the communities where they were brought up and their pre-war life style. So I sought more details from other survivors of the major Slovak Jewish communities. Dr Zergbaum, Chair of the Israel-Slovak Society in Jerusalem, introduced me to **David Steiner**. He spends his retirement studying documents at Yad Vashem on the history of Slovakian Jewry during World War II. He showed me a mass of original material that has been collected there - letters between Slovak and Nazi officials and with Jewish leaders, lists of deportations, records of Auschwitz prisoners and much else. These are the original reports, written in cold factual terms, gruelling to read. He also showed me a documentary made by Slovakian Television on the subject.[12]

David Steiner described the community life that The Hide-and-Seek Children had lost. He put me in touch with **Hetty Weiner-Fisch**, who was one of the group we had failed to locate, and he introduced me to **Shoshana Brayer, Edit Katz and Shmuel Klein.** Their stories relate closely to the main collection so I have obtained their permission to include them here. To these I have added the memoirs of my Slovak friends, **Bertha Fischer** and **Rachel Malmud.** What they have to tell has not been published before and it was through them this project emerged. So how could I leave them out?

David Steiner of Bratislava

David Steiner spoke to me in Hebrew about the Jewish Community of Bratislava and its history and his own story within it. His wife, Myriam, patiently and fluently translated for me when we met during June, 1998, and on several other occasions.

The Steiner family were antiquarian booksellers in Bratislava. Their business was founded there in 1847.[16]

They were active leaders in the Orthodox Jewish community. Unusually they saw to it that their children received a sound secular education. This was not customary amongst observant Bratislava Jews at the time. The Steiner's deep involvement in the book trade surely influenced their attitude. They had some connection with the Schonfeld family. Solomon's grandfather studied at the Bratislava Yeshiva. He mentions in his memoirs that he had meals with the Steiner family. It was customary and a *mitzva* for local families to feed the *yeshiva* boys.

David Steiner was brought up with a respect for German culture. He read Goethe and Schiller. German language and literature was respected among intellectual Slovakian families. Both his parents spoke English but he refused to learn the language because as a Zionist he felt strongly about the injustice of British policy in Palestine. His paternal grandparents lived in Mansell Street in London's East End. The grandfather, Eliezer, was known as Lesser Jamieson although the original family name was Baruch. He was in the quill and feather trade. His grave has a *shofar* depicted on the headstone. In recent years a relative presented David Steiner with his grandfather's *shofar*. It is now one of his most cherished possessions. His mother came from a German Jewish family but was born in London where she married. After her husband died she returned to live in Germany. Her parents are buried in East London.

In 1942 the Jewish community of Bratislava came under increasingly severe pressure. Most of the congregation was brutally rounded up and taken away. That was the last deportation until 1944. Any Jews left went into hiding, David Steiner among them. David hid at first with his parents in a cellar under the Great Synagogue. So did **Tamáš Reif** and his mother. Mrs Singer,

The Steiner Family Bookshop and Lending Library, founded in 1847 moved here to 22 Venturgasse, Bratislava in 1880. (DS)

Shoshana Brayer's mother, was also there. For three years David moved from place to place, sometimes with others, sometimes alone, continually planning where to hide next. One night he slept in the Reif family's former home and found a prayer book there. He kept it with him till they met again after liberation.

In April 1945, Russian troops ousted the Nazis. At first the Russians were welcome but the initial joy and relief was short-lived as tragic news spread of all those who would never return. The few who were still alive had lost most of their family members. Many surviving children were orphans. And Jewish leaders were profoundly concerned for the future.

David Steiner's father was the only one of eight children to return alive. Just seven of his many cousins survived. Of these four were liberated from Concentration Camps and three had been in hiding, protected by local friends. When the Steiners came back to Bratislava the gentile family they found living in their house took flight and they moved back into their old home.

For others it was very different. Living conditions were extremely crowded. There were pests in the houses and only buckets for toilets. Most survivors returned traumatised to face further deprivation. David Steiner was appalled to see a woman in the street wounded and bleeding, her little boy running after her, crying. He recognised them. It was Mrs Reif and her son Tamáš. She had been attacked by a Russian soldier. She was taken to a hospital where the nuns nursing her thought she would die. David Steiner tried to comfort her, calling her by her real name. This terrified her even more for she had disguised her origins and had been living among Christians. He was able to reassure her that the war was over, that she was safe and he would look after her son. And she recovered. Later he had the pleasure of returning to her the prayer book he had saved so carefully. In 1998, fifty-three years later, I was privileged to reunite **Tamáš Reif** with his mother's protector when he was visiting London.

Hetty Weiner-Fisch and **Tamáš Reif** recall David Steiner after the war as the dedicated leader of their Youth Group, B'nei Akiva. He collected surviving Jewish youngsters as they gradually emerged from their hiding places and worked indefatigably to restore their confidence. He told me how a soldier from the Jewish Brigade was amazed to find that any Jewish children had survived.

David Steiner (DS).

Before the war the Orthodox and the Reform (the Neolog) had separate facilities. Now they amalgamated and there was just one synagogue to serve all. Jewish Schools were set up. Children's Homes were opened by Agudath Israel and Beis Ya'acov as well as a seminary to train young women as teachers. Several youth groups were started again like B'nei Akiva and there were camps providing preparation for aliyah. All the institutions had become Zionist since the liberation. There were soup kitchens, an Old People's Home and a hospital. Survivors worked together to rehabilitate themselves and to rebuild their community.

Peace had come but anti-Semitism had not disappeared. A pogrom at Kielce in Poland in 1946 shocked Jews all over the world. This event propelled Rabbi Schonfeld to hasten over there and bring a group of children to recover in Britain. This was the first of his several post-war transports.

David Steiner eventually reached Israel himself in September 1948, one of the last Jews to leave Bratislava. Today he proudly states that he has demonstrated clearly his stand against Hitler. For he has produced four children and eleven grandchildren and all of them are observant Jews living in Israel today.

The Steiner family business was revived by his cousin, Zelma Steiner. She survived incarceration in Theresienstadt and returned to re-open the bookshop. It is a proud achievement. 150 years had elapsed since it was established, but there is now only a tiny Jewish community left in Bratislava.

Shoshana Singer Brayer of Bratislava

*This account is based on the book Shoshana wrote about her wartime experiences and an interview with her in June 1998 in my Jerusalem home. Shoshana was born in 1928 in Poland, the seventh of ten children. The family had moved to Bratislava shortly before the war. As conditions worsened they sought hiding places where they could stay together and avoid deportation. Shoshana stayed throughout those grim years with her mother and four of her siblings. Initially they were hiding under the Great Synagogue with **David Steiner** and others, he from a wealthy family, she from one of the poorest.*

Shoshana provides in her book a vivid account of a twelve year old's determination to survive. She describes fifteen moves between 1942 and 1945, from one bunker to another, some large and others tiny. Some were windowless, unheated cellars. One of these was the wood and coal store underneath the Bratislava Jewish Cultural Centre. Another was a hastily excavated, damp hole. Then she lived briefly with a sympathetic neighbour. But the difficulties only seemed to increase as she fled from place to place.

Food was always in short supply. They had no ration books yet her mother managed to produce dishes based on pasta and dried vegetables cooked over a kerosene lamp. During those incarcerations in bunkers the children sometimes played with a pack of cards they made from packaging. She tells of spending hours in pitch darkness and in total silence. When neighbours were at home they dared not make a sound - not even a whisper. So no small children could be included in the hiding place. A crying baby would endanger everyone. At least one infant was suffocated in such a situation. (See **Judit Ziegler**'s poem). Shoshana says she never despaired. Her mother was very strong. Ironically there was some relief when they were eventually found and arrested and imprisoned in Theresienstadt.

Childless neighbours gave devoted care to Shoshana's youngest brother. Another brother was found a place in a Children's Home said to be protected by the Fascists - but they broke that promise. Menachem, her baby nephew, spent several months hidden by a peasant family. Simcha, his young uncle, Shoshana's brother, kept visiting, bringing money and risking his life on every occasion. Later he managed to escape from a train on the way to Auschwitz using a small knife hidden in his shoe as he had been advised when a student at Nitra Yeshiva. After liberation it was Shoshana, then aged 17, who took full responsibility for the toddler, Menachem. She succeeded in reaching Israel with him, both of them as illegal immigrants.

Shoshana's passion once the war was over was to study. She read Comparative Literature, was a Bible Teacher in the USA and a High School Housemother for many years. Shoshana has three children. She used all her resources to ensure they had the best possible education. She stopped them helping in the kitchen so as to spend every moment on their studies. The elder daughter is a psychologist, the younger writes biographies. Her son presents courses on Judaism in Israel and in the USA for non-religious Jewish businessmen. Shoshana visits her Israeli grandchildren every *Shabat*. Her mother insists on living alone in Haifa despite her poor sight. Her children take turns in playing cards with her every evening. She is strictly Orthodox.

Shoshana has observed how she and two of her brothers have retained different memories and reacted very differently to their wartime experiences. David, the fifth child, is very religious like his father and is helped by that. Simcha, the sixth child, 18 months younger, recalls only sad things: that there was not enough food and too many children. As a teenager he had ensured his nephew's well-being. Shoshana, the seventh child, has retained a positive attitude to life as is clearly apparent today. Menachem, her nephew, now settled in Haifa, shows no obvious ill-effects from the grim events in his early childhood. He gave masses of toys to his children for he never had any.

Bertha Fischer of Rachov

Bertha told me her story in 2000. I sent it to Ben Helfgott, the editor of the Journal of the '45 Aid Society with the following note: "Here is a contribution from one of your girls. Bertha Fischer is among my oldest friends. Over the last two years I have taken down her story. It is her wish that you publish it. I have tried to convey her inimitable style. She has retained a remarkable command of English though she seldom uses it these days."

We lived in the small town of Rachov in the Carpathian Mountains, then in the Republic of Czechoslovakia.

Now it belongs to Ruthenia, a part of the Ukraine. Before the Second World War it had a population of about 13,000 and one third of it was Jewish. It was a place full of life as I remember it and so cheerful - until the war came. My father imported goods from abroad. He supplied the whole vicinity with groceries: tea, coffee, sugar and so on, and with building materials. He was the leader of the Jewish community when the war began. We lived in a house by the river and my paternal grandparents lived near by.

My mother's parents were much older than my father's. When my maternal grandfather died his widow was taken in by my father's parents. That was a great success and she lived very happily with them.

My aunt who today lives in Haifa, told me this extraordinary tale about her grandfather. He had died and his body was lying on his bed. Candles were lit and the burial awaited. Suddenly he woke up. It seems he had been in a deep coma. They found a red mark on his foot as if from a blow. He told the following story. He was "on the other side" and a big scale was weighing his good deeds against his bad ones. Someone came and put a cow on the scales and the good deed dropped right down. An angel came and hit him hard, "You are not ready to come here yet," he said, "We are sending you back." And he lived several more years.

We always celebrated the Sabbath and the Holy Days within our own immediate family - even *Seder* Night - but one of us children would go to the grandparents to ask the four questions. There were no guests unless there were strangers at synagogue when they would be included. Our Sabbath meals followed tradition. On the eve of *Shabat* there was carp and soup. For *Shabat* lunch we had *cholent* and for the third meal the rest of the carp with noodles, meat in a tomato sauce and compote. Later we would have apples.

*Rachov in the Carpathian Mountains, now in the Ukraine where
Bertha's father was head of the Jewish Community. (BF)*

*The Fischer family home beside the river in Rachov next to
Bertha's father's wholesale dry goods store. It had extensive yards
and outhouses behind. The imposing building on the right used to
be the Forestry Authority and is now the Town Hall. (BF)*

Bertha's paternal grandmother, Henja Geitel Fischer, on the left with her cousin, taking the waters at the spa in Karlsbad in 1935 as was fashionable in those days.(BF)

The entire Jewish community kept Orthodox practice; no one was secular then. There were three big synagogues. My father wore a *streimel* and kaftan on *Shabat*. The Rabbi played a big role in our everyday lives In later years he settled in Israel. The better off families looked after the less well off. We were a contented community. We children, both girls and boys, attended the local gymnasium. It was a big secular school with high standards. The school had a good library. Some years ago I went back to visit Rachov and introduced myself to present staff and children there.

Both my parents had their own books and read widely. That was how my mother relaxed. She also went to the cinema. The film was changed twice a week and she had a season ticket, much to the surprise of others in the local Jewish community. All of us read a lot. Books were always what I wanted as presents and I exchanged books with my friends. We kept them in drawers. Only religious books, beautifully bound, were kept on open shelves. My first book was about a Czech giant in the hills, and we enjoyed fairy tales by a famous Czech authoress. There were wonderful stories written by Karl May. We read, too, translations of many great classics including Dickens: "Oliver Twist", "David Copperfield", "Little Dorrit". I remember learning about the life of Mozart without knowing his music. At the end of the school day all of us Jewish children went to *cheder*.

At *cheder* we girls were taught to read and write - but only in Hebrew. We learned how to pray but without understanding the language. We learned by heart the daily services and those on *Shabat* but there was no translation in our prayer books. We learned the Bible stories and about the Festivals and the customs involved. The rules of *kashrut* we came to know from our parents but we learned nothing about the birds and the bees!

In 1944 German troops occupied our town. All the soldiers had to be accommodated. Several were billeted on us. It was *Pesach* and we sat down to *Seder* on both nights with those Germans sleeping in the next room. So we kept our voices low. The Festival ended. My mother packed away the special Passover dishes and at 5am next morning our father as head of our community was ordered abruptly to the Town Hall. He was instructed that all Jews must come with their belongings to the schoolhouse to await further orders. We stayed there for a week or two. Then we were crowded into cattle trucks and taken to Mátészalka. This had become a huge ghetto. Many Jewish communities in the region had been brought there. The cemetery was used as a camp site and at night we had to lie on the ground in pouring rain. I shall never forget it. Our bedding was soaked. Mother was crying. Father was helpless. There was no shelter anywhere.

406

Early in the war my father had been forced to hand over his business to Hungarians and so for the past four years we had been left very short of cash. Now father was accused by the police of not giving up all his money when ordered to do so by the Germans. He and my eldest brother Eli were brutally kicked by those police, back and forth, in front of mother, my sister and me. We were unable to intervene. Father and Eli were separated and interned. Mother pleaded to stay with us, her two young daughters. We moved into a loft in Mátészalka with several other families. We had some food. Then after two months we were ordered to go to the cemetery again.

Cattle trucks took us to Auschwitz. There Mengele was directing people, right and left. Celia and I were sent to the left, mother to the right. She tried to take Celia with her but Mengele stopped her. Then we saw Father and Eli running by from a different wagon. They called out "Where is mother?" We told them that we heard she had gone to an old people's camp. Father was crying bitterly. He seemed to know the worst. We never saw them again.

We were given bromide to make us docile. We just did as we were told. We were doped and only wanted to sleep. From then till we were liberated our menstruation stopped. I was fourteen. Two months later we were counted and commandeered to go to a Labour Camp. Celia, very small at twelve years old, was sent to one side with disabled and elderly people. At that time I did not believe the crematorium story. Later we heard about it from others who had been involved in building it. But I was determined that where Celia goes, I go. So I stood by her. There were two other young children and I saw an older woman pull them with her to be counted at the roll call. So I did the same, pulling us both into line with those due for the Labour Camp. That move saved us.

We went to Gieslingen, near Stuttgart, an enormous ammunition factory called Wurttembergische Metallwaren Fabric (WMF) making parts for aircraft and for pistols. It was a peculiar feeling to realise that we were making munitions that could be used against us and our people. We were guarded by kapos and we worked on twelve hour shifts, either day or night. Celia became ill and unable to work but the kapo had taken a liking to her. She was a gentile, a Sudeten German. She took her to the Camp hospital, looked after her and kept her there. Later on she wanted to adopt her though of course we would not hear of it.

It was *Yom Kippur*. The whole Camp decided to fast. We hoped that would lead to our release. I was on night shift and I, too, fasted. We returned to the barracks, terribly hungry to find that the SS had taken our food away. Every day we would queue, block by block, with our bowls. We were so hungry. It reminded me of "Oliver Twist". So, like him, I went

Bertha (indicated with an x) is the tallest girl in the second row, her sister Celia (also indicated with an x) two away on her left. These are the pupils of the "Jewish School at Rachov, June 25th, 1940", the cheder they attended after lessons at the local secular school. (BF)

and queued a second time. We all had to wear little caps. That was a factory requirement and as we all had shaven heads we all looked alike. However, after a few days someone recognised me in the queue for a second time. I got an awful beating. Never did I try that again.

One evening a heavily pregnant woman was put in our block. There were shouts and cries during the night. A baby was born but lived only a day or two. Both disappeared. We never heard of them again.

After Christmas there were bombing raids. The factory ran out of materials. So we were again pushed into cattle trucks. This time we were taken to Alach near Dachau. There was no work and little food during the two months we spent there. Everyone talked about cooking and recipes. It was utterly demoralising. My sister had stayed in the Camp hospital with the same kapo looking after her. I loved her very much and cried bitterly when we were separated, not knowing if we would ever meet again. I went alone when our women's group was marched off with no idea where we were going. After a while some 2,000 men were added to our contingent. They were Russian prisoners-of-war from Dachau. Back and forth we were marched between the Russian and American lines. I heard later they had intended to shoot us all but the SS wanted to protect their own skins by then, so avoided adding to their record of brutality. There was little food. Then we were put on a train. Suddenly we realised all our SS guards had disappeared, fearful of capture by the Allies. They had run into the woods. We were on our own. We were FREE. That was an unforgettable moment. Then American troops arrived. At first they thought our train was carrying soldiers and started firing. When we realised they must be Allies, we jumped off the train so that they could see we were not German troops but Camp survivors. We threw ourselves at the US soldiers and hugged and kissed them. An American Rabbi appeared. He told us we were going to a castle where we would be fed and cared for because, he warned us, a lot of SS men were hiding in the woods and we must be protected.

Next morning the POWs and all of us went a bit wild. For a few days we searched houses vacated by fleeing Germans. We looked for clothes and shoes; we had none and were covered with lice. We went looting, taking what we could, smashing what was left, letting off steam. All I wanted was a comb, a fine one, and some clothes. I so much wanted to clean myself up, to bring myself back to some normality. I kept those clothes for a long time afterwards - but the only pants I found were torn so I was careful not to lift my skirt!

We were taken to very large barracks, in Landsberg, last used by the SS. It was a place made famous because Hitler was living there when he wrote "Mein Kampf". When we arrived every block was occupied by a different nationality: Polish, Russian, Czech. We spent two months in the Jewish block. We had all starved for so long and here was food in plenty: sardines, meat loaves, sweets. We started to eat. For some it was too much. They could not digest the rich diet. Others were too weak to cope at all and died. We shared Red Cross parcels.

Our immediate priority was to make contacts, to seek any news of family and friends. So, together with Partisans and released prisoners-of-war, we Jews decided to make our way towards our home towns. I reached Pilsen and then Prague, searching all the time for any news, any at all. I found no one but I heard that my brother Eli was very ill in hospital. Some said he had died.

Word came that the Jewish Refugee Committee was giving out money in Bratislava. So I went there. I slept alongside men and women from all walks of life on straw mattresses in school halls. We were given food and a few clothes. We registered at their Information Centre where everybody was seeking news through a massive grapevine. That is how my brother Joseph learned I had survived. He had heard I was in Budapest and now came to fetch me. He had already found Celia. They were living in Romania. Now he sent me to join her, escorted by a friend of his, while he went to find Eli. In Prague he bumped into a man from Rachov who had seen him. Eli had asked him to make contact with his family and he directed Joseph to the hospital. That same friend later became chairman of the Rachov Survivor Group in Israel. Joseph found Eli very weak and bedridden. He had pleurisy and water on the lungs. He had been very confused and needed long medical treatment. He never spoke afterwards about his experiences in Buchenwald Concentration Camp.

Joseph found a house for us all about 3 km. from Theresienstadt in Bohemia. Eli joined us there when he was sufficiently recovered. He even found a piano for us - so typical of him. We were there until December 1945. All sorts of stories were being spread. We heard how many Czechs were openly becoming Communists. We wanted none of it. While visiting Prague, Eli heard about children's transports going to Britain. He put down my name and Celia's. A month later a telegram told us to be in Prague in two days' time. That was the last occasion I saw my handsome brother, Joseph. He saw us off from Prague. He settled in Australia where he married and had children who keep in touch with me.

We flew from Prague Airport to Prestwick, Scotland in January 1946. We were placed at Polton House, a farm school in Midlothian. It was a beautiful mansion with lovely grounds. Mary, Queen of Scots, was said to have been imprisoned in the Lodge at one time. We were there for about a year learning English, going to school in the village and discovering how to get on with each other. Many of us have stayed friends till today. Our Scottish teacher was Mr Harboth who had graduated from Heidelberg. He taught us arithmetic and the British currency system, weights and measures. From there, we joined the group in Bedford. Some were preparing to go to Israel. Others went to London hostels. Lots of them went on to the States.

At the Bedford Hostel all of us were interviewed and offered advice about how to plan for our future. Everyone had to decide what they wanted to do. My friend Hugo Gryn who was also from Ruthenia, chose to go back to High School. He became widely known as the Senior Rabbi of the Reform Movement in London and a celebrated broadcaster.[14] My choice was to be a mechanical engineer so I worked as an acetylene welder learning the trade at ORT. I wanted to do something different and not to be a typist like most of the other girls. From there we all were found lodgings in London. My sister and I had a room with the Whitman family in Stoke Newington for a short time; that was my first experience of landladies. It was hard to be accepted as a female welder. I found a place in a factory in Tottenham. But Eli was bombarding me with letters: "There is no future in this sort of work. Learn a profession, try a laboratory job." So the JRC found me a place in a dental laboratory. There I met Mayer Stern, who later on founded the Stern Gallery in Tel Aviv. He had trained as a dental technician and advised me to do so, too.

So that is what I did. I completed a five years' apprenticeship at the Borough Polytechnic but after all that I still found it very hard to find a job. I was advised to become a dental assistant and worked in a dental surgery for a year until I emigrated to Israel.

During those years in London the Primrose Club offered the only way we could keep in touch with each other. There I attended a pottery class and I joined a musical appreciation group led by Dr Barnett. This opened a new world for me. I had no previous knowledge of classical music for it was not known in my religious family. He taught us a lot. He got us to read about various operas and come and tell the others the stories. And to this day I enjoy classical music. I sing in the Amcha choir and am teaching the others English folk songs.

In 1953 I decided to join my brother Eli in Israel. But I was not going to miss the Queen's Coronation celebrations in London on June 2nd! After that event my friend Rose Laskier and I left for Israel. We went via Paris so as to enjoy the 14th of July festivities on the way. I had learned about the French Revolution as a child. My mother had given me a book about Madam Rolande.

My brother Eli had studied electronics in Paris. Then in 1948 he went to Israel where he joined the Haganah and fought in the War of Independence. He was an instructor in the Israel Air Force. He became an expert in his field and was a founder of Elbit Electronics where he worked for the rest of his life. Joseph also went to Palestine. I heard how he swam ashore with someone on his back, the two of them reaching there as illegal immigrants. He settled later on in Australia and my sister Celia joined him there in 1952.

My first need was to learn the language. Without Hebrew I could not get a job. It was a difficult time. I had got to the point of trying to borrow the money to travel back to England but my brother, Eli, bitterly disappointed, said he would not help me to leave and I must study Hebrew. He registered me at the *ulpan* on Kibbutz Shefayim. There I learned *Ivrit* and worked in the fields. But it was an Anglo-Saxon group and we talked far too much English and only a little Hebrew - but we had a good time. Despite that, I acquired a sound grounding in the language and made friends. From then on I was able to hold my own in Israel.

I came to live in Tel Aviv in the Anglo-Saxon Hostel and started job-hunting. While doing so I met Arieh and eventually we married. We had a similar background and a deep understanding and appreciation of each other. He was a survivor, too. It was a hard time for both of us. When we married we were penniless. With my last seven *lirot* I bought a lighter for Arieh. He still has it. Years later I heard that my aunt had toured round our relatives, telling them I was an orphan, had nothing and it was a *mitzva* to contribute to our future. So everybody gave us money. In the early days we lived with Arieh's brother and ate at my mother-in-law's place. Arieh had his own dental lab but no savings. Then I found work as a dental assistant and worked till my first baby was born. We called him Reuben. Dana arrived five years later.

In 1954 the Sokhnut gave us a house in Ramat Chen. It was our first real home. It has grown with us. We are still living there today. Our daughter, who also works in a dental clinic, lives with her children on the upper floor. Reuben is a geriatric consultant and lives on the edge of a *kibbutz* with his family. Arieh, who was an accomplished artist, had his studio in the garden that he nurtured, a garden that has become more beautiful with every passing year.

Arieh died in 2007. Now a widow and retired, I read widely and in English. This is a result of the eight years I spent in England where I studied and matured and absorbed another way of thinking and behaving that has enriched my life ever since.

Edit Katz of Košice

Edit's story I wrote from notes made when I visited her in Jerusalem in June 1998. She has two connections with the Hide-and-Seek Children. She was at school in Košice with Chaja Kurz who married one of her cousins. They live in the USA. Robert in Haifa and Gertruda Muller in London are also cousins of hers.

I was born in Košice in 1929. The Jewish community was not large. About half were Reform and half Orthodox. The Reform families were usually better off. Mine was a traditional family with "good genes". My father had a small beard and my handsome mother wore a *sheitl*. They were in the textile business and had a comfortable life. Both my parents were well educated. They read a lot, including the newspapers. After High School my father had attended a commercial school as well as the *yeshiva*. Our family doctor studied with him there. Later on they made an agreement that whenever the doctor paid a professional call to our house he was to stay to study a page of *Gemara* with my father.

On *Shabat* there were usually many visitors to our pleasant town. Every one of them would be invited for meals by local families. It was also customary to invite the *yeshiva* boys. We did, too. As a small child I wondered why my father always brought home two or three people from the synagogue. I came to the conclusion they were there to sing and in doing so drown out the unmusical voices of my father and brothers! There were no visitors on a Tuesday as it was laundry day.

I attended the Orthodox Jewish school in Košice. Some afternoons I went to Beis Ya'acov activities. It was a non-Zionist youth group in those days, financed by the Jewish community. My primary school fees were paid for by the Czech government. My mother and her friends collected clothing and distributed it to the children of poorer families before winter every year. I recall seeing long tables stacked with shirts and shawls and so on, and the children lining up to be decked out by the ladies. They also provided cups of milk at 10am every morning. Then Hungary took over that area and the school no longer received government funding.

The very religious preferred to send their children to the secular State elementary school to avoid the more liberal approach at the Jewish school. After the Hungarian take-over other parents sent their children there, too, except mine. I was the only girl from my class to be sent to the big school run by the Reform Jewish community. It cost them quite a lot.

All the Jewish institutions were run along democratic lines. My father and his colleagues often met at our house. There would be great discussions and elections to the synagogue committee and all the other organisations. The Jewish community had a home for the disabled, another for the elderly, a hospital for the psychiatrically-ill and an orphanage in a very nice building. I remember going there with my mother.

On Sundays we would often go by train for the day to see my maternal grandmother in Prešov, 32 kms away. Other times we would go to the countryside, into the hills. I thought of them then as high mountains so it was a surprise when I visited there some years ago to find them quite small. My parents sometimes went to take the waters at Kyrinica, a spa near Cracow, or at Karlsbad. It was the fashionable thing to do in those days - even for a child. When I was 6 or 7 years old they sent me off with a maid to drink the waters for a whole month hoping that would cure tonsillitis and a glandular infection. It did not do so. After the war my tonsils were taken out.

My mother, though, had a hunch long before troubles began that Czechoslovakia was not a good country for Jews. She had always wanted to move elsewhere although at that time Masaryk was the tolerant and much esteemed President and the government was pro-Jewish. When my father wanted to buy a house she said that the times were not secure enough. She was very much aware of the deeply instilled anti-Semitism among Roman Catholics in Slovakia. But where should we go? My brother and my uncle had been Zionists but my family in general had not been especially keen. To a big, liberal country perhaps like France? We moved to Prešov. We tried to hide but that failed. We were all deported to Auschwitz.

When I was liberated I was 16 years old and the sole member of my family to survive. I returned to Košice and found that the orphanage had became a centre for *Hasharah*-training and preparation for *aliyah*. Before the war my mother was a donor. After the war I became a recipient myself. That was very difficult to swallow. But I definitely wanted to go to Israel. No one had survived from my family and very few of my schoolmates had returned. For seven or eight months I trained there with about twenty boys and twenty girls living in two big dormitories. It was there I met the man I was later to marry. Our sole purpose was to get to Israel and to study. In 1947 I went off via Belgium and Cyprus and ended up in Israel.

My husband comes from the same background. We met again in Israel. There I worked as an accountant. We have two children and eight grandchildren. We both worked hard for many years and now enjoy our retirement.

Shmuel Klein of Nitra

Here are some recollections of a yeshiva boy from Nitra in peace time and his wartime experiences that followed. We met at his home in Jerusalem in June, 1998 and he added more details in 2007.

I was born in Nitra in 1928. My parents were born there, too. They had a shop where they worked very hard and for very long hours so my paternal grandmother took charge of the household. She stood between me and my mother when I was due for a hiding - usually with a wooden spoon - and got hit instead of me! She was a very good woman. At my home *Shabat* and *Kashrut* were strictly upheld.

My grandmother was very righteous and humane. She had a sound Jewish upbringing. She came from a farming family in Boleraz in Slovakia and all her family lived in and around Nitra. They were very hard-working people in those days. They baked their own bread of a very good quality so it kept well, easily for two weeks. My grandmother was very particular where she shopped and would walk a further thirty minutes or more to buy butter where it was made by Jews. Every *Erev Shabat* we carried the *cholent* to the baker's oven approved by my grandmother; the nearer one she considered not sufficiently *kosher*. The pot was very heavy, filled with liquid to make plenty of soup. On *Shabat* we boys had to fetch it. The job then was to find the right pot - for the bit of paper with our family name sometimes burnt up. Woe betide us if we brought back the wrong one! Every day of the week had its regular menu. On Fridays we always had *kasha* with goose fat crackling. For Friday night there was the traditional chicken soup with *lockshen* followed by meat in tomato sauce. Things went steadily on day by day. We had no thought of anything changing until suddenly our lives were turned upside down, and everything we had known fell into disorder.

The town of Nitra had about 30,000 inhabitants; these included 2-3,000 Jews. Most shops in the main street were owned by Jews so only a few were open on *Shabat*.

Let me tell you about my schooling there. All the Jewish children attended the elementary school belonging to the Jewish community. It was in a largely Jewish neighbourhood. The two storey building was kept spotlessly clean by the resident janitor. The Principal, Mr Shimon Feher, had taught my mother in her youth. He was highly respected. Our knees trembled whenever we were called into his office though I recall no punishments. We were well-disciplined. There were 300-400 pupils divided into grades 1 to 5 with parallel classes at each level and some 30-35 children in each one. Classes lasted till 1 o'clock. Religious boys then spent from 2 till 4 in intensive study of Rashi with Rav Herman.

I remember the teachers as being very kind. My teacher in Grade One was Miss Wasserburg who was newly-trained and very efficient. There was a washbasin for each class and if anyone wiped dirty hands on the clean towel she would get very upset. "Can't you wash your hands first?" She would inspect our fingernails and we felt very ashamed if she found them black or if our caps were askew on our heads. We tried to be good pupils. And my grandmother spoilt me. She would send her maid with a roll stuffed with hot scrambled egg for me for our 11.15 break. My grandmother was responsible for a great deal of what I am today. By her example she had a huge influence on me. She was killed in Auschwitz.

I can recall two or three senior teachers who were not good at the job. They could not keep order but were kept on as a duty to provide them with a livelihood. We teased them. Corporal punishment was normal. There were Mr and Mrs B who beat children badly. They were briefly dismissed for ill-treating their pupils. My auntie says Mrs B once hit her sister so my grandmother went and gave them a piece of her mind. That was why my aunt was kept in that same class for four years! Another teacher taught German. She once got in a rage and hit out with a wooden pencil box. Yet we learned a lot. Those who did best sat in the first two rows, the poorer students at the back. We were taught in Slovak but later on we had to master Czech, too. The languages are very similar so this was not so difficult. It was necessary for dealing with administrative matters because many of the civil servants in the tax office, post office and so on, were Czech.

Textbooks had to be obtained at the start of every school year. Some would be new, some bought second-hand from the older pupils. What was interesting and stuck in my mind was this: new books had coupons in them for further purchases. You needed ten coupons to buy another book. The teacher would tear these out and give them to those who could not afford to buy them. Children came from different income groups, rich and poor and quite a few were needy. But I saw no discrimination.

There were three strands of secondary schools where attendance was compulsory for three years. The better students went to the Roman Catholic Gymnasium where they were prepared for academic studies. There were two parallel classes. I was among five or six boys who received extra tuition twice a week in the month preceding the entrance exams and

I obtained a place there. Another pupil was Schumko, a judge's son who was particularly bright.

Other young people attended the Technical High School to train for an occupation. The third possibility was the Talmud Torah, a Jewish school where secular subjects were taught in the afternoon. Unfortunately teaching there was apt to be very poor. Jobs were too often allocated by *protexia* as still can happen today. I recall the very wild behaviour of those Talmud Torah boys. For example, one time needles were left in the holes in an unfortunate boy's seat, connected to a thread. When he sat down and the thread was pulled the boy jumped up, yelling, and he was punished for it.

At the Gymnasium there were bigger classes. Mr W was our teacher. If any of us failed to meet his demands there were punishments. You had huge amounts to write out and if you did not manage that then he doubled the amount. One poor boy, son of a lumberjack, was very small and very slow. He was beaten by Mr W. To our delight one fine day his father came and gave the teacher a bloody nose. But that only happened on rare occasions. The Jewish children had two teachers of religion: one class was for those from religious homes that kept a *kosher* kitchen and *shabat* strictly; and the other was for those from non-religious homes. Although the school was co-educational the religious boys were separated from the girls for this subject. They had a different curriculum. We learned to read and write Hebrew, we read the *Chumash* in Hebrew and in German. We were taught very well.

The parallel class had religious tuition at a different level. It was given by Mr Weiss. He loved children and they thoroughly enjoyed his lessons. I attended his class when my teacher was sick and was very impressed by his humour and his style. He was a most successful teacher. We were taught Jewish history by several staff, all very knowledgeable. Once in a while the Rabbi came, usually on a Sunday morning, and he would ask us questions, perhaps on Exodus or on Rashi commentary.

Later on religious boys studied at the *yeshiva*. It was housed in a big complex with two entrances. You entered through big gates. Probably this had once been the old ghetto. Within was the Great Synagogue and other small study groups. Some studied in two's and three's and others in larger groups. Within the compound too, were the Old People's Home in a beautiful garden, the orphanage and the rooms of a resident Rabbi and the *Dayanim*. And there was a *matza* bakery.

After *Chanuca* the *yeshiva* students would begin baking *matzot* under a Rabbi's supervision and any that were not *kosher* were thrown out of the window. The children would pick them up. We used to bring chickens to the slaughter house and they would hang on hooks. We had to hold the bird's head still after they killed them. Peasants who came twice a week to sell their produce at the Nitra market fattened up geese, forcibly fed, sometimes choking them. If that happened they would run quickly with them to the *shochet* in the compound or sell them at half-price to a non-Jew.

The Jewish Community of Nitra had brought Rabbi Ungar from Tarnow to establish their *yeshiva*. My grandmother had said that one day her grandson would study there and I did. (And I slept there briefly during the war). Rabbi Ungar became widely known. More than half the students came from all over the country. Routine at the *yeshiva* was very strict. We had to be at morning service by 8 am. The door was locked at 8.05. Anyone who was missing was reported to the Rabbi and you had to pay 5 *kroner* as a punishment. Study was intensive and lasted till 5.30. Some 300 pupils at a time would be sitting on benches at tables in a big hall.

When I was a *yeshiva* boy my grandmother would wake me at 6am. I asked her to pour water on me if I fell asleep again. Every morning she was up early feeding wood shavings into the stove to heat our two large ovens. Sometimes I worked at home, especially in the cold winter, and would arrive late. I would try to creep in unseen by the other gate left open for workers in the communal offices. Sometimes I went instead to the study group where Rabbi Vorhand taught but usually I tried to toe the line. After *Shabat* senior pupils would be examined in front of the *bemah*. They had to explain phrases from the *Torah* and quote Rashi. At 11am the Senior Rabbi would ask what we had learned during the previous week. At home before I was *barmitzvah* my parents introduced a young man into our house to give me extra teaching in Hebrew, *Chumash* and prayer. He had a strong influence on my life. He showed how one could be both humane and religious. "Just be a *mensch*," he would say.

There were several synagogues in Nitra. We attended where our parents chose; there was no connection with the school. The Great Synagogue held regular daily services. Then there were two or three small ones and the study group. For the "Three Day Jews" there was the Neolog, known as "the Big *Schul*" where they held *Shabat* services; it was a large and luxurious synagogue.

A very serious problem was army call-up. Some students feigned sickness. They would smoke cigarettes soaked in vinegar; one boy damaged his eyes permanently. Others went abroad. My teacher told me that some families failed to register their sons' birth so as to avoid army service.

The Antman family were religious Zionists. They led B'nei Akiva activities in their house. I attended every *Shabat* afternoon. We had a lovely time there. In 1936 that group made *aliyah* and settled in Kfar Saba. The matriarch of this family was my great-aunt, my grandmother's sister. She had six boys and four or five girls. The third generation are still living a religious life but their attitude has never been extreme.

I was not aware of coming problems until one *Shabat* in 1941 when we were walking in the park and airplanes dropped leaflets. These announced that Czechoslovakia had become a Republic and that "we had been chained till today but now were free". This was the start of hard times. The Hlinka Guard took over control of the town. From then on every knock on the window brought fear and distress. We knew that some day as Jews we would be forced to leave. Old school friends of my mother's, well-to-do and experienced people, knew the Hlinka chief and introduced us. Money changed hands. Some Jewish families refused to give bribes even if they could afford to do so. The Jewish community leaders were told that everyone had to register.

My maternal grandparents were arrested but the Hlinka commander released them. He really tried to help us. Then whole groups were taken away, first the teenage boys, and then the girls. By the time we left everyone had gone. Some had hidden, others managed to escape as we did in March 1942. My father organised cars and we went through the fields and across the Hungarian border to Budapest. The guides left. Some people were robbed on the way. My parents were later deported.

A few stayed on semi-legally in Nitra. I returned to the *yeshiva* with a number of others in 1943. In 1944 the *yeshiva* provided me with identity papers as a non-Jew but with my own photo. With these I went back to Bratislava and slept at a friend's house. All his family had been taken. German police arrested me. "He is not a Jew", my friend said. "It can't be helped", they replied; and they locked me in a detention centre in an underground car park. I spoke to the Commander. I told him I had to go to work. My papers showed I was from another part of the country so he could not really check them. "Take my address" I told him. I made out I did not understand German. So he let me go.

I found a room with two beds in an old German woman's home in the Street of the Wine Merchants. A Jewish family was in hiding in the courtyard. Next day I met a friend, sent him to the old woman and he moved in to the empty bed. Once while I lived there my mother visited me. I made out she was my auntie. People thought I was a funny boy; they would get me to repeat things I said. But you could never relax. I returned one day to find a huge commotion: the Jewish family had been taken away.

The battle front was coming closer. The whole population had to work for the Germans. Everyone's identity card had to be stamped daily to show where they worked. I was working with non-Jews. They saw that I was different and started making remarks like "He's a Jew". I was desperate. Every day someone was taken away. I wore an extra shirt and socks in case that happened to me. Then I realised that what was different about me was my language so I started to use their rough style. "Aren't you ashamed of suspecting your friend?" a German soldier said to the rest. From then on I assimilated very quickly. There were awkward moments - as in the public urinals with one's trousers pulled down. But I put on a good face. I was a good actor.

One week every month the Jewish Refugee Council gave out money to us from premises in a big block on the city outskirts. Our papers had a Police stamp to authenticate them, forged by the JRC. One day in 1944-45 I was on my way back to their office when I sensed something was wrong. It was too quiet everywhere. The JRC workers had been caught.

I returned to Nitra and was protected there by a policeman's wife. He was arrested later and killed by the Germans. Four of us shared one room. Then I escaped to Budapest, hiding in various places. Next I got myself a job as a supervisor in a children's prison and I found my sister there. We were housed in a large deserted building and slept on straw. One day it was announced that children under 13 could leave. I knew that the Budapest Jewish community was still at risk and if I did not get out quickly I never would. I realised that the long corridor of our building led to an exit. So I picked up my six year old sister in my arms and ran for it. We found our way to an uncle and he located an escort to take us back over the border to Nitra. False papers were provided for me under the name of "Andre Buber". I returned to Bratislava, moving from place to place.

I was working in a leather factory totally staffed by Germans. Every day our work permits had to be stamped. But at 4am one night there was banging on the door. I was arrested and taken to an underground car park. I insisted I must get to work, that I was not a Jew and eventually they let me go. For the final months of the war, when the Russians came, I hid in cellars. Then I got sick. I needed medical attention. So I attended the local clinic. They said they would send a doctor to visit me. And a tall German SS man came and began to examine me starting from my chest and as he moved down I thought my last moment had come - but he stopped at my abdomen. So I escaped yet again.

Both my parents had been taken to Auschwitz and both survived *with the help of the Almighty*. My father had hidden a gold coin in his shoe and with the proceeds of that he managed to buy bread for a time. Later he somehow extracted from his teeth a gold filling for the same purpose. He was a slave labourer in an underground factory where he had to carry long rails. His strength was extraordinary. In peace time he had been ill every winter – but not during the war. My mother meanwhile, a tiny but very strong woman, obtained extra bread for her duties as a translator as she had a good command of German. At one time she was beaten when digging potatoes and later had the grim task of marking dead bodies. Yet she survived all this to live to the age of 93.

After liberation I was active in B'nei Akiva. I taught mathematics and Hebrew at the Orphanage at Nové Mesto with my friend, the son of Rabbi Ungar from Nitra. A number of children from here were taken to England by Rabbi Schonfeld and we prepared a group of 500 child survivors for *aliyah* with youth leaders from the Zionist movement. Before the war we would never have worked together like this.

In 1968 I went to Australia and my parents settled there. That is where I first met my future wife. Later we met again in Israel where we were married. We returned to Australia and brought up three sons and a daughter. Recently we all came on *aliyah* and settled in Jerusalem. I established a stationery business in the central shopping area and ran it till I retired.

In the summer of 2005 Shmuel Klein went back to Slovakia for the first time and with his wife. He found no trace of the Jewish quarter in Nitra. Not a stone remained of the famous yeshiva complex. In the old city of Bratislava they felt quite uncomfortable. It was a harsh and tragic experience, a journey he will not repeat.

Rachel Malmud of Bratislava

This is the story Rachel related to me during the summer of 1999. **Bertha Fischer** *introduced us many years ago. She was married to Bertha's brother Eli. Rachel died in 2006 and so, to my regret, never saw this book. It was Rachel who initially introduced me to Olga Grossman in 1996.*

I was born in Košice, one of five children. When I was 5 years old we moved to Bratislava. My father, Samuel Malmud, was brought up in Košice and his parents, Edward and Helena Malmud, continued to live there. They were well-established and comfortably off. They had three daughters and two sons. The youngest girl was Ethel. She lived with her parents and was very helpful to us all.

Our father's business, like his father's, was the smoking and pickling of fish imported from Norway and Hamburg. He employed 30 to 40 people using modern methods of preparation learned from a German expert. Our mother was Dora Brandsdorfer-Weizman, from a religious family that had lived for centuries past in Slovakia. When her father became ill in Humenné, in East Slovakia, her parents came to live near us in Bratislava. My grandfather died in the Jewish Hospital from heart failure and was buried locally. He was 70 years old and seemed very ancient to me. My grandmother then came to live with us; I remember her as a good woman.

Our mother was not sent to High School herself but she always encouraged us to study. She was very intelligent and well educated. She read all the German classics. She had a strong personality, was open to new ideas and had a wonderful relationship with us. She was not just our mother but also our friend. In 1936, when 40 or 41 years old, she discovered she was pregnant again. She was somewhat ashamed but I told her she would enjoy having another child to look after when we were grown-up.

There were two Jewish Elementary Schools in Bratislava, one Orthodox, one Neolog (Reform). My sister Edit was 18 months older than me. We attended the Orthodox school where the main language was German and the second, Slovakian, was taught as a foreign language. Edit went on to the High School and had plans to continue at the Commercial Academy. I went to the German Gymnasium. I left there when it was becoming evident that Jewish students were not wanted. I moved to a Gymnasium for girls only, where the main language was Slovakian. But a year later, in 1941 I was forced to leave there, too, when new regulations forbade

Jewish students to attend any public schools. So the Jewish community set up a High School. It was there that among other subjects I first began to learn English; the teacher had spent several years in the United States.

In 1938 some German but mostly Austrian refugees had began to reach us. They had fled from their homes. They told us about terrible things happening to Jews under Nazi domination. An electric train connected Bratislava with Vienna only an hour's journey away. A year later the independent Slovakian Republic became a puppet state of Germany and the leaders were violent Fascists, assuring Hitler by their behaviour that they were faithful to him. It was learned later that the Slovakian government had agreed to pay 500 *Reichmarks* for every Jew deported to Poland from their soil.

Heavy demands were made on the Jewish community. First, property was confiscated. Then those with businesses were forced to accept Slovak managers. These, though quite inadequate for the task, were put in charge over the owners' heads. Once they had learned what they considered sufficient, the owners were thrown out. Not surprisingly these businesses floundered. Thus numerous Jewish families found themselves without work or income and becoming an increasing burden on Jewish Community resources. Further humiliating regulations followed. Cinemas, cafes and parks became out-of-bounds to Jews, dogs and gypsies. Jewellery, furs and electrical equipment had to be given up, even bicycles - though my little brother hung on to his much-loved bike, his present on his fifth birthday. It was prohibited to own a radio but on our top floor we listened, as did many others, to BBC news bulletins with deepening anxiety. By 1941 every Jew was required to wear a prominent yellow star.

Although Edit and I were proud Jews, we refused to wear that star. It was so very degrading. We were 17 and 18 years old and we continued to enjoy the company of our friends. As we were no longer allowed to meet in public places we met in each other's homes and tried to forget the horrors and dangers closing in on us. We especially enjoyed Sunday evenings. We came to know one young man from a secular family. He liked to spend Friday evenings and *Shabat* at our home; and he admired my sister Edit. His family were assimilated and did not keep the old traditions as we did. The father had a big stationery business and travelled a lot.

The young man's name was Hans James. He and his brother had gentile friends and one of them was a detective. One Sunday during 1942 the order came that all young women between 16 and 35 were to be home by 6pm. We were visiting our friends as usual. The detective warned the boys not to let us go home as there were rumours that there were to be

424

deportations. We warned our mother and told her we would return later. When we came home at 8 or 8.30 we saw her worried face at the window. She told us to come in quickly. The Hlinka Guards had come for us. She had told them she did not know where we were, that we were independent young women. So for the following night or two we stayed at the boys' home but dared not stay longer because we were putting them and their family at risk.

Our parents arranged for us to go to our paternal grandparents in Košice. That part of the country had by then been absorbed by Hungary. Our mother and little brother watched us leaving. That was the last time we ever saw them. I retain to this day the image of their faces in the window. Father took us to his former driver. He asked him to arrange for us to be taken across the border into Hungary. He had to pay a lot to manage this. He provided us with false birth certificates that made out we were far older women but luckily we met no guards. We spent two nights in the driver's simple little house till he found someone to escort us. The journey took much longer than usual - six hours instead of two. We were taken across where there were no guards. It was almost dark when he left us in a small town.

We were very hungry by then so we went into a restaurant. We were wearing smart green coats with cavalry trimmings and we did not look Jewish. A man in civilian clothes sat next to us. "What are you girls doing here?" he asked. "We are on our way to spend the Easter holidays with relatives", we replied "and our train does not leave till the morning". He recommended a boarding house where we could stay the night and took us there. He told the owner to make sure we were not disturbed and warned us to be careful as a lot of Jews were escaping across the border. We had a quiet night.

Who should we meet on the train next day but my school friend, Aviva, still my good friend today. She was travelling with a group of happy young people on their way to spend *Pesach* with their families in Budapest. She wanted us to stay with them. Edit told one of the boys we were refugees from Slovakia, a very risky thing to do. But we went on to Košice and arrived safely with our grandparents.

Grandfather was still living comfortably and managing his fish preserving business with a brother and a son. Our uncles and aunts lived in adjoining houses except for Bella. She lived in Zenta, a small town in South Hungary with her five children. She was pregnant again. The grandparents were very glad to see us but anxious that someone might recognise us as we had regularly spent the summer holidays with them.

So after *Pesach* they obtained our original birth certificates showing we were born in Košice. These gave us a legal right to live in what was now Hungary. But there was still a danger that some people would know we had escaped from Slovakia. Once we had these certificates we took the train again via Budapest to Zenta, to stay with our aunt where no one else would know us.

There was not a lot for us to do in Zenta. Our grandfather was sending us pocket money but we wanted to be independent. So we returned to Budapest. Jewish life was continuing freely there. The head of the community, Herr von Freudigger, took me on as governess as I knew German fluently. That language and culture was still considered prestigious by Hungarian Jews. They were not very kind to me. Perhaps they suspected I was a refugee.

They did not register me with the Health Service. So when after a month there I developed appendicitis and was seriously ill, there were problems. As I was under 18, a parents' permission was required to operate. Our wonderful aunt Elonka left her children and came and arranged for my care. She sat with me in the Jewish Hospital for five days. The appendix burst. My temperature reached 41°C. There was no penicillin then. I had an emergency operation. There was an air raid during the operation and the electricity was cut off. Fortunately the hospital had its own generator or I would not have survived. I returned to Zenta to recuperate. Edit came, too, as she was unhappy with her job. It took me six weeks to recover.

While staying in Zenta a postcard arrived from our mother in her beautiful handwriting. "We are on a train. They are deporting us. We do not know where. I hope you will be all right and we shall meet again. Take care. Your loving mother". That was the last contact we ever had with our parents.

This was in 1944. She had given the card to her brother to send on to us. He had managed to meet them on their train at the station at Zilina near the Polish border. All the transports went through there. They hoped he would find a way for them to escape - to no avail. When we found our uncle again after the war was over he told us how to his lasting sorrow he was unable to save them. He was a *hazan* at Zilina and he and his five children all survived the war. They spent the final months hiding in attics or cellars. Mother had sent our grandmother to them, a wise and wonderful woman. But by then she was very old and frail and was unable to climb up to attics. She did not survive the war.

I became very depressed, melancholy and feeling utterly helpless, crying at night, thinking how we should have tried everything to convince them to join us. Later I heard what had happened to our family. It was *Tisha B'av*. Deportations had started again. The family had joined others in a big cellar with all the children. They were fasting. Mother was feeling unwell and came out for a breath of fresh air. A German neighbour saw her and informed the police. The police searched and found them. They took away everyone in that cellar.

When I was well again Edit and I decided to go back to Budapest. Aviva was still working there and we had kept in touch. We wanted jobs, too. This time the Loewingers, a really kind Jewish family, asked me to look after their little boy. The mother was a highly intelligent lady and they had a beautiful home furnished with antiques.

A month later, on March 19th, 1944 German soldiers occupied Budapest and their army and the Gestapo streamed across Hungary. A few days after that Edit and I met a printer through our Jewish Slovak friends who provided us and many others with false papers without any charge. So we took on non-Jewish identities: Edit became Maria and I was Julia, from Gyor. I tried to urge the Loewingers to do the same. I moved into a small room in a boarding house. Edit was looking after children in a family nearby. We were careful not to meet too often. The password among Jewish Slovak refugees was at that time "And are you also a musician?"

Massive deportations were taking place of Jewish communities in rural areas, our grandparents and all the relatives in Košice amongst them. We were living under immense stress night and day, always on our guard. Yet somehow the values and mores imbibed from our earliest childhood stayed firm and conditioned our behaviour even under this formidable and excessive pressure. We faced continual crises. A time came when ration cards had to be renewed. Mine had been obtained illegally so I was wary of giving it up but eventually I faced the authorities and succeeded in obtaining a new one.

One day I returned to my room in the boarding house to find the big armchair was no longer there. I was horrified as I had hidden some false identity papers in it, intended to be passed on. I spent two or three hours in fear and trepidation, certain that at any moment the Hlinka would come to arrest me. Sure enough, loud voices began shouting from below. But no one came to my room and things quietened down. Then somebody knocked at the door. My heart jumped "It's the maid!" I asked her, in a voice as calm as I could keep it, what had happened to my armchair. She explained she had thought it too large for my little room and had moved it into the hall to give me more space. When she had left and the place was quiet I found my chair, sat in it slowly and felt along the seat. The papers were still there. What a relief!

I no longer felt safe there. I found a vacancy in a boarding house only for women. It was in Pest. I registered with the change of address in my new identity, relieved now to have authentic papers. One girl there had a Jewish friend; another who was blond and wore a crucifix, worked for the Gestapo.

A bit later I received a postcard from my uncle. He had been drafted into the Jewish Labour Unit of the Hungarian Army. Work there was so heavy and in such grim conditions that few were alive by the time the war ended. He wrote to tell me his wife and children were in the ghetto in Subotica where all the Jews of the district had been crammed. Then another postcard arrived saying they were being deported - destination unknown. We were terribly worried about them. Our aunt was due to give birth to their sixth child. At great risk I went to visit them and took some forged identity papers to help some of them escape. I got on to a train, found an isolated seat and sat down. A Fascist policeman came and sat next to me. They were on the look out for any Jews trying to escape from Budapest. A cattle truck passed by. It was full of Jews. The policeman said "There go the Jews to be made into soap." I stayed silent. "What! Do you like Jews?" "I don't know any," I replied. I could not curse my own people.

I walked into the ghetto. No questions were asked. People could come and go. But everyone was very worried. Now and then someone would be claimed, needed for the war effort. Then suddenly their permit to work would be invalidated. I found my aunt with the five children expecting the new baby any minute. We had a long discussion. I gave the two teenage girls the false papers but they refused to leave their mother in her plight. Their brother would have come but not without them. I made a speech to other young people, urging them to leave while they could. They were working in a factory. I told them to come to Budapest where it was safer but they argued they were needed there and seemed quite unaware of the danger they were in. I stayed till evening, deeply distressed that I was unable to help them. I was lucky to get away. For next day the ghetto was closed.

My uncle's postcards must have been seen by someone in the boarding house. They caused me a lot of trouble. They became the subject of the day among the residents. The landlady said I should not be associating with Jews. I told her the writer was a dressmaker I knew. She could have reported me but she did not. But I received a warning letter, then a second much stronger one, advising me to move away. I had no idea who sent them. After the war I tried to find out who it was. It was not the girl with a Jewish boyfriend but she explained that the girl wearing a crucifix was a Rabbi's daughter. It could have been her or the landlady who sent me the warnings.

So I went away quietly with a small suitcase to a room in a large house in Buda where an old lady lived alone with her maid. I told her I would be out working all day. Edit was living in the same street.

Slovak refugees were not well accepted by the Hungarians, or even by Hungarian Jews. They did not believe the stories that were circulating or that the atrocities would affect them. So it was very difficult for Slovak refugees to find jobs. Anyone without Hungarian citizenship had to keep off the streets. It was even more dangerous if they were Jewish and carrying false papers. There was always a risk of deportation or of being shot.

Just then I was fortunate enough to come across Lola Goldberger, a friend from Bratislava. She introduced me to a small watchstrap workshop owned by Mr Pappek. He knew my true identity and employed me. There I was with wonderful people, caring and affectionate. They gave me the strength to survive. I had little money and was short of food but Julia Sveda, Mr Pappek's sister-in-law, became a marvellous friend. She was divorced and lived with her mother and 13 year old daughter. She always made me welcome in her home though her situation was not easy. By befriending me she was endangering herself and her whole family. She did everything possible to help me.

I was protected by Mr Pappek. His was a safe place and my friends could visit me there. The Russian army was coming closer, only 30 km from Budapest and was shelling us from their tanks. The Allies were bombing us continually. So we spent hours in the shelter. We were glad this was happening and that the Germans were being attacked.

In the shelter we met a delightful young man and his mother. We would talk about music, play word games, anything to fill the long hours in cramped conditions and uncertainties of those heavy raids. He was strikingly handsome with blue eyes and wavy hair and appeared to be a Roman Catholic novice. He was very bright; he knew Hebrew and English as well as Czech. After liberation we discovered he was Jewish, and his name was Jan Weinberger. Julia hoped we would become a couple. In 1944 he was studying at the Rabbinical College in Budapest. After the war he worked at the Prague Museum and wrote to me. Then he went to study in London where Edit met him again many years later. He was by then a Reform Rabbi, serving in Rhodesia where he had married a well-to-do girl. In 1952 I came across him in Haifa. He introduced me to his wife "Meet my big love, Lily!" I, too, was married by then.

By Christmas time it was evident that it was only a matter of a few days before the Russians would be ousting the Germans and liberating us. It was then I came across Gita. She was homeless. I asked my friend Aviva if her mother would allow Gita to hide in their home. She agreed though it meant taking a huge risk. In those final hours of the Fascist regime anyone hiding Jews was shot on the spot. And their neighbours were suspicious "What are you doing with a Jewish girl in your house?" They told them she was a distant cousin, fleeing from the bombing.

Then at last Pest was liberated but I was living on the opposite side of the front line. For six more weeks I was in a shelter where 150 people were crammed in while the Russians and the German soldiers were facing each other in the street above. There were snipers, bombs, Katyushas. All I had to eat was a bag of dried pulses and I slept on a deckchair. A further danger faced me. A family with two girls came and sat near me. They were from the town I was supposed to be from - in my false identity. They asked which school I went to. Somehow I avoided answering. It was very tricky. Some Jews had just been found and were shot in the park on the Hill of Roses. The Roman Catholic priest held services in the shelter. I sat at the back, very scared because I was not familiar with their practices nor did I know how to make the sign of the cross. Another time, without thinking, I answered an SS man in German and that aroused suspicions. There were all sorts of risks.

Edit meanwhile was governess to two small children. The father had a bakery and he gave out bread during bombardments. It was a very cold winter. House to house fighting was going on. The German and Russian soldiers were attacking each other, fighting for control of Buda. The Russians took over the house where Edit was – No.16 Margaret Avenue. I was at No. 36. Five Hungarian boys, deserters from the losing Hungarian army, were helping the baker. Suddenly a strange young woman ran across the road. The boys pulled her in. Edit knew some Russian and explained what was going on. Then the Germans took over the house again and the woman left. A few hours later everyone in the house was taken for questioning at the German HQ. It turned out that the young woman was mistress of one of the German officers and had reported them. Edit was accused of being a Russian spy. In the bathroom she met a friendly Hungarian girl, mistress to another German officer, and told her of her plight. This girl assured her officer that Edit was no spy. So Edit and the family were freed but the boys were questioned continually day after day. Edit was taken on as the translator and she stood up to it.

These boys knew I had no food and they would rush across the firing line to bring me loaves of bread. Then just before the Russians broke through the five boys were shot and left dying in the snow. "This is what will happen to any traitors," said the Germans. Edit was fortunate: the Germans continued to use her as an interpreter.

Eventually Edit appeared with bread for me. She knew I was hungry. She told me that the Russians had broken through and taken over her house. We were liberated! We stayed on a few more weeks. There were no trains. So Edit and Aviva and I hitchhiked back to Košice. We had a lift in a Russian truck. On the way we stopped in a small village where the soldiers ordered a woman to make us a huge omelette. Then a very drunk Russian soldier saw us girls and started to molest us. An officer came by and saved the situation by threatening him with his revolver.

We reached Košice, hoping against hope some of our family would come back. My little suitcase with my few possessions was stolen on the way including the precious postcard from our mother. People returning from deportation began to tell us of horrific experiences. We scanned lists with information of anyone from our town but there was nothing about our family. We went on to Bratislava and to our house. No one had come back.

Edit found her childhood friend Hans again and married him. He was a good boy but it was not a suitable match and after reaching Israel together, they separated. I was a keen Zionist and saw Palestine as the best hope for the future. So I joined Hashomer Hatzair and went on *aliyah* with forged papers showing me as the wife of a Czech officer who fought with the British. In Israel I met Eliezer Peleg again, a survivor from Russian Carpathia, in Eastern Czechoslovakia. In July 1951 we married in Eilat and Edit married a second time two days later.

Many years later, after the Soviets gave up control in 1991, I went to see the land of my childhood. I was struck by the beauty of the mountains and the countryside. I put a plaque on my grandfather's grave and added the names of our mother and our two brothers lost in the *Shoah*. Only one synagogue was active in Bratislava and the old Jewish Quarter had been destroyed to make way for a new bridge and roadway. Nothing was left to show there had been 16,000 in Bratislava's pre-war Jewish community. The few Jews there today are elderly. Any children had assimilated or emigrated, mostly to Israel. Those few young people left wanted to know about Judaism and Jewish traditions for no religious practice had been permitted during Soviet times. Every year survivors from Bratislava gather at Gan Shmuel, an Israeli kibbutz, to honour all those we had lost in those terrible years. Near to Jerusalem is a forest planted in their memory.

Julia Sveda and I had kept in touch. She wrote wonderful letters to me. Then I came to Israel and soon after that the Iron Curtain cut off communication with Hungary. I was afraid to send more letters in case these would endanger her. Many years passed by. I thought of her often with pangs of conscience. Perhaps she was unwell or in difficulties. I wanted so much to do something for her after all she had done for me. Then in 1988 Eli and I travelled to Budapest to look for her. We found three Svedas listed in the local phone book. The first one was a medical doctor who was a niece of Julia's. She told me that Julia's daughter Elizabeth had married a Jewish boy. After the Uprising in 1956 they had emigrated to New York and five years later, when they had American citizenship, Julia had joined them.

The following year when Julia was 79 years old we finally met in New York. On my return I wrote a five page report and asked Yad Vashem to honour her as a "Righteous Gentile". They did this in record time. In May 1999 Julia received the Certificate and planted a tree. My daughter Dorit and her husband were also present. Julia spent two weeks with us and Eli took her on excursions all over the country. She has two granddaughters and one has a Jewish husband. In 1998 we met Julia's niece again so the link is retained with my so loyal friend and saviour. It is entirely due to her that today I am alive to enjoy my two children and two grandchildren. Thanks to her I stayed alive through those years of horrors and beyond the proverbial two score years and ten promised in the *Torah*.

Appendix A

Jona Laks and the Symposium: Biomedical Sciences and Human Experiments at Kaiser Wilhelm Institutes – the Auschwitz Connection.

Recent research into the activities of Josef Mengele in Auschwitz was presented to a conference in Berlin in 2001 at the Max Planck Society, previously the Kaiser Wilhelm Society. This was attended by Jona Laks who today represents the few surviving twins who Mengele incarcerated and tortured in his infamous unit. At the conference Jona gave a powerful response to an offer of apology and refuted any suggestion of "forgiveness".

She was introduced to me by **Olga Grossman**. I asked her if I may include her speech in this book and learned that she, too, with her twin sister, had been brought to London by Rabbi Schonfeld. That was in March, 1946. When he heard of the post-war pogrom at Kielce he had gone quickly to Poland to offer sanctuary in Britain for children who survived it. He brought Jona to London where she attended the Avigdor High School and was made a prefect. She rapidly learned English and, encouraged by Rabbi Schonfeld, was the first to give British Jews a first-hand account of Mengele's atrocities. Later she took a commercial course at Central Foundation Girls' School in London and then in 1948 travelled on a *laissez-passer* (an official identity document issued in lieu of a passport) ostensibly to Switzerland but in fact to Marseilles. She finally reached Israel as an illegal immigrant. There she was re-united with her much-loved older sister.

Jona married another Polish survivor and has three sons. She held a distinguished place in the Israeli parliament as a co-opted member of the Committee on Foreign Affairs. She was designated co-ordinator of the English and American desks as well as of Poland. She takes a special interest in anti-Semitism. She has yet to find time in her busy life to record her memoirs.

The Symposium was held in June, 2001 at the Max Planck Society, today a centre of scientific research of international repute. The purpose of the six year research programme was to clarify the activities of the predecessor organisation under National Socialism from 1933 till 1945.

Surviving Mengele Twins were invited to attend for the research team to learn from their experience. Eight individuals had the courage to do so including Olga Grossman's sister, Vera. They were traced through the organisation representing surviving Mengele Twins and today chaired by Jona Laks. In 2001 eighty remained alive from the 1,500 sets of twins and triplets subjected to Mengele's experiments. Many of the victims had long sought information about the gross maltreatment they had endured. "We were used as guinea pigs" one of them said. Her twin had barely survived. She wanted to know what had been done to them – and they learned some details about those horrific experiments.

The research commissioned by the Max Planck Society investigated crimes against humanity hidden under the guise of science, and there was concern, too, about the cover-up that followed. Fifteen staff of the staff of the Kaiser Wilhelm Institute were convicted at the Nuremburg Trials. Seven were hanged. Others escaped by claiming they were pawns but are now known to have been active accomplices. The Max Planck Society acknowledged that victims are entitled to ask for more information and that safeguards must be put in place to protect future generations.

An official apology was offered to survivors by Professor Hubert Markl, President of the Max Planck Society. To this Jona Laks responded on behalf of the surviving Twins. She spoke in English.

"Professors, Doctors, Researchers, esteemed Ladies and Gentlemen, I will begin by thanking the Max Planck Society and Dr Carola Sachse, Director of the research programme "History of the Kaiser Wilhelm Instutute in the National Socialist Era" for the very fact that you invited us to participate at this symposium. To our regret, we have long become accustomed to other people appearing in the name of victims of the Holocaust, on their own authority or their professional specialisation of that period - and then what appears is not the memory, but "the interpretation of the memory".

And I also thank you for the very fact that you are conducting an investigation of the connection between Dr Mengele's deeds and German medical institutions so many years after these things happened. Your sense of responsibility certainly assists in preventing their being forgotten. And everyone who assists in it merits our appreciation and blessing. So be blessed!

Dr. Mengele, a Doctor and an SS Officer, named "The Angel of Death of Auschwitz", served there from 1943 until the liberation of Auschwitz in January 1945. The connection between Dr Mengele and the Kaiser Wilhelm Institute is a fact. The connection involved necessarily people, correspondence and documents. Obviously, Dr Mengele was involved and active in the Institute itself. The people working there could not be mistaken about his activities. He corresponded with them in the language of medicine and this language aspires to be precise and realistic.

Dr. Mengele was not outside of history not outside of time and not outside of the networks that activate society, organisations, law, communications systems, archives and culture. Dr Mengele was not outside of Germany.

I would like to quote from an official Soviet report of January 1945:

"In the camp of Auschwitz special hospitals were set up, with operating histological laboratories and other institutions, in which German professors and doctors performed extensive experiments on absolutely healthy people: men, women and children. Experiments were conducted in making women sterile, castrating men, experiments on children, experiments in infecting masses of people with the diseases of cancer, typhus, fevers, etc. They investigated the effects of various chemical compounds on commissions from German commercial companies. On one occasion representatives of the German chemical industry, the doctor and gynaecologist Grauber from Königshütte, and the chemist Goebbel, purchased from the camp administration 150 women from among detainees there for such experiments."

Ladies and gentlemen, to speak about Auschwitz is difficult for me, but necessary. I am not a historian, not a philosopher, not an author or an artist. I do not have the ability to produce a new discourse about Auschwitz, a discourse that would sweep away clichés that have accumulated over the years to the point where they have dulled it and made it into a subject for philosophy or cinema, or a discourse that would block metaphysical commentaries, such

435

as that Auschwitz was all together outside of this planet. It was inside our planet and a part of it, perpetrated by human beings against the lives of other human beings. It was here, amongst us. There is no guarantee that it will not return again.

Ladies and gentlemen, human beings made Auschwitz. Dr Mengele was born to human beings. He and his wife were parents of human beings. I personally met Mr Rolf Yenkel - the son of Dr Mengele. He left the impression also of being a human being.

Who am I? I am Jona Laks from "there" marked with number A-27725. Now I am an Israeli citizen who does not cease admiring Israel for gathering in the survivors of the Holocaust at the time when Israel itself was fighting a war for its independence. I have no part in the position of the "new historians" who insinuate that the State of Israel was interested in refugees from the Holocaust mainly for its army. That position totally shocks me emotionally and mentally.

I am Jona Laks from Tel-Aviv, a human being. As I see it, a human being is a person who remembers. Memory requires cultivating nourishing partners. We are the last witnesses who remember but no longer by means of the living voice. All cultures prefer the living voice as a witness over the above-mentioned substitutes and reservoirs.

I remember Dr Mengele. I have come here to affirm it once again. I am a private individual and alive. I am not a representative of a state and not here as a means of arranging the balance of monetary agreements between Germany and the victims of the Nazis.

I am a representative of Mengele's victims. In other words, I am an emissary in the elementary sense of the word - an emissary of those of Mengele's victims who are still alive. An emissary, not a proprietor. And according to the law regarding emissaries in the Jewish code of observances (halakha) if I forgive in the name of the dead, I will be going beyond the bounds of the mission that I have taken upon myself to the point of distorting and destroying it. As for those of Mengele's victims who are still alive, those who are members of our organisation - I have received no permission from them to forgive on their behalf. Nor do I as an individual have the right to forgive. Hence, I have no one's power of attorney to forgive, but to remind you that forgiveness erases memory.

Let us adhere to Auschwitz as a physical fact. Let us not collaborate in the "culture game" in which Auschwitz is a metaphor, or a subject, or a "religious discussion" or an embodiment of the "evil" striving against the "good". We were there. Someone who was not there and does research on Auschwitz from a distance in time and from a psychological distance is tempted by the metaphor. We were there, which means that it is nevertheless fitting to hear our testimony and to relate to our words as at least equal to documents from the period.

Even I myself, who was there, am no longer sure of "language". Am I not inevitably recycling banal and quasi-religious images of Auschwitz? Are the Auschwitz-ian facts capable of transmitting themselves as they are? Is my audience - in the present case able - not merely willing - but able to experience my language in its plain sense?

Has the "discourse" about Auschwitz not narrowed extremely the possibility of "plain speech" about Auschwitz and Dr Mengele? Does not Mengele as the "symbol of evil" push Mengele into the category of a symbol and reduce the possibility of speaking about Mengele himself as a part of the German medical system of the time? I ask God to restore the power of plain speech.

Auschwitz was in Poland to the west of Cracow. Before the war it had 12,000 inhabitants, 4,000 of them Jews. Auschwitz was beside the Sola River, not outside the planet. Not in Hell. Not outside of culture, not outside of history, but like Treblinka, Majdanek, Belzec, Sobibór, Chelmno and all of them together.

Was Mengele "the embodiment of evil"? Certainly, he was an embodiment of evil in the reality itself, but to turn him into the concept "the embodiment of evil" casts a certain aura around him, as though he were a representative of the "evil" in its ongoing historical struggle with the "good". Mengele in my eyes, was not a representative, he was himself. All this discourse transforms Auschwitz and Mengele into images, severs them from the reality.

I was there and Dr Mengele was there. From there Dr Mengele transmitted his findings to the Kaiser Wilhelm Institute. My friends, the twins and I were then his objects. And that is how we arrived at the above mentioned Institute.

I would like to quote from the Bible: Joel I, verse 3, about memory in German: "Sagt euren Kindern davon und lasst es eure Kinder ihren Kindern sagen und diese wiederum ihren Nachkommen".[1]

Yes, I remember. I was there. I then am both a soldier and a witness in the long Jewish journey of memory. And here, ladies and gentlemen, we come to a cruel and exclusive thing: the victims' sincerity. We are the victims. You are the present heads of the Max Planck Society. You want "to clear up the Nazi crimes". We want to remember, but we ask not only ourselves to remember, but you as well. In other words, we are asking you to remember what you want to "clear up" and then perhaps forget. We will remember in any case. Will you forget in any case?

After we die, Auschwitz and Mengele will be remembered by means of video films, written literature, archives, remembrance days and Spielberg-style cinema. Will you see all these as a kind of "cultural solution" to past questions which were troublesome and have now stopped being troublesome and are now summed up in a monument or a video?

Now to "the victims' sincerity". Each day that passes intensifies our need to prove that our memory is sincere and honest. But every day that passes covers more and more the surface of the memory. As "findings of research", as a message in medical language, German doctors and researchers made use of Dr Mengele's reports from Auschwitz.

To remember, we have already grown weary from the vast quantity of automatic and official utterances about the Holocaust and memory. We have taken well the few precious and valuable things that have been written, such as those by Primo Levi. I will only note here, ladies and gentlemen, that as far as I know, only in Judaism is the instruction "to remember" a religious precept. Judaism commands its adherents: "Remember the days of the world, remember that you were a slave, remember what Amalek did to you" Deuteronomy XXV verses 17-19. Maimonides, one of the greatest Jews in history, a philosopher, a doctor of medicine, a statesman and codifier of precepts, who lived in the 12th century, explains in his "Book of Precepts", that the precept "to remember" is "the warning we have been given against forgetting".

According to Judaism, everyone has to see himself as though he himself had come out from slavery in Egypt. Everyone has to see himself as though he himself had been in Auschwitz and come out, or not come out of it. Everyone has to see himself as though he himself had been marked by Dr Mengele. According to Judaism, everyone of us at a certain moment represents all of humanity. The victim of Auschwitz represented it, and opposite him or her Dr Mengele represented it. Auschwitz was inside humanity, not in a play about humanity.

Memory assures continuity and has sustained Jewish tradition throughout all its generations. I mean that actual court verdicts against those who deny the Holocaust do not operate in a single and clear linear manner. True, they refute those that deny, but as they do so, they recycle the denial and its arguments. And somehow they do not banish it from the minds of the young generation. Absurd? No, not absurd - a well known deceptive mechanism.

Here too, today at this assembly, with its aspirations for purification, beneath the skin of this assembly, there is the feeling, though not expressed in words, that the sincerity of the victims is no longer outside of the discussion.

Ladies and gentlemen, I wish to thank again the Max Planck Society for conducting these discussions on the matter of the medical Kaiser Wilhelm Institute and Dr Mengele. Moreover, I feel obliged to thank Prof Hubert Markl, the President of the Max Planck Society, for his goodwill to offer us an apology.

Many thanks for your attention."

A note was added to the press release by journalist Adam Baruch. Jona Laks had asked him to help her prepare this reply. He said that the experience shook him to the core unlike that of any other. Jona Laks wants us to do something different about Auschwitz, to use a different language. The pressure put by the Max Planck Society on the victims by asking for their forgiveness put an intolerable burden on her. She and her group do not forget nor do they forgive. And another horrifying phenomenon has begun. The integrity of their own memories has been put under investigation in a number of ways. Now it is the victims who have to prove their honesty.

יונה לקס, נציגת קורבנות מנגלה. "בני אדם, ולא 'כוחות רוע' מטאפוריים, עשו את אושוויץ. ד"ר
מנגלה היה בן אדם שנולד להורים בני אדם, ולא 'סמל'. איני רשאית לסלוח" ● צילום: נאור רהב

Jona Laks, representative for the surviving Mengele Twins. "Human beings and not metaphors made Auschwitz. Dr Mengele was a human being born from human beings and not a symbol. I cannot forgive." © *Naor Rahav.*

Appendix B

The Beis Ya'acov Schools

Throughout the Schonfeld Archives and among the survivors' stories there is frequent mention of the Beis Ya'acov schools and seminaries for girls that spread across Orthodox Jewish communities in Europe during the twentieth century.

This school system was initiated in Poland by Sarah Schenirer. She became concerned that religious girls, unlike their brothers, were offered no education beyond an elementary level and so were frequently bored. Those attending non-Jewish primary schools were taught in the local language and became more familiar with the secular world. This easily led to their dropping Orthodox practice and marrying outside their community.

Sarah was born in Cracow in 1883. She worked as a milliner but she found time to attend *Torah* classes. She decided to pass on what she was learning to other women and she offered a class based on her notes. It was not very popular! One day a customer confided her distress: her older daughter had abandoned Judaism and she feared the younger one would follow. Would Sarah open a class for young girls? Sarah, through her brother, asked the Belzer Rabbi's approval. He gave her his blessing and she put all her energy into creating a unique movement that remains strong today. So the life of Sarah, a diminutive figure enlivened by her shining eyes, changed course.

Her first students came to meet Sarah after classes at the local Polish school. The girls loved her and her teaching and their numbers increased. Sarah had neither the money nor the organisation to sustain her activities but others helped and five years later she opened a modest teachers' seminary. There some forty to fifty teenagers seated on boxes in an attic room were given training in her teaching methods.

In 1924 Sarah met Dr Leo Deutschlander at an Agudath Israel Conference. He was an academic, educated at *yeshiva* and University and had helped inaugurate a Jewish school system in Lithuania. He was so impressed by Sarah's achievements that he found funding and sent books to assist her. He also arranged for her students to spend six weeks with her in the summer studying at Robov, a village in the Carpathian Mountains.

Meanwhile Judith Rosenbaum, who was born in 1902, had moved with her family to Germany. She was determined to go to Palestine to teach and prepared herself by attending a non-Jewish Teacher Training College in Frankfurt. But a German Rabbi had heard from Dr Deutschlander about Sarah Schenirer's summer school and persuaded Judith to join her there. Judith arrived in the village on a hay cart to find a lively group of enthusiastic young women. She never looked back. Four years later, encouraged by Sarah, she obtained from Frankfurt University a degree in Education, Physics and Psychology. In 1929 she received her doctorate. She emerged speaking German, Yiddish and French and returned to work with Sarah.

By then Sarah's school movement had spread across Europe. It offered a mix of traditional Jewish studies with industrial training. By 1929 there were 147 schools in Poland, 20 in Lithuania, Latvia and Austria. In 1931 more Teacher Training Seminaries were set up. Sarah provided the inspiration and Judith the intellectual strengths as her assistant. She also became Head of the school in Cracow. Sarah sent Fraulein Doctor Rosenbaum travelling across Europe. Her task was to impress parents to register their daughters and contribute funds for the schools. No wonder that Dr Isidore Grunfeld, then a law student in Frankfurt, deeply admired the charming and accomplished Judith. He followed her to Cracow. They married and moved back to Germany.

Then the Nazis came to power. Isidore Grunfeld sought work in Palestine but with no knowledge of English he failed to find any. Judith had intended to follow him there. Instead he reached London as a refugee and found work as a private tutor.

Dr J. H. Hertz, Britain's Chief Rabbi, had heard of Judith's work and asked her to come to London to raise funds for the *Beis Ya'acov* Schools. Dr Solomon Schonfeld listened to her speak and persuaded her to settle with her family in London and teach at his school. In 1937 she was teaching basic subjects and both the Grunfelds were learning English. The following year Judith became Head of the Avigdor High School. She remained there for the rest of her professional career and made a lifelong impact on the girls under her care.

But war clouds were gathering. On August 31st 1939 the

BBC announced "Pied Piper Tomorrow!" This was the coded signal broadcast on the radio for the evacuation scheme to commence from London schools. Dr Judith Grunfeld with the head of the boys' school became responsible for the full-time care of several hundred boys and girls, no longer merely day students but boarders, for the next six years. Among the pupils were many European refugees from the 300 that Rabbi Schonfeld had recently brought from Vienna who spoke only German or Yiddish. The children were billeted on local people scattered between six villages in Suffolk. Their hosts knew little if anything about Jewish people or their religion beyond some weird gossip. Judith spent her days cycling between the villages, coping with endless problems, encouraging girls and staff alike to adapt as best they could to the unfamiliar circumstances. All meals were organised communally and rules of *kashrut* were retained but with difficulty.[1]

When the war ended, the Avigdor High School returned to North London and absorbed many of the 2,000 girls that Rabbi Schonfeld had brought back from devastated Europe. These included **Olga Grossman** and her sister and friends from Clonyn Castle. The education they received there enabled them to make up for years of lost study. They emerged with fluent English and a keen appreciation of British culture as well as Jewish values. To this day they speak with immense pride of the fine mentor and inspiring role-model presented by Dr Judith Grunfeld. She was nicknamed "The Queen of Bais Yaacov" as is explained in a book with that title.[2] Dr Judith Grunfeld retired when her husband became ill. She died aged 95 in 1998, much honoured, and was buried in Israel. After the war Beis Ya'acov Schools and Seminaries spread to Belgium, France and Switzerland, to Uruguay and Argentina, to the USA, and to Israel as well as Britain where they are called Beth Jacob.

Appendix C

Facts and Figures

A closer look at the travel documents

The Collective Visas show authorisations from all embassies in Prague relevant for their journey. The six pages, 453-458, give the names of the children and show additional stamps marking each border crossing.

The Border Stamps on the document indicate the route they travelled: via Cheb (Czechoslovakia) - Schirnding (US Zone Germany) - Lontzen (Belgium) - Ostende (Belgium) - Dover (UK). These show that the party took the same or a similar route to the one you would take today, with no major diversions.

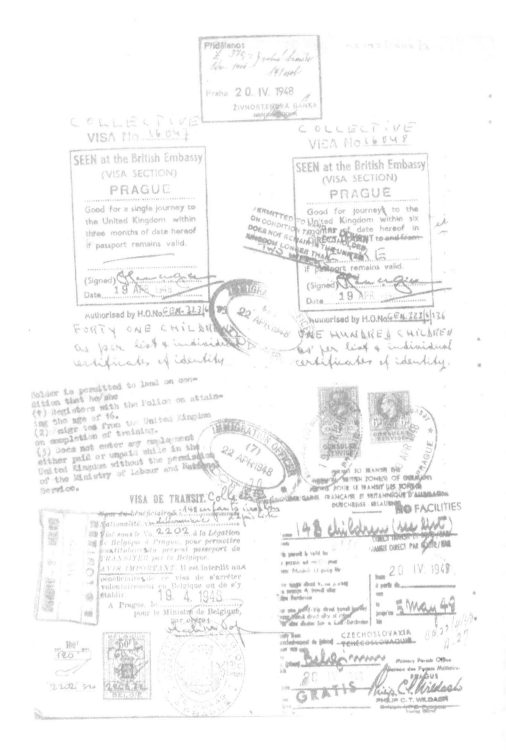

The Collective and Transit Visas from Prague to London.

Collective Visa No. 16047. (Opposite, top left) Seen at the British Embassy (Visa Section) Prague. Good for a single journey to the United Kingdom within three months of date hereof if passport remains valid.

Signed: 19 April 1948. Authorised by H.O.No.GEN.3273/6/?89

FORTY ONE CHILDREN as per list & individual certificates of identity. *On the attached typed label:* Holder is permitted to land on condition that he/she (1) Registers with the Police on attaining the age of 16. (2) Emigrates from the United Kingdom on completion of training. (3) Does not enter any employment paid or unpaid while in the United Kingdom without the permission of the Ministry of Labour and National Service.

Collective Visa No. 16048. (Opposite, top right) Seen at the British Embassy (Visa Section) Prague. Good for journey to the United Kingdom within six months of date hereof in direct transit to EIRE if passport remains valid.

Signed: 19 April 1948. Authorised by H.O.No.GEN 323/6/136.

ONE HUNDRED CHILDREN as per list and individual certificates of identity. *Stamped across document*: Permitted to land on condition the holder does not remain in the United Kingdom longer than TWO WEEKS.

Visa de Transit. Collectif *added by hand* (Opposite, lower left)

Names of beneficiaries: 148 Israelite children (*i.e. Jewish*) as on appended list.

Nationality: indeterminate

Visa stamped as No. 2202 from Belgian Legation in Prague.

Permits the bearers of this passport to travel in TRANSIT via Belgium.

IMPORTANT WARNING

It is forbidden to the beneficiaries of this visa to stop voluntarily in Belgium or to establish themselves to settle there.

Prague 19.4.1948 signed on behalf of the Belgian Ministry by order of: (*signature*).

(*overstamped*) Belgian Legation, Prague

(*stamps*) 2 Consular Stamps 50 francs and 100 francs

Issued by Belgian Legation in Prague for 148 children of indeterminate nationality to pass through Belgium by direct route.

Permit to Transit French, British Zone(s) of Germany
Permits for the Transit of the American, French and British Zones of Germany (*in French*) Transit-Approval (*in German*) (*overstamped*) NO FACILITIES 148 children (see list) 6889 (*stamped in English and French*) BY DIRECT TRANSIT BY ROAD (*deleted*)/RAIL

Direct transit by route from Czechoslovakia to Belgium from 20. IV. 1948 to 5 May 1948.
Fee GRATIS.
Military Permit Office, Prague.
Signed: Philip C. T. Wildash
British MPC Officer
(*initialled by Commanding Officer?*) C. O. 22/4/48. A-27

Stamped (Central Stamp) by Immigration Officer, Dover, 22 April 1948

The topmost stamp reads:
ALLOCATED
£370   ) with an illegible note
1000 Belgian francs)
148 Passengers
Prague 20.1V. 1948
ZIVNOSTENSKA BANKA
Signed

This was the sole Bank dealing with foreign currency at the time. My suggestion is that this is a permit allowing Rabbi Schonfeld to take these amounts of cash out of the country and that they are for payment at border crossings.

From the Ministry of Interior, Czech Republic:

Letter of Authorisation (Next page) for 148 persons of uncertain citizenship, temporarily staying in Czechoslovakia to travel abroad 20-29 April 1948 as a collective transport. Each of the persons named in the enclosures has to prove his/her/identity by producing a document containing his/her/photograph.

Stamped by the Ministry and by the British Passport Officer, Germany (British Zone) Departure 22 April 1948

Ministerstvo vnitra Československé republiky.
Ministere de l'Interieur de la République Tchécoslovaque.
Ministry of Interior of the Czechoslovak Republik.

Č. 1221/34-5/3-48-III/6.   V Praze dne 14. dubna 1948.

...o vnitra Československé republiky povoluje, aby 148 (jedno-
...osm) osob neurčené státní příslušnosti uvedených na tomto
listě, přechodně se zdržujících v Československé republice, vycestovalo
v době od 20. do 29. dubna 1948 z Československé republiky společným
transportem do ciziny. Každá z cestujících osob je povinna prokázati
svou totožnost průkazem opatřeným podobenkou.

Le Ministère de l'Intérieur de la République Tchécoslovaque donne
l'autorisation pour que les 148 personnes la citoyanité indéterminée
provisoirement domiciliie en Tchecoslovaquie énuméres dans les pages
adjointe voyagent depuis le 20 jusgu au 29 avril 1948 de la République
Tchécoslovaque a l'entranger dans un transport commun. Chaque partici-
pant de ce voyage est obligé a prouver son identité par une carte d'identité munie dúne photographie.

The Ministry of Interior gives hereby authority to the departure of
148 persons of uncertain citizenship, temporarily staying in Czechoslovakia quoted on the enclosed page to travel from Czechoslovakia to
abroad in the time from 20. to 29. april 1948 as a collective transport
Each of the persons named in the enclosures has to prove his /her/ iden
tity by producing a document containing his /her/ photograph.

Za ministra:
Pour le ministre:
For the Minister:

PASSPORT
DEPARTURE
2 APR. 1948
GERMANY (BZ)
BRITISH   OFFICER

---

*14th April 1948 Czech Ministry of the Interior approved 148
persons of uncertain citizenship to travel abroad between 20th
and 29th April. Countersigned in Germany.*   449

Telegrams : Alldep, London.
Telephone : CHAncery 8811.

Please quote the reference:—
Gen.323/6/156
Your reference:—

HOME OFFICE.

(ALIENS DEPARTMENT)

271-7, HIGH HOLBORN,

LONDON, W.C.I

1st January, 1948.

REC/S/L

Dear Dr. Schonfeld,

With reference to your letter of
14th December concerning the party of
up to 100 children for Eire, I am writing
to say that the necessary instructions
regarding the grant of United Kingdom
transit visas are being sent to the
Passport Control Officer, Prague, who
has been advised also that either you or
the duly accredited representatives of
the Chief Rabbi's Religious Emergency
Council will apply for these visas and
that so far as the Home Office is concerned, a "certificate" for production
to the Czech authorities may be supplied.

It is noted that the children will
travel either on individual travel papers
or group travel documents in which event
each child will be supplied with an
additional Certificate of Identity.

/It

Rabbi Dr. S. Schonfeld,
86, Amhurst Park,
London, N.16.

450   *1st January 1948. Letter permitting transit via the UK for 100*
           children travelling from Czechoslovakia to Eire.

BRITISH EMBASSY

VISA SECTION

Valdštýnská ul. 6

Prague III.

AF/10.919.

April 14th 1943.

Dr. S. Schonfeld,
Prague.

Sir,

Further to my letter of 7th April, I now
have to inform you that we have received authority
from London to grant visas in favour of the 50
(fifty) Jewish children for admittance to the
United Kingdom, provided they are full orphans,
not over sixteen years of age, and subject to
satisfactory documentation to this effect.

Yours faithfully,

Head of Visa Section.

HCLG/PD.

*14th April 1948. British Embassy approval for 50 children, orphans
under 16, to be admitted to the UK.*

Observations

Some of the restraints imposed on this manoeuvre can be drawn from these sparse documents. Officialdom made tough demands. It took several years of hard negotiation by Rabbi Schonfeld, with the Irish, with the Czechs and with the Communists who were about to take control, and with the British, in order to bring these children and young people away. The dates on travel permits were very tight for so large and complex an expedition and conditions varied from day to day.

A long search for present addresses of the children located only 94 from the original 148 and only half of these contributed. So it was not possible to verify or complete the information collected. From other sources it is clear, though not evident in the official documents shown here, that the Czech officials had to believe that none of the children were Czech nationals. In fact the vast majority were. The records show only 35 born in other European countries, 15 of these in Hungary. The British authorities required all of them to be orphans. Both Czech and British officials required entrants to be under 16 years of age. The list shows 41 born in or before April 1932 but I know of at least 8 who were older than that. When several families withdrew their children at the last minute the precious places were hastily filled by others. There was no time to alter documents so substitutes were given not only their places but their histories, birth dates and even their names. Maximilian and Lenke Rubin appear widely separated on the Visa list and given the same year of birth but in fact they are brother and sister two years apart. Such complications, as with age discrepancies, created difficulties later. Some only learned why their names had been changed from the present research. And numbers do not always tally. For example see Collective Visa No. 6047 that only covers 41 children and not 48.

- I -

Z á j e z d n í   s o u p i s k a .

- -

1.	LOWY	Olga	9.7.1932	Lowy, Olga, 9.7.32
2.	AMENT	Helena	10.6.1938	
3.	BINET	Gaspar	15.1.1938	
4.	BINET	Robert	20.6.1939	
5.	BOCK	Robert	7.9.1934	
6.	BRENNER	Zwi	25.5.1933	
7.	DANZIG	Tibor	17.3.1937	
8.	DOHAN	Oto	17.2.1935	
9.	RUBIN	Maximilian	7.3.1932	RUBIN, Maximilían, 7.3.32.
10.	FEUERSTEIN	Judith	25.6.1935	
11.	FISCHER	Richard	21.5.1937	
12.	FISCHER	Vera	3.1.1942	
13.	FRIEDMANN	Desider	2.9.1934	
14.	FRIEDMANN	Hedviga	2.1.1933	
15.	FRIEDMANN	Josef	14.9.1938	
16.	FRIEDMANN	Judita	15.5.1937	
17.	ROSENFELD	Dezider	24.12.1932	ROSENFELD, Dezider, 24.12.32.
18.	GOTTLIEB	Tamás	11.11.1938	
19.	GROSS	Juraj	6.12.1932	
20.	GROSSMANN	Emerich	13.8.1935	
21.	GROSSMANN	Olga	23.4.1938	
22.	GROSSMANN	Vera	23.4.1938	
23.	HERZ	Alfred	9.11.1936	
24.	FLEISCHMAN	Ester	14.4.1932	FLEISCHMAN, Ester, 14.4.32
25.	HERZOG	Matilda	31.1.1936	

453

Names covered by the Collective Visas - Page 1

Zájezdní soupiska.

- -

26. 3½ HAUPT ✓	Eva	5.5.1935	
27. 3½ HIRSCH✓	Mordechaj	10.10.1935	
28. 2½ HOCHHAUSER✓	Manfred	26.2.1937	
29. HOCHHAUSER✓	Moric	4.7.1935	
30. 3½ KATSCHER✓	Ivan	25.4.1934	
31. 3½ KATSCHER✓	Anna	6.2.1936	
X 32. ○ KOHN	Judit	25.12.1941	
X 33. ○ KOHN	Margit	8.10.1938	
34. 3½ KUMMELDORFER/Ervin		15.6.1936	
35. 3½ KUMMELDORFER/Sonja		15.5.1940	
36. LEBOVITSCH ✓	Jichel	8.8.1932	
37. LEBOVITSCH ✓	Michael	7.5.1932	
38. LENZ ✓	Alexander	9.5.1932	
39. 3½ MANGEL ✓	Gertruda	14.8.1932	
40. 3½ MANGEL ✓	Viktor	14.8.1933	
41. MASTBAUM✓	Alexander	18.7.1936	
42. MULLER ✓	Gertruda	23.5.1934	
43. 3½ KURZ ✓	Chaja	9.8.1931 — KURZ, chaja, 9.8.31.	
44. 3½ REICH✓	Israel	29.3.1939	
45. 3½ REICH ✓	Oskar	4.4.1935	
46. 3½ REICH ✓	Richard	4.6.1938	
47. 3½ REICH ✓	SUsanna	25.1.1936	
48. 3½ REIF ✓	Tamás	22.5.1935	
49. ROTH ✓	Markusz	26.4.1932	
50. RUBINSTEIN ✓	Eva	26.2.1938	

Českosl. pasová kontrola
v CHEBU
21 -4.1948
ODCHOD

Names covered by the Collective Visas - Page 2

- III -

Z á j e z d n í   s o u p i s k a .

51.	RUBINSTEIN Ernst		5.6.1935
52.	SCHNEBALG Chajim		1940
X 53.	SCHNEOR	Peter	4.11.1936
54.	SCHONBERGER Moric		15.5.1932
55.	SCHWARZTHAL Ella		16.1.1939
56.	SCHWARZTHAL Rozsi		16.1.1939
57.	SCHWARZTHAL Gizella		11.9.1933
58.	STEINER	Mihály	13.10.1938
59.	STEINER	Péter	7.8.1934
60.	STEINER	Ruth	17.4.1942
61.	STEINER	Tamás	29.9.1937
62.	STRAUSZ	Alexander	30.7.1936
63.	STRAUSZ	Gizella	4.10.1934
64.	STRAUSZ	Leona	2.9.1932
65.	TAPPER	Martha	2.6.1935
66.	TEMPLER	Sendi	1.6.1932
67.	WEINBERGER Artur		17.2.1937
68.	WEINBERGER Emanuel		8.8.1942
69.	WEISS	Jakub	5.6.1932
70.	WIESEN	Franklina	23.5.1939
71.	WIESEN	Vera	21.5.1942
72.	WIESNER	Agi	15.6.1933
73.	WIESNER	Judit	2.10.1932
74.	ZIEGLER	Alfred	10.7.1937
75.	ZIEGLER	Judit	17.12.1936

455

Names covered by the Collective Visas - Page 3

MS182/1002/3 (Lot6)

Z á j e z d n í   s o u p i s k a .

26. 32 ZIEGLER	Olga	9.4.1938
27. BOCK	Erich	12.1.1934
28. BRODMAN	Stella	28.3.1935
29. DANZIG	Eugen	18.6.1933
80. DANZIG	Miklos	7.8.1934
81. ICZKOVITS	Lenke	7.3.1933
82. Kaiser	Mirjam	12.7.1932
83. KAISER	Sara	25.3.1933
84. KLEIN	Mragaretha	4.5.1932
85. 32 KLEIN	Max	1942
86. KOHN	Erika	5.6.1935
87. 32 KRAUSZ	Pál	19.10.1934
88. 32 KRAUSZ	Tamás	31.7.1936
89. LANDAU	Rifkah	13.7.1934
90. LEICHT	Alfred	19.5.1932
91. LIPSCHUTZ	Simon	31.1.1933
92. 32 MANNHEIMER	Judith	4.8.1936
93. PALÁN	Vera	11.8.1934
94. 32 PRISSEGI	Gyorgy	1942
95. 32 REISZ	Jakab	13.12.1942
96. SCHREIBER	Judith	6.5.1933
97. 32 STEINER	Eva	6.3.1939
98. STERN	Erika	5.8.1934
99. WEINER-FISCH	Hetty	30.5.1932
100. WEISZ	Erika	21.1.1933

Českosl. pasová kont
v CHEBU
21 -4.1948
ODCHO

Names covered by the Collective Visas - Page 4

Z á j e z d n í   s o u p i s k a .

- - - - - - - - - - - - - - - - - - -

101.	WINKLER	Oskar	20.4.1941
102.	ADLER	Hermann	2.6.1932
103.	BIRNBAUM	Livia	7.5.1934
104.	BLEIER	Viola	5.2.1932
105.3½	DEUTEL	Helena	18.5.1932
106.3½	EHRLICH	Kornelia	6.11.1932
107.	EIGNER	Agatha	8.6.1932
108.	FEDERWEISS	Blanka	25.4.1932
109.	FELDMANN	Edit	14.2.1933
110.	FRIEDMANN	Relly	11.11.1932
111.	GRUNFELD	Rachel	21.9.1932
112.3½	KRAUSZ	Rozália	24.4.1932
113.	LIEBERMAN	Aliz	14.11.1933
114.	MAUSKOPF	Rozie	6.5.1932
115.	OSTERREICHER	Magda	15.9.1932
116.	SICHERMANN	Helena	26.7.1932
117.	SINGER	Helena	25.7.1932
118.	STEINBERGER	Eva	2.6.1932
119.	BLEIER	Relly	16.3.1932
120.	FISCHER	Helena	19.6.1932
121.3½	GRUNSPAN	Edith	10.5.1932
122.	ICKOVITC	Josef	11.3.1934
123.	KAHAN	Alfred	1.10.1932
124.	KAHAN	Samuel	12.7.1932
125.	KALMAN	Klara	2.6.1932

z á j e z d n í   s o u p i s k a .

126.	φKOHN	Frida	20.8.1932
127. KUMELMANN		Sába	1.2.1933
128.	LEHNER	Tibor	13.12.1932
129. LOWINGER		Lily	6.11.1932
130.	LOWY	Gustav	4.8.1932
131.	MULLER	Robert	7.8.1932
132.	FELDMAN	Elizabeth	9.6.1931 – FELDMAN, Elizabeth, 9.6.1931, –
133.	RUBIN	Lenke	23.3.1932
134.	SCHWARZ	Ervin	8.6.1932
135.	KRAUS	Viola	9.7.1932 – KRAUS, Viola, 9.7.1932.
136. ADLER		Helena	21.9.1931 – ADLER, Helena, 21.9.1931.
137. STAHLER		Gyury	31.3.1939
138. STAHLER		Istvan	6.5.1938
139. STAHLER		Marianna	14.7.1942
140. STEINMETZ		Chaja	2.9.1932
141.	STRULOVIC	Leib	1.6.1932
142. WEINBERGER		Judit	21.4.1933
143. KLAROVÁ		Malvina	24.8.1939
144. LOWY		Alexander	14.2.1939
145. LOWYOVÁ		Judita	21.6.1941
146.	MAIEROVIZ	Marie	24.6.1932 – MAIEROVIZ, Marie, 24.6.32.
147. SCHWARZ		Eva	11.7.1934
148.	KAUFMAN	Robert	3.8.1932

US ZONE
GERMANY
Schirnding Post
Exit ____ Entry
Signature
6th Con. Sq.

Českosl. pasová kontrola
v CHEBU
21 -4.1948
ODCHOD

Names covered by the Collective Visas – Page 6

Dispersal in April 1948

Following their arrival in London 48 stayed in Britain. Of these some joined relatives, others were placed in hostels. All of them were probably orphans as required by the British authorities. 20 teenage boys stayed in Dublin. They were hosted by Jewish families until a hostel was opened. 80 children were accommodated at Clonyn Castle.

Dispersal during 1949

By January 1949 only 45 children remained at Clonyn Castle. In April the 20 remaining moved to Dun Laoghaire with the last 12 boys from the Dublin Hostel. By June 20th Mrs Eppel records just 18 remained.

During 1949 at least 32 children went to Israel on *aliyah*. Nine settled in Canada, five of them inter-related but none of these were traced despite one anonymous contact via the Irish Jewish Genealogical web site. At least 30 obtained entry to the USA.

From September 1949 The Central British Fund took over responsibility for those remaining in Britain until they were financially independent.

Those attending schools and *yeshivot* in London mostly lived in hostels including:-
95 Stamford Hill, N16 - for the Talmudic College
The Joint Synagogues Children's Hostel:
   90-92 Cazenove Road, N.16
The Boarding Houses of the Jewish Secondary School Movement:
   12 West Heath Road London NW3
   and 63 Lordship Road, N.16
Refugee Children's Hostel: 32 Woodberry Down, N.4
The Hostel for Religious Girls: 10a Woodberry Down, N.4

Others lived with foster parents in Stamford Hill and Golders Green.

Nearly one hundred of the original group were eventually traced. These are almost evenly distributed today between the UK, North America and Israel. Their stories published here include 36 from individuals in the Slovakian transport. These represent 50 (allowing for 12 siblings), a third of the original group. The present whereabouts of a further third have not been traced. The other third chose not to contribute. Five are known to have died before 2000 and sadly more since then.

In 1954 those who had remained in the United Kingdom, and were orphans, were offered British citizenship by the British government.[1]

Relationships within the group

Amongst them there are cousins, former school friends and neighbours, marriages and lasting friendships. Here are some examples.

There were two marriages within the first generation: Tibor Lehner and Grete Muller, Oto Dohan and Ruth Steiner - and one between grandchildren of the next: Pál Krausz' daughter married Eva Steiner's son. Benjamin Pels, a son of Henry Pels, Rabbi Schonfeld's administrator in London, married Séndi Templer. Chaja Steinmetz was introduced to her future husband by the Dublin Ladies. The Friedmann sisters are cousins of Alfred Herz. Four girls who shared a turret room in the Castle stayed friends. The two Alfreds, Leicht and Kahan, met at the Dublin Hostel and retained a lasting friendship. Judith Mannheimer and Anna Katscher were cousins. Anna Katscher's father, Judith Mannheimer's grandmother and Israel Reich's uncle, post-war Chief Rabbi of Prague, were friends of Rabbi Schonfeld. David Steiner's parents gave hospitality to his grandfather. David Steiner knew several of "the Schonfeld Children" before and after the war, including Hetty Fisch, Shoshana Brayer and Tamáš Reif. Séndi Templer visited Mrs Reif in hospital in 1945. Ervin and Sonia Kummeldorfer were neighbours of the Steiner family in Bratislava. So was Rachel Malmud.

For Mr. Hersh Schwarz

LIST OF CHILDREN AT PRESENT AT CLONYN CASTLE
NEAR DUBLIN.   OR AT 143 KIMMAGE ROAD, DUBLIN.
(LATTER CASES MARKED D)

NAME	AGE	PLACE OF BIRTH.	PROSPECTS OF BECOMING SELF SUPPORTING.
1. ADLER Helena *now UK.*	17		Able to start earning.
2. BINET Caspar } *Ahava Tora*	10	Nove Zamky, C.S.R.	Youth Aliyah in due course.
3. BINET Robert }	9	Nove Zamky, C.S.R.	" " "
4. BOCK Erich { *left 24.1.49*	14	Bielsko, Poland	Youth Aliyah Candidate
5. BOCK Robert } *Israel*	13	Bielsko, Poland	YOUTH ALIYAH Candidate
6. DEUTL Helena	16	BUDAPEST, Hungary	Able to start earning.
7. FEDERWEISS Blanka	16	Mako *U.S. Student Candidate*	"
8. FISCHER Helena *now UK*	16	Rimiscara *UK. set of family to*	
9. FISCHER Vera	6	Tarnow *UK. 10ª*	
10. FLEISCHMAN Esther	16	*UK. 10ª*	Able to start earning.
11. FRIEDMANN Hedvig *left*	16	Miskolc	Youth Aliyah
12. FRIEDMANN Judita } *24.1.49 Israel.*	11	Miskolc	"
13. GOTTLIEB Tamas	10	Sopron *27.4.49 to Paris, from there with parents USA.*	
14. GROSS Juraj	15	Bratislava, C.S.R. *may go back to parents Able to start earning.*	
15. GROSSMAN Olga } *UK*	10	Lodz, Poland	
16. GROSSMAN Vera } *10ª*	10	Lodz, Poland	
17. GRUNSBAN Edith *left 14/61 Israel*		1, Poland	Youth Aliyah Candidate
18. HAUPT Eva *now all UK.*	13	Halnau *10ª*	Youth Aliyah Candidate
19. HERZ Alfred "	12	Presov	*Ahava Tauro*
20. HIRSCH Mordechaj /	13	Prague, C.S.R.	*Switzerland*
21. HOCHHAUSER Manfred "	11	Kosice	"
22. HOCHHAUSER Moric "	13	Kosice	"
23. ICKOVIC Josef /	14	Oradea	*Ahava Starnes.*
24. KAHAN Alfred *left for US, Israel Sept 49*		row, *Israel Sept 49*	D Looking for a job
25. KAHAN Samuel	16	Bielsko, Poland	D Looking for a job
26. KALMAN Klara *David*	16	Halnau	Youth Aliyah Candidate
27. KAUFMANN Robert	16		D Working as trainee, one year's training required.
28. KLAROVA Malvina *left 9 24.1 now Israel*		, Poland	Youth Aliyah.
29. KUMELMAN Saba "	15	*— 24.1 Israel*	Youth Aliyah Candidate
30. KUMMELDORFER Erwin "	12	Bratislava, C.S.R. *24.1 Israel*	Youth Aliyah in due course.

Early summer 1949. Plans for the remaining children show those who
went to Israel in January and suggested destinations for the rest
(Page 1 of 3)

LIST OF CHILDREN AT PRESENT AT CLONYN CASTLE
NEAR DUBLIN. OR AT 143 KIMMEAGE ROAD, DUBLIN.
(LATTER CASES MARKED D)

NAME	AGE	PLACE OF BIRTH.	PROSPECTS OF BECOMING SELF SUPPORTING.
31. KUMMELDORFER Sonja *4/28*		*Israel* Bratislava, C.S.R.	
32. KURZ Chaja *expected to go to UK 10th in August*	*19*		Starts work soon
33. LEBOVITSCH Jichel	16	Gerla	D Looking for a job
34. LEBOVITSCH Michael	16	Cluj, Roumania	D "
35. LENZ Alexander	16	Mako	D "
36. LIEBERMANN Alice *left 15 28 Israel*		Budapest, Hungary	Youth Aliyah Candidate
37. LOWY Alexander	" 9	Sabinow *24.1.49 Israel*	Youth Aliyah in due course.
38. LOWY Judita	" 7	Sabinow *24.1. Israel*	"
39. LOWY Olga	" 16		Youth Aliyah Candidate
40. MANGEL Victor *Sunderland 15*		Szombathely *Sunderland*	
41. MAIEROVIZ Marie *left 16*		*24.1. Israel.*	(Will either go to relatives in Switzerland or start earning)
42. PRISSER Gyorgy	" 6	*24.1 Israel*	Youth Aliyah Candidate
43. REICH Israel	9	Mako *UK. Gateshead Board.Sc. relatives pay.*	
44. REICH Richard *left*	10	Miskolc *24.1. Israel*	Youth Aliyah in due course.
45. REICH Susanna	12	Mako *UK address: 33 Hall, NW 7 relatives*	
46. ROSENFELD David	11	*UK Ahavas Tora.*	
47. ROTH Markus	16	Vác	D Waiting for permit to start work.
48. RUBIN Lenke	16	Miskolc	Able to start earning.
49. RUBIN Maximilian	16		Able to start earning.
50. RUBINSTEIN Ernst	13	Debrecin *Sunderland.*	
51. RUBINSTEIN Eva	10	Debrecin	
52. SCHONBERGER Moric	16	Budapest, Hungary	D Looking for a job
53. SCHWARZ Ervin	16	Sarvar	D "
54. SCHWARZTHAL Ella *left 8*		Topolcany	Youth Aliyah in due course.
55. SCHWARZTHAL Gizella *15*		Topolcany *24.1. Israel*	"
56. SCHWARZTHAL Roszi	" 9	Topolcany	"
57. STASNY-STAHLER Gyury	9	Michalovce	"
58. STASNY-STAHLER Istvan	10	Michalovce	"
59. STASNY-STAHLER Marianna	6	Michalovce	"

462

Early summer 1949. Plans for the remaining children show those who went to Israel in January and suggested destinations for the rest (Page 2 of 3)

LIST OF CHILDREN AT PRESENT AT CLONYN CASTLE
NEAR DUBLIN. OR AT 143 KIMMEAGE ROAD. DUBLIN.
(LATTER CASES MARKED D)

NAME	AGE	PLACE OF BIRTH	PROSPECTS OF BECOM SELF SUPPORTIN
60. STEINER Mihaly	10	Budapest, Hungary.	Youth Aliyah in du course.
61. STEINER Peter.	14	Budapest, Hungary.	"
62. STEINER Tamas.	11	Budapest, Hungary.	"
63. STEINMETZ Chaja	16	Mad.	
64. STRAUSZ Alexander	12	Vienna, Austria.	Youth Aliyah Candi
65. STRAUSZ Gizella	14	Vienna, Austria.	"
66. STRAUSZ Leona	16	Vienna, Austria.	"
67. STRULOVIC Leib.	16	Beszprein.	D Working as trai
68. TAPPER Martha	13	Satorujhely	
69. WEISS Jakob		Targ	D Looking for job
70. WIESEN Franklina	9	Krakow, Poland	
71. WIESEN Vera	6	Krakow, Poland	
72. WIESNER Agi	15	Arad	Going to U.S. near futu
73. WIESNER Judith	16	Arad	"
74. ZIEGLER Alfred	11	Kosice	
75. ZIEGLER Judit	12	Kosice	
76. ZIEGLER Olga	10	Kosice	

NOTE: Costs of maintenance amount to £3.6.0d. per head per we

Early summer 1949. Plans for the remaining children show those who went to Israel in January and suggested destinations for the rest (Page 3 of 3) 463

Appendix D

The Resilience of Young Survivors

In earlier years there was a school of thought that deterred victims of terror from looking back and advised them not to re-examine the past. **Olga Grossman** suffered long and acutely from this approach. She was prescribed strong tranquillizers.

> They gave me injections - the horrors of Auschwitz all over again. I felt like a shadow, as if I did not exist, disconnected from this world when all I wanted was to be a good wife and a loving mother. But this treatment meant I was denied involvement in my family and it cut me off from any social life for many years.

She makes a plea to doctors to avoid medication, to encourage the ousting of traumatic memories and above all to listen. Olga has told how years later she eventually freed herself from undue dependency and heavy medication to lead an independent and satisfying life. In doing so she showed remarkable determination and resilience.

This astonishing resilience shown by so many young Holocaust survivors has drawn much attention from the helping professions. Those studying human behaviour or providing support services for victims of traumatic situations and gross ill-treatment are usually confronted with people in severe shock with profound damage difficult to repair. So what was different about those like the Hide-and-Seek Children who have demonstrated an extraordinary ability to move forward?

Among the numerous writings that have emerged on this subject a few stand out for me. Dr Kerry Bluglass has made a fascinating study of Hidden Children[1] and the resilience of so many she has encountered. She reminds us of John Bowlby's Attachment Theory[2] and of what can be learned from Donald Winnicott's deep understanding of the mother/child relationship.[3] She recognises that Hidden Children were born into typically caring families where they had experienced "good-enough" mothering – a term coined by Winnicott - before external forces had brutally intruded on that vital relationship. The urgency of the situation put children suddenly into wholly unfamiliar surroundings and in mortal danger unless they adapted immediately. Those who survived discovered in themselves the strength and the coping mechanisms to do so. These attributes Dr Bluglass recognises as derived from sound bonding in early infancy, innate intelligence and astonishing adaptability.

Judith Mishne came to similar conclusions.[4] She also suggests that the younger the child is when losing their parents the more likely are they to succeed in bonding afresh when the shock is lessened. Much depends, too, on the quality of any future role models they find as they grow up. That could be a friend, a teacher or a spouse, or the impact of their religion that provides enough solace and encouragement without recourse to formal therapy. Perhaps that is why a number of survivors have chosen to marry a fellow survivor.

Recently a French research team has made a study of children institutionalised in Romania.[5] There, too, they found that many severely deprived youngsters once freed, and in a reasonable environment could reach a point where they could move forward. These children avoided the notion of victimisation by delegating the period of trauma to the past. But this does not and cannot obliterate horrendous memories.

Dr Shamai Davidson was particularly concerned about victims of the *Shoah.* He grew up in Scotland as the Nazis took control across Europe. He saw the impact this had on his Polish father, the only member of his family to have escaped persecution, and that never left him. He trained as a psychiatrist and I met him when Director of Shalvata Hospital in central Israel. There he inaugurated innovative mental health services for the local community, both social and therapeutic, and found that increasing numbers of survivors were using them. He set about a study of their specific needs. Sadly he died young but Professor Israel Charny, his colleague and friend, published his writings.[6] This contains seminal work of immense insight and original thought.

A Note on Play

Donald Winnicott, my revered teacher, compared children's play to the work of adults as a natural and necessary preoccupation and of vital importance.[7] He and his wife, Clare, showed how through trial and error, by experiment and imagination and phantasy, children from babyhood to adolescence make use of play.[8] They explore and test out relationships and situations, both animate and inanimate, within their environment. In doing so they slowly acquire understanding and coping mechanisms. These are crucial in preparation for managing their adult lives. But there is a prerequisite. A child can indulge in play only where he enjoys freedom within safe boundaries. Then the simplest of materials are sufficient to experiment and explore his thoughts and phantasies. These conditions were so often missing for the Hide-and-Seek Children whilst in a world controlled by Fascists or Nazis. Yet even in the direst situations examples are recorded in images at Yad Vashem of children entering into play, clinging on to life in the starkest of environments. Eisen has written about this.[9]

On reaching Clonyn Castle the younger children demonstrated their recognition of newly-found freedom and safety by their joy in play. Several mention this. But the older ones needed longer to throw off the shackles of the past when "Hide-and-Seek" had been no game.

Notes

Introduction

1 Taylor, 2009
2 Marks, 1993
3 Smith, 1998
4 Leverton and Lowensohn, 1990
5 Gottleib, 1998
6 Schonfeld, 1959
7 Emmanuel and Gissing, 2001
8 Smith, 1998
9 Linnea, 1993
10 Mieszkowska, 2010
11 Gottleib, 1998
12 Gilbert, 1996
13 Schonfeld, 1959

Chapter 1

1 The circumstances remain controversial but it seems that Hitler convinced Tiso that Hungary and Poland were about to invade Slovakia, and declared that he could not prevent them unless Slovakia was an independent state and an "ally". Thus Hitler simultaneously obtained powerful influence over Slovakia at the same time as the excuse he needed for invading the Czech territory.
2 Brayer, 1995
3 Cohn, 2001
4 Steiner, 1949
5 Rothkirchen, 1984
6 Fuchs 1984
7 Rothkirchen, 1961
8 Gilbert, 2010
9 Vrba, 1963
10 Gilbert, 2008
11 Rothkirchen, 1961
12 Levi, 1947, 1958
13 Simpson, 2001
14 *www.upn.gov.sk*
15 Gilbert, 2008
16 After liberation Rabbi Frieder worked hard to bring together all survivors of Jewish communities. He represented the Neolog Synagogues (as the Reform movement was called) together with the Status Quo group (who were more like today's Modern Orthodox) to work with the mainstream Orthodox. All his immediate family perished in Auschwitz except one brother who has published his writings and recorded the impact of the war on Slovakian Jews (Frieder, 1991). Rabbi Frieder died at the early age of 35 in 1946.

Chapter 2

1   Fuchs, 1984.
2   Tomlin, 2006
3   Fuchs, 1984.
4   Orczy, 1905
5   Korobkin, 2009
6   Kranzler, 1968
7   Curio, 2004
8   In Hebrew, each letter possesses a numerical value. *Gematria* is the calculation of the numerical equivalence of letters, words, or phrases and relates to different concepts and it explores the interrelationship between words and ideas.
9   Grunfeld, 1979

Chapter 3

1   Schonfeld, 1959
2   Arthur Moses was born in Romania and was a student at Bratislava Yeshiva. In 1938 one hundred students were offered visas to Manchester in England. He accepted one but was turned back at the Channel. A stamp was missing on his passport. A complete stranger found him crying, sorted out the problem and gave him five English pounds.
3   The Irish Republic, initially named the Irish Free State, was established in 1922, as a dominion within the British Commonwealth. In 1949, the last formal link with the UK was severed when Ireland declared itself a republic and formally ceased to be a dominion. Consequently it left the then British Commonwealth, having already ceased to participate in that organisation for several years. During British rule and initial independence Ireland was one of the poorest countries in Western Europe and had high emigration, but in contrast to many other states in the period remained financially solvent as a result of low government expenditure. The protectionist economy was opened in the late 1950s and Ireland joined the European Economic Community (now the European Union) in 1973. An economic crisis led Ireland to start large-scale economic reforms in the late 1980s. Ireland reduced taxation and regulation dramatically compared to other EU countries. Today Ireland is a member of the EU, the OECD, and the United Nations.
4   Shillman, 1945; Hyman, 1972.
5   Keogh, 1998
6   Quinn, "The Jerusalem Report", March 30, 2009
7   Briscoe, 1956
8   See Further Reading
9   By chance, I came across the fact that in 1620 a certain David Sollom, described as a "Jewish Merchant" is recorded as having bought an estate in Meath, Ireland. This is remarkable because at that time it was rare for Jews to acquire any property in the British Isles. (Hyamson, 2007)
10 Eppel, 1992
11 Gilbert, 1996; Dow and Brown,1946
12 Gilbert, 1996
13 Bertha Myer's husband, Emanuel Fischer, came to Britain on Rabbi

Schonfeld's Vienna transport in 1938. He trained as a *hazan* and officiated at Southend and Westcliff Synagogues, then in Perth, Australia. They are retired now in Jerusalem. Mr Fischer is collecting names of the numerous refugees Rabbi Schonfeld brought from Europe both before and after World War Two.

Chapter 4

1 Marshall 1980

Chapter 5

1   Schonfeld, 1980
2   Hoffman, 1989
3   Child Survivors Association, 2005 p 63
4   Cyrulnik, 2009
5   Mikes, 1959
6   Kirschen, 1996
7   Oz, 2005
8   Gilbert, 1996
9   "Amcha" is the codeword that was used by Jewish survivors after World War II to identify themselves.
10 Leverton and Lowensohn, 1990
11 Sadon, 1999
12 Documentary Films, 1996, 2000
13 "Shoah", 1985
14 Epstein, 1979

Part Two

1   *Kings XI v.4-13*
2   *Genesis XV v.2*
3   The Swedish diplomat, Wallenberg, on a mission to save Jews, rented thirty-two buildings in Budapest and declared them to be extraterritorial, protected by diplomatic immunity. He put up signs such as "The Swedish Library" and "The Swedish Research Institute" on their doors and hung oversize Swedish flags on the front of the buildings to bolster the deception. The buildings eventually housed almost 10,000 people. (Courtesy of Wikipedia)
4   Hanna Szenes, an Israeli, was dropped by parachute into Hungary to assist the Partisans but was caught and executed in November 1944.
5   see Chapter One
6   In 2007 Hetty told me that her husband had designed and made a plaque for a Catholic Convent in Zilina to record the fact that the nuns had hidden 9 Jewish children there during the war. A particularly dangerous moment was on Christmas Eve 1944, when the Mother Superior invited local German officers to a carol singing. A small boy sang to them in German. But in general, only Jews had known German. However the chief officer hugged the boy and said: "You and your sister will be safe with me!"
7   This must have been when the last remaining Castle children moved near Dublin

8   The "Altalena" was a ship purchased by the Irgun to bring weapons and fighters to Palestine during the War of Israeli Independence. On arrival there was a violent dispute between the Irgun and the newly-formed Israel Defence Forces over the control of the weapons, which ended with the shelling of the Altalena. The ship was abandoned and sank with the weapons. Most on board were able to swim to shore but the whole affair remains notorious and controversial because 35 men had been killed by fellow Jews.

9   See Appendix B

10   Séndi Templer commented later "Blanka was such a loyal friend that when Rabbi Schonfeld asked me to go to London to run the girls' hostel, she delayed plans to go to join her sisters in the USA and insisted on coming with me."

11   A Unit of the British Army

12   Ceska Televisia, 1999

13   Trancik, 1995.

14   Gryn, 2000

Appendix A

1   "Tell ye your children of it, and let your children tell their children, and their children another generation."

Appendix B

1   Grunfeld, 1979

2   Zakon, 2001

Appendix C

1   Gottleib, 1998; see Chapter One.

Appendix D

1   Bluglass, 2003

2   Bowlby, 2004

3   Winnicott, 1965

4   Mishne, 1997

5   Lecompte, 2006

6   Charny, 1992

7   Green, 2005

8   Kantner, 2004

9   Eisen, 1988

Bibliography and Further Reading

Introduction

BOLSHOVER, Richard: *British Jewry and the Holocaust*. The Littman Library of Jewish Civilisation, 2003.

EMMANUEL, Muriel & GISSING, Vera: *Nicholas Winton and the Rescued Generation, Save One Life, Save the World*. Library of Holocaust Testimonies, 2001

GILBERT, Martin: *The Boys, Triumph Over Adversity*. Weidenfeld & Nicolson, 1996

GOTTLEIB, Amy Zahl: *Men of Vision – Anglo-Jewry's aid to victims of the Nazi regime 1933 – 1945*. Weidenfeld & Nicolson, 1998

KARPF, Ann: *The War After: Living with the Holocaust*. Minerva, 1996

LEVERTON, Bertha & LOWENSOHN, Shmuel: *I came alone, stories of the Kindertransports*. The Book Guild, 1990

LEVERTON, Bertha (editor): *Kindertransport 60th Anniversary 1939-1999*. Produced for the Reunion, June, 1999

LINNEA, Sharon: *Raoul Wallenberg: The Man Who Stopped Death*. Jewish Publication Society of America, 1993

MANN, Jessica: *Out of Harm's Way*. Headline Publishing, 2005

MARKS, Jane: *The Hidden Children*, Bantam Books, 1993

MIESZKOWSKA, Ann: *Irene Sendler, Mother of the Holocaust Children*. Praeger, 2010

PARSONS, Martin L: *"I'll take that one", dispelling the myths of civilian evacuation 1939 – 1945*. Beckett Karlson, 1998

SADON, Inge: *No longer a stranger*. Published privately, Jerusalem, 1999

SCHONFELD, Solomon: *Message to Jewry*. Jewish Secondary Schools Movement, 1959

SMITH, Michael: *Foley, the Spy who saved 10,000 Jews*. Hodder & Stoughton, 1998

TAYLOR, Derek: *Solomon Schonfeld: a Purpose in Life*. Valentine Mitchell, 2009

Chapter 1

BRAYER, Shoshana Singer: *Childhood Lost*. Published privately, 1995

CESKA TELEVISIA: *Among Blind Fools*, TV Documentary, 1999.

COHN, A Romi & CIACCIO, Dr Leonard: *The Youngest Partisan – a young boy who fought the Nazis*. Mesorah Publications, New York, 2001

FRIEDER, Emanuel: *To Deliver Their Souls – The Struggle of a Young Rabbi During the Holocaust*. Tauber Holocaust Library, 1991.

FUCHS, Abraham: *The Unheeded Cry – the gripping story of Rabbi Weissmandl, the valiant Holocaust leader who battled both Allied indifference and Nazi hatred*. Mesorah Publications, New York, 1984

GILBERT, Martin:
    The Routledge Atlas of the Second World War. Routledge, 2008
    "Rudolph Kastner" in the *Journal of the 45 Aid Society*. Issue no. 34, 2010
GRYN, Hugo with Naomi GRYN: *Chasing Shadows – memories of a vanished world*. Viking, 2000
HUMPHREYS, Rob: *Czech and Slovak Republics: The Rough Guide*. Rough Guides, 1996
LEVI, Primo:
    Is This A Man. Einaudi, 1958
    The Truce. Einaudi, 1947
MORRIS, Jan: *Europe: an Intimate Journey*. Faber and Faber, 2006 pp 111-117
ROTHKIRCHEN, Livia:
    The Destruction of Slovak Jewry: a documentary history. Yad Vashem Archives, Vol iii.1961
    "The Slovak Enigma: A Reassessment of the Halt to the Deportations", *East Central Europe*, Vol 10, 1-2, 1984
    "Escape Routes and Contacts during the War" In *Jewish Resistance during the Holocaust: Proceedings of the Conference on Manifestations of Jewish Resistance, Jerusalem, April 7-11, 1968*. Yad Vashem, 1971
    "Hungary – An Asylum for the Refugees of Europe", *Yad Vashem Studies*. Yad Vashem, Jerusalem, 1968
SCHWEID, Alexander: *Personal memoir*. Unpublished, (in German). Weiner Library, London, 1951
SIMPSON, John: *A Mad World, My Masters: Tales from a Traveller's Life*. Pan Books, 2001. See Chapter 3 "Villains" pp 94 -104
STEINER, F (editor): *The Tragedy of Slovak Jewry*. Documentation Centre of the Central Union of Jewish Religious Communities, Bratislava, 1949
TRANCIK, Martin: *Between the Old and the New – the History of the Bookseller Family Steiner in Pressburg*. Marencin, Bratislava, 1995
VRBA, Rudolf and WETZLER: *The Auschwitz Protocols*. War Refugee Board, 1944
VRBA, Rudolf & BESTIC, Alan: *I Cannot Forgive*. Sidgwick & Jackson, 1963

www.loc.gov/rr/european/cash/cash3.html. Bibliography of Czech and Slovak History sources, Jews and Jewish Affairs on the Library of Congress Catalogue.

Chapter 2

CURIO, Claudia: "Invisible Children", *Shofar, an Interdisciplinary Journal of Jewish Studies*. Volume 23, I, 2004 pp 41-56
FUCHS, Abraham: *The Unheeded Cry – the Gripping Story of Rabbi Chaim Michael Dov Weissmandl, the Valiant Holocaust Leader who Battled Both Allied Indifference and Nazi Hatred*. ArtScroll History, 1984
GRUNFELD, Dr Judith: *Shefford: The Story of a Jewish School Community in Evacuation 1939 -1945*. Soncino, 1979
KATZ, Rubin: "Bending the Rules: the Unsung Hero Rabbi Solomon Schonfeld", *AJR Journal*. London Association of Jewish Refugees, December 2007

KOROBTKIN, Frieda Stolsberg: *Throw your feet over your shoulders: beyond the Kindertransport.* Devora Publishing, 2009

KRANZLER, David & HIRSCHLER, Gertrude: *Solomon Schonfeld – his page in history.* Judaica Press, New York, 1982

ORCZY, Baroness Emma: *The Adventures of the Scarlet Pimpernel.* Blakeney Manor, 1905

SCHONFELD, Solomon: *Message to Jewry.* Jewish Secondary Schools, 1959

TAYLOR, Denis: *Solomon Schonfeld: a Purpose in Life.* Valentine Mitchell, 2009

TOMLIN, Chanon: *Protest and Prayer: Rabbi Dr Solomon Schonfeld and Orthodox Jewish Responses in Britain to the Nazi Persecution of Europe's Jews 1942-1945.* Peter Lang, 2006

Chapter 3

BIELENBERG, Kim: "The Shamrock and the Swastika", *Irish Independent*, January 6th 2007

BRISCOE, Robert: *For the Life of Me.* Little, Brown, Boston 1958

DOW, J W & BROWN, M: "Evacuation to Westmorland from Home and Europe 1939-1945", *Westmorland Gazette.* Kendal 1946 pp 50-59

EPPEL, Cissie: *A Journey into our Ancestry – Chronicles of the Rosenheim, Levy and Eppel Families.* Bennie Linden, 1992

GILBERT, Martin: *The Boys. Triumph Over Adversity.* Weidenfeld and Nicolson, 1996

HYAMSON, A M: *A History of the Jews of England.* Macmillan, 1907 p.144

HYMAN, Louis: *The Jews of Ireland from the Earliest Times to the Year 1910.* Irish University Press, 1972

KEOGH, Dermot: *Jews in Twentieth Century Ireland, Refugees, Anti-Semitism and the Holocaust.* Cork University Press, 1998

MILLISLE PRIMARY SCHOOL, Co. Down, Northern Ireland: *A Kinder Place, a Different World,* DVD 2004/5

O'DONAGHUE, David: " Neutral Ireland's Secret War", *Sunday Business Post*, Dublin, December 21st 2006

QUINN, Conall: "The Death of Harry Leon", Review of a new play, *The Jerusalem Report*, March 30th, 2009

SCHONFELD, Solomon: *Message to Jewry.* Jewish Secondary Schools, 1959

SHILLMAN, Bernard: *A Short History of the Jews of Ireland.* Eason, Dublin, 1945

HISTORY CHANNEL: *Ireland's Nazis: The Support of the Regime,* 21st, 28th June 2007

www.hetireland.org. Holocaust Education Trust, Eire

www.secondworldwarni.org. Second World War in Northern Ireland

Chapter 4

MARSHALL, Robert: *In the Sewers of Lvov – the last sanctuary from the Holocaust.* Collins, London, 1980.

Chapter 5

ABRAMOVICH, Solomon and ZILBERG, Yakov: *Smuggled in Potato Sacks – Fifty Stories of the Hidden Children of the Kaunas Ghetto.* Valentine Mitchell, 2011

CHILD SURVIVORS' ASSOCIATION OF GREAT BRITAIN: *Zachor – Child Survivors Speak.* Elliot and Thompson, 2005

CYRULNIK, Boris: *Resilience.* Penguin, 2009

EPSTEIN, Helen: *Children of the Holocaust.* Putnam, 1979

GILBERT, Martin: *The Boys. Triumph Over Adversity.* Weidenfeld and Nicolson, 1996

HOFFMAN, Eva: *Lost in Translation.* Heinemann, 1989

KIRSCHEN, Yaacov: *What a Country: Dry Bones Looks at Israel.* Jewish Publication Society, 1996

LEVERTON, Bertha & LOWENSOHN, Shmuel: *I came alone, stories of the Kindertransports.* The Book Guild, *1990*

MARRIS, Peter: *Loss and Change.* Routledge & Kegan Paul, 1974

MIKES, George: *How to be an Alien.* Andre Deutsch, 1946

MIKES, George: with BENTLEY, Nicholas: *Milk and Honey – Israel* Explored. Wingate, 1959

SADON, Inge: *No longer a stranger.* Published privately, Jerusalem 1999

SCHONFELD, Solomon: *A New-Old Rendering of the Psalms,* The Uniby Press, 1980

OZ, Amos: *A Tale of Love and Darkness.* Harcourt, 2005

Documentaries and Films

LANZMANN, Claude*: Shoah. 1985*

SPIELBERG, Steven: *Schindler's List.* Universal, 1993

HACKER, Melissa: *My Knees Were Jumping: Remembering the Kindertransports.* DVD 1996

HARRIS, Mark Jonathan and OPPENHEIMER, Deborah: *Into the arms of strangers, stories of the Kindertransport.* DVD 2000

SLESIN, Aviva: *Secret Lives: Hidden Children and Their Rescuers during World War II.* DVD 2003

Web Sites

The Second Generation: *www.2ndgeneration.org.uk*
Beth Shalom: *www.holocaustcentre.com*
The Shoah Foundation: *dornsife.usc.edu/vhi*

Part Two

CESKA TELEVISIA: *Among Blind Fools,* TV Documentary 1999.

TRANCIK, Martin: *Between the Old and the New – the History of the Bookseller Family Steiner in Pressburg.* Marencin, Bratislava, 1995

GRYN, Hugo with Naomi GRYN: *Chasing Shadows – memories of a vanished world.* Viking, 2000

SCHWEID, Alexander: *Personal memoir.* Unpublished, (in German). Wiener Library, London, 1951

Appendix A

LAGNADO, Lucette Matalon & DEKEL, Sheila Cohn: *Children of the Flames – Dr. Josef Mengele and the untold story of the twins of Auschwitz.* Sidgwick & Jackson, 1991

KOENIG, Robert:
"Nazi Research: reopening the darkest chapter in German science". *Science Magazine* Vol. 288, Issue 2, June 2000
"Nazi Research: Max Planck offers an apology". *Science Magazine* Vol. 292, 15th June 2001

HEIM, Susanne, SACHSE, Carola, and WALKER, Mark: *History of the Kaiser Wilhelm Society under National Socialism.* Cambridge University Press, 2009

Appendix B

BENISCH, Pearl: *Carry me in your Heart – The Life and Legacy of Sarah Schenirer,* New York, 2003

GRUNFELD, Judith: *Shefford: a story of a Jewish School community in evacuation.* Soncino, 1979

ZAKON, Miriam: *The Queen of Bais Yaakov: The story of Dr. Judith Grunfeld.* Feldheim, 2001

Appendix C

GOTTLEIB, Amy Zahl: *Men of Vision – Anglo-Jewry's aid to victims of the Nazi regime 1933 – 1945.* Weidenfeld & Nicolson, 1998

Appendix D

BLUGLASS, Kerry: *Hidden from the Holocaust: Stories of Resilient Children Who Survived and Thrived.* Praeger, 2003

BOWLBY, Richard: *Fifty years of Attachment Theory.* Karnac, 2004

CHARNY, Israel W (editor): *Holding on to Humanity: Message of Holocaust Survivors - The Shamai Davidson Papers.* NYU Press, 1992

CYRULNIK, Boris: *Resilience.* Penguin, 2009

EISEN, George: *Children and play in the* Holocaust – *games among the shadows.* University of Massachusetts, 1988

EPSTEIN, Helen: *Children of the Holocaust.* Putnam, 1979

GREEN, Andre: *Play and Reflection in Donald Winnicott's Writings.* Karnac, 2005

HOFFMAN, Eva: *Lost in Translation.* Heinemann, 1989

KANTER, Joel (Ed.): *The Life and Work of Clare Winnicott.* Karnac, 2004. See Chapter 3 *"Children who cannot play"*

LECOMTE, Jacques: *Recovering from Childhood's Wounds.* Free Association Books, 2006

MARRIS, Peter: *Loss and Change.* Routledge & Kegan Paul, 1986

MENDELSOHN, Yitzhak (editor): *Child Survivors; forms of intervention.* Amcha, 1996

MISHNE, Judith: "Memories of Hidden Children". *Journal of Social Work and Policy in Israel*. Bar Ilan Press, 1997

SCHLINK, Bernhard: *Guilt about the Past*. Beautiful Books, 2010

SZEKACS-WEISZ, Judit & WARD, Ivan (editors): *Lost Childhood and the Language of Exile*. Imago East West and Freud Museum Publications, 2004

WINNICOTT, D W: *The Maturational Process and the Facilitating Environment*. Hogarth Press, 1965

Glossary

Prepared by Colin Barnett, Oron Joffe and John Speyer.

Abbreviations used in Glossary:
G German   H Hebrew   S Slovak   Y Yiddish

Note: Where Hebrew terms are listed with variant spellings, the first spelling is the scholarly transliteration and the second reflects the pronunciation used by Ashkenazi Jews.

Adath Yisroel, *Adass Yisroel*   H. Congregation of Israel, *often abbreviated to Adath or Adass: the name of the parent synagogue of the Union of Orthodox Hebrew Congregations, established by Rabbi Victor Schonfeld.*

Afikoman, Afikomen   H. *A portion of matza hidden at the start of the Passover Seder celebration. At the end of the festive meal it is customarily searched for; if not found the children receive a reward. (see also Seder).*

Agudath Israel, Agudas Yisroel   Jewish Union: *the political arm of Eastern European orthodox Judaism, founded in 1912 with an anti-Zionist orientation.*

American Jewish Joint Distribution Committee (The Joint)   *A worldwide Jewish relief organization established in 1914 to assist Jewish communities around the world.*

Aliyah   Going up: *to migrate to Israel.*

Aliyat Hanoar
See also Youth Aliyah   *Organisation that arranges immigration of youth to Israel and sets up Youth Villages there.*

Amcha   H. Your people: *a code word that helped survivors identify fellow Jews in Europe after World War II. Taken as the name of an Israeli organisation founded in 1987 by Manfred Klafter, a Dutch survivor, to provide social activities and therapeutic services for Holocaust survivors and their children across Israel.*

Anschluss   G. Connection: *the annexation of Austria by Nazi Germany in March 1938.*

Arba minim   H. Four species: *four plants used together in the ritual for the festival of Succot (Tabernacles), namely the etrog (citron) a palm frond, a willow branch and a sprig of myrtle. The branches are bound together around the palm (lulav).*

Arisator   S. *Gentile given ownership of Jewish business or property by the Fascist government in Slovakia.*

Aryanisation   *The exclusion of non-aryans from business and the confiscation of their property by the Nazis in the 1930s.*

Ashkenazi   H. *Jew from Central or Eastern Europe.*

Bagrut	*H. School leaving exam in Israel.*
Bais Yaacov, Beth Jaakob,	Y. **House of Jacob:** *school system for orthodox girls.*
Beis Ya'akov	*See Appendix B*
Barmitzvah, batmitzvah	*H. coming-of-age ceremony for Jewish boys on reaching the age of 13, girls at 12.*
Baruch HaShem	*H.* **Blessed be The Name:** *roughly equivalent to "Thank God".*
Benching	*From Y.* bentshn, *to bless. Grace after meals.*
Berit	*Y.* circumcision.
Beschert, Bashert	*Y. (more commonly Bashert):* **Predestined.**
Beth Din	*H.* **Court of Jewish Law.**
Beth Hamidrash, Betei Midrash	*H. small orthodox synagogue.*
Beth Jaakob	*See Bais Yaacov.*
B'nei Akiva	*H. a religious Zionist youth movement, named after a famous 2nd century Rabbi.*
CBF	**The Central British Fund for German Jewry:** *established 1933 by the British Jewish community to help Jewish victims of the Nazis. Based at Woburn House, West London.*
Chadar ochel	*H.* **Dining room.**
Chametz	*H.* **Leavened (bread):** *forbidden during Passover.*
Chanuca, Hanukkah	*H. Winter Light Festival commemorating the rededication of the Temple during the Maccabean revolt against the Seleucid Empire.*
Chasidishe	*Y.* **Chasidic:** *this refers to the mystic Chasidic movement, founded in Poland in the 18th century.*
Cheder	*Y. Classes, for Jewish children usually held after regular school hours where they study Judaism and Biblical Hebrew.*
Chol Hamoed Succoth	*Weekdays of the festival of Tabernacles: The middle days of the festival, when work is allowed (unlike on the first and last days).*
CRREC	**The Chief Rabbi's Religious Emergency Council.** *Executive Director: Rabbi Solomon Schonfeld.*
Cholent, cholnt	*Y. Stew served on the Sabbath, kept warm from the day before to confirm with the prohibition of cooking on the Sabbath.*
Choshuv	*H. Y. Distinguished, respected.*
Chumash	*H. The Pentateuch.*
Chutspah	*H. Cheek, arrogance, temerity!*
Daven	*Y.* To pray.
Dayanim	*H. judges, often rabbis, in a religious court.*
Divrei Toire	*H.* **Words of Torah:** *discussion or commentary on the first five books of the Hebrew Bible.*
DP	**Displaced Person:** *those left stateless following World War II.*

Eretz Israel	H. **The land of Israel.**
Erev Pesach	H. *The first evening of Passover known as Seder Night, a traditional celebration.*
Esrog, etrog	H. *A citrus fruit grown in Israel, similar to a lemon and known in English as a citron. It is used in the ritual of the festival of Succot (Tabernacles) – see* **arba minim** *and lulav.*
Fleishig	Y. *Kosher foods that contain meat and may not be eaten with dairy food.*
G-d	*Abbreviation used by orthodox Jews to reflect the tradition that His (Hebrew) name may not be spoken.*
Gadol	H. **Big, great.** *Sometimes used to refer to a prominent religious leader.*
Gemara	**Talmud.** *Strictly refers to rabbinic discussions on the* **Mishnah** *(the first Rabbinic codification of Jewish Law, dating from c. 200AD), contained in the Babylonian* **Talmud** *(compiled c. 500AD) and the Palestinian* **Talmud** *(compiled c. 400AD). By general convention, gemara (from an Aramaic word meaning to study) refers to the Babylonian Talmud.*
Gematria	H. *Traditional Jewish numerology, in which rabbinic commentators use the fact that each letter of the Hebrew alphabet has a numerical value to uncover hidden meanings in religious texts and in everyday life. Rabbi Schonfeld enjoyed this practice.*
Haaretz	**The Land:** *the Land of Israel.*
Haganah	H. **Defence:** *a Jewish paramilitary organization in British Mandatory Palestine from 1920 to 1948.*
Halakha	H. *the generic term for Jewish religious laws.*
Hamapil	H. **Who causes to fall:** *The name of a prayer recited by children at bedtime, asking God to "cause the bands of sleep to fall over my eyes".*
Hamidrash	*See Beth Hamidrash.*
Hasharah, hachshara	H. **Preparation:** *a kibbutz model (collective agricultural settlement) set up in Europe after World War II to prepare Jewish survivors of the Holocaust for migration to Israel.*
Hashem	H. **The Name:** *one of the traditional ways of referring to God.*
Hashomer Hatzair	H. **The Young Guard:** *Socialist Zionist youth movement founded in 1913 in Galicia, Austria-Hungary.*
Hasmonean	*The orthodox Jewish secondary school founded by Rabbi Schonfeld in London in 1944, named after the Hasmonean dynasty which ruled Israel from 140 to 37 BC.*
Hatikvah	H. **The Hope:** *the name of the Israeli national anthem.*

Havdole	H. *ceremony that marks the end of the Sabbath and the beginning of the week.*
Hazan	H. *Cantor who leads the chanting of prayers in a synagogue.*
Hesed, chesed	H. Kindness, love, grace.
HIAS	Hebrew Immigrant Aid Society, *established in New York in the late 19th century to support Jewish migrants to the USA.*
Hlinka	*The Fascist Guards of the Slovak People's Party while they were in power.*
Hora	H. *A popular Israeli folk dance.*
ICRC	International Committee of the Red Cross.
Ivrit	H. *Hebrew language.*
JewishGen	Jewish Genealogical website
JRC	Jewish Refugees Committee: set *up under the auspices of the CBF to assist Jews fleeing from the Nazis (see also CBF).*
Judenrein	G. Cleansed of Jews: *a term used by the Nazis to denote their successful expulsion or murder of Jews in an area under their control.*
Kadish	Aramaic. *the prayer for the dead.*
Kaftan	*Long loose garment.*
Kapo	G. *A concentration camp prisoner in charge of a group of other prisoners.*
Kashrut	H. *the system of laws governing diet and the preparation of food.*
Kehilla	H. *Jewish community.*
Kiddush	H. *blessing of wine and bread before a meal on a holy day.*
Kindertransport	G. *the pre-war rescue of 10,000 unaccompanied Jewish children from the Nazis, brought to the UK from Germany, Austria, Poland and Czechoslovakia.*
Kipa	*Head covering worn by orthodox males.*
Kolel	*Advanced Yeshivah.*
Kosher	Y. Fit, legitimate (for use): *food in accordance with Kashrut rules.*
Kotel	H. *the Western Wall in Jerusalem. Only part of the temple still standing, hence an especially holy place for Jews. Traditionally people write prayers on pieces of paper and push them between the stones.*
Kristallnacht	G. Night of (broken) glass: *a pogrom in Germany and Austria on 9-10 November 1938, in which synagogues were burned, Jewish shops destroyed and looted, and about 35,000 Jewish men sent to concentration camps.*

Lirot	H. **Pounds:** former *Israeli currency.*
Lockshen, lokshn	Y. **Noodles.**
Lulev, lulav	H. *palm branch: a ritual object used at Sukkot (Tabernacles), made from a palm branch, two willow branches and three of myrtle tied together. See also esrog, arba minim.*
Madrich, madrichim	H. **Guide, guides:** *male instructors or youth leaders.*
Madricha, madrichot	H. **Guide, guides:** *female instructors or youth leaders.*
Magen David	H. **Shield of David:** *the six pointed star, used as a Jewish symbol since the 19th century.*
Matmid, masmid	H. **Persevering, diligent:** *a student who shows commitment and consistency in his study of Torah.*
Matza, matzot	**Unleavened bread:** *eaten instead of bread during the Festival of Passover*
"May you live to 120"	*As did Moses – i.e. "Long Life".*
Mazkir	H. **secretary.**
Mensch	Y. *a decent and responsible person, someone of integrity and honour.*
Mesivta, metivta	Aramaic: *religious academy (see also yeshiva).*
Metapelet	H. **Nursery nurse, nanny.**
Mezuzot	H. *Small cylinders containing two of the three paragraphs of the **Shema prayer,** which are attached to the doorposts of Jewish homes and buildings.*
Midrash	H. *collections of commentaries and teachings on the Hebrew Bible.*
Milchig	Y. **Dairy:** *Kosher foods that contain dairy products and therefore cannot be eaten with meat.*
Mincha	H. *Afternoon service.*
Minyan, minyanim (pl).	H. *the quorum of at least ten Jewish males over the age of thirteen required for communal Jewish prayer. Used sometimes to describe a small congregation that meets regularly for prayer.*
Mitzva	H. **Good deed:** *derived from the Hebrew word meaning commandment (see also bar mitzvah).*
Mizrachi	*Jews from Middle Eastern and Asian countries.*
Moshe Rabenu	H. **Moses our Teacher:** *the traditional way of referring to the biblical Moses.*
Motzei Shabat	**The ending of Shabbat:** *Saturday evening.*
Nachlath	H. **heritage:** *Name given to Dublin Jewish Community's bi-monthly magazine.*
Neolog	*A Jewish movement that made modest changes to religious practice in and around Hungary in the late 19th century.*
Ohel David	H. *Tent of David*
ORT	*Organisation offering Educational Resources and Technological Training for Jewish Youth established worldwide in 1880.*

Parasha	H. Section, portion: *weekly reading from the Pentateuch during Sabbath morning service.*
Parnose	Y. *Living, subsistence.*
Pirkei Avot	H. *usually translated as* Sayings of the Fathers, *a Tractate (section) of the Mishnah containing often-quoted proverbs and maxims (see also Gemara).*
Protexiu, protektsia	Y. *Favouritism, patronage, influence. Favoured treatment obtained through personal contacts or nepotism.*
Rabbenu	H. Our leader: *often used as a term of reverence for a rabbi or religious figure.*
Rashi	Rabbi Shlomo Yitzhaki: *Leading commentator on the Hebrew Bible and the Talmud; French, 11th Century.*
Rav	H. Rabbi.
Reb	Y. Mister: *a traditional and polite title*
Rebbe	Y. Rabbi, teacher.
Rebbitzen	Y. A rabbi's wife.
Rosh Hashono, Rosh Hashana	H. Beginning of the year: *the Jewish New Year.*
Sabra	H. *A native-born Israeli.*
Savta	H. Grandmother.
Schnorrer	Y. beggar: *collector for charity*
Shochet	H. *Jewish ritual slaughterer*
Seder	H. Order: *ceremony conducted in the home to mark the start of the festival of Passover, commemorating the exodus from Egypt.*
Sephardi	H. Spanish: *descendants of Jews who were expelled from Spain and Portugal, their religious practice slightly different from Ashkenazi Jews who had settled in other parts of Europe. Also used broadly to include Jews from middle-eastern countries.*
Sepher	H. Book.
Shabbos, shabbat	H. Sabbath.
Shaliach	H. *Israeli representatives working in Jewish communities abroad.*
Shammas, shames	Y. Caretaker *or beadle of a synagogue.*
Sheitl	Y. Wig: *worn by Orthodox women to hide their hair.*
Shema	H. *the main traditional prayer, recited daily.*
Shemot	H. *the Hebrew name for the Biblical book of Exodus.*
Shidduch, shidduk	Y. Match: *an introduction or arranged marriage.*
Shiur, siur	H. *a discussion or class on a religious subject (pl. shiurim).*
Schnorrer	Y. Beggar.
Shoah	H. Catastrophe: *the Hebrew name for the Nazi Holocaust.*
Shochet, shochetim	H. *Ritual slaughterer of animals according to Jewish dietary laws (see also Kashrut).*

Shofar	*H. Ram's horn, blown during services on the New Year and Day of Atonement (see also Rosh Hashonoh and Yom Kippur).*
Shul	Y. Synagogue.
Shulchan Aruch	*H. An authoritative codification of Jewish law written by Rabbi Joseph Karo in the 16th century.*
Siddur	H. Prayer book.
Simches	*Y. Parties, celebrations: derived from the Hebrew word for joy.*
Sokhnut, sochnut	*H. the Jewish Agency , now called "The Jewish Agency for Israel", established under the terms of the British Mandate for Palestine to promote Jewish immigration and to administer the affairs of the Jewish community in Palestine. After Israeli independence it became a government department facilitating economic development and the absorption of immigrants.*
Sonderkommando	G. Special command: *work units of Nazi death camp prisoners who disposed of the bodies of those killed in the gas chambers.*
Streimel, shtreimel	*Y. Fur-trimmed hat worn by some Chassidic rabbis and men during the Sabbath and festivals.*
Sukkesz, Succot,	H. Tabernacles: *the autumn harvest festival.*
Succah	*H. Temporary shelter where traditionally meals are eaten during Succot; usually decorated with fruit and foliage.*
Tisha B'av	H. Ninth of Ab: *fast day commemorating the destruction of the two Temples in Jerusalem.*
Talet, tallit	H. Prayer shawl: *worn by men at morning services.*
Tashlich, tashlikh	*H. ceremony on the afternoon of the Jewish New Year, in which the previous year's sins are symbolically "cast off" by throwing pieces of bread into a river.*
Torah	*H. The Hebrew Bible, the Old Testament, or specifically the Pentateuch.*
UHU	Slovak Central Economic Organisation *set up by Tuka, the Hlinka Prime Minister, to deal with Jewish matters in Slovakia.*
Ulpan	*H. Intensive course in modern Hebrew.*
United Synagogue	*Confederation of 42 Ashkenazi orthodox Congregations and 24 affiliated, in Britain and the Commonwealth, led by the Chief Rabbi.*
UNRRA	United Nations Relief and Rehabilitation Administration, *set up during World War II to provide relief to areas liberated from the Axis powers.*
UZ	*The Jews' Centre: a committee of Jews set up in Slovakia to carry out orders from the UHU.*

WIZO	Women's International Zionist Organisation.
Yad Vashem	H. *the Holocaust Martyrs' and Heroes' Remembrance Authority, founded in 1953 in Jerusalem.*
Yartzeit, Yahrtzeit, Yahrzeit, Yarzeit	Y. **Anniversary of death** *when surviving relatives recite the mourners' prayer and light a memorial candle (see also Kaddish).*
Yeshiva	H. *Jewish religious academy (pl yeshivot)*
yidishkeit	Y. **Jewishness, Judaism.**
Yisroel, Yisrael	H. **Israel.**
Yom Kippur	H. **Day of Atonement:** *annual fast day, ten days after the Jewish New Year (see also Rosh Hashono).*
Yom Tov	Y. **Festival, holiday.** *from the Hebrew for good day.*
Youth Aliyah	*Organisation founded in 1932 to save Jewish children from persecution and bring them to Israel.*
Zechut	H. *merit, virtue.*
Zyklon	G. *The poisonous gas used by the Nazis in gas chambers at the death camps.*

Index

A

Abrahamson, Professor Leonard 79, 161
Adath Yisroel 52, 53, 54, 68, 176
Adelaide Road Synagogue Dublin 203
Adler, Helen 158
Aegis Trust, The 197
Agudath Israel 117, 400, 441
Ahavas (Ahavat) Torah Yeshiva
    Boarding School 255, 294
Alach 355, 410
Alexander, Duro 47
Aliyah 29, 42, 79, 129-131, 164, 191,
    207, 208, 223, 240, 243, 256, 266, 271,
    317, 318, 326, 333, 341, 357, 373, 375,
    400, 415, 420, 422, 431, 459
Allies; Allied Forces 70, 75, 363
Alony, Rabbi 98, 116, 203, 205
Amcha 195, 319, 342, 349, 412
American Joint Distribution
    Committee, The ('The Joint') 72,
    73, 74, 244, 255, 293, 324, 356
Antman family 419, 420
Antwerp 91, 161
Arrow-Cross 173
Ashkenazi 13, 52, 54
Auschwitz 29, 31, 34, 36, 37, 75, 161,
    194, 206, 209, 220, 222, 224, 230,
    243, 247, 248, 253, 259, 266, 271,
    281, 292, 297, 316, 324, 325, 331,
    337-339, 341-345, 347, 350, 352,
    354, 356, 358, 361-364, 373, 377-
    379, 393-395, 402, 407, 415, 417,
    421, 433, 435-440, 464
    see also Birkenau
Auschwitz Protocols, The 36
Austria 78, 249, 250, 258, 279, 330,
    360, 442
Austro-Hungarian Empire 20, 28
Avigdor High School 53, 54, 57, 59,
    68, 164, 202, 207, 221, 241, 279,
    280, 286, 327, 345, 346, 386, 433,
    442, 443

B

Bacsi, Micklosh 247, 248
Banská Bystrica 36, 231, 243
Bardejov 330
Barnett, Barbara xvi, 12-18, 175, 177
Barnett, Richard 13, 412
Baruch, Adam. Journalist 439
Bedford/Bedfordshire 68, 412
Beis Ya'akov (Beis Ya'acov; Bais
    Yaacov; Beth Jacob) 5, 42, 71, 108,
    210, 279, 345, 349, 353, 384, 400,
    414, 441, 442, 443
Békéscsaba 277, 278, 284
Belgium 5, 75, 91, 97, 244, 295, 340,
    357, 358, 378, 415, 443, 444, 447, 448
Belzec 437
Benedict family 375
Benes, Edvard. 22, 26, 45
Ben Zvi Institute 333
Bergen-Belsen 78, 223, 224, 226, 229,
    259, 352, 386
Berlin 7, 9, 299, 306, 308, 339, 351, 433
Berlitz Secretarial College 317
Bernadotte, Count Folke 374
Bet Hakerem 379
Beth Hamidrash 52
Beth Jacob   see Beis Ya'akov
Beth Shalom 195
Bilke 360, 361, 364
Binet, Gaspar v, 26, 123, 195, 338-34, 373
    Miriam 338-341, 373
    Robert 123, 338-34, 373
Birkenau 266, 267, 270, 339, 343, 344, 350
    see also Auschwitz
Bleier, Rabbi and family 95, 109, 203,
    204, 207
B'nei Akiva 117, 304, 333, 398, 400,
    419, 422
Bock, Erich 33, 37, 39, 111, 123, 130,
    191, 243, 244, 245
Bock, Robert 243, 244
Bohemia 28, 219, 411
Boleraz 416
Bournemouth 47, 176, 394
Bratislava 4, 20, 22-26, 28, 29, 31, 33,
    34, 39, 41, 42, 51, 71, 96, 209, 210,

219-221, 224, 231, 233, 239-241, 252,
258-260, 262, 266, 267, 276, 290,
292, 293, 299, 300, 304, 309, 310,
313, 316, 317, 322, 324, 329, 338,
352, 353, 356, 367, 375, 385, 386,
388, 391, 396-398, 400, 401, 411,
420-424, 429, 431, 460
Braunhorf 343
Brayer, Shoshana Singer 41, 395, 398,
401-402, 460
Brazil Rabbi and Mrs 176, 394
Briscoe, Robert 78, 85, 205
British Branch of the Anti-
Tuberculosis League of Israel 91
British Friends of Magen David
Adom 89
Brodie, Dr Israel 164, 165
Brooklyn, NY 245, 249, 251, 255, 256,
298, 353
Bucharest 248, 333, 364
Buchenwald 224, 363, 364, 411
Buchvarm, Rabbi 373
Budapest 9, 21, 22, 51, 209, 219, 253,
259, 277, 282, 284, 296, 297, 323,
330, 340, 356, 360, 364, 366, 367,
391, 411, 420, 421, 425-428, 429, 432
Burkhardt, Cecil 38

C

Caplan, Trudy 178
Carpathia 365, 366, 431
Carpathian Mountains 21, 366, 403,
404, 442
Casanova, Daniella 377
Catholic (s) 9, 22, 25, 26, 33, 77, 78,
108, 266, 324, 326, 330, 415, 429,
430
Catholic School (s) 258, 284, 377, 417
CBF The Central British Fund for
German Jewry 9, 12, 13, 56, 59,
83, 91, 94, 131, 137, 158, 161, 164,
165, 192, 202, 241, 358, 459
CCCCC The Committee for the
Care of Children from the
Concentration Camps 12, 13
Cheb 292, 293, 444
Chelmno 437
Cheshunt 174
Christian (s) 31, 57, 195, 228, 229,

258, 259, 277, 284, 296, 312, 323,
340, 355, 356, 360, 398
see also Catholic and Gentile
Clonyn Castle Children's Hostel,
Delvin v, 4, 63, 75, 79, 82, 84-
86, 91, 94, 98, 108, 110, 125, 131,
134, 141, 144, 168-170, 173, 176,
178, 185, 189, 191, 193, 201, 202,
204-208, 210, 212, 221, 223, 226,
230-232, 237, 241, 243-246, 254,
258, 260, 274, 275, 277, 294, 297,
329, 332, 334, 345, 352, 353, 358,
360, 368, 373, 385-388, 393, 443,
459, 466
Clonyn Castle Football Team 125
Clonyn House Hostel, Dun
Laoghaire 107, 134, 142, 143, 144,
148, 149, 159, 164, 260, 262, 294,
459
Clyne family 203
Cohen, Rabbi Israel 4, 91, 94-96, 98,
105, 107, 108, 116, 117, 120, 123,
126-128, 168, 174, 177, 178, 193,
201-204, 245, 294, 332, 358, 387
Cohen, Trudi 4, 91, 94-96, 98, 105,
107, 109, 114, 126, 127, 168, 174,
176, 193, 201-204, 212, 358
Cohen, Romi 31
Committee of Six, The 34, 36, 299, 326
Cooper, Anthony Ashley 52
Cork 77, 476
Cracow 253, 296, 352, 415, 437, 441, 442
Cromwell, Oliver 77
CRREC The Chief Rabbi's Religious
Emergency Council 51, 56, 57, 58,
71, 83, 85, 90, 131, 134, 161, 205, 206
Cyprus 267, 415
Cyrulnik, Boris 192, 475
Czechoslovakia 17, 20, 21, 25, 26, 28,
37, 40, 64, 70, 71, 168, 207, 209,
219, 221, 231, 237, 239, 245, 249,
254, 255, 284, 295, 298, 329, 332,
350, 352, 354, 356, 357, 383, 385,
386, 391, 403, 415, 420, 431, 444,
448, 448, 450, 482

D

Dachau 24, 340, 355, 356, 410
Danube 20, 25, 51, 239, 293

Danzig 123, 377
David, Nicole 5
Death March 361, 363, 378
Delvin 82, 95, 108, 110, 128, 129, 149,
    202, 204, 205, 244, 294, 393
Deutel, Helena 161
Deutschlander, Dr Leo 441, 442
de Valera, Eamon 77
Dobsïná 292
Dohan, Oto 460
Dohany Ucca 284
Dolny Kubin 230
Dov, Avrom see Prissegi, Gyorgy
Dover 244, 295, 326, 387, 444, 448
DP (s) Displaced Person (s) 39, 61,
    255, 298, 363, 364
Dublin 19, 63, 75, 77- 79, 83, 89, 94,
    95, 98, 105-107, 109, 110, 116, 117,
    120, 126, 128-131, 134, 138, 140,
    158, 161, 164, 173, 178, 182, 189,
    202, 203, 205-208, 241, 244, 245,
    254, 294, 340, 357, 358, 367, 368,
    387, 393, 459, 460
Dublin Hostel at 143 Kimmage Road
    98, 368
Dublin Ladies (including the Dublin
    Jewish Ladies' Society; the
    Dublin Jewish Ladies' Voluntary
    Aid Committee; and the Ladies
    Committee from the Dublin
    Synagogue) 8, 78, 79, 110, 164,
    205, 206, 208, 393, 460
Dunaszerdahely 352
Dunner , Rabbi Abba 176, 177, 185, 212

E

Eire 4, 75, 85, 204, 206, 267, 293, 450
Engel family 266, 267, 273
Eppel, Olga (Mrs Eppel) 4, 19, 78, 79,
    85, 89, 91-96, 98, 105, 109, 110, 115,
    116, 120, 126, 128-131, 134, 137, 140,
    146, 149, 158-161, 164, 168, 173, 191,
    201, 202, 205-208, 241, 246, 260, 271,
    333, 367, 368, 393, 459
Epstein, Helen 198
Epstein, Stella 241
Europa Plan, The 34

F

Federweiss, Blanka (Blanche) 40, 99,
    108, 117, 121, 170, 176, 189, 193,
    203, 212, 245, 294, 332, 333, 352,
    353, 386, 393
Feher, Shimon 416
Feintuch, Zvi 333, 335
Feldman, Alice 207
Filakovo 388
Final Solution, The 33, 198, 361
Fisch, Dr Geza 30, 299
Fisch, Jeanette (Hartvig) 299
Fisch, Hetty see Weiner- Fisch, Hetty
Fischer, Bertha (Betty) xvi, 13, 198,
    217, 395, 403-413, 423
    Celia 407, 408, 411, 413
    Eli 407, 411, 412, 413
    Henja Geitel 405
    Joseph 411, 413
Fischer , Helena 158
Fischer , Mordecai 123
Fischer, Richard 99, 104, 111
Fischer, Vera 99, 213, 216
Fischer, Emanuel see Myer, Bertha
Fischers 293
Fitzsimmons, Mr and his daughter
    Norma 117, 203
Fleischman, Ester (Esti) 116, 158
Fleischman, Gisi 34, 35, 299, 301
Foley, Frank. Diplomat in Berlin 9
Frankfurt am Main 53, 91, 442
Fried, Ivan 47
Frieder, Rabbi Armin 36, 42, 45, 47,
    49, 267, 284, 326
Friedmann, Hedviga (Hedy) 25, 115,
    228-230, 460
    Judita 228-230, 460
Friedmann, Oscar 94
Friedrichstrasse Station 7
Fuchs, Abraham 34

G

Galanta 373, 375
Gateshead 212, 221, 241, 326, 394
Gentile (s) 12, 29, 39, 41, 77, 219, 220,
    238-240, 252, 253, 259, 266, 304,
    323-325, 330, 331, 365, 398, 407,
    424, 479

see also Non-Jew(s) *and*
Righteous Gentiles
Gematria 66
Gerafy, Mr 324
Germany 6, 13, 28, 38, 55, 75, 244,
319, 326, 328, 339, 340, 355, 363,
364, 365, 373, 377, 396, 424, 435,
436, 442, 444, 448, 448
Gieslingen (WMF Wurttembergische
Metallwaren Fabric.) 407
Gilbert, Martin 13, 36, 41, 193
Ginsberg, Thea 57
Glass House, The (Budapest) 284
Gnazdach 228
Goldberger, Lola 429
Golders Green 174, 286, 358, 375, 459
Goldring House, The 29, 31, 246-248
Goldring, Peter 246-248, 251
Goldwater, Mrs Erwin 78, 131, 134,
206, 208
Gomez de Mesquita, August 52
Goodman, Harry 79
Goodman, Bertha 108, 126, 203, 373,
375
Gottlieb, Tamáš 123
Green, Mr 110
Green family 203
Green Lanes 54, 57, 317
Greenville Hall Synagogue 98, 106,
205, 358
Greenwood family 375
Greenwood, Freddy 373, 375
Grossman, Emerich 123
Grossman, Olga v, xvi, 15, 26, 123,
170, 194, 195, 198, 213, 216, 217,
342-351, 423, 433, 434, 443, 464
Grossman, Vera 213, 216, 217, 342-
351, 434, 443
Grunfeld, Dr Isidore 442, 443
Grunfeld, Dr Judith 6, 68, 178, 279,
345, 349, 442, 443
Grunfeld, Rachel 99, 104, 213
Grunwald, Dr Judith 286
see Grunfeld, Dr Judith
Gryn, Hugo 412

H

HIAS Hebrew Immigration Aid
Society 364

Haifa 130, 228, 230, 245, 256, 317,
342, 343, 347, 349, 375, 383, 402,
403, 414, 429
Handler, Arieh 207
Handy, Maria 377
Harboth, Mr. (Polton House,
Scotland) 412
Hartvig, Jakob and Thekla 306
Hartvig, Egon and Ursel 308
Hasmonean Grammar School 66,
108, 161, 207, 286, 288, 388
Haupt, Agi 388, 389
Haupt, Eva 173, 174, 210, 388-390
Herman, Mrs 286
see also Hasmonean Grammar
School
Herman, Rav 417
Hertz, Rabbi Dr J.H. 54, 55, 56, 57, 442
Hertz, Leon 13
Herz, Alfred 99, 111, 123, 460
Herzog, Rabbi Isaac 77
Herzog sisters 220
Hidden Children 5, 18, 41, 63, 105,
197, 218, 464
Hide-and-Seek v, 5, 69, 91, 169, 170,
191, 194, 197, 198, 201, 217, 221,
393, 395, 414, 432, 464, 466
High Tatra Mountains (High Tatras)
21, 46, 231, 260, 284, 324, 326, 327
Hirsch, Rabbi Samson Raphael 52
Hirsh, Mordecai 245
Hlinka (Hlinka Guards) 26, 28, 33,
42, 170, 173, 266, 281, 300, 309,
310, 312, 313, 321, 361, 420, 425,
427
Hochhauser, Manfred 123
Hodickova, Helena 223, 224
Holocaust, The 3, 13, 18, 41, 64, 78,
91, 97, 193, 195-197, 221, 253, 254,
271, 296, 326, 349, 353, 369, 371,
372, 379, 391, 434, 436, 438, 439,
464
Holocaust Memorial Day 197, 271
Holyhead 164, 294, 357
Home Office, The 59, 75, 78
Honig, Mr N 57
Hope Square, Liverpool Street
Station 8
Horneburg Philips Factory 374, 375
Howarth, Mr and Mrs 277

Humenné 423
Huncovce 326
Hungarian Uprising in 1956 432
Hungary 20, 28, 29, 31, 36, 71, 209,
    219, 246-250, 253, 258, 259, 277,
    278, 282, 284, 297, 328, 330, 333,
    338, 340, 354, 356, 357, 360, 366,
    372, 373, 386, 414, 425, 426, 427,
    431, 452

I

Ickovitc, Josef (Yossie) 117, 184, 241
ICRC The International Committee
    of the Red Cross 38
Immigration Committee, Dublin
    Congregation 79, 158
Ireland xv, xix, 3, 63, 74, 75, 77-79,
    82, 83, 89, 98, 110, 120, 126, 129-
    131, 161, 164, 168, 202, 210, 212,
    221, 226, 230-232, 245, 250, 254,
    255, 263, 266, 278, 281, 286, 297,
    329, 334, 340, 345, 357, 367, 368,
    369, 372, 383, 385-387, 391
Irish Red Cross, The 77, 110
Isaacson, Miss 126
Ivanka 259

J

Jakobovitch, Rabbi 131
James, Hans 424
Janner, Greville 322
Jerusalem Report, The 39, 41
Jewish Agency for Israel, The
    (Soknut) 241, 271, 317, 413
Jewish Brigade, The 378, 398
Jewish Museum, The. 3, 10
Jewish Museum Atlanta, The 360
Joint Synagogues Children's Hostel,
    The 459
'The Joint' see American Joint
    Distribution Committee
JRC The Jewish Refugee Committee
    56, 317, 411, 412, 421

K

Kahan, Alfred 29, 40, 173, 189, 246-
    251, 360, 369, 460

Kaiser sisters 317
Kaiser Wilhelm Institute 433-439
Kaiser Wilhelm Society see Max
    Planck Society
Kalman, Klara (Gellu) 109, 158, 204
Kalmanowitz, Rabbi 249
Kapo (s) 373, 374, 377, 407, 410, 482
Karlsbad (Karlovy Vary) 71, 292,
    373, 405, 415
Katscher, Anna 15, 110, 111, 114-117,
    121, 122, 173, 174, 176, 178, 183,
    184, 210, 213, 216, 277-280, 281,
    282, 388, 460
    Giselle (nee Mannheimer) 282
    Ivan 123, 277-279
Katscher family 284, 286
Katz, Edit 42, 197, 395, 414, 415
Katz family 375
Kežmarok 29, 326
Kfar Hanoah Hadat 230
Kielce 39, 70, 400, 433
Kindertransport 6, 7, 57, 79, 195, 278
Kiryat Bialyk 237
Klein, George 340
Klein, Max 99
Klein, Schmuel 31, 395, 416-422
Kluj 326
Knocke 358
Koenisberg 54
Komaron 277
Kook, Rabbi Abraham Isaac 52
Kophaza 277, 278
Koplewitz, Dr Lionel 89
Košice 21, 28, 29, 39, 71, 221, 229, 252,
    254, 297, 330, 331, 340, 343, 345,
    348, 349, 354, 356, 383, 414, 415,
    423, 425, 426, 427, 431
Kramer, Rachel 380
Krausz, Pál 47, 97, 99, 104, 261, 286,
    324-327, 460
Krausz, Tamás (Tom) 47, 99, 261,
    324-327
Kristallnacht 6, 365
Kumelmann, Saba 115
Kummeldorfer, Ervin 40, 123, 170,
    171, 460
Kummeldorfer, Sonja (Sonia) 81, 170,
    171, 460
Kupler, Judy 242
Kurtansky, Mrs 234

Kurtz, Chaja 109, 158, 213, 414
Kyrinica 415

L

Laks, Jona 6, 18, 337, 351, 433-440
Landsberg 356, 410
Langner, Gordon 37
Lanzmann, Claude 195, 478
Lapian, Rabbi Chaim Shmuel 385
Laskier, Rose 412
Lehner, Tibor (Tommy) 207, 460
Leicht, Alfred 39, 107, 129, 168, 189,
    194, 198, 206, 246, 360-372, 460
Letchworth 221
Leverton, Bertha 195
Levy, Jacob (Yankel) 79, 82, 94, 95,
    134, 140, 178, 202
Levy, Malkeh and daughter Shula 82
Lewis, Rabbi 98, 116, 205
Lichtenstein 207
Limerick 77
Limoges 358
Lipstadt 339, 340
Lithuania 53, 85, 441, 442
Liverpool 8, 205, 244
Liverpool Street Station 7, 8, 195
Lodizhin 91
London 3, 4, 6, 7, 10, 12-15, 17, 19, 42,
    47, 51-58, 60, 61, 68, 70, 79, 85, 91,
    95, 97, 98, 105, 109, 110, 117, 120,
    126, 130, 131, 149, 158, 161, 164, 173,
    174, 176, 189, 192, 197, 203, 205, 207,
    210, 215, 219, 221, 222, 229, 233, 237-
    239, 241, 244, 250, 255, 262, 278, 279,
    281, 286, 289, 293, 294, 298, 299, 317,
    319, 322, 326, 329, 331, 340-342, 345,
    347-350, 353, 357, 358, 360, 373, 375,
    383, 385-391, 394, 396, 398, 412, 414,
    429, 433, 442-444, 459, 460
Lontzen 444
Lowinger, Lily 121, 122, 172, 207,
    213, 271, 275
Lowy, Alexander 123
Lowy, Gustav 206
Lowy, Judith 208
Luknar, Amiel 47, 49
Lunzer, Ruth 202
Lvov 109

M

Majdanek, Lublin 219, 437
Majercik, Dr Michael, Anna his wife,
    and family 309-316, 320, 321, 322
Makó 219
Mala Torona 354
Malmud, Rachel xvi, 15, 29, 31, 217,
    342, 395, 423-432, 460
Manchester 82, 91, 161, 187, 202, 207,
    237, 358, 390, 394
Mangel, Gertrude 207
Mangel, Trudi 115, 317
Mangel, Victor 122, 245
Mannheimer, Judith xxi, 44, 104, 213,
    216, 278, 280, 281-287, 460
Mannheimer, Arthur, Bella, Morris,
    Renka and Robert 281-285
Marava 377
Margulies, Mr and Mrs 109, 140
Marienbad (Mariansky Lazne) 249, 357
Markl, Professor Hubert 434, 439
Marseilles 130, 207, 226, 245, 378, 433
Masaryk, President 22, 25, 26, 45,
    239, 415
Mastbaum, Alexander 123, 328-329
Mátészalka 406, 407
Max Planck Institute, The 6, 351
Max Planck Society, The 433-439
Maxwell, Elizabeth 197
Maybaum, Fela Cajtak 217, 374, 376,
    377-381
Mayer, Dr Paul Yogi 13, 16, 66
Mayer, Rita 375
Mefice School 316
Meisler, Frank 6, 7
Mely Litnip 228
Mengele, Dr Josef 6, 337, 342-344,
    351, 354, 373, 374, 378, 407, 433-440
Michalovce 258, 259, 343
Michelovsky 210
Mihalik, Mihal, his wife, and
    daughter Helena (later Helena
    Hodickova) 223, 224
Mikes, George 192, 477
Millisle Farm Children's Home 79
Mishne, Judith 465
Mizrachi 117, 357, 394
Mobile Synagogue Ambulance 61, 62

Mocenok 223, 224
Modra 324
Montreux 375
Moravia 28
Morocco 212
Morris, Jan 41
Moses, Arthur 71
Mount Kisco 53, 282
Muller, Gertrude (Grete) 175, 210,
  388, 414, 460
Muller, Robert (Robi) 114, 123
Mullingar 260
Mundheim 109
Munich 319, 364
Munk, Rabbi Eli 53
Munkach 246
Murphy, Dr Kathleen 77
Myer, Bertha 98

N

Nagyvarad 246
Namesto 219
Neolog 22, 193, 326, 400, 419, 423
Nitra 29, 31, 39, 53, 219, 220, 223, 277,
  278, 281, 282, 386, 402, 416, 419-422
Nitra Yeshiva 53, 281, 282, 402
Non-Jews, Non-Jewish v, 5, 9, 31, 57,
  105, 204, 207, 209, 218, 219, 221,
  240, 244, 253, 254, 258, 266, 281,
  296, 297, 300, 304, 313, 324, 328,
  356, 385, 419, 420, 421, 427, 441, 442
  see also Gentile (s) and Righteous
  Gentiles
Northern Ireland 79, 202, 478
Nováky 31, 36, 231, 243, 244
Nové Mesto Nad Váhom 36, 42, 231,
  260, 284, 326, 338, 422
  see also Villa Sylvia
Nové Zámky 338, 373
Novitak 209
Nurock, Dr 129
Nussbaum, Manfred 176, 183

O

Ohel David 36, 44, 45, 49, 50, 71, 231,
  267, 284, 326

Oliver (Caretaker at Clonyn Castle)
  120, 202, 203, 260
O'Neill, Mr 208
Operation Shamrock 77
Oradea 246, 247, 248
Ostende 97, 221, 230, 244, 295, 357,
  387, 444
Ovadia, Arie 7
Oz, Amos 193

P

Pappek, Mr 429
Paris 130, 207, 245, 412, 413
Partisans 5, 21, 29, 31, 34, 41, 218,
  228, 229, 243, 266, 292, 309, 313,
  318, 331, 348, 411, 469
Passport (s) 75, 281, 293, 295, 319,
  389, 433, 447, 448, 468
  Irish 81
  See also Visa (s)
Peleg, Eliezer 431
Pels, Benjamin 85, 89, 108, 118, 119,
  204, 215, 353, 358, 460
Pels, Henry 19, 85, 90, 120, 12-131,
  134, 138, 149, 153, 154, 158, 161,
  168, 460
Pels, Séndi see Templer, Séndi
Petry, Osnat 343
Pichler (neé Prissengen), Magda 276
Piešťany 324
Pilsen 356, 411
Pinkesz, Isaac 185
Pinkesz, Pinches 384
Podhradie 22
Poland 39, 61, 64, 70, 71, 109, 237, 253,
  297, 316, 333, 377, 388, 400, 401,
  424, 433, 437, 441, 442
Pollak, Rabbi Artur and Mrs Olga
  98, 358
Polton House 411
Pomeranz, Eva Gisela 267
Poprad 228, 229
Porpa 374
Posen, Rabbi and family 345, 383, 386
Prague 3, 9, 10, 37, 70, 71, 74, 75, 78,
  96, 97, 108, 116, 173, 209, 221, 228,
  229, 237, 240, 241, 244, 249, 278,
  293, 316-319, 331, 347, 353, 356-

358, 375, 388, 393, 411, 429, 444,
    447, 448, 460
Prešov 21, 228, 229, 331, 415
Pressburg 20, 22, 51, 385
    see Bratislava
Prestwick Airport 411
Primrose Club, The (Belsize Park) 13,
    14, 97, 244, 245, 412
Prissegi, Gyorgy (Avrom Dov) 34,
    99, 111, 172, 189, 207, 208, 266-268,
    271-273, 276, 323
    Michael 271
Prissegi family 266-268, 271

R

Rachov 403, 404, 406, 408, 411
Ravensbrück 259, 343
RCM The Refugee Children's
    Movement 57, 59
Red Cross, The 37, 38, 77, 89, 97, 110,
    220, 221, 267, 284, 340, 374, 375, 411
    see also ICRC and Irish Red Cross
Refugee Children's Hostel, 32
    Woodberry Down 97, 326, 459
Reich, Israel v, 29, 37, 123, 134, 174,
    189, 219- 222, 323, 360, 460
    Susannah (Susie) 29, 219-222, 332
Reich, Richard (Yehuda) 111, 123,
    191, 223-227
    Oskar (Aharon) 123, 223-227
Reichman, Rabbi Ayreh 385
Reif, Tamáš 25, 26, 40, 174, 175, 210,
    239-242, 385, 396, 398, 460
Reunion, The Rabbi Dr. Solomon
    Schonfeld's Childrens Transport
    Jubilee 4, 15, 17, 51, 105, 173, 174,
    177, 178, 181, 185, 189, 191, 193,
    201, 219, 223, 228, 231, 233, 239,
    246, 253, 277, 279, 292, 296, 328,
    329, 330, 342, 352-354, 360, 383,
    385, 386, 388, 391, 393, 394
Reunion Committee, The Jubilee 15,
    174, 178, 219, 292, 388
Richer, Rabbi Emeritus Herbert 54
Righteous Gentile (s) 41, 224, 247,
    277, 319, 379, 432
Rivlin, Rabbi 255

Robov 442
Roman Catholic see Catholic
Romania 29, 71, 246-250, 326, 360,
    364, 366, 369, 385, 393, 411, 465
Rosenbaum, Esther 255
Rosenbaum, Judith 442
    see also Grunfeld, Dr Judith
Rosenfeld, Dezider 111, 123, 170,
    174, 292-295
Rosenfeld, Judith 317
Rubin, Lenke 104, 213, 452
Rubin, Maximilian (Max) (Michel)
    104, 114, 122, 123, 452
Rubinstein, Ernst 114, 123
Rubinstein, Eva 104, 213, 216
Ruthenia 37, 403, 412

S

Sandelson, Enid Oppenheim 85, 89
Sátoraljaújhely (Satoralja Ujhel)
    (Satorlsa) 259, 354
Schenirer, Sarah 349, 441, 442
Schiff, Otto 56, 59
Schirnding 444
Schnebalg, Chaim 203, 207
Schneider Yeshiva 294, 329
Schonfeld, Jeremy 83
Schonfeld, Jonathan 15, 174, 178, 191
Schonfeld (nee Hertz), Judith 13, 54,
    55, 60
Schonfeld, Rabbi Dr Avigdor 51, 52
Schonfeld, Rabbi Dr Solomon 3-6, 9,
    13, 17, 18, 34, 42, 43, 51-76, 78-80,
    82, 83, 85, 89, 91, 95-98, 105, 116-
    119, 126, 128-131, 134, 139, 149,
    158, 161, 164, 168, 173-176, 178,
    179, 181, 185, 188, 193, 198, 202,
    204-210, 212, 216, 217, 221, 229,
    231-234, 239-241, 243, 246, 252-254,
    260, 267, 278, 279, 281, 282, 284,
    286, 287, 291, 293-295, 297, 317,
    326-329, 331-333, 338, 340, 342,
    343, 345, 346, 348-350, 353, 354,
    357, 359, 360, 367-369, 373, 375,
    383, 385-389, 391, 393, 396, 400,
    422, 433, 441-443, 448, 452, 460
Schonfeld, Moses 291
Schonfeld, Victor 55

Schonfeld Children's Reunion
see Reunion
Schonfeld Square 68, 176
Schwab family 221
Schwartz, Matilde 345, 349
Schwartz, Moshe 241
Schwartzthal, Ella 47, 49, 99, 111,
121, 168, 231-232
Gizella (Grete) 47, 49, 231-232
Rozsi (Rozie; Ruzena) 47, 49, 99,
111, 121, 168, 231-232
Schwartzthal family 33, 39
Schwarz, Ervin 26, 38, 39, 122, 123,
130, 184, 203, 240, 354-359, 375
Eva 28, 76, 114, 117, 175, 184,
210, 233-238, 388
Schweid, Alexander 221
Sendler, Irena 9
Sephardi 13, 77, 384
Sered 31, 37, 220, 224, 259, 344
Shakovitsky, E 108
Shefford 202
Sherwood, Dr 98
Shishi, Malka 89
Shoah, The 195, 247, 319, 431, 465
see also Holocaust
Shoah Foundation, The 18, 197, 393
Shtern , Rabbi (Marienbad) 357
Sichermann, Helena 99, 213
Sighet 246
Simpson, John BBC Journalist 38-40
Sinsovitz, Yakir 344, 345
Skadany 243
Skolska Ulica 292
Slobodka 53, 85
Slopak, Dr 74
Slotover, Peggy and daughter Jill 92
Richard 89, 91, 93
Robert 93
Slovak National Uprising 1944 36,
224, 228, 231, 243, 244, 309, 324, 331
see also Partisans
Slovakia xi-xv, 3-6, 20-22, 25, 28, 33,
34, 37, 38, 40, 41, 43, 53, 71, 78, 85,
198, 210, 217, 223, 224, 226, 228,
229, 243, 244, 259, 262, 277, 278,
279, 281, 287, 297, 300, 319, 331,
343, 344, 350, 354, 356, 375, 415,
416, 422, 423, 425, 426

Smat, Leah. Journalist. 379
Smith, James and Stephen 195, 196
Smith, Miss 126
Sobibór 437
Soknut see Jewish Agency for Israel
Sopron 277, 278
Spielberg, Steven 18, 197, 438
Stahler, Gyury 47, 96, 111, 123, 258-262
Istvan (Ivan) 29, 47, 96, 97, 99,
104, 111, 123, 182, 184, 258-265
Marianna 44, 47, 96, 99, 104, 213,
216, 258-262
Zelma 400
Stalin, Josef 45, 221, 329
Stamford Hill 56, 57, 68, 69, 98, 255,
280, 286, 341, 345, 357, 388, 394, 459
Status Quo 22, 467
Steinberg family 203
Steinberger , Eva 375
Steiner, David 31, 299, 313, 318, 395,
396-400, 401, 460
Gustav 24
Myriam 396
Steiner, Eva 46, 286, 290, 460
Steiner, Mihaly 123, 164
Peter 111, 114, 164
Tamáš 99, 123, 164
Steiner, Ruth 460
Steinmetz, Chaja v, 98, 164, 168, 173,
182, 184, 188, 193, 241, 393-394, 460
Stern, Erika (Erica) 217, 338, 373-376
Stern, Marci (Bacsi) and Ilinka 282,
284, 286
Stern, Mayer 412
Sternberg, Rachel Leah 52
Sternberg, Sigmund 68
Sternberg family 241
Sternbuch, Judith 108, 203
Stoke Newington 51, 242, 326, 412
Strauss, Gita 114
Strausz , Alexander 123
Stropkov 344
Sudetenland 26, 238
Suffolk 443
Sveda, Julia 429, 431
Sweden 210, 267
Szatmar 366

T

Tajtelbaum, Isaac 176
Tannebaum [Watchmaker, Budapest]
282
Tatra Mountains
see High Tatra Mountains
Taylor, Professor Derek 4, 51
Tel Aviv 230, 232, 317, 412, 413
Templer, Séndi 4, 85, 99, 108, 116,
117, 161, 170, 193, 201, 203, 204,
207, 209-216, 240, 279, 294, 332,
345, 352, 353, 358, 386, 388, 393,
460, 470
Temporary Shelter for Jewish
Immigrants, The 3, 12, 13
Tešín 266
Tewkesbury 89
"The '45 Aid Society" see "The
Boys"
"The Boys" 10, 12-14, 16, 94, 140, 193,
403
Theresienstadt (Thereisenstadt) 37,
220, 259, 400, 401, 411
"The Vatican" [Nitra Yeshiva] 29, 219
Tidworth 89
Timishora 248
Tischauer, Mr and Mrs 241
Tiso, Jozef 26, 27, 28, 31, 33, 239
Tomlin, Rabbi Chanan 53
Topoľčany 39, 231, 243
Transit Camps 31, 33, 34, 36, 37
see also individual Camps by
name
Transylvania 230, 246, 247, 248, 333
Treblinka 377, 437
Trenčín 293
Tuka, Vojtech 28, 31
Turiani 343
Two Alfreds, The 189, 190, 191, 370
Tyrnau 53

U

Ukraine 37, 360, 365, 403, 404
Ungar, Rabbi Solomon David 53,
419, 422
Union of Orthodox Hebrew
Congregations 57, 351 see also
Adath Yisroel

UNRRA United Nations Relief and
Rehabilitation Administration
244
Unsdorf 326
Uprising see Slovak National
Uprising

V

Vasovi 377
Vatican in Rome 31, 33
Velvet Revolution, The [1989] 40
Verbove 220
Vexnia 85, 89
Vienna 20, 22, 52, 56, 57, 241, 255,
279, 298, 317, 322, 424, 443
Villa Silvia 42, 44-46, 49, 231, 260,
261, 324
see also Nové Mesto Nad Váhom
Visa (s)
British Visas 56, 57, 158, 388
Collective Visa (s) 74, 96, 266, 444,
447, 452-458
Czech Republic Letter of
Authorisation 448
Group Visa 17, 174, 217
Irish Visas 129
Permit to Transit French, British
Zone (s) of Germany 448
Visa de Transit Collective 447
see also Passport (s)
Vogel, Mr and Mrs 48, 49
Vorhand , Rabbi H 71, 221, 375, 419
Vrba, Rudolf 36
Vyhne 31
Vylok 258

W

Wallenberg, Raoul 9, 253, 297
Warhaftig, Helen 289
Warhaftig family 286
Wasserburg, Miss 417
Weil, Pálo 47
Weinberger, Artur 99, 104, 296-298, 329
Emanuel 99, 111, 123, 168, 253-257
Judy, sister of Artur and
Emanuel. See their accounts
Weinberger, Jan 429
Weinberger, Sarolta 46

Weiner-Fisch, Hetty 30, 35, 38, 39,
    194, 299, 303-305, 395, 398, 460
Weiss, Mr 418
Weissmandl, Rabbi Chaim Michael
    Dov 29, 34, 53
Weisz , Dr 292
Wellstead, Miss 75
Westmeath 82, 204, 205, 370
Wetzler, Alfred 36
Whitman family 412
Wiesel, Elie 230, 246
Wiesen, Franklina 111, 184, 185, 213, 216
    Vera 40, 111, 184, 185, 213, 216,
    383-384
Wiesner, Agi 110, 114, 116, 184, 186,
    206, 207, 353, 391
    Judit 173, 184, 186, 206, 207, 353,
    391, 392
Windermere 12, 91, 94, 202
Winton, Nicholas 9
Wisliceny, Dieter 34, 326
WIZO Women's International
    Zionist Organisation 300, 317
Wolfson family 98, 393
Woodberry Down Hostel for
    Religious Girls 210, 213, 241, 293,
    353, 375, 388, 459
Woolgar, Professor C.M. 18
World Agudath Israel 42, 79 see
    also Agudath Israel

Y

Yad Vashem 18, 31, 41, 195, 196, 224,
    225, 319, 320, 344, 349, 378, 379,
    395, 432, 466
Yenkel, Rolf 436
Yeshiva, Yeshivot 26, 82, 130, 164,
    221, 241, 251, 255, 326, 333, 384,
    385, 396, 419, 420, 422, 441, 459
Yeshiva
    Ahavas Torah 255, 294
    Bet Hakerem 379
    Galanta 373
    Gateshead 212, 241, 326
    Karlsbad 71
    Košice 414
    Letchworth 221
    Marienbad 249, 357
    Mirer 249

Mount Kisko 53, 282
Netzath Israel 255
Nitra 29, 31, 53, 219, 278, 281, 282,
    402, 416, 418, 419, 420, 422
    Pressburg/Bratislava 22, 52, 71,
    367, 385, 396, 468
    Ramaz and Frisch 334
    Schneider 294, 298, 329
    Slobodka 53, 85
    Staines 385
    Sunderland 128, 130, 385, 387
    Tyrnau 53
Yeshiva boys 56, 66, 247, 249, 250, 278,
    384, 385, 396, 414, 416, 418, 419
Yeshiva Torah Vodaas High School
    255, 385
Yodanken family 203
Youth Aliyah 79, 129, 130, 207, 223
    see also Aliyah

Z

Zahn, Moishe Lozor 128, 204
Zahn, Rabbi 128, 130
Zahradnik family 259
Zenta 425, 426
Zergbaum, Dr 395
Ziegler, Alfred (Buby) 123, 330-333
    Judit (Judita; Judith) 41, 97, 108,
    330-336, 401
    Olga 330- 333
Zilina 36, 281, 304, 319, 426
Zlati Mikolas 293
Zofia, Sister 324, 325

Lightning Source UK Ltd.
Milton Keynes UK
UKOW040405180312

189164UK00002B/4/P